7970
2 vol
50

THE
PATTON
PAPERS

"By perseverance and study and eternal desire any man can be great."

—George S. Patton, Jr.,
Cadet Notebook, 1906–1909

THE PATTON PAPERS

1885—1940

MARTIN BLUMENSON

II

ILLUSTRATED WITH PHOTOGRAPHS
AND WITH MAPS BY SAMUEL H. BRYANT

HOUGHTON MIFFLIN COMPANY BOSTON

CHAPTER 24

Langres to Bourg

"I am the absolute boss and it seems strange at first not to have to ask any one any thing at all."

On February 1, Patton conducted the first close-order drill of tank men in the history of the U. S. Army. That afternoon he started working on tank drill regulations.

Letter, GSP, Jr., to Beatrice, February 2, 1918
We have been having some most interesting lectures on special subjects and all of them go to show what a complex war we are in and how much we have to learn. It seems more and more certain to me that we cannot punch a hole [through the German defenses] with out tanks. There are too many instruments of death in the way but I believe that Tanks well backed up will do the job. I hope the war lasts long enough for us to try our hand.

The tanks have attracted a lot of good men and I get requests from them to transfer nearly daily.

According to a cable received from the War Department, 100 American-built Renaults would arrive in France in April, 300 would be delivered in May, and 600 would come every month thereafter. It would turn out to be a wholly overoptimistic assessment of American tank production.

Patton traveled to Chaumont and had a long talk with Rockenbach, who authorized him to select two General Staff officers from the Staff School at Langres to help Patton run his organization. Rockenbach also said he was recommending Patton for promotion to lieutenant colonel. As Patton explained, "I have not sufficient rank [as a captain] to get proper subordinates. He told me that I was to organize the 1st Tank Center and see to biliting arrangements for 12 companies [of] light tanks he had asked for."

Carrying out Rockenbach's instructions, he called on the appropriate offices at Langres about securing billeting areas for the tankmen who would be coming to the tank school and made tentative plans for organizing the staff of the 1st Tank Center.

He wrote Beatrice that if everything worked out well, he would have 1400 men under him by May. Rockenbach wanted him to go to England to take a course at a school there, but Patton would try to put this off until Beatrice, who had been ill, was strong enough to visit her sister in London. He was elated by Rockenbach's formal recommendation for his promotion, for this meant —if the War Department complied—that he would have sufficient rank to command the first two battalions of light tanks.

Attending a meeting at the Army Staff School, where assignments of graduates were arranged, he asked for two officers by name. The chiefs of staff of all the divisions and of the I Corps were present for the same purpose, and their appearance disturbed him. "They were not an impressive lot, yet there are none better available."

Letter, GSP, Jr., to Beatrice, February 5, 1918

We have done about all we can organizing till we get some machines. I have been trying with some success not to fall into the habit of doing every thing my self but of directing others to do it and seeing that they do. Still one has a natural tendency to try to pull all the strings one self. My only crytocism of J. [Pershing] is that he is over prone to do that. It is a great mistake.

Rockenbach telephoned to say he was having trouble getting tanks from the French. He directed Patton to go to Paris and see what he could do.

In Paris for two days, he secured a promise that the French would deliver several tanks to him by the middle of March, these to be used for training at the center. He extracted the pledge, no doubt, by sheer persistence coupled with charm, the latter enhanced by his highly original yet completely fluent use of the

French language. He characterized his accomplishment as quite a feat, for he had given up hope, he said in some exaggeration, of ever getting any tanks at all.

Letter, GSP, Jr., to Beatrice, February 8, 1918
I bought my self some more leather junk [in Paris]. A saddle store has a hellish fascination for me as you know and I always buy something . . .
Asto my staying in the Tanks after the war I doubt it because it is a specialty. And specialists don't get supreme command. Besides we will have another war in Mexico and Tanks would be useless there so I will be back in the Cavalry. At least that is my present notion . . .
I want you to be the same age when I get back as when I left. Also die your hair for I don't like gray hair at all.

He was drawing up tables of organization and equipment for quartermaster and ordnance supplies of tank companies when Rockenbach telephoned and told him he would soon have to go to Blois to select men for the first light tank company.

Letter, GSP, Jr., to Beatrice, February 11, 1918
Don't send me any more sweaters this year as I have six. Gen. P. has twelve and 14 pairs of heavy socks. I was at the house last night and counted them.
Former Secretary of War [Henry L.] Stimson is going to join my mess and live in the house . . . Mr. S. is now a Lt. Colonel . . .
This is a soldiers war not a staff officers [war] for as all the attacks are frontal there is little strategy possible only a vast mass of detail to arrange like a cleark. If we or when we break through things will be different but first we must make the hole with the Tanks.

With four of his lieutenants—Borland, Hebert, Sweeny, and Winters—Patton tramped all over the site of his tank camp. He instructed his junior officers on how to unload the tanks if they arrived while he was away at Blois. He showed them what he wanted done to prepare the land for tank exercises. He made some notes to instruct his adjutant. He wrote the following letter to an old friend with whom he had served in Mexico.

My dear Col Burt. Sir: I respectfully call your attention to the fact that I am about to procede in a most unmilitary manner. My excuse for so doing is that I desire if possible to get some results and my experience, limited as it is, leads me to the belief that "Channels" are not built according to the mathematical axium "That a straight line is the shortest distance between two points."

Between the Langres-Dijon road and the Bois-sur-Marne, Foret Du Mont woods there is a tract of ground one and a half Kil. long extending north from the Cross Roads at Burg. It is my intention to use this ground for Battle Practice with the Light Tanks. There are three lines of trenches crossing this ground. In Tank operations it is most important to correct maps with Aeroplane Photographs. I have heard that Col. Alexander, Intelligence section, G.S. has asked to have some pictures taken near Langres. If possible I would like some pictures of this ground taken at the same time . . . so that I can use them to instruct officers in conjunction with a map I now have . . .

If I am wrong in assuming that the Air Service takes these pictures or if a more formal request is necessary will you please inform me.

Very respectfully.

Letter, GSP, Jr., to Beatrice, February 12, 1918
It is hard to get out of the habit of doing every thing my self but absolutely necessary and it is the sign of efficiency or lack of it in an officer. Those who can only do them selves are not much good as human power is limited while those who can make others do have the world to pick from.

The trouble is that my officers have all been N.C.O's and lack initiative. Still they do what they are told and that is something.

His travel orders having arrived, he went to Chaumont and left for Blois. His train was delayed, and he was two hours late when he reached St. Aignan-Noyers, the headquarters of the 41st Replacement Division, which served as a manpower pool and furnished men to fill ranks and positions in other units. Discovering that Lieutenant Colonel F. B. Hennessy had gone ahead with the selection of men and had already gathered what appeared to be a fine group, he accompanied Hennessy to Montrichard and inspected another group; these men pleased him too.

He obtained an automobile to drive to St. Aignan-Noyers and the train, but the car skidded off the road and was damaged. He walked five kilometers to town, missed his train, and slept on a stretcher in the hotel lobby. He managed to send a telegram to his adjutant:

> Two hundred men should arrive Friday morning. They will have equipment C with three blankets. Draw one hundred extra blankets two field ranges [stoves] and two march kits [for] cooking. Get permission to use stjoemes [the nearby village of St. Geosmes] for temporary billets if Burg [Bourg] not available.

Taking the train to Saumur—like Langres, Saumur was a great AEF school center, but for artillerymen—he found many old friends "all were dilighted to see me." He rode to Tours, dined at the Hôtel de l'Universe, boarded the Army special train that evening, and arrived at Chaumont in the early afternoon. He reported to Rockenbach the results of his trip.

From Rockenbach he received a copy of Tank Corps AEF General Orders 2, dated February 14, which assigned Patton formally to command the 1st Light Tank Center.

Rockenbach accompanied him to Langres that evening and left after supper. Both were elated by the way things were working out.

On Saturday, Patton completed the arrangements for the proper reception of his new men.

Letter, GSP, Jr., to Beatrice, February 16, 1918
I have two hundred men coming to day for the first two companies I hope that they are good men . . .

I also got the inclosed order [assigning him to command the tank center] yesterday. A center is two or more battalions.

Col. Fox Conner got wounded last week. They were inspecting and came to a part of the trench full of water. They climbed out on the top and ran along to avoid the water when just as they were jumping in again a shell blew up and cut Col C's nose and throat. He is all right again and will get a wound badge which is nice.

About this time, several buildings began to appear on his camp site. The former Coast Artillery officers assigned to him, plus a few infantry officers who had also joined, had been constructing workshops, getting water piped in, and preparing barracks. Patton had secured, by proper and legal means, some lumber with which to build a tank shed. In addition, he later wrote:

[six buildings mysteriously] sprang up in the night like mushrooms and they looked strangely like French barracks . . . freely daubed with serial numbers . . . each number backed with large obtrusive U.S. A still closer examination would have revealed places where other numbers had been removed with a plane. But why be inquisitive.

Major Farman of his West Point class came for a visit on Sunday morning. He was two places above Patton on the promotion list, but he said that Patton had been promoted to Major on December 15. This was hardly official notice,

but after much debate [with himself] I decided to put on my [major's] leaves and now I am wearing them. I feel sort of like a thief but that does not bother me at all as there are so many militia majors around here that one must have leaves to keep ones self respect.

Soon after Patton put on his new insignia, a soldier addressed him as "Lieutenant"—"which proves that I am still not 'old' looking."

"Inspite of my increased rank," he wrote Beatrice, "I still love you."

Actually, his date of rank as major was January 26, but the War Department order announcing the promotion would be issued only on March 11 and arrive in France still later.

That Sunday, February 17, the men of his first two companies reached Langres. Patton was at the railroad station to meet them.

He marched them to St. Geosmes and to temporary billets in a tent camp—"195 men all told good lot." Most of them, including one officer who accompanied them, had volunteered for the tanks. As though he had not enough to do, Patton received a telegram from Braine in Paris. Braine expected to leave Thursday for the United States, and before he departed he wanted to talk with Patton—"will need help to carry out your plans." Patton was too busy to attend to Braine, who, he probably figured, had enough ability to make his own way and do all that was expected of him.

Letter, GSP, Jr., to Beatrice, February 18, 1918
My two companies arrived here yesterday and I have them Bileted in a Town near here. They are very well fixed and my officers are good and efficient. When the men got in they found a hot dinner waiting for them, and a nice latrine all dug.
I think all the villagers thought we were digging for gold as they came out and watched the operation.
The sgt. Mjr. [sergeant major—the highest enlisted man] is part owner of Mark Cross [Stores—Fred Murphy] and a graduate of Yale. Twenty other men are from big colleges. Quite forty owned their own machines inclusing a couple of Pierce-Arrows. They are really a very fine bunch of men much above the ordinary. All drafted men.
I must stop now. I love you.

He inspected the billets, arranged for medical support, and ordered lumber for more buildings.

GHQ AEF issued provisional drill regulations for the light tank service with an acknowledgment that they had been prepared by Lieutenant Colonel George S. Patton, Jr., who was still, so far as anyone knew officially, a captain. In pencil, written a dozen or so years afterward, he noted: "This was wholy original with me. GSP Jr."

Drills or exercises on foot, Patton specified, were to follow generally the instructions in the Infantry *Drill Regulations*. Machine drills on foot were to accustom the men to signals and to the proper intervals and distance between tanks. Commands were to be given by signs, visual or touch, by sounds, voice or Klaxon (horn), and by the example of leaders. For instance, touch signals between crew members: to turn, the gunner in the turret pressed the right or left shoulder of the driver, who turned in that direction as long as the pressure lasted; to go faster, repeated pats on the back of the driver's neck; to halt, pressure on the top of the driver's head; forward from halt, the same as faster; backward, the same as halt followed by several pats on top of the head. "By Claxton. One long blast means attention. Other signals," it was candidly admitted, "not worked out."

He designated drills by platoon and by company and drew diagrams to show how the tanks were to move. It was all quite typically Patton, detailed and thorough.

Patton was at the camp at 8 A.M. on Tuesday, February 19. He gave the men a talk on discipline and behavior. He had an officer lecture them on camouflage. He himself went to the gas course that afternoon. In the evening he sent Rockenbach a list of proposed ranks for tank officers.

"Things are looking better for us now in the Tanks," he wrote Beatrice.

The gas course was a great bore, particularly since his thoughts were with his troops at the tank center. One type of mask made him look like a member of the Ku Klux Klan, another like an incubator baby—

> a most unplesant disguise in which to fight . . . Each form of specialist like the gas men or the aviators or the artillery or the Tanks talk as if theirs was the one useful weapon and that if there were but enough of that sort the war would end. As a matter of fact it is the dough boy in the end who does the trick.

When he wore his mask in a chamber full of tear gas, along with everyone else taking the course, he found to his surprise that the "resperator absolutely nutrilizes gas."

On February 22 he moved his two companies, now named Companies A and B, to Bourg and their permanent billets. He inspected the old quarters they had occupied at St. Geosmes and found them clean. He heard that a tank had arrived and became terribly excited before learning that it was only a mistake due to his adjutant's imperfect understanding of the French language. After telephoning Rockenbach and requesting several vehicles for his tank center, he received—that afternoon, which was quick work on Rockenbach's part—a Dodge sedan, a motorcycle, and a truck.

Letter, GSP, Jr., to Aunt Nannie, February 22, 1918
I have my battalion in a town of my own near here and am very independent. Tanks are Army Troops so we are not bothered by little superiors which is a great help.

My town is the dirtiest place in the world full of cows and chickens but it has a fine view being on the edge of a cliff over a long and beautiful vally.

We had a rumor to day that our first tank had arrived but it proved only the result of bad French. The station agent said one was going to arrive which we knew already.

Letter, GSP, Jr., to Beatrice, February 22, 1918
We moved down [to Bourg, about 5 miles south of Langres] and got settled. It is a nice little town full of manure and smells but we are the only troop in it so are not bothered, every thing is quite well fixed. I rented a room for a soldiers Club at 7 F[rancs] a week and they ought to be quite comfortable. I am the absolute boss and it seems strange at first not to have to ask any one any thing at all.

I can see how hard it must be for officers who have been subordinates longer than I to ever do any thing for them selves.

It is a good experience. I also inspected my old town to see that things were done right. The men did well. Every thing was neatly put away and cleaned. I have a Q.M. who is a good one and does lots on his own initiative. We will start drills monday and will spend tomorrow removing the manure to a degree.

Just as I got through an officer rushed up shouting that a tank was at the depot. I dashed there but found that he was mistaken. The man [station master] had simply said some were coming in two weeks.

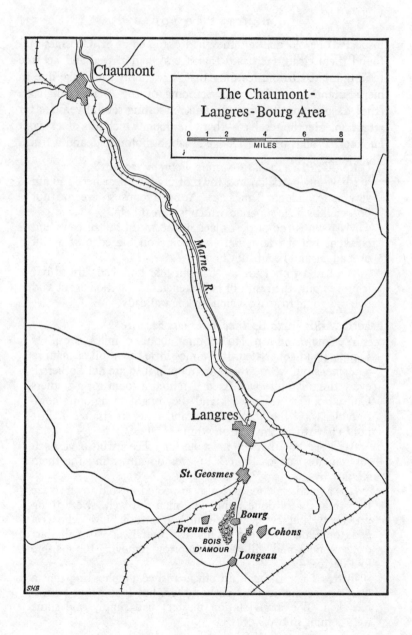

Chaumont

Marne R.

The Chaumont-
Langres-Bourg Area

0 1 2   4   6   8
MILES

Langres

St. Geosmes

Bourg
Brennes   Cohons
BOIS
D'AMOUR
Longeau

SKB

I may move down to the town [Bourg] to live as this place [Langres] is pretty far away.

Saturday, Patton held the normal inspection and found the men dirty and unshaved. He "raised hell and [also] disciplined [the] Doctor for not keeping heels together" when standing at attention. He took a bath, saw and briefly spoke with General Leonard Wood who was visiting the American Expeditionary Force (having been denied a high command in it by the Wilson administration) and who seemed somewhat puffy and old-fashioned, even lost, quite different from the Pershing type of officer.

That afternoon, in a written memorandum to his adjutant, Patton laid down the law on how he wanted the tank center and school to operate. All communications to the Chief of the Tank Corps, he specified, were to be headed "Headquarters 1st Light Tank Center, AEF" and signed "G. S. Patton, Commanding"; all communications to the Commandant, Army Schools, were to be headed "Army Tank School, AEF" and signed "G. S. Patton, Director." This made a nice distinction between his dual functions as commander of troops and director of a school.

Morning drills, he ordered, were to be held strictly as follows: from 8:20 to 8:30, close order drill and saluting, with special attention to exactness and precision; from 8:35 to 9:25, calisthenics, games, running, and jumping; 10:05 to 10:35, instruction in guard duty, military courtesy, challenging, posting sentinels, and the like; 10:45 to 11:15, foot drill by platoons; 11:20 to recall, close order drill by companies.

All officers will set their watches with that of the Adjutant at breakfast daily and will conform exactly to the times specified. No "rests" except those specified will be given.

All officers not on other duty will attend all drills . . . [All officers] younger than thirty five [would take part in calisthenics].

Afternoon drills were to consist of the following: 1:00 to 1:45, all officers and ten noncoms from each company to receive pistol instruction from Major Patton; 1:50 to 2:30, all officers except the Officer of the Day to receive instruction from Major Patton in machine and foot drill by platoon and company; 2:50 to 4:00, classes in the theory and operation of gasoline engines.

The men were to be occupied during the afternoon by what was known as company fatigue, that is, duties in housekeeping, the maintenance of property and grounds, and the like; they were also to perform what Patton called town fatigue, that is, keeping the village of Bourg clean and neat.

Morning reports were to be turned in to the adjutant every evening before taps was sounded. Company commanders were to inspect personally the billets of their men at least once every day. Officers were to leave camp only after reporting at the adjutant's office their time of departure, destination, and expected time of return.

Letter, GSP, Jr., to Beatrice, February 23, 1918

I think it will keep them fairly on the go for a while till we get the tanks. It is absolutely necessary to do so as there is nothing else to amuse them and as they live in stables and lofts so can hardly be said to have much home life if any.

I have always thought and still more strongly think that our chief fault as an army has been that of taking things too easily. When the days get longer I can work them more which will be a help to them.

You ought to see me brace when they can look at me. And already it has so I fancy given them a better carriage.

The officers have a nice mess and one well located so things ought to go well.

I was issued a truck, a motor cycle, and an auto yesterday so shall have to hoof it less but still fear that I will unduely develop my legs and hence not look so well in boots . . .

I make the chauffeurs wash their machines after the last trip each night no matter what the hour. This I got from the english . . .

Gen. Wood was here to day and looks quite well. He was most cordial and asked after you.

Riding ten miles on Miss Green [his horse] daily has improved her disposition and my health vastly.

I also had the pleasure of militerizing my doctor. To day
he was talking to me with his heels apart but will not offend
in the future.

Letter, GSP, Jr., to Mr. Ayer, February 24, 1918
I have two companies of Tank Soldiers here. About seventy
percent of them are drafted men and of an exceptionally high
class. Three sergeants are Yale graduates and many other colleges are represented. It is a pleasure to work with them because they are so quick to learn.
If we have only luck getting material we should have two
battalions ready to fight by June. That does not mean that we
will fight but that we may.

Letter, GSP, Jr., to Beatrice, February 24, 1918
Madame La Baronne Pig and Sheep which is her name [an
inaccurate approximation of Madame de Vaux de la Porquière,
a distinguished French family with whom he would be friends
for the rest of his life] has asked me to tea at her chateau
which is in my town. Her husband is a colonel in the French
Army and she is quite nice and safely old.
(Maj) Stanley Rumbough is here at the school also Farman. They are both to mess with me.

Letter, GSP, Jr., to Beatrice, February 25, 1918
I am getting all sorts of applications for officers in the tank
corps and they are a good lot young and full of pep. But we
will need a lot to keep things going.
I have got them [my men] pretty well to heel as I am very
mean with them every once in a while.

Letter, GSP, Jr., to Beatrice, February 26, 1918
I ate dinner at the officers mess [in Bourg] and had just
the [same] effect Col Pitcher [the commanding officer] used
to have at the mess at [Fort] Sheridan. It was most amusing.
They all ate hurridly and went out. They have a very nice
mess and a good cook.
Through some mistake the Motor Transport Service . . .
issued me two autos. I told them that I only had asked for one
but they said I must take both which I have done.
The poor Dr. is so scared of me that he giggles when I

speak to him and is almost incoherent. It is quite amusing. If I ever get to be an "old general" I fear that B Jr. & R.E. [his daughters] will have a fiew suitors. Or perhaps many for "bootlick."

The man I have for a Q.M. is certainly good (Lt. Borland) but I can't say so much for my adjutant. He rushes around a lot but does little work so far as I can judge.

I am getting to talk to you about my Battalion as much as you used to talk about the children. As I objected to that I will stop this.

I started pistol practice again to day and found I needed it. So I shall devote more time to it here after. It might come in handy as in Mexico. I hope I get another close up like that. I rather think that they are rare in this war.

Letter, GSP, Jr., to Beatrice, February 27, 1918

When this war is over I am going to insist on using a single bed for *both* of us at the same time. There is perhaps more than one reason for this, but the only one which the censor and modisty will allow me to mention is that I am tired of being cold and especially of getting into a large and empty bed full of cold sheets. Hence you will have to go to bed first.

You see we have only enough wood for one fire in the house and that is in the parlor. So when I go to bed my room is like a vault and the bed like a shroud. Besides a large double French bed, just like the one we had at Saumur, is not sociable.

Letter, GSP, Jr., to Kay Merrill [Beatrice's sister in London], February 27, 1918

At last after all the reserve officers in the world have been promoted they have made us majors. So I am very grave . . .

I have a battalion of Soldiers (Tankers) under me now but as yet no tanks. Still I have hopes . . .

I am pretty busy and quite well but still too d—— safe.

Diary

February 28: "Went to drill. Found B. Co. not out on account of rain. Got them out."

Patton expanded the provisional drill regulations for tanks into a larger "Tank Drill and Training Manual (Proposed)." Chapter I, the introduction, was pure Patton:

Success in battle presupposes the destruction of the enemy. This is brought about by killing and wounding his men so as to reduce his strength and destroy his morale. The above happy results may only be looked for when the training has been intelligent and thorough, so that the men are educated in what to do and have the discipline to do it.

Commanding officers are responsible for the proper training and discipline of their units . . .

Simple movements, elastic formations and iron discipline are the essentials to success in battle.

The drill regulations are furnished as a guide . . .

In interpreting the regulations the spirit is to be sought. Quibbeling over minutiae is a demonstration of failure to grasp the spirit.

Diary
March 1 (Friday): It snowed. Got hut from Gen Shipton. Unloaded lumber for shops. "R[ockenbach] sent me a scheme to train 116 off. and 1638 men in no time. Worked out [an improved] scheme."

Letter, GSP, Jr., to Beatrice, March 1, 1918
I just got an order to train 40 Companies in no time with nothing and it has put me to it to find means. I finally got a scheme for training 32 Companies in a fair sort of way but my temper is shot to hell as a result. For fear of showing it I will stop. I love you.

He wrote a memo to Rockenbach and suggested altering the program of having 400 tanks and 40 companies by June 30 to one of having 400 tanks but only 28 companies. The reason was a problem that was hardly specific for tanks alone but was a universal difficulty whenever shipments of equipment any kind—and of men were made, particularly overseas. The process of requisitioning a specified amount of men and matériel for delivery to a certain place by a certain time was in and of itself simple. But the execution was infinitely complex. To gather together an entire and balanced kit or package, consisting of different parts coming from different places, then to load it and ship it, and finally to check it upon arrival comprised an operation that was a nightmare. Success demanded an extremely high level of organizational and logistical competence.

Patton's memo was very clear and to the point.

Memo, GSP, Jr., to Rockenbach, March 2, 1918

The shipment of Tanks is absolutely dependent on the space allotted by the shipping board. Hence we must have a definate promise from them in the case of each shipment, otherwise we would get more men than we could possibly use and whose space could be better utelised by infantry.

There should be an officer of the Tank corps with rank and experience on duty in the U.S. as your representative to coordinate the shipment of both men and Tanks for the reason that the elements of Tank units are handled by three different departments. The Ordnance, the Q.M. and the Adjutant General. Now if tanks were held up by the shipping board the Adjutant General [who assigned personnel] would not know it and the men would come and be in the way.

It is a well established military principle that men should travle with their units. This is particularly true with a new unit like Tanks. You know what happened in the case of our trucks. Bodies landed in one place. Chassis another and both were useless. No spare parts came at all. Tanks would be in even worse case. A Q.M. told to ship them would not know what comprised a unit and would send off what he had on hand with the result that he would get incomplete tanks or that the spare parts would get sent to some truck park.

To obviate this your representative should coordinate the shipments of men and tanks and an officer of the unit should have a list of the shipment so that he could supervise the loading and have a complete list of all prepared. Then he and his men could see that the stuff was collected on debarcation.

To my mind the foregoing are absolutely prerequisite to success. The men must be shipped with regard to the tanks . . .

I take the liberty of repeating that the men should syn-cranise in quantity [numbers] and time [of arrival] with the tanks.

The expanded training program would work because billets available in Bourg and in the neighboring communities of Noidant and Cohons could accommodate 51 officers and 1645 men. But he would need several prefabricated huts, each of which housed 17 officers; he strongly recommended sending Lieutenant Robinson and Sergeant Major Murphy to the replacement division to select new men for the tank center and school.

Diary

March 2: Took memo and went to Chaumont to see Col R about training. Recommended that Tanks have a representative in U.S. R. said no.

Somewhat depressed, Patton was pleased to be invited by Pershing's aide Boyd on Sunday to go on a short trip with the general that afternoon. Patton accepted, not only because he always enjoyed being with Pershing but also because he felt that a change in routine would do him good.

He accompanied Pershing to the headquarters—near Toul—of the 1st U. S. Infantry Division, which was occupying a quiet front-line sector under the French. Pershing wanted to compliment the division on its recent repulse of a German raid. He discovered that Premier Georges Clemenceau, who made it a practice to visit units at the front every Sunday, had come also to congratulate the American division. Clemenceau, characterized by Patton as "quite an active little chap and nice to meet," was enthusiastic over the conduct of the American troops.

Learning that there was to be a "show" that night, Pershing decided to stay. General Summerall, the division commander who knew Patton since his West Point days, promised Patton he could watch the action from an advance OP—observation post. But when Pershing saw Patton getting a helmet, he said, "Where in hell are you going?" Patton had to tell him, and Pershing forbade it. So Colonel Purrington took Patton up the road to General Duncan's brigade, a safer place.

The barrage was to start at 1 A.M. with 90 guns, and Patton stayed up to see it. The shoot started exactly on the designated second, and in three minutes the Germans came back with their own artillery fire. The regiments were supposed to attack at 1:20, but the infantry was unable to get started, and the preparatory shelling was halted. The German guns continued for almost twenty minutes. Then all was quiet. Everyone went to bed around 2:30.

Somehow Patton found time to write to Beatrice about an imagined slight on the part of his sister.

> I think you and nita and all got much excited over nothing. I feel sure that J's sentiments are as always but what you all don't know is the pressure he is under over here . . . He is still fond of me . . . am sorry I made Nita angry.

Pershing and his party left the 1st Division that morning, and Patton went on to Langres. That afternoon he was at Chaumont where, with Rockenbach, he took the train for Paris. They boarded the train for Boulogne.

Patton managed to write to Beatrice.

> J. was most contrite over Nita. Neither of us imagined that she would be hurt and we are both sorry. There are no doubts that he feels the same as ever only more so and he said he wished they had married. Of course don't tell him I said so.

Rockenbach and Patton were going to England to consult with the British on tank training, to visit the British tank training area at Wareham, and to make preliminary arrangements for the reception of a battalion of American heavy tankers.

In London Patton met several interesting people at his sister-in-law's, accepted an invitation from Mrs. Leverton Harris, wife of a deputy secretary in the Ministry of the Blockade, to see *Faust*, and enjoyed the opera, which was sung in English.

He and Rockenbach spent nearly a week in England. They examined a new tank model—"I argued in favor of four speeds, but was ruled an ass. Time will show. Also think there are too many guns." They looked at new tanks in production, visited tank schools, observed machine gun practice, watched tank guns firing at the target range, saw antiaircraft guns in operation, and inspected the site of what would be the American heavy tank area.

Letter, GSP, Jr. (Langres), to Beatrice, March 12, 1918
I feel pretty tired and dirty [after the trip]. We have a stupendus job and little time and none of my officers are worth a damn. I have to instruct all of them in every thing under heaven except infantry drill and I have to check them up at that. I have to teach maping, Visual training, Aiming, gas Engines, signaling, reconnaissance, Intelligence, and some other things that I cant recall. I send them out to teach classes and have to watch them for mistakes. I hope to get Viner [whom he had known in Mexico] soon and that will be a help but so far I have gone on alone to the detrement of my temper.

I am going to bed early to night and will feel better in the morning.

Rockenbach wrote to Hennessy at the replacement division to whom he was "greatly obliged . . . for your continued interest in the Tank Corps . . . The prospects in the Tank Corps are, I believe, better than anywhere else, considered from every point of view." The tank center needed officers with knowledge of mechanics and experience as commanders. Would Hennessy please try to find and send five majors, who could look forward to promotion to lieutenant colonel "when tried out and found effective"; 34 captains, who would have a good chance of promotion to major; a large number of first lieutenants—the best 119 would be promoted after trial; and quite a few second lieutenants—249 would eventually win promotion.

On impulse, Rockenbach drove to Bourg. He inspected the tank center and was extremely impressed with what he saw.

Letter, GSP, Jr., to Beatrice, March 13, 1918
I am sorry I stired up such a mess over Nita. It was well ment but shows that with out your advice I am apt to make mistakes of judgment . . .

I got a fine letter from Mr. Ayer in which he said he took great pride in my efforts. It delights me to have him think so and I hope I justify his confidence.

When I realize that I am with out question a very superior soldier and yet realize as I do my many shortcomings I can but feel sorry for Gen P. [who is] served by men worse than I. I am not fishing [for compliments] but telling the exact truth.

Col. R. Inspected camp this P.M. and was much pleased. I was glad as I had not known he was coming so things were just as they usually are.

Patton had a fine athletic field for the soldiers, and they enjoyed it. They had 45 minutes every day for hard-played games, and each man participating worked up a fine sweat. "To day we had a sort of polo on foot using a round foot ball"—he was referring to the game of soccer—"and kicking it was fine exercise. I plaied and found I was shockingly short of wind. I bought some camp clothes and am going to train a little."

He had a good view from his headquarters building "in my town," Bourg—a nice old garden with a statue, an iron fence, and a high terrace looking about 30 miles down a green valley with a lake in the distance and a Roman road down the middle. On a hill about 200 yards away were the ruins of a robber bishop's castle.

Visiting the French tank center at Martigny-les-Bains, he watched an attack maneuver in which four Schneider tanks worked with a battalion of infantry. He was pleased to hear the commanding general of the 18th French Division say that no attack would ever be made again without tanks.

He sent Rockenbach a run-down on some of his thoughts on personnel. He had talked with a cavalry major who was a student at the Army Staff School about joining the tanks, but the major was dubious of his ability and wished to suspend judgment until he saw a tank. Since he was a Regular officer "and almost a temporary Lt. Col. I believe we had better let him make up his mind." A classmate of Patton's who had failed to graduate from West Point was at Langres; he was "quite military and has not got much

intelect. He might do well as I believe him brave." Captains
Chamberlin and Cramer, old friends of his, were to be relieved as
instructors at the Military Academy when they were promoted to
major, and Patton suggested that Rockenbach ask for them. Would
he please request the transfer to the Tank Corps of Captain Sereno Brett, who was an infantryman, a Regular officer of long
service, an expert operator of and instructor in the machine gun
and the 37-mm. gun, and who was eager to join the tanks. The
only man Patton had who could speak French was Sergeant Major
Murphy, and Patton was recommending him for commission as a
second lieutenant. Lieutenant Miller had been on duty for three
days and seemed well versed in military matters and in paper work.
Lieutenant Hebert was neat and soldierly but failed to get on
well with some of the company commanders.

Diary
March 17 (Sunday): "Had Elsie Janis [the favorite American singer and entertainer of troops in France] and her
mother to lunch. She is not pretty but quite amusing though
common in her pronunciation. She wore an artificial Lepord
skin coat. Met Secretary [of War Newton] Baker and went
around with him for a while. Seemed interested and intelligent."

He wrote Beatrice: "The Sec of War was here yesterday and I
saw him. He is a little rat but very smart."

Patton delivered to his officers and men a lecture on discipline,
which he defined as "instant, cheerful, unhesitating obedience."
Obeying instantly and cheerfully was

very good but it is not good enough, in that you do not obey
automatically.
For example: A group of you are sitting talking. An officer
approaches, one of you calls "Attention." What happens? You
look about, see the officer, and then come to attention. Your
discipline is good, in that it is almost instantaneous and quite
cheerful, but it is lacking in that it is not automatic. You have
failed in the vital thing, the rest is useless show.

After a long illustration on the response to the quarterback calling the signals for a football team, he continued:

> . . . just as surely as the automatic obedience . . . will give you the edge on the other team which will win for you, and the lack of which no amount of star tackling and blocking will replace, so no amount of bayoneting or shooting will win the battle if you are late, slow, owing to lack of automatic obedience . . .
>
> Lack of discipline in war means death or defeat, which is worse than death . . . The prize for this war is the greatest of all prizes—Freedom.
>
> In battle as in fistfights or football, man cannot reason. What he does for good or evil he does automatically—subconsciously.
>
> The reason the Bosch [Boche] has survived so long against a world in arms is because he is disciplined. Since 1805 he has bred this quality as we breed speed in horses; but he is neither the inventor nor the patentee of it. Philip of Macedon had as high a discipline three hundred odd years before Christ. The great Alexander saw its value and by its aid his phalanxes were victorious against odds of fifty to one . . .
>
> The legions of Rome were disciplined and conquered because of it . . .
>
> We cannot wait until A.D. 2018 to breed discipline as they [the Germans] have done. But we are as intelligent as football players, far more intelligent than the Greeks or the Romans or the Persians or the Gauls of two thousand years ago . . . You must get it likewise: instant, cheerful, and automatic discipline, so that when we the quarterbacks give the signal of life or death in the near day of battle, you will not think and then act, but will act and if you will, think later —after the war. It is by discipline alone that all your efforts, all your patriotism, shall not have been in vain. Without it Heroism is futile. You will die for nothing. With DISCIPLINE you are IRRESISTIBLE.

This became a standard lecture Patton gave all new officers and men reporting to the tank center. When speaking to officers alone, he added several paragraphs, stressing that officers could hardly expect discipline in others unless they were capable of imparting it themselves, and pointing out that many officers used unnecessary words when giving commands or directions, for example, "Will you please," or "Kindly."

There is nothing harsh in brief words of command any more than there is impoliteness in the brief wording of a telegram. Commands simply express your desire, your signal, in the briefest and most emphatic language possible. If you are to obtain automatic obedience from your men your language must express your meaning concisely and with emphasis, further each meaning must always be expressed in precisely the same language; so that when you give commands in battle the unreasoning mind of the soldier, unreasoning for the time being on account of the stress of battle, shall automatically carry out the identical directions to which at drill this set of words this signal has accustomed him. On you rests the responsibility, to you goes much of the glory. Hence it is inexcusable for you to express yourselves in an ambiguous or hesitating manner.

These thoughts were impressive, primarily because they were spoken with firm conviction. These were the precepts by which Patton himself lived.

Another lecture he delivered from time to time was on the sense of duty or obligation, which, he said,

are inseparably connected. In fact, duty is but discipline carried to its highest degree. Like discipline also, it must be automatic . . .

The sense of duty is hard to acquire, because it is made up of so many tiny things. But in essence it consists in doing the task set, however small, absolutely, perfectly, and better than it was ever done before . . .

It is not enough to perform a task so that you can get by with it. That is easy and worthless . . .

[For example] to-morrow at reveille, it is raining or cold, and bed is so very pleasant; your undeveloped sense of duty lets you stay in bed two minutes too long. You must make the formation. Have you done your duty? You have not! . . .

unless your sense of duty is so undeveloped that you can lie to yourself . . . leniency to self . . . is inimical to duty—hence to victory.

Unless you . . . do your best, the day will come when, tired and hungry, you will halt just short of the point you were ordered to reach, and by so halting make useless the efforts and death of thousands . . .

This imperious sense of obligation is the mark of the thoroughbred in men as in horses. The cold-blooded horse quits in the "Stretch" when the race is all but won. The thoroughbred passes the wire at his best though he dies for it. The thorough-bred man . . . does not argue. He goes until his duty is done or he is dead.

You must develop this thorough-bred sense of duty, otherwise you had better never have been born to wear a uniform you will inevitably disgrace . . .

If this iron conscience, this sense of obligation could not be developed, it would be futile to talk of it, but it can be developed and to beat the Germans, it must be.

Do not talk or think of your rights or your fatigues or of what the other fellow has failed to do. War is the struggle of nations, you are in it but as an individual and hence your feelings as such do not exist . . .

In doing your utmost, even unto death you are conferring no favor, you are privileged to be able to do so much for your Country . . .

To wear the uniform of an officer of the United States Army in any other frame of mind is to live a lie.

Strong words, they were effective in stirring his listeners.

Still another paper Patton wrote in March—whether to deliver orally, to be read by his officers, or simply for his own guidance —consisted of instructions for training the Tank Corps. It was eight pages of single-spaced type containing the principles and maxims on which he himself modeled his actions.

Commanders will train the troops they lead into action. This is a principle which must never be departed from, and nothing in the following instructions, the object of which is to co-ordinate policy and system and so to arrive at uniformity of doctrine, is to be held to relieve Commanders of their initial responsibility . . .

The object of all training is to create a "Corps d'Elite," that is a body of men who are not only capable of helping to win this war, but are determined to do so. It cannot be emphasized too often that all training, at all times and in all places, must aim at the cultivation of the OFFENSIVE SPIRIT in all ranks . . .

The requirements were "a high Efficiency and a high Moral"—plus mental alertness and bodily fitness, discipline, organization, and skill, pride, smartness, and prestige. Lessons must be explained, demonstrated, and carried out as an exercise. Instructions must be interesting. Work requiring brain power should be followed by work entailing physical exertion.

Order is best cultivated by carrying out all work on a fixed plan. Order is the foundation of discipline. Small things like marching men always at attention to and from work, making them stand at attention before dismissing them, assist in cultivating steadiness and discipline . . .

It is an essential part of training for war that the men are taught to care for themselves so as to maintain their physical fitness. To this end the necessity for taking the most scrupulous care of their clothing, equipment and accoutrements will be explained to them.

The importance of obedience to orders will be impressed on all ranks and prevention of waste rigorously enforced . . .

The men must understand that the skill they gained during training would have a result on their lives as well as on the battle. Instruction was not a matter of getting through a definite subject or time period, but of employing time to the fullest advantage.

"Tactics are the foundation of all training, for training has as its object the preparation of the soldier for war." Realism in training must always be sought, for "the value of training is greatly enhanced if the men's interest can be roused."

The principles Patton enunciated in these papers were fundamental to him. On them he staked his career, his hopes, his desires as a soldier.

Writing to Major Daniel D. Pullen—who had defeated Patton in the broadsword tournament finals at West Point, who had been captain of the football team, and who had graduated in the class after Patton's—he asked for suggestions on improving his map course. After explaining his training program in some detail, he concluded, "This keeps everyone pretty well occupied and I have had only one drunk inspite of pay day."

He told Beatrice he hoped to have some tanks soon, though "It will be the greatest surprise in history if I do." He had moved into a new office "in my town," had his adjutant and quartermaster in the same room and his sergeant majors in an adjoining room. "I feel just like Col Pitcher," the post commander at Fort Sheridan.

He closed on what was for him a normal comment: "I have got this place so well organized now that there is nothing for me to do and I am getting nearvous again."

CHAPTER 25

Bourg

"Some times it seems to me that all I have ever done has been in preparation for my present job."

Diary

March 19: "Got telegram from B congratulating me on promotion to Lt. Col. Have not heard of it yet."

Letter, GSP, Jr., to Beatrice, March 19, 1918

I am not so hellish young and it is not spring yet still I love you just as much as if we were twenty two on the baseball grand stand at W.P. [West Point] the night I graduated . . .

I fear he [Willie Horton who had written to ask whether there was a job for him in France] is suffering the fate of rats who cling too long to a sinking ship. He could have come earlier but yearned for the "Flesh pots" of Washington. Still I owe him so much that I will do all I can to help him out . . .

[Tate was living in his house, and Chaffee and Haverkamp were in Langres, together with a lot of other classmates and friends, but] as I am out here [in Bourg] all day I don't see a great deal of them . . .

If I am a lt Col. I have surely gone some and feel like an imposter though dangerous modesty is not one of my many faults.

Well this is the second letter I have written you to day. I only wish it were not necessary and that I could hold you in my arms and squeeze you. I have almost forgotten how soft you are even with corsets on to say nothing of your softness in your wedding nighty. I love you so B.

Letter, Pershing to Mr. Patton, March 19, 1918

George is looking well and seems to be very well satisfied with his new job with the tanks.

Letter, GSP, Jr., to Beatrice, March 20, 1918

Darling Love (Beatrice) I add the parenthesis for fear you might think you were reading a letter to some other lady of my acquaintance. That shows how careful I am even in small details. I have been sitting around all day like an expectant mother waiting the advent of a child in the shape of a train load of tanks but thus far there have been no premonitory symptoms.

Still if the things did get here on time it would probably upset the entire French nation and they would declair a public holiday to celebrate the first occasion on which they were ever on time. Not that we have any thing to boast of in that reguard either.

Some times it seems to me that all I have ever done has been in preparation for my present job. As an instance some of the men could not visualize a contour so I made a mineature hill out of a potato and cut parallel horizontal slices out of it the way Gen. F. C. Marshall [his first company commander at Fort Sheridan] used to do in "K" Troop years ago. And then as now it worked.

I suppose however that in any exact science like war the same would be true and that genius as Napoleon put it is simply memory of detail. I have a hell of a [good] memory for poetry and war.

We are going to have a track meet here on Saturday . . . By having track meets we make the men exercise with out their knowing it.

I have just heard over the phone that the tanks have left Paris so they should be here tomorrow night.

Before the tanks arrived, he received a cablegram from Mrs. Ayer. Beatrice's father had died. Patton wired sympathy to Beatrice and her mother, then wrote Beatrice a fine and sensitive letter.

. . . it is with out question a direct interposition of Almighty God that this war made it necessary and possible for you to be with him for had it not occured you would have been in the Phillippines and absent at the time so priceless to him.

It is a great source of pleasure and pride to me that Mr. Ayer who is the most perfect mortal I know of took an interest and pride in my present work, and his last letter to me will ever be an inspiration to me in this or any other work.

Beatrice Jr and Ruth Ellen should be wonderful children with such a grandfather.

Fearing that Beatrice's sister Katharine would feel guilty over being away from home when her father died, he wrote to his brother-in-law, who was with the State Department in London and toward whom Patton never felt close. "My dear Keith . . . I feel sure she [Katharine] almost sacrificed her love for you in order to stay with her family." But he knew that Mr. Ayer was delighted with Kay's marriage and happy that all his children were happily married.

Especially Kay who had given up so much for him and for Ellie [Mrs. Ayer]. Tell Kay how much I sympathize for her but that I also envie her the satisfaction she must feel in having been such a fine daughter and unfailing source of comfort to her father. I hope she is reconsiled to her absence [from home] and my personal opinion is that her duty is to stay with you but that is none of my d—— business.

Letter, Pershing to GSP, Jr., March 23, 1918

My dear Patton. Please accept my sincerest sympathy for yourself and family especially for Beatrice and her mother in the great loss that has come to them . . . I have cabled to Mrs. Ayer . . .

I am getting sane letters from Anne again and suppose she is over her rage—poor girl, it is hard for her to be anything but open and frank, so I can fully appreciate her abhorrence at anything that looked like subterfuge.

I was sorry you did not have a tank to show the secretary [Mr. Baker] the other day.

Glad to see you looking so well—the trip around with the secretary did me a lot of good, and I have started to ride every day—hope to keep it up.

Sincerely

Letter, GSP, Jr., to Beatrice, March 23, 1918

There is a strange thing that happened on the seventeenth. I was most restless and worried and all the people at the mess noticed it. I thought of you every moment and longed to be with you more than usual which is always a lot.

Of course I don't know when your father passed away. Think it must have been about then. Although at the time of your operation I did not have similar feelings.

Patton suggested to Rockenbach that cutaway models of the parts of the tank engine be furnished to facilitate instruction—specifically, to show the workings of the valves, the camshaft, the oil pump, pistons, spark plugs, carburetor, and so on. One model of each was sufficient because "it is my opinion that after july we will have enough wornout tanks to supply similar models to each battalion if it becomes advisable." He had sent Lieutenant Baldwin to Nevers to get some spare parts, and he requested authority to do so whenever necessary in the future so that at least the driver could draw his two dollars a day—per diem pay—for being away from his home station.

Pershing cabled the War Department on March 22, saying that Patton was the "best qualified officer to command light tank centers, due to previous experience." Pershing renewed his recommendation, initiated earlier by Rockenbach, for Patton's appointment to Lieutenant Colonel, Tank Corps.

On March 23, ten light tanks, so long anticipated, finally arrived at Bourg. They reached the Langres-Marne railroad station about 3 P.M., and Patton arranged to unload them opposite the Bois d'Amour, his training area at Bourg. The train moved to that place at 8:40 and stopped at unloading platforms that Patton had had constructed. All the tanks and spare parts were taken off without accident, and the tanks were run under their own power to the tank park at the center, then camouflaged in the wood. By midnight, the entire operation had been completed. Three tailboards on the flat cars were slightly damaged, but no other injury to the railroad was discovered.

The tanks were in excellent condition, although they lacked

jacks, weapons, and turret foreplates for guns. Patton requested Rockenbach to have these deficiencies remedied at once. He called attention to the excellent work performed by all the officers and men who helped detrain the tanks, especially Borland, the Supply Officer of the 1st Light Tank Center.

Diary

March 23: "I backed seven [tanks] off the train and Lt. Baker the other three."

Later versions of the episode had Patton driving all the tanks off the train because he was the only one who had ever seen a tank. After nine of the most experienced drivers were shown the gearshift—it was dark by then—they drove the tanks to the Bois d'Amour, a mile away. "This shows the adaptability of the American Soldier, for totally inexperienced as they were, they drove the tanks by night . . . over two kilometers and landed them without accident at the designated point."

Diary

March 24 (Sunday): Moved tanks into sheds and arranged to have them oiled Monday.

Letter, GSP, Jr., to Beatrice, March 24, 1918

The Tanks are here. Ten of them . . . The french were much impressed [with our unloading] as they said it would take us 15 hours and we did it in just three.

It was a beautiful moonlight night and ideal for the purpose. When the procession of ten started across the fields I was delighted as I have been living on hopes for the last four months.

They certainly are saucy looking little fellows and very active. Just like insects from under a wooden log in the forest.

No one but me had ever driven one so I had to back them all off the train but then I put some men on them and they went along all right. I took one through some heavy woods this morning and it just ate up the brush like nothing.

Tomorrow they will all be oiled up and we will start active business making drivers on Tuesday. It will be fine having

something to work with as up to now I have had one old
truck [the Atlas] . . . and had to teach all about driving with
it . . . I am a little tired to day due to excitement I suppose
but am feeling fine.

It was just as well, to help get over his excitement, that he had
to take the train to Paris that Sunday afternoon to get his
car, which he had left to be repaired. He reached the city in the
midst of an air raid. On the following morning, long-range German guns put shells into Paris every fifteen minutes between seven
and ten, "but no one paid any attention to it as the chances of it
killing any particular person are so small." The shells did little
harm because they carried little explosive. The range was said to
be 120 kilometers, and the hits were well grouped, most of them
near the Gare de l'Est. "It is a hellish affair but a great scientific
achievement. Just think of shooting a gun 75 miles and hitting
even so large a target as the city of Paris."

Returned to Langres, he assured himself that the tanks were well
oiled. He trained eight men quickly so they could act as instructors in driving. He arranged a schedule designed to teach, in three
weeks, 96 men and 3 officers to drive the tanks and fire the guns.

Letter, GSP, Jr., to Beatrice, March 26, 1918
My tanks are going full blast this afternoon and I feel very
cheerful over the prospect of getting something done. Of
course I have only a few [tanks] but they are much better
than none . . . It is wonderful how fast the men pick up
driving tanks. They will learn it 50% faster than the French
do I feel sure.

He had the tanks working ten hours each day to instruct the
men not only how to operate them but also how to keep them in
repair. The latter would prove somewhat difficult for the tank
center was initially short of monkey wrenches and screwdrivers.

Diary
March 27 (Wednesday): Started schedule; things did not
work well. Examined the nearby village of Brennes as possible
location for the tank center.

Letter, GSP, Jr., to Beatrice, March 27, 1918

[Sends letter from Pershing about Mr. Ayer's death, which] was certainly a nice thing to do . . . the last tribute of the greatest American soldier to the greatest American civilian. It is a rare privlage for little people like me to have two such associations. I hope I may be worthy of the good thoughts which I flatter my self these two men have had of me.

To day however I hardly feel like I was worth much consideration as I have been having the duce of a time making things go and one of the two trucks broke down right in the middle of the morning . . .

[The YMCA opened a canteen for the men, and he was pleased because there were no amusements in town.] The only advantage is that they are working so hard that they go right to bed . . .

[No disease and hope to keep it out, which is easy if the men take proper precautions.] Of course I know that your remidy would be but I don't approve of that as men who are apt to be killed are entitled to what pleasures they can get even if they are not considered shick [chic] by some.

Letter, GSP, Jr., to Mrs. Ayer, March 28, 1918

We are now wearing a gold V on our left sleaves to show that we have been in the zone of the armies for six months. I wonder how many we will have on before we get through this business? If we get wounded we wear the same on the right arm for each wound. I would like to be hit in some nice fat part so I could get one.

Patton reconnoitered another piece of ground nearby at Brennes, twenty minutes' marching time from a proposed railroad siding in Bois St.-Georges-le-Gros. It would be suitable for establishing billets and training facilities for additional tank Corps units.

He had six tanks working in training exercises, but firing the tank guns proved a complication, for the French were afraid of stray bullets.

Letter, GSP, Jr., to Beatrice, March 28, 1918

All my present officers are former soldiers [enlisted men]

and have no push at all. I have to keep kicking them to get any speed out of them and it is rather a bore and very hard work . . .

Col. Rockenbach is realy fine and does not bother me at all and we get on quite well all things considered especially his reputation [as a difficult man to work with].

He received a letter from Brigadier General F. C. Marshall, his first troop commander at Fort Sheridan, who thanked Patton for the stars—insignia of rank—that Beatrice had sent him upon his promotion to general officer rank.

Patton thanked Beatrice for doing so, saying it was "very thoughtful and like you to do it."

Marshall's letter, sent from the 165th Field Artillery Brigade, Camp Travis, Texas, reproached Patton lightly, but seriously nonetheless, for having gone into the tanks. "I wish you would get out of vadevile [vaudeville] and get into the legitimate—you ought to be preparing for a high command, which you will surely get, if the war lasts long enough, and you have not specialized too much."

Patton was far too busy to answer Marshall immediately. Perhaps he was somewhat displeased that his old company commander should try to throw cold water on what was rapidly becoming a growing enterprise. The Tank Corps overseas was supposed to have more than 15,000 officers and men, including one brigadier general, 4 colonels, 10 lieutenant colonels, 34 majors, 119 captains, 249 first lieutenants, and 505 second lieutenants—not a bad opportunity for an ambitious man.

He had to abandon his training schedule in order, as he noted in his diary, to "groom the tanks," for Rockenbach was bringing Major General W. M. Black, the War Department Chief of Engineers who had come to France with Secretary Baker, to visit the center. To get ready, Patton was in and out of everything. Once when he was under a tank to inspect its bottom, he received about a pint of black oil in his face. After getting cleaned up, he demonstrated how the tank should be operated, and he drove one through some heavy woods to show its power.

Rockenbach had, as requested, obtained Captain Sereno E.

Brett for the tanks, and Brett reported in. Patton was pleased to have him at the center helping him run things.

By then he had 98 men in Company A, 99 in Company B, 59 in Company C, and an unspecified number in the battalion headquarters. An additional 23 noncommissioned officers, 6 mechanics, and 30 privates were unassigned. Three more men were under orders to join and had yet to arrive.

Patton suggested to Rockenbach that sufficient privates be obtained to complete Company C and the battalion headquarters. He had enough noncoms and private-specialists. Since 100 light tanks to be constructed in the United States had been promised for delivery to the eastern seaboard by April 15, he suggested that Rockenbach ask for deck space so that the tanks could be shipped to France and put into service at the earliest possible date.

Letter, GSP, Jr., to Pershing, March 31, 1918
    I have ten tanks here now and eight of them work every day from eight fifteen A.M. to five P.M. I would consider it an honor if you could inspect them some day. If you would let me know in advance I could arrange a small maneuver for you. I regret that they did not arrive in time for Mr. Baker's inspection. I have had very good accounts of my family especially of Anne. I have as yet no details as to the death of Mr. Ayer. Very respectfully.

A group of celebrities visited his tank center, were curious to see tanks in operation, and seemed much impressed with the show Patton put on.

Donald M. Call, who had volunteered for the tanks, who would later be commissioned, and still later be awarded the Medal of Honor, recalled immediately after the war that when he arrived in Bourg he

    found things rather discouraging. The Tank Corps was just beginning to take shape and there were many hardships to go through before things really became organized. There were ten little French tanks and most of the time was spent cleaning and repairing them.

On April 1, Patton visited the dentist in Chaumont and had several teeth filled. He went to Pershing's house for dinner. When General Harbord entered the dining room and saw Patton, he said, "Hell oh Colonel." General Alvord, the adjutant general, came in behind Harbord and confirmed Patton's promotion to Lieutenant Colonel, Tank Corps, National Army, as the result of a message just in from the War Department. The AEF order formally announcing the promotion would be issued two days later.

"I feel more or less a fool being a colonel," he informed Beatrice, "but it will wear off . . . How do you feel being a Mrs. Colonel. We never thought to reach it so soon did we."

His old headquarters troop at GHQ AEF had grown to a battalion of about 2000 men, so he would have been promoted even had he remained with Pershing. But he had no regrets. He was working his men very hard and keeping them very military.

As a matter of fact, he was working his ten tanks so hard that they required more than normal attention. He asked Rockenbach to transfer two first lieutenants who were skilled mechanics to the tank center. Then he changed the training schedule to get even more men at work.

Letter, GSP, Jr., to Beatrice, April 3, 1918

Darling Beat: I got your letter about the horses and at once wrote Pa to sell Cotton but to keep the rest even if it does cost something. I would rather have them and the ponies will be all right for polo even in a couple of years. Though I hope to ride them before that. I would rather kill both Mugador and Spy than to sell them and have them abused. They have both been very honest horses and I owe them something better than the bone yard or the plow . . .

Gen P. had a hell of a time getting me promoted as they said I was too young but he finally put it over.

. . . I wish you would send me a couple of pair of silver leaves [lieutenant colonel's insignia] and send Col S. D. Rockenbach a pair of nice silver stars with his initials on them and the words "Tank Corps."

He will be a B.G. [Brigadier General] in a few days.

I am keeping my gold leaves as I will need them ten years

hence when I get to be a major again. At least Williams [my striker] thinks so for he put all my Captain's pins carefully away for future use.

Of course all that depends on the length of the war.

Well there is nothing but the usual thing to say—I love you.

He sent Rockenbach a rough drawing of a device—probably something like a compass—to help a tank crew orient the tank toward its objective when under heavy fire. It was Captain Brett's invention "and is in my opinion mechanically practical and of great value more especially to the Liberty type tank where the visibility [from inside the tank] is bad." He recommended that Rockenbach examine it personally, and that, if he thought it useful, he refer it to the proper source for production. No one at the tank center was capable of making the necessary mechanical drawings, but perhaps someone in the AEF Engineer Section could do so under Brett's direction.

Enough new men arrived to complete Company C. He found the men good, the noncoms poor. They were all somewhat "wild," he wrote Beatrice, but they would soon be put into proper shape.

Am as busy as can be but have to hang around an office too much to suit me . . . It seems funny to think that so short a time ago we thought a Captain was some pumpkins—and will think so again?

Saturday, after the usual personal inspections, he supervised the cleaning of the tanks—they were probably the most immaculate in the world—and worked on plans for a platoon maneuver. He also wrote a formal letter notifying a lieutenant that he was confined to town for two weeks as punishment for an infraction of the rules.

Memo, GSP, Jr., to First Lieutenant Will G. Robinson, April 6, 1918, subject: Absence.

In the military service there can be no hazy uncertainties. Your excuse for your absence comes under that category.

Owing to the fact that your service thus far has been excellent, I will not take the action I at first contemplated but will resort to disciplinary measures here. You will not leave the town of Bourg except on a military duty until after retreat at Saturday, April 20, 1918.

Letter, GSP, Jr., to Beatrice, April 8, 1918

[Training] is certainly a cut and dried business and takes a long time to arrange but then this war is not a sparkling affair and so many officers are inexperienced that we have to definately prescribe each seprate movement.

Letter, GSP, Jr., to Beatrice, April 9, 1918

Col. R was down yesterday and was most complimentary and pleased. He threatens to recomend me to be a [full] colonel. I hope he waits a while or people will accuse me of using "influence." But I guess there is little danger of any ones taking him seriously.

I work pretty hard but seem to do so little. Still I have some fine men under me and they are very soldierly.

That afternoon he received a telegram from Beatrice telling him that her mother had died. His letter to her in reply was sensitive and compassionate, all that a letter of heartfelt sympathy could be. In part, no doubt, to divert her thoughts from her mother, in part to express his own deeply felt emotion, he concluded: "I do not think I would care much about keeping on if you were gone. Because if you were not around to admire what I did what the rest thought would make little difference to me."

He phoned Collins and asked him to see whether Pershing would send Beatrice a telegram of sympathy.

On the same day, he received from Beatrice a letter devoted mostly to her father, who had died two weeks earlier. Patton wrote into his diary:

[Mr. Ayer] often read my letter to him saying that his letter to me had decided me to enter the tanks. Last letter he got was one from B announcing my promotion to Lt. Col. He said now that George has his start he will go higher.

Letter, GSP, Jr., to Beatrice, April 11, 1918

It is a source of great pride and joy to me that he [Mr. Ayer] took such an interest in me and I am so glad that the news of my promotion reached him.

Of course he knows what is going on now too but to have had him express his satisfaction in words is fine. I hope his prophicy will come true.

If the war lasts long enough to give me a chance I shall try to justify his opinion . . .

I wish I could be with you [now that her mother was gone] but hope that mama and nita were. They are so solid and natural that I feel sure they would have been a great comfort.

He wrote a long and grateful letter to Colonel Draine, Ordnance Officer of the Tank Corps in Paris, who was helping to expedite shipments of men and matériel to the tank center. He thanked Draine for having sent several replacement depot officers to visit the center, for "Now they know by personal observation just what we are up against. And it is some problem"—meaning it was difficult to find qualified men for the tanks. Captain G. D. Sturdavent, president of the Grant Six Auto Company and a first-class engineer, had come for a few days, and Patton had profited from his advice. Sturdavent was taking to Paris a list of parts and tools needed at the center, and Patton hoped that Sturdavent could return to help him from time to time. Could Draine push the shipment of the first hundred tanks from the United States—or any part of them? He hoped that Draine would at least prod Rockenbach, who

has much more respect for your views than for mine. Please follow example of the British at Cambrai and [in the legendary words of General Elles] do your damnedest.

Of course if the tanks come equiped so much the better but tanks tanks and yet more tanks with or without guns are what we want to train our men on. . . .

It is I hope useless to add that I look forward to a visit from you as soon as possible.

Letter, GSP, Jr., to Beatrice, April 13, 1918

The men of this command are certainly a fine lot and work

like the duce. We work saturdays the same as other days and have inspection on Sunday so they don't get much time off . . .

right now I am more like Henry Ford than a soldier only my product is Tankers instead of cars. I think that I might have been a manufacturer if I had put my mind on it but I am glad I did not. Because you might never have married me if it had not been for my brass buttons?

His chest and forehead had been itching for several days, but he entered the hospital only after Captain Joseph Viner reported for duty at the tank center and assumed some of his burdens. He remained in the hospital for three days, staying in bed with a wet dressing applied to his chest, for what the doctors diagnosed as "dermatitis veneneta on anterior chest and left of brow."

Pershing sent a telegram of condolence to Beatrice, adding, "I hope Anne is with you to comfort you."

He also wrote to Patton to express his sympathy for the loss of Beatrice's mother, a hard blow coming so soon after the death of her father.

Patton replied, thanking the general for his kind letter.

There is one good feature connected with the death of Mrs. A[yer] namely that now Beatrice will be able to stay in California [with his parents] which will be a comfort to both she and Anne. Mrs. A's health was so bad that she would have been a constant worry to her self and family so that my statement is not as heartless as it sounds.

Talking his way out of the hospital, he rushed to Bourg to watch a maneuver he had planned. He had secured the cooperation of a battalion of the 16th Infantry, and infantry and tanks were to participate together in a practice attack to seize trenches in the Bois d'Amour and the Bois-sur-Marne, small wooded areas near Bourg.

Diary
April 16: Maj. J. F. Hughes Morris who was to command the infantry got mad at not being met so went home. Maneuver worked out fine.

Letter, GSP, Jr., to Beatrice, April 16, 1918

We had our first tank manuver to day and I came out [of the hospital] to direct it. It went fine better than I had hoped.

I had to have some of my men act as infantry but they did not do well as they had no training [in infantry tactics] . . .

One of my cannon blew up . . . but did not hurt any one much though it scared a lot [of people] pretty well.

This was the beginning of a series of exercises, maneuvers, and practice movements in simulated combat. Patton wrote and supervised the preparation of field orders, instructions, movement directives, and the like, to cover a variety of problems and combat situations. Typical of Patton was a thoughtful detail: "On leaving Bourg, each tank will carry 10 gallons gasoline on its tail in order to start fight with full tanks." It was all very serious.

Patton was finally able in mid-April to reply to his former troop commander, General Marshall, who was at Camp Travis, Texas. He was delighted to get Marshall's interesting letter and to know that he liked his job, and that he had received Patton's letters. "I know how deep your interest must be in the present great battle" —he was referring to the Ludendorff spring offensive, by which the Germans hoped to crush the French and British before the Americans could put a trained army in the field—

and wish that I could tell you about it but I cant for the very good reason that I know nothing and that if I did I could not tell. It is a great effort on the part of the Bosch but in my opinion it is not as so often stated his "Swan song." He is not so badly off in the way of resources as we could hope. Nor have the losses all been on his side . . . There was a brief period of very fine open war and had it not been for the magnificent work of the cavalry of the allies he [the enemy] might have made a hole [through the Allied defenses]. One french division in particular made a most stupendus march and then formed a line dismounted and fooled him [the enemy] into thinking that infantry supports had arrived. This was facilitated by the fact that the Bosch was out of the air [had been denied reconnaissance by planes, either because of bad weather or Allied air supremacy]. So [the Boche] could not tell what was in front of him . . . The bosch cavalry seems to me to have been too cautious. I believe that in their place I would have gone through. The tanks were caught with their pants down owing to their being in the act of changing equipment so did not do so well as could have been hoped. This proves my contention also that the big tank is like a very heavy gun and is also only good for a prepared assault. The light tank on the other hand with its mobility can act like field guns . . .

we have a great general and a great army and when it all gets here he [Pershing] will use it like Gen. Grant would have. I hope to God that I will be in at that time. It will be a great day and some show . . . I was offered the chance [for tanks] when no one else would take it just before [the battle of] Cambrai and it was better than any thing in sight. It gave me a chance to get off the staff. I staid awake all night debating the problem and finally put the pros and cons on a piece of paper and added them up. It seemed to me that the pros had it so here I am. Now I must see it out. I have got a fine outfit and work Hell out of them. In twenty days with only four guns and ten tanks I qualified 88 men who had never seen a tank as drivers gas engine expirts gunners M.G. [machine gun] and 37 mm. [gun] signalers and pistol shots. The British with all the facilities in the world take a hundred days. But then they take tea also. We work from six A.M. to five P.M. and have school at night. We do it saturdays too and have full pack inspection on Sunday. God forgive me [for being so tough on the men].

After the war I am never going to work for a month and then start getting ready for the next [war].

I am inclosing a pistol course which I made up. It is good for quick results and takes no machinery as the men can see the holes [in the targets]. Putting men on fatigue who fail to qualify is also a great insentive. One thing about being over here no one watches you and you can go to hell or heaven in your own way. So long as you do something and get results. I think I have.

I must stop now and get up a lecture for to night. I have 66 officers under me here and nearly two battalions. I will eventually have three, and 116 officers.

With sincere reguards to Mrs. Marshall and Mrs. Page. I am Most sincerely

On April 19, Colonel Maxie brought a battalion of men—students attending various schools in Langres—to Bourg for a rehearsal with Patton's tanks for a tank-infantry maneuver.

Letter, GSP, Jr., to his father, April 19, 1918

This drive [the Ludendorff spring offensive] that is now on is pretty bad but we all hope that it will be stopped eventually and that it will take all the blood out of the Bosch. Still the english have been very roughly handled. Unfortunately we have no tanks so I am out of it though there is consolation in the thought that there are very few Americans enjoying it either. The regiment I would have been in had I gone to the infantry is one of those at it now. That ought to please Mama.

We just got through our first Tank [tank-infantry] maneuver a few moments ago. It worked out fine and we are all very pleased with our selves. It is a very complicated affair to get all the guns and infantry and tanks to the same place at the same time and as I had to write all the orders I was delighted to find how well they worked out. The directing tank got to the first trench with in ten seconds of the time I had planned it would. Of course there was no one shooting at it but on the other hand none of the crews had ever seen a tank on the last day of March and they were the result of my personal effort so I was very proud of them. In fact the Lt. commanding came over [to France] in the Headquarters troop with me. I made him a sergeant then a Lt. and finally a tanker so he is my personal property as much as a man can be.

Sylvia [his horse] thinks the tanks are some new sort of racing animal. She is not afraid of them but snorts in contempt when she passes them as if in derision of their lack of speed. Sim [his horse] wont even get out of the way. They are very sensible horses.

I have had the itch for about a week and had to go to the hospital to get it cured but it is all but well now . . .

With much love to all. Your devoted and disgustingly safe son

Letter, GSP, Jr., to Beatrice, April 19, 1918

Lt. Boland does not belong to the class of society who give dances at the Somerset. He was a sergeant of C.A.C. before the war.

Stanley R.[umbough] is better than he used to be but pretty much of an ass just the same.

We do have games in the athletic period running, jumping, shot putting, hurdle races, rope climbing, socker foot ball, and boxing. We can't play regular foot ball because it is too hard to get clothes and we could not store them if we had them. We also have baseball.

B. Jr had better not be too stuck on being a Miss Colonel as I will probably go back to a Captain after the war.

As I have frequently told you I am not in the battle and very few Americans are . . .

P.S. Here are two poems I wrote in the Hospital. Please don't throw them away. What do you think of them.

Letter, GSP, Jr., to Beatrice, April 19, 1918

I have traveled far and fast since [Mexico] . . . I miss you more all the time and long so to see you but I guess there is little use hoping for any thing but the end of the war. If the Bosch keep on as they are doing the end may come sooner than we want [by] a d—— sight. But I feel sure that they will be stopped and chased the other way shortly. Of course this is the time for them to do their damndest and they are. We can't do a thing for a while yet but will make a fine show when we get started.

Letter, GSP, Jr., to Beatrice, April 20, 1918

We got the parts [probably meaning weapons] for our tanks this morning and now look quite war like on a small scale.

The big hospital at G. H. Q. is giving a dance tonight quite shick [chic] with invitations and I am going. It will get me to thinking about something besides Tanks if it is only corns for all the nurses dance horribly.

Letter, GSP, Jr., to Beatrice, April 21, 1918

The dance last night was lots of fun. We danced till one o'clock and the party was still going on when I left.

I had a letter from Braine [who was in the United States trying to expedite the production and shipment of light tanks] to day saying he had seen [her brother] Frederick and hoped to see you. He also was most discouraging about the tanks but I hope he is pesemistic asto when they will get here. We could use them right now. He needs more money than his travel allowance to see all the people and get things moving so I am going to write him to call on Frederick for a thousand dollars if he needs it. He would be more apt to ask Fred than you and you if he takes it can deduct it as war bonds . . .

We are going to have a big show in the morning. I inclose some of the dope [orders, memoranda, and other papers] in various letters as it comes to hand. You can Peace [piece] the thing together as it is only a problem. It is all right to send it to you and I feel sure it will interest you.

I love you.

The letter from Braine to Patton was a long report. Ordered to Washington on tank matters, Braine had loaded a tank turret, a 37-mm. gun, several tank cannons and mounts, and other pieces of equipment on a train bound for the port of St. Nazaire, then had his things put on a ship. With that as the only cargo and he the only passenger, he sailed to New York.

He obtained a tugboat and unloaded his matériel at Governors Island. He took the train to Washington, where he had difficulty finding the proper ordnance office. He finally saw Colonel Alden, whom he had met in England, and gave him the blueprints of the 37-mm. gun that Patton wanted.

Braine returned to New York, hired a truck, and moved the model gun from Governors Island to Washington. He traveled to Dayton, Ohio, by fast train, taking the turret and turret drawings, plus a list of changes Patton wanted made in the tank. "They were waiting for this information so as to get this turret job into production."

Back in Washington, Braine attended a conference on the truck-and-trailer idea for transporting tanks, then consulted with the Engineer Office on building and producing a machine-shop truck.

After going again to Dayton to answer questions on the turret, Braine proceeded to Detroit to offer guidance on the tank transmission and to try to convince the manufacturer to publish a book of maintenance instructions.

Off to Cleveland, he inspected a sample or mock-up of the tank to be manufactured in the United States.

It would probably be, he estimated, three or four months before tanks were actually in production, longer to get them built and forwarded for shipment overseas. He was attending a production meeting that day of all the manufacturers who were making different parts of the tank. He expected to leave that evening for Chicago and Harvey, Illinois, to see the motor. He would then go on to Peoria and Rock Island.

> This is just a hurried line to give you some idea of what I am trying to do, and I believe they will try to keep me over here, but I do not see what good I can do after getting a general line on the whole situation. Please keep me advised as to your wishes. Have been on the move every minute since I arrived, and I doubt very much if I will even get a chance to get home for a few days. Things are now as far along as I had hoped, but will do all that I can to impress upon everyone the necessity of getting some [tanks] over there as quickly as possible. Am taking it upon myself to get around and see as much as I can. This new Department, as you will see by the letter head [—War Department Engineering Bureau, Office of the Chief of Ordnance—], has just been organized; and I may never get any money for my travel and at that will never cover expenses as I am trying to get in with everybody in this whole job.

Diary
April 22, 1918 (Monday): "manuver in heavy rain. Barage of grenades. Fine show. I was much complimented both on the show and on Sylvia's looks [his horse]. About 200 officers were present. One tank fell in a hole but we got it out before five [P.M.]."

Letter, GSP, Jr., to Beatrice, April 22, 1918
Darling Beat: The show came off all right except that it

was raining hard and very cold so that one tank got stuck in a shell hole but I had a reserve one ready and every thing went on fine.

We made a fake barage of grenades and burning steam and it worked fine. I was realy more than pleased.

The only accidents occured in the case of general staff officers who fell off their horses. Williams said he saw six fall off. They certainly are rotten riders. I hope you get the copies of the orders for the show as they will interest you a lot. And as I wrote them all and they are correct so you might keep them.

I am all wet and cold so will stop and change my clothes.

I love you.

The copies of the orders Patton referred to were those that defined the exercise, instructed the participants, set the objectives, and gave the starting and finishing times.

He had written to the Director of the Army General Staff College, Lieutenant Colonel A. W. Bjornstad, a few days before the demonstration to advise him that tanks would operate in conjunction with infantry, the whole supported by two battalions of artillery. Bjornstad, as Patton hoped, instructed his student officers to attend and distributed to them orders, maps, and sketches of the exercise, as well as an explanation of tank characteristics, capabilities, and organization—all furnished by Patton. After the demonstration, many student officers examined the tanks and asked questions.

It was a nice package tied to perfection by Patton, not only for training his own men but also for impressing the faculty and students at the staff college. The latter, after graduation, would be staff officers of tactical organizations and would plan attacks that, hopefully, would utilize tanks.

Across Bjornstad's memorandum, Patton later wrote: "1st Problem. Col Maxey [later] killed at Cantigny commanded the infantry in this manuver. The same tactics were used at Cantigny. GSP Jr." Still later he wrote: "I ran this show. It was the first Tank Maneuver ever held in US Army. GSP Jr." He had every right to be proud.

Several years after the war, when he wrote a humorous account of his experiences with "Tanks, Tankers, and Tactics," he referred to this demonstration, saying:

> The enemy was unintentionally represented by the members of the General Staff College. These officers, for whose benefit the affair was staged, attended mounted . . . the horses objected to the tanks, and one officer was seen leaving the final objective on foot, after having been thrown five times. He held the record but the competition was close and general.

In a more serious vein, he said he was sure that the maneuver was "largely responsible in convincing a great number of the staff officers who witnessed it, of the efficiency of the light tank."

Somehow in the midst of his activities, Patton found the time to write to Pershing. He invited attention to a lecture presented under YMCA auspices by a Dr. Palmer, who had assured his listeners that the war would end in a year. Patton recommended that lecturers, both civilian and military, be prohibited from prophesying such events.

Four of Patton's officers, Brett and three others, departed to visit a somewhat inactive sector of the front near Montdidier held by French troops. Patton wanted to go too, but Rockenbach forbade it. Brett and the others were gone about a week and returned with valuable information on how the front was organized and how troops behaved in the actual presence of the enemy.

Letter, GSP, Jr., to Beatrice, April 25, 1918

They are certainly piling officers in on me and I am having a hard time putting them away but so far have managed to do it but it is like a sardine factory. This town has only room for eight and there are fifty in it and more on the way.

Still I got a compliment out of it for Col R. told his adjutant that he could send them to me as I had never kicked yet. It is the old thing of the willing horse being ridden to death . . .

[Had an amateur night for his men at the YMCA tent and some boxing matches.] I made a speech. They had a song about me which is most complimentary and says that "We will follow the Colonel through hell and out the other side."

I don't see why they like me as I curse them freely on all occasions. But the drafted man is just like the regular which is a surprise to me.

On April 28, he organized the 1st Light Tank Battalion. His three tank companies were commanded by Captains Viner, Brett, and Herman. Patton himself was the battalion commander. This position was a significant step up the command ladder.

CHAPTER 26

A Glimpse of the Front

*"If a person does his best and keeps doing it it usually
pays though not always."*

Diary
April 29: Lt Sewell suggested that adding to the length of
the tail of a tank could make it jump further and therefore
cross trenches more easily. None of us had ever thought of it
before. He said that it was so obvious he feared to mention
it. This is an important discovery and can be done easily.
Discussed the essentials of a tank with Major Champlin and
wrote them out.

If lengthening a tank gave it the capacity to cross wider
trenches, was this really what the designers of tanks ought to
strive for? Or were other capabilities more important?
Considering these questions, Patton clarified a significant issue
in tank design and grasped an essential tactic of tank warfare.

*GSP, Jr., Headquarters, 1st Tank Center, Memo on the
bridging of Trenches and the essential qualities of a Tank,
April 29, 1918*
It appears to me that the single feature of crossing very
large trenches easily has so obsessed the minds of the designers of tanks that they have neglected other and more important essentials. In order to discuss this question I set down
here in the order of importance the desirable features of a
tank as I see them.
1. Mobility of strategic employment.
2. Speed and radius of action on the battle field.
3. Ease and cheepness of construction.
4. Command for the guns and vision.
5. Ability to cross trenches.

With these as the basic principles, Patton went on to say that the strategic mobility of tanks varied inversely with their weight. In other words, the heavier the tank, the less useful it was. "The perfect tank would travel on its own wheels" while moving over roads to the scene of combat "and mount its self on catipillars on entering battle."

This statement was a prophetic vision of the experimental model tank that designer Walter Christie would build in the 1920s and 1930s.

"From this sublime animal" capable of operating both on wheels and tracks—theoretically the most effective machine possible—conventional tanks were useful in a descending scale according to whether they could be transported on trucks or trailers, on standard railroad wagons, or solely on carriages specially built to haul them. Thus, the factor of weight was the most important element in tank construction, for the lighter the tank, the easier and faster it could move—not only in battle, but also in the approach march to the combat zone. For what good was the best tank if it could not quickly get to the battlefield?

Speed of movement, then, both strategic and tactical, was the most valuable tank characteristic, and to that end

> we must reduce the vulnaribility of the tank by making it so fast that it like the [naval] cruser is hard to hit. More than this we must give it a radius of action of sixty miles. This means more gass, hence added weight which must be compensated by reductions in useless armour.

Because the tank was a special vehicle-weapon, it was expensive to build. "The perfect tank from the point of view of construction would be a converted truck. The probable tank [in the future] will be a mean between these two."

Tanks had been invented to cross trenches. But huge trenches, like those in the Hindenburg Line, were rare. There was, then, "no reason to make the crossing of such onomolies as [the Hindenburg trenches the] one determinate feature in the design of tanks, any more than it would be sensible to scrap all but huge howitzers in the artillery." In other words, there was no need to make enormous and unwieldy, consequently less mobile, tanks simply to provide a means of crossing large trenches.

Since the Hindenburg Line was a special obstacle, a special solution was better, for example, the use of explosives, which were far less expensive than "huge machines which have many unsermountable defects and the one advantage of great [trench] bridging ability."

The average trench was no wider than nine feet. Therefore, all tanks should be built to cross trenches of that size. To get across wider obstacles, a tank "should be equiped with a bomb throwing catipult and a certain number of large peterds." A petard containing six pounds of high explosive would do enough damage to any trench to allow any tank to cross. The petard, he felt

> should have a perforated outer envelope of some such substance as tin, the space between the two envelopes to be filled with a phosperous compound which would start smoking and squirting fire in three seconds after discharge, while a thirty second fuse would give the tank time to back off out of the way. The explosion would scatter the phosperous and so render the immediate passage of the tank possible.

Five bombs of this sort and the throwing apparatus would weigh about 100 pounds. But each foot added to the length of a tank—the longer the tank, the wider the trench it could cross—would add about a ton to its weight.

From a theoretical engineering point of view, a tank weighing about ten tons and able to cross a nine-foot ditch could be manufactured to go twenty miles an hour on its tracks and thirty on its wheels. Because of

> its speed the chances of its getting hit will be so reduced as to more than compensate for its reduced armour. We have the authority of Col. Fuller [of the British Tank Corps] for the statement that "Any machine which will cross nomans land and make a noise like a machine gun will be fully as useful as the biggest tank ever made."

When I get a machine shop [at the tank center] I request the permission to make such a machine. I will personally bear the necessary expenses and will so conduct the work that it will in no way interfere with the training of any unit under my command.

Patton was exhilarated by his thoughts and discussions of the features of tanks, for tank design and tank tactics were inseparable. The characteristic he sought above all was speed, the cousin of mobility. Movement, maneuver, and firepower became his passions.

Several papers he wrote in May showed his willingness to reduce armor and consequently weight. Compensation for the diminished protection offered tank crews could be gained in part by designing a tank with more favorable angles and a better silhouette, in part by increased mobility.

Letter, GSP, Jr., to Beatrice, May 4, 1918
Don't worry about me. I am disgustingly safe and feel more like a slacker than a soldier.

I have made an invention which I believe is of great value and hope to be able to put it in operation shortly to the great discomfort of the Hun and his friends.

I cannot tell even you what it is but it is a slight alteration where by with an increase in weight of only 250 lbs the value of a machine is more than doubled without the least sacrifice to speed or handeness. It may be a day dream but I think not and I think not on the judgement of men far smarter than my self so far as mechanics goes . . .

I am having a parade followed by inspection this P.M. so must stop and learn my commands.

A letter from Braine prompted him to write: "I think him a very good man and expect a lot out of him when he gets back. I hope he is not so aloof as he was."

Braine was still traveling around the country, to St. Louis, Camp Colt, New York, Washington, and elsewhere, trying to bring some order to the fragmented production of tanks, tank parts, and tank guns. "Not more than twelve people working on all tank work," he later wrote, "including light and heavy, when I arrived in Washington." No tools or spare parts had been ordered. When he insisted that the tank gun be put into immediate production, he was overruled.

He was appalled by the organizational chaos in the Army. Separate groups were working on motor equipment, small arms, ammunition, explosives, cannons, machine guns, automatic weapons, equipment, and supplies, and no one had the authority to coordinate the whole.

After being in the United States three weeks, he discovered, quite by chance, that Colonel Welborn was the director of the Tank Corps in Washington. Braine went to see him and exposed the disunity in the tank program, but Welborn was powerless to weld the various and often divergent, even conflicting, efforts into a single meaningful operation.

Braine finally met Benedict Crowell, Assistant Secretary of War, and, by his description of the haphazard procedures, interested him in the problem of tank production. The arrival of Colonel Draine from Paris helped. Eventually, a civilian was appointed to take charge of the entire work. And, finally, two tanks were constructed and made ready for shipment.

It was Braine who arranged to take these to France. He had some trouble getting authority to leave the United States, for various groups had found him knowledgeable and useful, and they clamored for his assignment to them. But he persisted and succeeded in obtaining clearance.

Traveling to Cleveland, Braine secured the two tanks, personally convoyed them to port, had them loaded on a ship, and himself sailed for France with them. His two American-built tanks would arrive in Bourg and the tank center after the war was over.

Letter, GSP, Jr., to Beatrice, May 5, 1918
Did I ask you to send some sheet music for piano and quartetts of voices for the men. Not very many as there is only one piano.

Letter, GSP, Jr., to Beatrice, May 6, 1918

I am thinking of taking the General Staff course next term if I can manage it. I don't see when I will get the time but hope I can manage it as it is a most valuable course.

But I am getting nearvous. I will have to take a leave I fear or do something different. This thing of doing the same thing every day as hard as I am is getting me a little.

Letter, GSP, Jr., to the Deputy Chief of Staff, GHQ AEF, May 6, 1918, subject: Tank Tactics and Strategy

Presuming upon your interest in the Tank I am sending you herewith . . . a problem which I have gotten up as a basis for further instruction and in the hope of exciting discussion and consequent interest.

In the problem you will notice a halt of eleven minutes on the intermediate objective. Subsequent reflection on my part has convinced me that this halt is an error. The second wave of infantry supported by a line of tanks preceding them should "LeapFrog" on at once. For the reason that if they do not the enemy will have nothing on his mind except the shelling of the tanks and inft. at the intermediate objective, while if the line goes right on he will have something else to think about. Any tanks surviving the attack . . . should help mop up and then go on as fast as possible to thicken the leading line [of] tanks.

The British supports [supporting troops] follow in short columns, the French in skirmish line. I am uncertain which is the best formation and request an opinion from you.

Before the wilderness campaign Gen. Grant told the President that in his opinion the Union Army had never been fought to its limit. Please pardon my presumption in suggesting that the same is true of the Tanks.

About this time he received a letter that pleased him enormously. Captain R. I. Sasse, a cavalry officer with the 1st Division, had made four applications to transfer to the tanks but was being held because he "was needed here." He asked whether Patton could do "anything . . . toward a successful approval of my transfer." Patton would get Sasse into the tanks, and they would become close friends.

Letter, GSP, Jr., to Aunt Nannie, May 9, 1918

I am getting ashamed of my self when I think of all the fine fighting and how little I have had to do with it . . .

[Someone was recently wounded in the fleshy part of the leg.] I rather envie him as now he can wear a wound chevron and pose as a hero . . .

I have a very good place and have been frequently complimented on the good appearance of things and on the discipline of the men.

This is at least satisfying and I hope will lead to something for the good opinion of those above you is a source of great advantage.

I am very well and in no danger of any thing but getting fat.

Letter, GSP, Jr., to Beatrice, May 9, 1918

We will not get the tanks so soon as we had hoped and that is indeed too bad. Still the "darkest hour is just before the dawn" and we may find that we are getting Tanks sooner than we had hoped.

Yesterday I was all for transferring to the infantry but now think I will not first because probably they would not let me and second because having made my bed I think the sporting thing to do is to lie in it. I have never quit yet that I know of and though it is discouraging to be kept out of the fight so long it may pay in the end. If a person does his best and keeps doing it it usually pays though not always.

Letter, GSP, Jr., to Beatrice, May 12, 1918

I was feeling very low over lack of material but some has just turned up and we ought to do fine. I will have ten times as many machines as I have now. You see luck always changes if you do your best with what you have.

I have been working on a [tactical] problem for 3 days and it is finished so I feel better . . .

Just about a year ago we were rushing around like every thing to get my dress uniforms. I have never had them on since.

Letter, GSP, Jr., to Beatrice, May 13, 1918

I fear that the tanks will not do much for many months except perhaps a few raides for practice.

When "a lot of milk toast YMCA women" came to Bourg to see the tanks, Patton put on a show for them. In the process he experimented with crossing trenches at relatively high speeds. The results were surprisingly good.

Letter, Mr. Patton to Beatrice, May 17, 1918

[Returning some of his son's papers, orders, maps, and poems.] The article on tanks is very interesting and the spelling really spectacular. He certainly misses his "Editor" . . . He was very wise when he left the Staff. What he needs is action—and I have not the slightest doubt he will succeed— He always has.

Diary

May 19 (Sunday): "Col. R came down and talked a lot but said nothing. It was very tiresome. He told me I could go to French front Tuesday."

May 20: Got ready to go. Wrote letter to B which I gave to Viner to forward in case I am killed.

Letter, GSP, Jr., to Beatrice, May 20, 1918

Of course if I am reported killed I may still have been Captured so don't be too worried. I have not the least preminition that I am going to be hurt and feel foolish writing you this letter but perhaps if the thing happened you would like it [the letter] . . .

I think I am too high ranking to be allowed to see much [of the action]. Of course you know I will try to see all I can.

Beatrice there is no advice I can give you and nothing that I could suggest that you would not know better than I. Few men can be so fortunate as to have such a wife.

All my property is yours though it is not much. My sword is yours also my pistol the silver one. I will give Sylvia [his horse] to Gen Pershing and Simalarity [his horse] to Viner.

I think that if you should fall in love you should marry again. I would approve.

I have some money here which Viner will send to you.

The only regret I have in our marriage is that it was not sooner and that I was mean to you at first . . .

If I go I trust that it will be in a manner such as to be worthy of you and of my ideals.

Kiss Beatrice Jr and Ruth-Ellen for me and tell them that I love them very much and that I know they will be good.

Beat I love you infinately.

Diary

May 21: I went home early and sat in sun to cure itch. Gave party in mess. Champagne.

Letter, GSP, Jr., to his father, May 21, 1918

I am leaving in a few moments for the French front to go with a bunch of french tanks. I am hoping that the Bosch will start something but the prospects are not good and besides I have too much rank to see any thing . . . Still there is a great deal of gas in that sector and they may get me. In order to forestall that eventuality I have left some instructions with Capt. Joseph Viner as to my affairs which of course are simple . . .

I left a box containing my dress uniforms and some other things at a fencing room . . . [in] Paris. I have told Viner about it and he will send them to B. if any thing happens. As I said before nothing will.

Patton and five of his lieutenants, Will Robinson, T. C. Brown, W. H. Williams, Nelms, and Morrison, traveled to the Montdidier-Noyons sector.

Diary

May 24, 1918: "Did not speak a word of English all day but talked incessantly."

Letter, GSP, Jr., to Beatrice, May 25, 1918

We are about six miles from the front and you can hear the guns all the time but it is simply a constant roar as there are so many guns you can't distinguish any seperate explosion. At night the sky is quite bright . . . every once in a while you can hear a machine gun above all the other noise . . . All this shooting does little harm but is supposed to worry people. I hope to get up closer for a day or two and can then tell you how it feels when it is hitting nearer.

There are manuvers here every day with Tanks . . .

The French have much less office work than [is] usual with

us. This is a command of 3 battalions and it has one typewriter. At my place we have six. All busy.

The French are awfully nice and I get on fine with them.
None of the ones here speak a word of English. We get on
fine and tell jokes.

Still I some times wish I had gone in the fantry for there
is too damned much waiting in the tanks.

Commandant (Major) La Fevre took Patton to St. Martin-aux-
Bois. There was a fine eleventh-century church in the village, but
"I did not look at it"—meaning he had no time to visit it. On a
hill crowned by an old mill, which gave a commanding view of
the German lines, La Fevre explained what troops did on entering
the front, and "I wrote it all down."

Letter, GSP, Jr., to Beatrice, May 26, 1918
One interesting thing about life is that one can never tell
what is going to happen. It is like fishing. You always expect
a "strike" yet when it comes you have all the pleasure of
surprise . . .

These people know a lot that I should know but it is like
pulling teeth to get it out of them . . . They take for granted
that one knows it also.

To show Patton what the front was like and, more particularly,
where the French usually placed their tanks, La Fevre took Patton
in an automobile through St. Martin to Menevillers. Leaving the
car—it was unsafe to drive farther toward the front—they walked
through a ravine, passing a battery of 155-mm. howitzers well
hidden under nets. La Fevre pointed out several good positions
for tanks, discussed the reasons why they were good, and talked
about the best approach routes to them. Walking along the railroad in search of additional positions, they saw two batteries of
75-mm. howitzers in action and also several German planes receiving antiaircraft fire.

Letter, GSP, Jr., to Beatrice, May 29, 1918
The French are certainly nice and do everything they can
to help us. They are some soldiers too. Personally I like them
much better than the British possibly because they do not

drink Tea. Which to my mind is a most hellish and wasteful practice . . .

I have hardly spoken a word of english for a week and am quite surprised at my fluency. I can now easily understand conversations between Two French who I happen to overhear. Which is a test of any language.

Diary

May 30: With Commandant La F in auto at 7:30 to Godenvillers; walked along a bayou to a farm near Robescourt; 2 shells fell 100 yards from us; there were many shell holes; we crossed a field on a hill 300 to 400 yards from Bosch but they did not shoot, "which seemed to me foolish as they could have easily gotten us." Neared Ployron while it was being shelled, but when we entered, the soldiers were walking about unconcerned. Visited the Colonel and had some wine; he had a fine abri [shelter].

Letter, GSP, Jr., to Beatrice, May 30, 1918

Darling Beat: I had a most interesting morning. We The Maj. and I left here at 7:30 and went by motor to with in about 1500 yds of the front line. Most of the way the road was screened with camouflage. Sacking about 12 feet high on Frames it keeps the enemy from seeing what is on the road so he can not fire on it. In places there were shell holes in the road quite large perhaps five feet deep and 12 ft accross. We left the machine at last and armed with walking sticks tin hats and gas masks we started accross a wheat field toward the front line. (Our purpose was to locate the departure position for tanks.) The sun was shining and it was as peaceful as could be but no one was in sight. Except for long snake like trenches. Communication trenches—there was no sign of war. Pretty soon we passed some green sacking on the ground. Under it was a whole battery [of artillery] with little caves for the men. They were all asleep. At last we came to the support position about 1000 yards from our front line. There were lots of shell holes and a whole battalion under some sacking died green to look like trees.

There were several bunches of soldiers walking about armed with walking sticks like picknickers. The guns began to shoot a little just then.

Then we went on up a hill to a farm. It was all shot to pieces. On going round the corner we saw a line of trees about 400 yds away. (The length of the avenue at Pride's.) The Maj said "There are the bosch." It was their line but not a thing was to be seen not even a trench. He said that they could see us which was quite evident so we walked along in the shadow of a hedge.

Two shells came and blew up about 100 yds away at most perhaps less. I went over to the hole and picked up a piece for you. It was still hot. I was not scared but a little thrilled. We went behind the house and you could hardly walk for shell holes but here a rise hid us from the Bosch. We came to a communication trench and I was rather hopeful we would get in it but the Maj said that the walking was better on top so we came to the top of the rise and there was our trench like a ditch for pipe with a little wire in front of it and there was the line of trees—the Bosch, 200 yds away . . .

He then said we had best be going or some "sallebut" [sale bête—dirty dog] will shoot at us. So we went down the rise to my great relief and moved behind it to a little wood where the trench was just in front of it. Here we looked for Bosch 200 yds away but none were to be seen. Behind the wood was a new grave with (UN Soldier Alemande) written on a nice wooden cross. He had been killed by a patroll this morning . . . The Maj. Paused to show me what a magnificent field of fire the Bosch had but I could not help noting that we were the only avalable target and the range was deadly. I hated to have my back to them as it would be awkward to explain a wound in the back. We went diagnally accross this field in plane view. It is the biggest field in the world I think. At least it seemed so. Right in the middle of it the maj. Stopped to fix his legging exposing his bottom in a most tempting way to the Bosch whom he assured me were watching us. To express contempt equal to his I removed my helmet and lit a cigarett. Finally we got over the ridge. Really it is funny to picture a Col and a Maj. strolling along in broad day light the only living things in sight and not a shot. One does not feel scared but has a great curiosity as to why in hell the Bosch don't shoot.

It was about the same thrill as riding a steeplechase.

As we were in the sector of an inft. Col. we knew we went to call on him. As we approached the village two french batteries in the back edge of it opened fire and shot to beat hell for about five minutes.

Then they stopped and the Bosch started shelling the village while we walked towards it. Then they stopped and when we were about 200 yds from the village the French started again. This provoked the major for he said, "Now the Bosch will be shelling back when we get there." In my mind I advocated waiting till the Bosch were through but of course did not mention it. The French stopped and just as we entered the place the bosch started we were in one street and the shells were mostly landing in the next. It was not heavy about 5 a minute. There were lots of soldiers in the place and they did not pay the least attention but walked about smoking.

The Col. lived in an abri about 30 feet below the ground it was a fine place with bed rooms and telephones. He apologized for having no electric lights but the oil lamps were ample. We had some Ciro and talked about the war in 1914 and how much more chick it was than the present one.

The Maj said "Ah comme j'adore sette guerre de movement, c'etait passionelle. Mais celue ce est tres embetant." [Ah, how I loved that war of movement, it was exciting. But this one is every annoying.] I hope that is the way to spell what he said? All Frenchmen talk of 1914 with longing and never speak of the present "salle affaire."

When we left the col. we watched the batteries for a little while. The performance was must amusing. Every thing is covered with camouflage. The Bosch stop firing. Pretty soon the French rush out of their caves and shoot to beat hell. Then they stop and rush back to the caves . . . They keep this up all the time with out the slightest chance of hurting each other.

The major told me it was perfectly useless but necessary other wise they would forget they were at war. Once in a while they shoot at the infantry trenches but not often. Of course in an attack it is different and they stay by their guns and shoot all the time . . .

This long account gives you an idea of how safe this sort of war is. Also I have been here a year and it is the nearest I have ever been to a bosch so you see I am quite safe. Send this to Papa when you have read it as it may interest him. The whole show appeals to one as funny more than dangerous.

On Friday, May 31, Patton drove through Breteuil to a farm east of Paillart, where he visited a French tank unit. These tankers had made an attack two days earlier with part of the American 1st Infantry Division at Cantigny. The Americans had lost 300 men, including Patton's friend, Colonel Maxie. Patton spoke to the tankers and learned the details of the battle. He discovered that not a single tank had been hit by an enemy shell.

Traveling to the 1st Division headquarters at Le Mesnil, Patton obtained the American side of the tank-infantry operation. He talked with Colonel King, the chief of staff, and Captain Johnson, who had commanded the assault wave of infantry working with the tanks. Johnson was "most enthusiastic" about the machines.

Patton was in Paris on Saturday and went to the theater. After a fairly lazy Sunday and Monday, he returned to Chaumont, where he had a satisfactory talk with Daniel D. Pullen, Rockenbach's new chief of staff. Patton believed that things would move along better now that Pullen was helping Rockenbach.

Then to Langres, where he found everything in fine shape, especially the mess hall, which the officers had decorated while he was gone "as a surprise for me." They had covered the walls and ceiling with camouflage burlap to which they attached branches of trees. But they had refrained from cutting the camouflage material, for they would take it down and use it when they went to war. "One has to be careful not to waste a thing and we don't."

Best of all, he learned that the Commandant of the Army Schools, "Col [Harry A.] Smith [had] said that the Tank Corps was the first [leading] unit in this district and that its smartness and enthusiasm enspired all the other units. I am well pleased as we are having a pretty hard time for not getting Tanks. Still we are doing our damdest."

Smith had complimented Patton's tank center in a memo he had issued "to all concerned":

Too many officers and men salute as though they had creeping paralysis. All freak salutes will be avoided . . .

The officers and men at the Tank School rank number one so far as saluting is concerned.

Smith was a man after Patton's heart, and they would become good friends.

"Capt. Viner did well while I was gone so that every thing is in fine shape." After catching up on his correspondence, Patton began translating the French tank regulations for the benefit both of himself and his officers. For several days he ran what he called a "Cook's Tour," showing people around the center and introducing them to tanks. "It is most useful as I use my well known and fatal charm to get them on my side. The last victim was the Chief of Ordnance and he is all for us." Another important visitor thought little of light tanks until he saw them at work, and then, according to Patton, went wild over them and promised to do all he could to help.

On June 6, Patton reorganized the tank center in order to accommodate a second battalion. With this larger command under him, Patton needed a larger staff. He therefore appointed Gibbs his chief of staff, Hebert his adjutant, Knowles reconnaissance officer, and Robinson supply officer. He placed Captain Viner in command of the 1st Battalion—formally named the 326th Tank Battalion (later it would be redesignated the 344th), with Company A under Compton, Company B under Weed, and Company C under English. He put Captain Brett in command of the 2d Battalion—formally the 327th Tank Battalion (later redesignated the 345th), with Company A under Semmes, Company B under Williams, and Company C under Bernard. Lieutenant Baldwin commanded the 301st Repair and Salvage Company, which serviced and repaired the tanks.

With Patton in command of this organization, he became the equivalent of a regimental commander, another significant step up the chain of command.

With two full battalions now formed, with more men and tanks expected soon, he suggested to Beatrice that she stop trying to get to England—"after all the work I have done I should hate to be sent home that way," meaning because her coming might be construed as a breach of regulations.

"Brief Notes on the Tactical Employment of Tanks," dated June 10, indicated the growing maturity of Patton's ideas of warfare, for he was now thinking of how to employ the machines in different types of operations—the assault, the counterattack, the exploitation of a success, advance and rear guards in a war of movement, raids with cavalry or special infantry units, and small, independent operations—and he described how tanks could be so utilized. For example:

> We are all aware of the over cautious movements of advance guards. A few shots are fired. The point lays down and signals enemy in sight. The advance party sends out a patrol or deploys and finally perhaps even the support is involved in dislodging a squad with a machine gun in a barn or thicket. Much time is lost and the enemy has made us do just his bidding . . . Time is the great factor in war. The light tank in open war is an uneaqueled time saver.

Unarmored troops working as rear guards performed "a difficult and dangerous proceeding and most exhausting. Also there is the constant menace of being taken in flank by hostile cavalry." But a company of light tanks in this duty was something else.

> Cavalry cannot hurt it as a tank has no flanks. The light tank on account of its small size can be hidden in barns thickets or rolls on the ground and from these concealed places will surely take heavy toll of the hostile advance parties . . . It will frequently be put out [of action] but that is the fate of all soldiers and it will cost the enemy untold hours in the priceless element of time.

Speaking of special operations involving a few tanks:

> The hostile barrage might put out one tank on the return trip but since it costs only $8000.00 it would be much cheaper than a barrage to cut the wire . . . Besides it would be a complete surprise and hence would reduce the losses of the infantry.

It must never be forgotten that boldness is the key to
victory. The tank must be used boldly. It is new and always
has the element of surprise. It is also very terrifying to look
at as the infantry soldier is helpless before it.

He could have been speaking of blitzkrieg in World War II, 21
years still in the future.

*Letter, Will G. Robinson (Secretary, South Dakota Histori-
cal Society, Pierre, S.D.) to Lieutenant Colonel Arthur J.
Jacobson, July 6, 1961*

I went to France in 1917 with the 147th F.A. [Field Artil-
lery] and one day, General Patton, then a captain, came down
to Montrichard looking for an adjutant, as St Aignan nearby,
was the replacement center . . . He made the Tank Corps
look good to me and I got 200 volunteers from the 147th and
other troops down there, truck drivers, mechanics and machine gunners and went up to B[o]urg, a little village near
Longue [Langres], where the Light Tanks had their headquarters.

Not long after arriving, some Division, or the advance elements came in, I believe it was the 82nd, and they had
shoulder patches. The first we had ever seen. Patton, at mess
that night, said "I want you officers to devote one evening to
something constructive. I want a shoulder insignia. We claim
to have the firepower of artillery, the mobility of cavalry and
the ability to hold ground of the infantry so whatever you
come up with it must have red, yellow and blue [the traditional colors of artillery, cavalry, and infantry] in it." I was
billetted with a medico, Lt. Howard and we spent all that
evening with some crayons . . . in front of a fire place figuring out use of the colors and a design . . . At breakfast the
next morning everybody showed up with their attempt. I
guess we were the only ones that had managed to get color
on ours. In any event Patton adopted our design [a pyramidal
figure] and pulling [out a] $100 dollar bill, the first I had
ever seen or at least held in my hand, he told me to take one
of the . . . vehicles . . . and go into Longue [Langres] and
get as many of our shoulder patches made up as I could get
and get them back by Retreat. I managed to get the three
colors in felt at the Belle Jardineer a big store on the Place

Diderot and took them into a hat and cap shop next door and persuaded the old lady in charge to start her crew making shoulder patches. They did a good job of them and I had one sewed onto my overseas cap, as a possible idea of a new use of them and got two or three hundred of them out to B[o]urg before retreat.

Patton was tickled about it. If there was anything he wanted it was to make the Tank Corps tougher than the Marines and more spectacular than the Matterhorn. That triangle [shoulder patch] was the first step. A few days later he conceived the idea that our overcoats were all too long and he ordered them cut to knee length and the surplus made into belts. We were different all right.

Another indication of his unorthodox methods in some matters:

Letter, GSP, Jr., to Beatrice, June 15, 1918
I am in a little trouble my self over some Pipe I "stole" for the Center here. The Engineers are very mad at me and the inspector General is coming down to investigate the affair. I will probably get reprimanded for cutting red tape but it ought not hurt me as I am only guilty of too much initiative. Which is a quality often missing over here. Don't worry about me. The inspector . . . lived next to us at [Fort] Myer.

Brett moved his battalion to new facilities at Brennes, two kilometers from Bourg. Then Patton arranged for Viner, Brett, Gibbs, and himself to take the General Staff course at Langres.

Letter, GSP, Jr., to Beatrice, June 12, 1918
Things are very stupid here now and I have little to do but wate and twist my thumbs. I am going to take the next course at the Staff College which starts on the 17th when I will be very busy indeed but that agrees with me more than doing nothing or only a little . . .

I am certainly living a healthy life. I get up at six go to bed at ten and eat very simple food and drink only water. Not even Port Wine.

I have to do a great deal of writing on regulations etc as there are none for the tanks, also being a C.O. one can have no friends and though I never much cared for them I find the total loss a little of a bore.

Sometime in June, when it became apparent that there would be no American-built tanks in France in any quantity before 1919, Pershing secured a promise from the French that they would equip two American battalions—Patton's—with Renaults.

Meanwhile, Patton instituted night combat training and was immensely pleased when a tank company traveled 10 kilometers in just under three hours without straying once from a designated route. That the tankers were able to work through gullies and thick woods under simulated battle conditions indicated a sense of self-assurance on their part that delighted Patton.

Diary

June 13: Col. Rockenbach came down and said that probably one battalion would get into a fight in August. "I fear we will have no such luck. But hope for the best."

Letter, GSP, Jr., to Beatrice, June 13, 1918

[Camouflaged tanks were] awful and wonderful to behold close up though at a distance they cannot be seen at all. It is very funny how the bright crazy colors blend with the most ordinary colors. We had one under a net the other day and some staff officers thought I was lieing when I told them that there was a tank with in 100 yds of them. They could not see it at all.

Letter, GSP, Jr., to Beatrice, June 13, 1918

One year ago to day we reached Paris full of desire to kill Germans. We are still full of desire but so far as I am concerned there are just as many Germans as there were then. Some times I deeply regret that I did not take the infantry last November instead of the Tanks. The regiment I had the chance to join has been at it now for five months. Of course I have done a lot but I keep dreading lest the war should finish before I can realy do any fighting. That would destroy my military career or at least give it a great set back.

The only cheering prospect is that there are very many infantry Battalion commanders and only a few Tank commanders.

If the war lasts long enough it will work out greatly to my advantage but the unknown is always full of terrors and I wake up at night in a sweat fearing that the d—— show is over.

I am having two much routine for my health at least health of mind.

I trust that it is doing my character a lot of good for I keep at it inspite of constant difficulties and descouragements. But unless I get into a fight or two it is all wasted effort.

CHAPTER 27

Bourg and Langres: Staff School

*"I will have to develop even a meaner look than I
now have but that will only be my official face."*

PATTON attended the third course of studies at the Army General
Staff College in Langres. It was a good experience, for he came to
understand the complex duties of staff work in a modern army,
and he came into contact with some of the best soldiers in France.

Brigadier General Harry A. Smith, the commandant, directed
a no-nonsense operation that sought to train staff officers, by
means of an extremely compressed curriculum, as quickly as possible. A French Mission headed by Colonel J. L. Koechlin-Schwartz
and a British Mission headed by Lieutenant Colonel Sir T. A. M.
Cunningham contributed the experience of their armies. Major
John Millikin, who would command a corps in World War II,
assisted. Major Adna R. Chaffee, an old friend of Patton, was
an instructor. Visiting lecturers included General Trenchard, the
foremost British authority on air power, Brigadier General George
Van Horn Mosely, Pershing's G–4 or Supply Officer, Lieutenant
Colonel George C. Marshall, who would be the U.S. Army Chief
of Staff in World War II, Major Alexander M. Patch, who in
World War II would command the Seventh Army during the invasion of southern France and throughout the rest of the Euro-
pean campaigns, and Patton himself, the leading American expert
on armor.

Among those who would graduate with Patton's class were
Major H. R. Bull, who would be the G–3 or Operations Officer of
Eisenhower's Supreme Headquarters, AEF, in 1944–45, Major
W. H. Simpson, Patton's classmate at West Point who would com-
mand the Ninth Army in Europe during the same period, Captain

Joseph Stilwell, future theater commander in China and Burma, and Major John S. Wood, later the commander of the 4th Armored Division and probably the most intelligent disciple of Patton and the most vigorous exponent of his methods of tank warfare.

Although Patton had little interest in becoming a General Staff officer—he wished instead to be a commander—he worked hard at the school. He was motivated by his admiration of and respect for General Smith, who had helped and supported Patton at the tank school. He was motivated too by his professional interest in all aspects of soldiering, and he understood that the immensity of the World War had raised to unprecedented importance the role of the military administrator, organizer, and coordinator—whose functions would, many years later, be combined under the term "manager." Finally, he was motivated by the demon that drove him, his quest for perfection and attainment.

He was extremely busy, so busy that he was unable to write Beatrice as frequently or as lengthily as he wished. He was too busy even to write his normal few lines in his diary; between June 24 and August 20, he made but one entry.

There were several reasons why his time was so fully occupied. Classes at the school started at eight A.M., and the students were usually unable to leave their desks until close to five o'clock. The instructional materials were so concentrated that he marveled how "any one but a regular [officer] of considerable experience" could finish the assignments. Although he would leave the school about ten days or two weeks before the conclusion of the course and the brief graduation ceremony, he would receive credit for the entire work.

Another reason why his days were so full of activity was his continued interest in his tank center and school. He remained in close touch with what was taking place at Bourg and Brennes. In addition, he wrote and delivered lectures to his tankers, drew up drill regulations, and prescribed training exercises and schedules.

"I am now taking a cold bath at six each morning and am feeling fine."

On Monday, June 17, the day Patton started attending the General Staff College, fifteen new French Renault tanks arrived for the center. In less than an hour they were driven off the train and down the ramp and on their way to the tank park. It was a fine performance by well-trained men.

The arrival of the new tanks, giving the center 25 in all, made it possible to have company maneuvers. Patton consequently modified the drill schedule in order to have the companies, in rotation, train as a unit every afternoon, and the platoons, each in turn, work on night maneuvers every day after dark.

From seven until noon, some men from each company took driving instruction while the rest trained on the guns and practiced such activities as message writing, grenade throwing, and gas-mask wearing; from one in the afternoon to six, one company held a maneuver as a unit while the other troops worked with the pistol, learned how to assault trenches, and exercised physically. From seven-thirty to midnight, each platoon had an exercise that featured night driving.

Patton later wrote:

> The spirit of the men during all this time was most wonderful for in spite of working six days a week and having inspection on Sunday and in spite of building roads, buildings, sheds, etc. there was not the least complaint, each man and officer doing his very best each moment of the day.

Some of the lectures he was writing and delivering were on the tactical employment of tanks, the use of ten-ton trailers to move tanks, and the like. One paper, headed "Speaking Notes," consisted of 42 topic sentences, among them:

> 26. I propose instead the following method of employment—
> 27. Diagram V and VI
> 28. But in order to make these actions of the tank useful.
> 29. Here it may be permissable to point [out] a defect I have occasionally noted . . .
> 39. Now I shall take advantage of my position to respectfully prepound a question to you. Is the creeping Barrage

worth while. [In the later stages of World War II, it was completely eliminated—26 years after Patton posed the question.]

   40. Next do you give enough thought to transient targets.

   41. Do Tanks get as much support as they deserve.

Another paper detailed a training schedule for a nine-week period—with subjects to be studied and hours to be spent listed daily, including recreation—the whole culminating in a week-long battle practice.

So well had he placed his imprint on the men under him that Major C. C. Benson, one of his officers, could himself sound like Patton when lecturing. All company officers must, Benson said firmly, "stay on the job until all machines of the convoy are in . . . Platoon Commander stays on the job until all parts of his groups are parked in camp." Command responsibility in the Patton school of thought could not be delegated.

Letter, GSP, Jr., to Beatrice, June 21, 1918
Things look pretty blue for our getting into the fight soon. We will have to go on training I fear for some time yet.
I must stop now and study.

Letter, GSP, Jr., to Beatrice, June 22, 1918
Still no mail. I know it is not your fault but that of the war. Still I miss hearing from you very much. We had another map problem to day and worked from 8 till 4 with out lunch so feel rather empty. I did not do very well as I am lazy when it comes to stupid details. Still I probably did better than many others.

Enclosed—because it was a "stupid" letter—was the one he had written on May 20 and left with Viner to send in the event Patton was killed during his visit to the French sector of the front.

He was quite tired as the result of doing double work at the college and the center, but he felt that his studies were worth the effort, for he might thereby avoid the necessity of attending the college at Leavenworth after the war. As for tank matters in general, he felt much easier in his mind knowing that Pullen was Rockenbach's chief of staff. To Beatrice he reported talk of giving him six battalions instead of four—"That will be some command. But I can handle it all right if I get the buildings, and the Tanks."

He took a break one Sunday afternoon and rode his horse Sylvia Green to Chaumont. It was a beautiful day and a beautiful ride, 40 kilometers, about 25 miles, along the poplar-lined tow path of the canal. It took him three and a half hours. There were "cows and cow girls in the green fields on both sides. Each girl had at least one soldier in attendance so I fear that more than calves will be approaching in nine months." He had dinner with Pershing, left his horse stabled in Chaumont, and returned to Langres by auto.

Beatrice was thinking again of trying to visit Kay in England, but Patton was against it—unless "you can get things arranged so as not to get me in trouble." He had a bright idea. "I think you had best get a divorce then you can come at pleasure. It realy might be a good idea?"

Letter, GSP, Jr., to Beatrice, June 27, 1918
Four of my officers got put in arrest last night for drinking publicly with women. We are getting full of virtue here. Personally I don't think much of it. The French do as they please so why not we. People who are going to be killed deserve as much pleasure as they can get. This does not mean that I am one of these pleasure seekers but that I approve of the principal.

Letter, GSP, Jr., to Beatrice, June 30, 1918
We have just come back from a most interesting experiment in driving tanks over shell holes at an artillery target range near here. There were a lot of generals and people out to see [us]. The tanks could not have done better. In fact it was as fine a performance as I have seen. Every one was very complimentary. One hole was ten feet deep and over 30 feet across. One tank got stuck in it but another one came and pulled it out in a minute.

They also raised hell with some wire entanglements and had a great time.

I am going over to the artillery school for dinner to day and so must stop and clean up a little.

Letter, GSP, Jr., to Beatrice, July 1, 1918

I am getting to be a regular devil on telephones and use them on all occasions. Remember how I used to hate them. Now I even talk french over them which is a truly great feat for me; both as a linguist or a telephonist.

The Director Army Staff College told me I was doing well. This was a surprise as I have not had time to do any studying . . .

It is remarcable how soon they [his tankers] improve with a little night work.

Letter, GSP, Jr., to Beatrice, July 2, 1918

Next time you go to Washington make it a point to see Brigadier Gen. Hugh S. Johnson who lived with me in Mexico. He is now in very close to the chief of Staff and is also a good friend of mine . . . You could talk to him quite freely about me and might pump him about John [Pershing] but he is pretty smart so you will have to be careful on the pumping. Still I think that he is susceptable to good looks and you have them. That is one of the many reasons why I love you.

Letter, GSP, Jr., to Beatrice, July 4, 1918

[Holiday] not doing much. I did not get up till eight o'clock which is better than my usual 5:30 habit. Or rather necessity for I never want to get up and never will develop that practice . . .

I have a double sort of existence. With you and away from you. One has a time scale quite different from the other like a creeping and Fixed barrage tables.

I miss you terribly but there is no use dwelling on that as we both know it.

Letter, GSP, Jr., to Beatrice, July 5, 1918

Darling Beat: We have been having much excitement to day. The people to put in my Rail Road arrived also . . . to put in the roades and build houses so I feel like a leading manufacturer putting up a new plant. Which is in fact just what I am at present.

We also did some shell hole stunts for a large crowd of people 250 field officers. The tanks did fine and just played in and out of the holes in a most approved fashion.

It is realy inspiring to see the little beasts climb in and out
of the holes in fine style even [though] I always expect them
to get stuck but they never do.

See if you can find out why Col. R[ockenbach] is not made
a general. He has been recomended time and again and there
must be some one gumming up the game. Is it Col. Welborn
[chief of the Tank Corps in Washington].

There is another hitch in the mail so I have not heard from
you for some days. I love you. George.

Patton traveled to Hammel, where 60 British tanks, 10 Australian infantry battalions, and 2 American infantry companies had
carried out a battle operation. He read all the orders and reports,
examined the battlefield, inspected several tanks, and talked with
participants—the tank brigade commander, the tank battalion
commanders, many staff officers, and a few tank commanders.
One senior officer explained that too many tanks had been employed on too small a front. As a result, many tanks masked other
tanks and prevented them from firing. Two collided. The tanks
had nevertheless been of great assistance.

Returning to Langres, Patton wrote a report of four single-
spaced typed pages entitled "Tank Action at Hammel." His conclusion: "Infantry well trained with Tanks is the most powerful
and least expensive answer to the German machine gun." Then
he passed the paper to his battalion commanders, Viner and
Brett, and asked them to study the operation and comment on it.

Letter, George to Beatrice, July 7, 1918

A tank which I have had altered will get here in the morning. It has some things on it which render it perfectly silent
and it holds more men and gas. If it comes up to my expectations it will be more than twice as good as the present machine and ought to be a truly great invention which will give
me prestige as an inventor.

The trouble with me is that I can do too many things fairly
well and nothing hellish well and so nothing I have done is of
any great use in getting me medals or decorations . . .

It is funny all we do is for the effect it will have on people
later. And all I try to do is for the effect it will have on you.

In fact my attitude towards you is more that of a lover uncertain of his chances than of a husband. Still it is a good way to be.

Letter, GSP, Jr., to Beatrice, July 11, 1918
I think you would be a fool to try and do war work in addition to your other duties. There are a lot too many people doing it any way. And the work you could do would have no real value. Most of this alledged war work is realy histeria.
    Col P. Echols was here to day to see the tanks. I was very nice to him though he did turn me back a year [at West Point] and keep me from marrying you that much longer.
    Col R is now Gen. R having just been promoted to day. I am glad of it as it will give the T.C. [Tanks Corps] more prestige.

Letter, GSP, Jr., to Beatrice, July 12, 1918
We are going to have a map Problem [at the General Staff College] tomorrow which by all indications will be a stinker so I must stop and study it a little. This is the first time in my life I was not after tenths [of points in his school grades] as I don't want to be a staff officer and only am taking the course for general information and to have it on my record. The result is that I am doing very well indeed.
    I just got orders to day to arrange buildings for 4 new battalions. That will make 8 here. I don't know whether I shall command all of them or not but I rather think I will. It will be quite a young army about 4000 men. So I will have to develop even a meaner look than I now have but that will only be my official face and not for you.

When about 50 promotions in general officers' ranks were announced, Patton told Beatrice:

the list was fine active men and we ought to do a lot with such leaders. I am afraid people of my time are out of luck. We are too young for this war and future wars will have to use up all these [old] chumps before we get a show. When we do we will be too old to accomplish much.

Letter, GSP, Jr., to Beatrice, July 17, 1918
I shall have to give a lecture to a lot of colonels here to-

morrow but as I know my subject I have not the least apprehension but that I shall make a go of it.

Letter, GSP, Jr., to Beatrice, July 18, 1918

I gave a lecture to the Line School to day and five or six officers told me it was the best lecture they had ever heard over here. One said it was the best lecture he had ever heard by soldier or civilian. It was just after lunch and as people are always sleepy I got off a joke every few minutes to keep them awake. The idea worked fine and none of them went to sleep. I had a lot of notes but did not have to use them. I certainly know the subject and could talk right off which is the best way of doing. After wards I had a demonstration for them [at the tank center] and it was a fine performance.

So I feel quite elated over the day . . .

We [in the Tank Corps] will never get any recognition until we have been in a fight and showed that we could do business.

His lecture was on the cooperation between tanks and the other arms, especially infantry. "No claim is made for originality," he began disarmingly.

The ideas are simply a restatement of the ideas advanced by the French and British with some slight changes made necessary by our organization and in conformity to our desire to employ the Tanks more offensively.

There were, he said, "two very patent but none the less frequently neglected truths." These he had presented in his very first lecture—that the advance of infantry was limited by the physical endurance of men, and that the advance of tanks was limited by obstacles incident to the terrain; thus, it was futile to attack where the ground rendered tanks impotent and when infantrymen were expected to follow tanks at a speed or for a distance beyond their endurance.

Tanks in common with all other auxiliary arms are but a means of aiding infantry, on whom the fate of battle ever rests, to drive their bayonets into the bellies of the enemy.

. . . the liaison between the tanks and infantry must be of

the closest. It must be worked out in the most minute detail for so complex is its nature that hazy ideas or ill digested plans will become abortive or ruinous in the excitement of the close fighting where the cooperation must be put into practice.

. . . cooperation must be more than a mere matter of routine. Tank and Infantry officers must associate and by conversation at mess and elsewhere interchange ideas and so become thoroughly conversant with all the difficulties which beset their respective arms. . . .

Infantry should enter the [barbed] wire at least fifty yards behind the tank so as not to be tripped by trailings . . . They must not crowd around a tank nor yet follow it like mourners after a hearse. If they do they may change places with the late lamented. They should move up taking advantage of the ground and probably by rushes.

It was a good performance, and it allayed any suspicion that infantry officers might have had that the members of the Tank Corps were about to usurp their missions or claim that tanks could supplant the foot soldier.

Patton was supposed to attend an officers' smoker at the club, but was pleased when he did not have to go. "Pullen was here and we were busy until late on some details caused by things having taken a turn for the better so far as Tanks are concerned."

A lecture to the students at the General Staff College restated some earlier ideas, lifted earlier paragraphs he had written, but his talk was effective.

In order to properly impress you I shall preface my remarks with the statement that the theory of tanks or of mechanical offensive machines to overcome mechanical defensive measures, was evolved about 300 B.C. That is, during the siege of Tyre by Alexander, moving towers were first used to assault the walls which were so well made as to resist other means of attack.

Now again, that inverted wall—the trench—has become too strong to be overcome by normal means of offence, and we have, once more, evolved a mechanical appliance—the tank—to crush it. . . .

Considering that only 51 [of the 75 tanks in a light tank
battalion] . . . go into the fight, we may appear to have an
excessive reserve. This, however, is not the case. The tank is
a delicate animal, and when you have got your fighting tanks
tuned up and ready for action it is best for all concerned to
leave them severely alone. Yet since the men must be trained
other tanks are necessary, and it is here that the reserve mentioned comes in . . .

The infantry win the fights, the tanks only and always help
the infantry to win them. Any other theory of using tanks is
utterly wrong . . .

At the Battle of Juvaincourt the tanks were put in arbi-
trarily by the Infantry Commander, who did not take the
trouble to consult the tank officers. The result was a loss of
76% for the tanks and no gain for either the tanks or the
infantry. Again at Malmaison, the Infantry Commander, disregarding the recommendations of the tank officers, required
the tanks to commence their attack before daylight, with the
result that over 50% of the tanks became hopelessly lost in
a swamp and did no good to either themselves or the
infantry . . .

It must never be forgotten that boldness is the key to victory. The tank must be used boldly. It is new and always has
the element of surprise. It is also very terrifying to look at, as
the infantry soldier is helpless before it.

Letter, GSP, Jr., to Beatrice, July 22, 1918

I got off my lecture to the Gen. Staff class this morning
and it was very well received. In fact I surprised my self at
my fluency of utterance but as I have been soaking in Tank
dope for a long time I suppose when the plug was removed it
naturally flowed out all right.

I was walking around inspecting things just now when all
at once a completely new tank tactics popped into my head.
It is realy a great idea and I believe it is pregnant with far
reaching possibilities. I hope so at any rate. The only thing is
that it is so darned simple that I don't see why it has not
been thought of long ago. Perhaps there is some equally obvious flaw in it but I don't think so.

All war is simple and we all err by allowing its complexities
to divert our minds from the few basic truths . . .

I am going to G.H.Q. Tomorrow and expand this revolutionary theory of mine. For truly it is just that, you may have
a genius for a husband yet.

He set down his thoughts at once. "In my opinion the time has
now arrived to diverce tank tactics at least to a considerable
degree, from the stereotyped formations heretofore thought essential." The proper use of tanks, he believed, should be their employment with a sudden and violent burst of artillery fire mixed
with a copious use of smoke to paralyze the German front, which
would make possible an assault by light tanks followed by infantry
echeloned in density from rear to front. Each jump of the barrage
—that is, the progressive advancement of the artillery fire targets
—should, he thought, be moved forward, not the standard 100
yards but rather in intervals of 200 to 400 meters, even longer;
they should come to rest on defensive lines from 30 minutes to
one hour, depending on the length of the jump.

Since he anticipated the utilization of tanks for the most part
in enemy territory, he foresaw the need for definite refilling centers for gasoline, oil, and ammunition in hostile country—and this
was a new idea also. The large or heavy tanks should take care of
establishing these dumps. Each heavy could also tow by chain at
least two guns mounted on wheels, plus a supply of ammunition.

"There is nothing original in this mode of progression," Patton
modestly wrote, "except the utilization of tanks to produce the
effect heretofore produced by machine guns and pack artillery."

But there was, indeed, much more involved, and he directed
that experimental training of this sort be conducted at the tank
center.

In "Further Notes on the Use of Tanks in Various Operations
including Open Warfare" (what would come to be called Mobile
Warfare), written perhaps later that evening or later that summer,
Patton said, quite contrarily:

The ideas herein advanced are purely original, or if they
have been advanced by others it is unknown to me. Hence
no virtue is claimed for them but they are simply stated as a

basis for criticism in the hope that they may lead to some good results.

Proposing that the light tank could be used in several basic types of operation, he warned:

> Tanks must not expect to do these things for nothing; they will be put out [of action] but that is what they are paid for and the loss of a few tanks and men will be a cheap price to pay for . . . [success].
>
> It seems to me that . . . they [tanks] should never be distributed along a front as sort of Pill Boxes in the way the British seem to have done in front of the Fifth Army. Tanks like cavalry must depend on rapidity and shock for success, or as a rear guard in an active retreat but never as adjuncts to a passive defence . . .
>
> Tanks are only partially known and like all new weapons they justify extreme boldness, even rashness, in their employment.

Patton's cavalry upbringing and training were showing, but the qualities of boldness, mobility, and shock action would characterize his deepest military beliefs.

Whatever paper on tactics he sent to Rockenbach's office at GHQ AEF, he received a rapid reply from Pullen, who acknowledged receipt of Patton's outline of proposed new tactics and his belief in their soundness. But he thought that it was no time to propose novel techniques. The first job of the Tank Corps was to get tanks, the second to get tank units into combat. After tank formations had been in several shows, as battles were then familiarly called, the tankers would be in a better position to talk new tank tactics. They would be able to say exactly what they wanted, for

> at the present time a great deal of what we say will be looked upon as hot air.
>
> As far as I can find out, the General Staff entirely approves Tanks and is not hostile to the Tank Corps. However, they take the stand that they have approved a Tank program and now it is up to the Tank Corps to produce some Tanks and get them on the fighting line.

What Pullen said made a lot of sense. It was the thinking of the intelligent officer who was well adjusted to and well integrated into the establishment. To him, unorthodoxy, at least at that moment, was out of place. And he was probably right. Patton, the maverick, was out of step, but he had the perception to recognize the truth of what Pullen said.

Letter, GSP, Jr., to Aunt Nannie, July 23, 1918
[His adjutant, Captain Hebert, who was a First Sergeant, Regular Army, for nine years] is realy a most efficient man. I have . . . a lot of officers who were former non coms and with only two exceptions they are fine officers. We never appreciated our sergeants as much as we should. I have one 1st Lieutenant who was a sergeant 27 years and he is a hell of a good officer and one of the best dressed I have ever seen.

In fact all my men are well dressed and I inspect the officers clothes every week.

He delivered a lecture on morality and gambling to his officers, and when he learned that some were losing more than a month's pay in a single night,

I made them stop all together.
They think me very cruel but if they will not play for a one cent limit they must not play at all.
They all think that I am so old that I was probably a class mate of Gen Pershings.
. . . things are looking much better for the tanks now. Some French tanks were in [battle] for thirty hours and only lost eight percent which is nothing . . .
Gen. P. congratulated the 1st and 2d Divisions in a general order. I do hope we can get mentioned when we go in. We will certainly try to deserve it.
But sometimes I fear that we will all die of old age before we get a chance.

He lectured his officers on the points he had earlier raised with Pullen, probably to stimulate his tankers into thinking about the best methods of employing tanks in combat.

When he lost the first of his men, a soldier who died of pneumonia, he published a general order to remark the death and wrote a letter of sympathy to the man's father. In part, it read:

> Though he was not spared to die in battle yet he as truly gave his life for his country as if he had fallen on the field of battle. During the short time he was under my command he impressed me as a very fine type of man and soldier. You should feel proud to have had such a son. I know that in cases such as this sympathy is difficult to express but I beg that you will accept mine and extend it to the other members of your family.

He mentioned this in a letter to Beatrice, then said, "I guess I will have plenty more such letters on this subject to write." His statement was matter of fact rather than callous.

Presenting a lecture to his officers on the "points to be considered in the execution of a tank attack," he concluded:

> Having to the best of my ability told you what to do and so far as is possible how to do it I will now tell you what not to do.
>
> Do not cross trenches diagonally.
>
> Do not cross on traverses. You will fall off.
>
> Do not run away from your infantry.
>
> Do not stall your motor.
>
> Do not bunch. The rally [position] as defined previously is abolished.
>
> If one tank sticks [gets knocked out] thank God it is not your tank and go on.
>
> Do not take prisoners. [There was no way of getting them to the rear.]
>
> Do not go nearer than five yards to a trench when you are mopping up. You may side slip into it.
>
> Do not allow your tank to be taken [by the enemy]. Death is better than a life of shame [being a prisoner of war].
>
> To sum up. You must be elastic like a reubber.

Letter, GSP, Jr., to Beatrice, July 29, 1918
Some of my men deserted the other day in order to [go to the front and] get into the fight. That shows an excellent

but lamentable spirit which if persisted in would cause us more casualties than war.

Letter, GSP, Jr., to Beatrice, August 7, 1918

Gen. P. got decorated with the Grand Cross of the Legion of Honor yesterday morning and the president of France kissed him on both cheeks. But the President is so little that Gen. P. had to stoop down. This amused the soldiers a great deal and some who were not in ranks laughed as loud as they could. Gen. P. will have the K.C.B. pinned on him by King George this week also.

He published and had put up on the tank center's bulletin boards a list of 18 *don'ts*. For example: "Don't fool with the magneto or carburetur and don't dissect them . . . Don't tolerate loose wires or poorly made connections. FIX THEM AT ONCE . . . Don't leave your tank standing with motor running." The last one was: "Don't read this only ONCE and think you know all the Don'ts."

Letter, GSP, Jr., to Beatrice, August 10, 1918

Quekemeyer and Bowditch were here yesterday and I think that I impressed them largely [very much] with tanks. I did my best so as to have them in turn make talk at Headquarters as they are both aides to Gen. P.

The way things look now the english and others are doing so well that I fear the war will be over before I get in. That would certainly be a shame. So I shall hope for the best.

There is a fine Rumor that the Staff college will be over in ten days. I hope that this may prove correct as I am getting tired of it and besides would like to devote more time to inspection of Tanks.

The more I see of Gen. R. [Rockenbach] the less I think of him. He is nothing but a good hearted wind bag. I truly believe others would have pushed this show along much better and that we could have been fighting even now.

I hope to hear that Blaine and the first lot of Tanks have left [the States] even now and that he and my watch will soon be here.

I must go to school now. I love you.

Letter, GSP, Jr., to Beatrice, August 11, 1918

Darling Beat: A lot of people in the Staff Class were Promoted last week so last night they gave a smoker to which all were invited. It was a very nice affair with only French Beer which as you remember is perfectly harmless. There were also a lot of funny speeches and poems but I am not a gregarious person and such parties bore me to death so I left early at 11 o'clock and went to bed. I slept until ten this morning then got up and had the luxury of dressing for an hour.

Speaking of dressing I often think with regret of how badly I used to dress especially at Ft Myer. In fact Col Vidmer was the first person who impressed on me the virtue of neatness. Now I am a regular Beau Brummel. I wear silk khaki shirts made to order, Khaki socks also made to order. I change my boots at least once during the day and my belts are wonders to see they are so shiney and polished. I have the leather on my knees blancoed every time I ride and my spurs polished with silver polish. In fact I am a wonder to behold.

But the whole army is like that. You can spot a newly arrived officer instantly by the fact that he is not slicked up like us vetrans. I think that among the many good things the war will do an improvement in dress will be most noticable. This is largely due to the fact that having no cits [civilian clothes] at all one takes more interest in ones uniform.

We have a fine big Y.M.C.A. here now and next week the officers are giving a dance to all the nurses and telephone girls at this place about forty five of them in all.

I am going to lunch with some english officers to day so must stop and dress some more.

I love you with all my heart.

Despite his studies at the General Staff School and his duties at the tank center, he composed at least four papers during the first three weeks of August: "Tank Drill Regulations (Provisional)," "Notes for the Guidance of Battalion and Company Reconnaissance Officers," "Instructions on Tank Driving," and "Duties of the Platoon Leader." All were well thought out, detailed, firm, written with spirit, and to the point. He exhorted junior officers to lead at all times by example and instruction, to give careful attention to saluting, dress, and hygiene—"Neat clothes and a clean body help to keep up the spirit of your men"— and to look personally into the health of every man.

Letter, GSP, Jr., to Beatrice, August 13, 1918
. . . we are to put over a big demonstration for a lot of general staff officers on Friday so I have been writing up the problems.

I hope we get time to do the necessary practising to get it down well.

I just got a very nice letter from Gen Harbord. I wrote him congratulating him on his promotion. He has been put in command of the service of supply.

[Henry] Ford is bothering us to death with his machine but I believe it is too small and it would be absurd to run things into the ground with too small a machine [tank].

Pullen has been made a full Colonel and is leaving the Tanks. All my class mates in the Engineers are colonels also. They certainly have been getting rapid promotion.

A full and tiring day was normal. For example, one day Patton was at the Staff College until 5:00 P.M. At 5:15, he rehearsed men and tanks for a maneuver showing tanks and infantry working in cooperation. Because he was unable to secure infantrymen to participate in the exercise, he trained his own men in that role. When the rehearsal was over, he drove to Chaumont to see Rockenbach on business. He returned home at 10:30.

Letter, GSP, Jr., to Beatrice, August 15, 1918
It is remarkable how much easier these [drafted] men are to teach than the old soldiers we used to have. They had no brains at all. These men have plenty . . .

I am certainly some tank profit [prophet] . . . Three months ago I submitted a memo on Tank possibilities to Col. Eltinge. Even he thought I was crazy.

Among other things I advocated night raids by a few tanks. Three weeks later the British pulled one. I said that the seccond line should be half the strength of the first instead of the other way around after the Fight at . . . The british said it was correct.

I advocated using cavalry & tanks in raids. People said I was clearly crazy. In the present battle the British are doing just that.

Lastly I said that tanks should replace the creeping barrage and that all guns should be used for counter battery. People nearly died of horror at such a thought. Today we had a lecture by a British artillery general advocating my idea in toto.

Hence I have a swelled head for which I ask no pardon. But I still love you more every day.

Letter, GSP, Jr., to Beatrice, August 16, 1918

Here is a poem I wrote a while ago. I went to bed and for a wonder did not go to sleep at once so I composed poetry to put my self to sleep and rather fancying this [poem] I got up and wrote it, it was a moon light night. I think it is rather disconnected though some of the individual verses sound well.

The officers as I think I told you are giving a dinner dance to night. I did not find out until today that it was for me. All the programs being headed "the Colonels Party." I wish you were here to enjoy it or at least make me [enjoy it]. The guests are rather assorted. One countess two barronnesses. To [two] reporters wives of doubtful cast. The best nurses and telephone girls. I hope that they will have a good time. It may be a sort "of revrilly by night in Belgiums capital" [the night before Waterloo] for some of them as I think one Battalion will be out of here by the 1st of Sept. Of course not many will be killed but if they do their duty some are bound to. Still that rather adds zest to the entertainment as each hopes it will be the other and none are sure.

The demonstration we gave yesterday was a great success. Both the tanks and the infantry did fine and no one was hurt by the grenades. There were over 300 officers looking on and nine generals. Three of whom were Major Generals.

The candy etc you sent by Gen Marshall arrived to day and I have just eaten a lot as I had no time to get lunch.

I have seven or eight sweaters and four or five helmets also some heavy socks so use the wool for something else. In fact stop doing war work and keep young as I am doing.

Patton's scenario of the tank demonstration held for the Army General Staff College on August 16 included such problems as how to replace a dead tank driver and how to knock out an enemy 37-mm. gun. On the program distributed to the observers to enable them to follow the events being staged, Patton had written:

> Note to Observers. The infantry taking part are only tank soldiers and may not do as well as trained infantry . . . Other problems have been spoiled by staff officers and other observers getting into the ranks of the infantry and fearlessly braving the supposed barrage. It is requested that this be not done.

At this time he had 900 men and 50 fully trained officers in his center. They were still using only 25 tanks. The French said that tanks had to be completely overhauled and the parts replaced every 50 miles of operational use; Patton's tanks often ran for 500 before being refurbished.

Since July the tankers had been working hard on target practice. At first they fired from a makeshift wooden tank mounted on and rolling along an uneven track, which gave them the motion of a "seagoing platform." Later they worked on a more orthodox range constructed by Major L. K. Davis a few kilometers west of Bourg.

In August, to harden his men physically, Patton instituted a new program. Every morning before breakfast, each company ran one kilometer at double time in a column of squads. It was the forerunner of special physical conditioning that elite units, such as Rangers and paratroopers, later took such pride in.

About this time Rockenbach rated Patton's performance. He wrote:

> The splendid results obtained by this officer in the Tank School show him to be zealous and of good judgement and intelligence. His command is well disciplined and very soldierly in appearance.

Another rating by Rockenbach in the summer of 1918 read that Patton was "energetic, efficient, does much good work with little assistance. Qualified and especially fitted to command a tank brigade."

On Tuesday morning, August 20, while Patton was attending a lecture at the General Staff College, a note was delivered to him. It read: "You will report at once to the Chief of the Tank Corps accompanied by your Reconnaissance officer and equipped for field service."

This had to be a trip to the front at the very least, more probably participation in a "show." It had to be combat; otherwise the note would have told him more. He decided that the summons meant the opportunity at last to lead his tanks in battle and, further, that more tanks were about to arrive in Bourg.

In some excitement, he immediately went to Bourg, where he turned over command of the center to Viner, making him assistant commandant. He also wrote a letter to his father, saying that he had just received a message to go somewhere, a place where there was the

danger of remaining longer than one wishes on such trips perhaps for ever . . .

[If I die] please do what is best with any property I may have. Personally I hope you and mama keep it as beatrice has plenty. I will send her my sword. I will give one horse to Gen. Pershing and one to Maj. Viner. I told you on a former occasion where my dress uniforms are in paris . . .

Of course dont get alarmed over me. I will wire you or Beat. or both of my safe return long before you get this letter.

You and mama and Nita and Aunt Nannie know well my unending love.

VII

Combat

"*Things are most interesting and getting more so.*"

CHAPTER 28

Preparations for St. Mihiel

"This is our big chance; what we have worked for."

AFTER TURNING OVER COMMAND of the tank center to Viner on Tuesday, August 20, Patton, accompanied by Lieutenant Maurice K. Knowles, drove to Chaumont, picked up Rockenbach, and continued to Neufchâteau, where the headquarters of the First U. S. Army was located. On the way, Rockenbach briefed Patton on a proposed operation in which the tanks might take part. The St. Mihiel offensive, as it would be called, was tentatively scheduled for September 5 or 7. It would involve several American corps under the First Army, commanded by Pershing, who would retain also his position as Commander in Chief, AEF.

At Neufchâteau, Patton secured from Colonel Hugh Drum, now First Army chief of staff, maps of the area where the attack was to be launched. While Rockenbach remained to work with the First Army staff, Patton and Knowles drove to Ligny-en-Barrois and reported to General Burtt, V Corps chief of staff. He had dinner with Burtt, an old friend from Mexico, who gave him more information on the action being planned.

Diary

August 20: "Was rather overwhelmed at size of task [for tanks] but it cleared up after eating."

Wearing field artillery insignia to conceal the plan for using tanks in the impending operation, Patton and Knowles drove to the Third French Army to reconnoiter the battle terrain. With permission to visit the appropriate units in the area, the Americans proceeded to Ancemont and the 10th French Colonial Division. The division commander, General Marchand, impressed Patton enormously, for Marchand had been decorated with five palms, six wound stripes—Patton counted them—and the Grand Cross of the Legion of Honor. Marchand believed that the Woevre plain, the ground envisaged for tank action, was too marshy for the machines.

Unwilling to accept this disappointing news secondhand, wanting to see the ground himself, Patton received authority to visit the battalion there. After reporting to the battalion command post, Patton and Knowles walked to an observation post. Through field glasses they studied the terrain. Still unable to determine the actual condition of the ground, Patton asked whether the two Americans could accompany a patrol that night into no-man's-land.

They joined one of the patrols making a routine sortie beyond the French trenches after nightfall, and moved about 1500 meters into no-man's-land. They met no Germans, but several enemy soldiers whistled at the patrol when some Frenchmen cut a few strands of German barbed wire. The ground was pretty soft, but Patton decided it might be passable for tanks.

Letter, GSP, Jr., to Beatrice, September 1, 1918

I was out on a patrol in No mans land last week. It was most interesting and not at all exciting. We went along with the "Burglars crawl" for about a mile and a half till we came to the Bosch wire. This we examined and the Bosch whistled at us and we whistled back and having seen what we wanted went home. No one shot at us but we saw some bosch walking along about 100 m. [meters away]. Both sides were anxious not to disturb the others. Coming back we came through a village from one house to another by holes in the walls. The village had been destroyed a long time and looked like a skeleton in texas.

I picked some dasies for you in the bosch wire and will send them back . . . it was on the whole a most interesting evening and not up to expectations.

I rather hoped we would have a patrol encounter but nothing happened. The Bosch seems to be catching it pretty well and is more or less on the run but is a long way from being dead yet.

A later version by Patton:

The raid itself was a very tame affair, the party penetrated two belts of wire and was approaching a third when someone in front in the dark whistled, on this the raid [patrol] stopped and began to retrace its steps. The French noncom in charge explaining that the whistle meant that if the raid had been pushed further the Germans would reluctantly be forced to fire . . . Anyhow the raid had been a success, the ground was fine for tanks.

Back in the French lines at 2:30 A.M., Patton thanked the officers at battalion headquarters for their help. Then he and Knowles drove to an American unit, the 59th Railroad Artillery, and found a place to sleep.

They returned to the French battalion on Thursday and walked again to the observation post. Once more, this time for two hours, they studied the ground. Very tired and hot, they proceeded, after lunch, to another OP for still another look at the ground that interested them.

Having examined the terrain to his satisfaction, Patton drove to the rear and, with Knowles, inspected the closest railroad detraining point. It was excellent, not far from the front and hidden by woods. After stopping at Ancemont to pick up more maps and after dinner at Bar-le-Duc, Patton and Knowles reached Ligny. They were tired and went to bed immediately.

Patton spent most of Friday writing a terrain report and a suggested plan for employing tanks. The corps staff members were most helpful; Burtt, Farman, Cotton, and Russell were old friends. That evening Patton returned to Neufchâteau.

Early Saturday morning, he and Rockenbach brought each other up to date. Rockenbach, on temporary duty with the First Army, had studied the operational plans issued by the Army, the corps, and the divisions. A large number of tanks would take part in the attack—three U.S. heavy battalions coming from England with 150 British tanks, three French battalions with 225 light tanks, and two U.S. battalions, both Patton's, with 144 French light tanks. As a matter of fact, the first of Patton's new tanks were beginning to arrive at Bourg that day.

Telling what he had done, Patton said that his reconnaissance "showed the absolute necessity for a tank officer to personally see the ground." All the intelligence reports indicated that the ground to be used by the tanks was an impassable swamp further blocked by dreadful barbed wire; and his observations from OP's confirmed these reports. But his participation in a raid convinced him that the ground and the wire were neither impassable nor dreadful. An attack could be made.

Then he and Rockenbach went over his written report. The proposed battle terrain, according to Patton, was "a very flat and marshy plain drained by numerous small streams" and ditches. Trees and bushes along the waterways offered cover to "prone lines of skirmishers." A protracted hot, dry spell of weather had made the ground hard. Infantry and tanks could easily cross the streams. But two days of rain would "render this sector quite difficult to tanks." Late in September, the wet season would make the area impassable "except along the roads."

He described the roads and the shell craters. Some of the wire entanglements, he said, were strung on iron posts that could "be readily flattened by tanks." The rest of the wire was attached to wooden posts which had been there for several years and were rotten— "It was possible to push these posts over by hand."

After considering the hostile trenches and gun emplacements, which posed no great problem, he mentioned that the villages, all destroyed by shell fire, "were potential centers of resistance" because many walls were still standing.

Patton suggested tank attacks in four sectors and discussed detraining points. He recommended forgoing a long artillery preparation—"it tears up the ground" and made tank movements difficult. He further suggested the use of artillery smoke shells to screen the tanks from antitank guns. He hoped that at least "one low flying airplane" would be assigned the duty of maintaining liaison by wireless radio between the tanks and the supporting artillery. He warned that road space should be requested to guarantee the arrival of gasoline trucks for the second day of operations.

After his discussion with Rockenbach, Patton returned to Chaumont, where he talked about the operation with several GHQ AEF staff members during lunch. He then traveled to Bourg.

Letter, GSP, Jr., to Beatrice, August 24, 1918

I have been so rushed for the last four days that I have had no time to write. So you must forgive me. I am perfectly all right and love you very much but some new soldiers are arriving to be trained and I have to work every minute at that. Then there are other things.

I will try and write every two or three days and will wire from time to time.

I love you with all my heart.

With the men at the tank center—officially designated the 302d Tank Center—working feverishly under Viner's direction to tune up the new tanks and get them ready for combat, Patton put Viner in charge of the school and training facility. He placed Brett in command of the 1st (326th) Tank Battalion, and gave Captain Ranulf Compton command of the 2d (327th) Battalion. These two battalions would operate in battle under Patton's headquarters, called the 304th Brigade, Tank Corps (later it would be known simply as the 1st Tank Brigade). Patton was now a brigade commander—like his grandfather in the Civil War.

That evening Patton drove to Ligny, taking Borlan and Heilner with him. They arrived late, but Knowles was waiting for them. The tank operation at St. Mihiel, he said, would be a smaller show than originally planned.

One of the two battalions of American tankers training with heavy tanks at Wareham, England, since April would be, at the end of August, on its way to France with 47 British-built Mark V's. But the unit would arrive too late for St. Mihiel.*

* Assigned to the 27th U.S. Division, the battalion would enter battle on September 29 at Le Catelet, working with American and Australian infantry. Later it would operate with the 30th U.S. Division. By October 23, it would have only 12 tanks in operating condition.

As soon as Rockenbach learned that the heavies would be un-available for St. Mihiel, he asked the French to furnish four bat-talions instead of three for the operation—this in addition to the equipment they were sending Patton's battalions. Unable to do so, the French added 12 St. Chamond and 24 Schneider tanks to the Renaults they were contributing to the attack.

Rockenbach was concerned. He feared that the infantry at St. Mihiel might lack sufficient tank support.

Patton moved with the V Corps headquarters to the attack area. His three lieutenants set up a command post, reconnoitered the area, determined the best tank detraining and troop assembly points, located command post sites, traced routes to the front, and laid telephone wires from the corps headquarters to the tank com-mand posts.

Diary

August 25 (Sunday): "wrote plan for attack simply rough draft . . . Billeted in old monestary in a cell with all sorts of praying apparatus. Good bed."

Letter, GSP, Jr., to Beatrice, August 26, 1918

I am very well and have nothing to do so will either get fat or nearvous I cant say which . . . I don't think I have changed much unless it is that I look meaner.

Diary

August 27: "Truck arrived with nothing in it. I was very mad."

August 28: "Worked for revised plan on the use of Tanks showing in detail the operation of nearly every Tank . . . Hebert & Gibbs got in at 10:30. But truck and clearks were lost."

Patton issued his field order, indicating in detail the enemy line forming the St. Mihiel salient, the V Corps plan of attack, and his own instructions to the tankers. It was, he later said, quite easy to write, for the Allied front ran along high bluffs overlook-ing the assault area, which lay spread out like a map.

Memo, GSP, Jr., to V Corps, August 29, 1918, subject: Plan for the Use of Tanks.

The greatest danger to Tanks is from direct fire of A-T [antitank] guns on the flanks or sweeping roades . . . If a creeping Barrage is used it should have a proportion of smoke shells (I believe 20% is about right but that is an artillery question) . . . In each sector where tanks operate there should be a special air plane detailed to fly low and spot anti Tank guns. On locating any it should signal the support battery [of artillery] by wireless or by special light signal. The battery will at once fire on the designated spot with H.E. [high explosive] and smoke.

Rockenbach proposed a tank maneuver at Bourg for the infantry commanders and staff members of the divisions that were to work with the tanks. The infantrymen would thus become somewhat familiar with tank capabilities.

Diary

August 29 (Thursday): "Sent word to have Brett & [his subordinate company commanders] Semmes, Weed, and English to come up. I went to Ligny to see Gen R. [Rockenbach]. He told me to let no one come up but they had [already] started . . . Gave Brett and his capts a talk on their duties. Truck got in and we got office started."

August 30: "Went to see Gen [Clarence R.] Edwards [26th Division commander] at 1:30. He was most interested and asked me how I wanted him to employ his infantry [with the tanks]. I told him and he was eager to agree. Went to see Gen G. Bell [George Bell, Jr., 33d Division commander] at Tronville. He was also eager to help and I could not have had a better reception. Went to Langres [to prepare tank maneuver for infantrymen] but had motor trouble and did not get in until 1 A.M. Arranged to give shows for officers [of] 26 and 33 Divs."

August 31: "Talked over every thing with Viner & found every thing o.k. Went to see new tanks. All were in but 30. They were in fine shape. Gen R[ockenbach] came to lunch.

Had demonstration with one Bn[Battalion]. Every thing
went fine. 90 [infantry] officers . . . present.

Letter, GSP, Jr., to Beatrice, August 31, 1918
[The demonstration was] Better than I could have hoped.
One tank fell off a cliff and rolled clear over then went on
again with out any difficulty . . .
At last we have all the equipment we want even a little
more and every thing is coming in fine and fast. The woods
are full of tanks over 150 of them all nice and new and in fine
shape.
I only got three hours sleep last night so will stop and go
to bed.

September 1 (Sunday): "Arranged for Brig[ade] reserve
with Viner. Got pigeon baskets . . . Left with Capt. Etheridge
at 1:30 P.M. Stopped at Chaumont then came on to Ligny by
Joinville & St. Dizier. Passed 200 French trucks full of Americans. Had dinner with Gen R. Saw Col DeWitt G4 1st Army
about Detraining [tanks]. Got in at 12:30 A.M.

He was at the V Corps headquarters on September 2 when he
learned that the attack zones had been changed somewhat. This
required some adjustments in his own arrangements. He moved
his office, had Etheridge draw up a memo on detraining and sent
him to talk with Rockenbach, and himself reconnoitered the area
immediately behind the intended battleground.
Everything was set for the operation—telephone wires were
laid, orders distributed, maps disseminated—when without warning, everything was changed. The First Army decided on September 3 that Patton's tanks would work, not with the V Corps, but
rather with the IV Corps and in a completely different area. The
attack was postponed.
Word reached Patton late that afternoon—as he was picking
blackberries. After "some profanity and much regret" because all
the preliminary work had been for nothing, he instructed Hebert,
his adjutant, to move the tank brigade headquarters to the new
area without delay. Patton packed his things and drove at once to
Ligny. Pullen met him there, and as they rode together to the IV
Corps at Etrouves, near Toul, they discussed the new situation.

Pullen had already drawn a tentative plan for the tanks, but Patton objected to the large amount of frontage Pullen had assigned each battalion.

At IV Corps on Wednesday, September 4, Patton talked to the chief of staff and G–3 and had them reduce the length of the tank frontage. Then, still disguised by field artillery insignia, he reconnoitered the terrain near Beaumont, where the new attack would be made.

On Thursday he visited the front, made a daylight inspection in no-man's-land—it was quiet—walked up the fairly large stream called the Rupt de Mad looking for tank-crossing sites, discovered that three smaller streams running through the attack zone were perfectly dry and no obstacle to tanks. The bridge at Marvoisin was intact, but he thought he saw evidence that the Germans were mining it. Since he could not count on the Marvoisin bridge as a sure method of crossing, he found another site 700 yards away where the water was shallow and fordable. After examining the ground from an OP in the Bois du Jury, he decided that the ground would be difficult for his Renault tanks but passable unless it rained. That evening he wrote his plan of attack.

The attack to reduce the St. Mihiel salient—a bulge pushed forward by the Germans into the Allied line—was the first independent offensive to be launched by the First U. S. Army. The salient had been in German possession since September 1914, and though it covered a sensitive position, the Mézières–Sedan–Metz railroad and the Birey iron basin, there had been no large-scale fighting there since 1916.

Pershing hoped to start his attack on September 7, 1918, but bringing the scattered American units together, assembling the necessary artillery support, and constructing a host of new installations—all at night in great secrecy—consumed more time than anticipated. D-day was eventually scheduled for September 12.

On August 29, Pershing moved his First Army advance headquarters from Neufchâteau to Ligny-en-Barrois, 25 miles southwest of St. Mihiel, and on the following day assumed command of the sector. In the attack he would direct three U.S. corps and several French divisions.

The IV U. S. Corps and I U. S. Corps were in position on the southern face of the salient with the I Corps on the right (east). The IV Corps headquarters was at Toul, the I Corps at Saizerais, northeast of Toul. Over on the left and separated from the other American corps by several French units was the V Corps, in position on the western face of the salient. The attack, simply stated, was to have the I and IV Corps drive to the north and meet the V Corps advancing to the east.

Three battalions of the 505th French Tank Regiment, plus one half of the groupement of St. Chamonds and Schneiders the French had added, were to work with the I Corps. Patton's brigade of two U.S. tank battalions, reinforced by the other half of the French groupement—the 14th and 17th Groupes, would work with the IV Corps.

More specifically, Patton's American and French tankers would support the 42d Division, which was in the center of the IV Corps zone, and the 1st Division, which was on the immediate left (west).

Patton disposed his tanks as follows: The 327th Battalion (Compton), less 25 tanks held in Brigade Reserve, but augmented by the French groupes (under Major Chanoine), would operate with the 42d Division. The 326th Battalion (Brett) would be with the 1st Division.

Brett on the left, with the support of the Brigade Reserve, was to cross the Rupt de Mad and lead the infantry to the objectives. In the center, Chanoine's heavier Schneider tanks, which would have more difficulty than the Renaults crossing streams, were to follow the infantry. Compton, operating on the right of the French, was to stay behind the infantry initially, then pick up speed, pass through the infantry, and lead the foot soldiers into Essey and Pannes.

Letter, GSP, Jr., to Beatrice, September 5 ,1918
I have been being shelled yesterday and to day but not much. I was out in no mans land to day and it was fine till

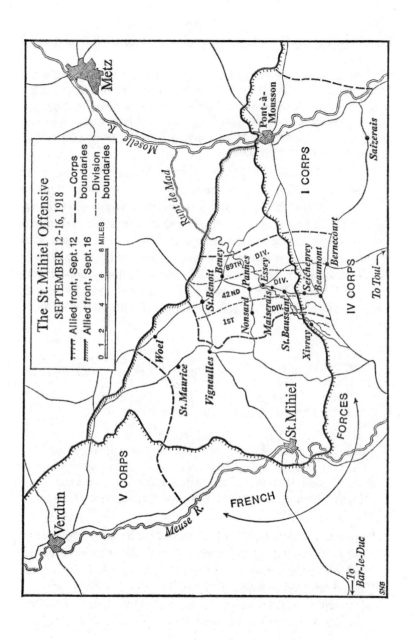

The St. Mihiel Offensive
SEPTEMBER 12–16, 1918

Allied front, Sept. 12
Allied front, Sept. 16
Corps boundaries
Division boundaries

0 1 2 4 6 8 MILES

Metz

Moselle R.

Pont-à-Mousson

Saizerais

Rupt de Mad

I CORPS

To Toul

89TH Beney
DIV.
Pannes
Essey
DIV.
Seicheprey
Beaumont
Bernecourt

St. Benoit
42ND
Nonsard
Maizerais
St. Baussant
Xivray

IV CORPS

1ST

Woel

St. Maurice

Vigneulles

FORCES

St. Mihiel

V CORPS

FRENCH

Verdun

Meuse R.

To Bar-le-Duc

SHB

we started back. I hated the idea of being shot at from behind.

It is funny how little notice one pays to shells after a short experience. I was talking to a major in the middle of a street to day and they were shelling hell out of a church about a block away. The bosch shoot so accurately that when you see what they are aiming at you simply have to avoid that spot and are quite safe for the rest . . .

Things are most interesting and getting more so.

From the configuration of the terrain, it was apparent that the tanks would have to start their attack 300 meters behind the infantry, which Patton disliked. It was also apparent that if the tanks were to move through the marshy ground assigned to them, they would need grousers or mud hooks. Only one had ever been made as an experiment, but it seemed to work. Patton therefore telephoned Viner at Bourg and told him he needed 1000. Viner said, "Very good sir, when do you want them?" Patton had them in three days.

Diary

September 6 (Friday): "Changed [my plan] . . . on advice of Chaffee. Went to see 42 Div C of S [chief of staff] Lt. Col [William N.] Hughes [Jr.]. Thought him an ass. Maj. Chanoine reported. Gen R. [Rockenbach] called."

September 7: Visited 1st Division, saw Gen. Summerall and others, "all most obliging and did all I asked. Went to 42 [Division] Maj Murphy G3. Found that they had adopted my plan in total. Thought Col Hughes less of an ass. Fixed up plan for French . . . Tanks shipped from Langres. Gen. R. called."

Patton was pleased with the cooperation he was getting from the 1st Division, which had worked with tanks at Cantigny. Also, he had complete confidence in Brett, and he was sure that the tanks and infantry would cooperate well together in that sector.

Although the 42d Division was cooperative too, it had had no previous experience with tanks. In addition, he had some concern about Compton. It was these factors, probably, that led him to be somewhat oversolicitous in his arrangements with the 42d Division.

He wrote a memo for the division G–3, specifying certain requirements for moving the tanks from their detraining point to the battlefield. For example, he requested that a bridge be built, pointing out that plenty of trees in the nearby woods were available for the construction. He also worried about the lack of time —everyone was extremely busy getting ready, and this precluded a training maneuver to familiarize infantry commanders with the tanks. He therefore recommended that some of Compton's officers give several brief lectures to the platoon and company commanders of the infantry assault battalions. "No other means of training is available. This will be better than nothing." There was no time even for that.

Half of Chanoine's tanks arrived by train during the night of September 7. Most of them moved to places of concealment in the Bois de la Reine. A small group descended by mistake eight miles away and temporarily fouled up the arrangements for assembling the tanks.

Patton inspected the French units on September 8, arranged to have them move to another wood so that the rest of the French tanks, as well as his own, which had started from Bourg on the previous day, could move swiftly off the trains and into concealed bivouacs.

Still concerned about operations with the 42d Division, he called on the assistant division commander, General Michael J. Lenihan, and spoke with him about getting smoke into the plan. Lenihan referred him to Murphy, the G–3.

Major Grayson M. P. Murphy was a competent officer. A West Point graduate who resigned from the Army after several years of active duty to enter banking, he became head of the American Red Cross in France when the United States entered the war. After organizing that service, he applied for active duty and was assigned to be Operations Officer of the 42d Division. Very busy preparing for the St. Mihiel operation, probably feeling somewhat harassed, particularly by a tank officer who was constantly making suggestions or demands, he refused Patton's request to add a provision for smoke shells in the division plan, which he had to reproduce in many copies and distribute to higher, subordinate, and neighboring units by a certain time.

Diary

September 8: "Maj Murphy told me he could not put smoke in plan as stencil was already cut. The biggest fool remark I ever heard showing just what an S.O.B. the late chief of the Red Cross is. Told Col. Heintzelman [division chief of staff] of remark & said that if tanks fail in 42 Div it will be his Murphy's fault."

He was angry because he was tired and because he was concerned about the attack. The fact that it was raining did nothing to improve his temper and disposition. If the rain continued, the Woevre plain would turn into a quagmire, and the ground would be unable to hold the tanks.

That night the rest of Chanoine's tanks arrived. The rain had become a downpour.

Letter, GSP, Jr., to Beatrice, September 8, 1918

I have been having a hell of a time for the passed two days getting things arranged. I command among other things a French outfit and it is a job requiring great tact but so far I have managed all right.

Yesterday every thing bad which could happen did but I got things clear by supper time to night. Among other things an engine jumped the track and one band of fools detrained eight miles from where they should have.

I met a few militia staff officers who were such polite men that they would say neither yes nor no and refused to do any thing that they could get any one else to do.

West Pointers stand up like light houses in a fog. They do their best and don't shirk responsibility which the rest do all the time . . .

All the Allies seem to be doing very well in deed and the Bosch is catching it on all sides.

Patton issued his field order on September 9, setting forth the missions of his units and how they were to attack.

Diary

September 9 (Monday): Got dump of 10,000 gallons of gasoline; no oil or grease. Very bad weather, wet and raining.

That night two trains bringing half of his battalions reached the area. Since each train could carry one-and-a-half companies, Patton had specified that half of the 326th and half of the 327th come first, the rest later. He had hoped that all the men and equipment would arrive early enough before the attack for the men to get some rest and the tanks some minor adjustments and a tune-up. But frequent delays and sidetracking of trains disrupted schedules. Blocked tracks near the front sometimes required detraining at places other than those selected and consequently meant longer drives to jump-off positions, as well as traffic congestion.

Diary

September 10 (Tuesday): 327th unable to detrain because French had put ammunition on tracks and we could not move up. "Things look bad but we will do our best to get them off." Lt. Colonels Mitchell [commander of the American heavy tanks] and Viner came to observe the operation.

The second section of the brigade was unable to leave the train because French railroad officials would not or could not stop the cars where the tanks could get off. The train engineer was finally threatened with bodily harm and forced to halt. Viner got most of the tanks off.

The last tank company to reach the general area was on the ground at 3 A.M., September 12, a scant two hours before the attack was to begin. The company started at once on an eight-kilometer march to its jump-off point. Patton made a last-minute adjustment in his orders, shifted the company to battalion support, and the tankers got into position at 4:50 A.M. The men had not slept for two nights but were anxious to fight.

Probably the best summary of his activities before the battle of St. Mihiel opened was his own description several days after the attack.

Letter, GSP, Jr., to Beatrice, September 16, 1918

Darling Beat: The news is out so I can give you a brief account of the Battle of St. Mihiel etc. At 10 A.M. August 22 I got a telephone message to report to Gen. R. with my reconnaissance officer ready for protracted field service. I did, at 3 P.M. we were at Army Hq and had been told the plans which as you know contemplated the attack by 3 corps. I was to command the tanks in the 5 Corps. The rest of the tanks were to be supplied by the French. At 6 P.M. I reported to your old friend Gen Burtt (Capt in Mex) who was chief of staff. Next day I went to French Corps Hq. to get permission to visit the Front. On going there I was told it was a marsh where tanks could not move. As I did not believe this I went out with a French Patrol that night to the Bosch wire and found the ground hard and dry though in winter it is probably a marsh. We worked hard and got already to fight also got our tanks. For on August 22 we had only 22. I had to patrol and make plans and then travle back to the center every other night, a four hour ride, to arrange things there. We thought that "D" day would be sept. 7. On Sept 4 I got ordered to leave the 5th Corps and report to the 4 Corps near Toul. Here I got a new job and had to start all over again which was a bore still it had to be done. I walked down the Rupt de Mad by day to the bridge at Xivray which is in no mans land and was not shot at. I had to do it to see whether we could cross the stream.

Then we started to detrain and that was awfull. For 4 nights the French made every mistake they could, sending trains to the wrong place or not sending them at all. The last company of the 327 Battalion detrained at 3:15 A.M. and marched right into action.

Meanwhile, on September 11, the day before the operation was to start, the commander of the French Tank Corps sent Rockenbach a message. Referring to the new tanks recently furnished Patton's brigade, he warned that Renaults required a twelve-day period for breaking in. They should not, he said, be used in action until then. Rockenbach was unperturbed. He replied "that the mud would act as lubricant and that the tanks would operate."

With his tanks moving into position for the attack, Patton issued special instructions. He wanted all cooking completed before dark, no lights or fires to be shown after darkness, no flashlights used. He warned that water in the streams was likely to be contaminated by gas. Then, having warmed up to exhortation, he concluded:

From a tactical point of view the present operation is easy. A complete success insures the future of the Tank Corps in which all have shown by their long and cheerful work that they are fully interested . . . Remember that you are to make paths in the wire and put out machine gun nests for the infantry; hence do not leave them [the infantry], never get more than a hundred and fifty yards ahead of them and never let them get ahead of you or if they do hurry to regain your place. No tank is to be surrendered or abandoned to the enemy. If you are left alone in the midst of the enemy keep shooting. If your gun is disabled use your pistols and squash the enemy with your tracks. By quick changes of direction cut them with the tail of the tank. If your motor is stalled and your gun broken still the infantry cannot hurt. You hang on, help will come . . . you are the first American tanks [in battle]. You must establish the fact that AMERICAN TANKS DO NOT SURRENDER . . . As long as one tank is able to move it must go forward. Its presence will save the lives of hundreds of infantry and kill many Germans. Finally This is our BIG CHANCE; WHAT WE HAVE WORKED FOR . . . MAKE IT WORTH WHILE.

Diary

September 11 (Wednesday): Viner got tanks off the railroad after working all day. "I wrote B a letter ate as much as I could hold and went to see Compton at Bernecourt. Then tried to get to P.C. [command post] fell in hole and got shelled. It was very lonely in the wet dark being shelled and all. Found P.C. and went to sleep."

CHAPTER 29

St. Mihiel

"the feeling, foolish probably, of being admired by
the men . . . is a great stimulus."

Diary
September 12 (Thursday): "D. Day [Our] Artillery started at 1 A.M. and the Bosch put up pathetic little Flares but made no reply. At 5 the show started at 5:30 could see tanks beyond Xivray having a hard time. Moved at 7 to Seicheprey. Saw some prisoners & wounded . . . got some shelling . . . at 9:30 took Pannes at 10:40 attacked Beney got shot at by m.g. [machine gun] & had to recall tank as . . . [infantry] would not go in. Saw Brett at Nonsard. He had 326 T[ank Battalion] up. Reported to corps very tired."

This extremely compressed account of Patton's activities during the first day of the St. Mihiel offensive was supplemented by several fuller accounts. Patton sent an interim report to the IV Corps on September 13 and an operation report on the following day, wrote to Beatrice on the 16th and to his father on the 20th. In response to a request from Rockenbach in December, he and other tank officers submitted individual papers on their personal experiences in the war, including St. Mihiel. Sometime later he wrote a humorous sketch of the tanks. He also contributed much to, probably composed by far the greater part of, the less personal "304th Brigade Operations Report on the St. Mihiel Salient" and the "History of the 304th Brigade." The substance of all these narratives concerning Patton painted a similar picture. From them emerged the following story.

"We have all been in one fine fight and it was not half so exciting as I had hoped, not as exciting as affairs in Mexico, because there was so much company [in France]."

"We attacked at 5 A.M. on Thursday Sept 12" but before that, "at 1 A.M. 900 plus guns opened and shot till 5. It was dark with a heavy rain & wind. I was on a hill in front of the main line where I could watch both Battalions and 30 French [tanks] that I had also under me."

"When the shelling first started I had some doubts about the advisability of sticking my head over the parapet [of the trench], but it is just like taking a cold bath, once you get in it is all right. And I soon got out and sat on the parapet."

Sending periodic messages of the tanks' progress to the IV Corps, he made his first communication by telephone at 6:10, reporting that tanks were passing Xivray, that the French tanks were invisible to him because of the fog, and that the Germans were making very little reply to the American shells.

He telephoned at 6:30 to say that the tanks were advancing.

"I could see them coming along and getting stuck in the trenches. It was a most irritating sight. At 7 o'clock I moved forward 2 miles"—"and passed some dead and wounded. I saw one fellow in a shell hole holding his rifle and sitting down. I thought he was hiding and went to cuss him out, he had a bullet over his right eye and was dead. As my telephone wire ran out at this point I left the adjutant there and went forward with a lieutenant and 4 runners to find the tanks, the whole country was alive with them crawling over trenches and into woods."

At 7:20 he sent a motorcycle messenger with the information that at least sixteen tanks were heavily engaged and that the smoke screen laid down by the division and corps artillery was excellent.

At 8:20, from a hill 800 meters northwest of Seicheprey, he reported that the tanks were preceding the infantry on the fronts of both the 1st and 42d Divisions. Only five tanks were out of action so far as he could tell, but he was unable to determine the cause.

He transmitted news brought by a runner from the 327th Tank Battalion at 9:15 that Compton's tanks—with the 42d Division

—were being delayed by bad ground. He himself had a poor view of the action from where he was, and he could see none of the tanks working with the 1st Division.

"I had to see something so I took an officer and three runners and started forward."

"I could not see my right battalions so went to look for it."

"There were very few dead in the trenches as the Bosch had not Fought hard but you never saw such trenches—eight feet deep and 10 to 14 wide."

"We passed through several towns under shell fire but none [of the exploding shells] did more than throw dust on us. I admit that I wanted to duck and probably did at first but soon saw the futility of dodging fate, besides I was the only officer around who had left on his shoulder straps [many officers had removed this identifying mark distinguishing them from enlisted men because they feared that the enemy would concentrate fire against the leaders] and I had to live up to them. It was much easier than you would think and the feeling, foolish probably, of being admired by the men lying down is a great stimulus."

"At the first town we came to St. Baussant the bosch was still shelling and it was not pleasant . . . I found the French stuck in a pass under shell fire. I talked to the Major [Chanoine] and went on. I had not gone 20 feet when a shell 6″ [a large shell] struck the tank he was working on and killed 15 men. I went on towards Essey and got into the front line infantry who were laying down. As there was only shell fire I walked on smoking [his pipe] with vigor. Most of the shells went high."

"I walked right along the firing line of one brigade. They were all in shell holes except the general (Douglas Mcarthur) who was standing on a little hill."

"Here I met Gen McArthur (Douglas) . . . he was walking about too."

"I joined him and the creeping barrage came along toward us, but it was very thin and not dangerous. I think each one wanted to leave but each hated to say so, so we let it come over us."

"We stood and talked but neither was much interested in what the other said as we could not get our minds off the shells. I went up a hill to have a look and could see the Bosch running beyond Essey fast."

He walked to Essey, "then five tanks of my right battalion [Compton's] came up so I told them to go through Essey. Some damed Frenchman at the bridge told them to go back as there were too many shells [falling] in the town. The Lt in command obeyed. This made me mad so I led them through on foot but there was no danger as the Bosch [was] shelling the next town."

It was only later that a story, perhaps mostly legend, arose out of the action at Essey. Someone said that the bridge was mined or prepared for demolition by the Germans. Perhaps some inhabitants thought this was so. Whether Patton was aware of it at the time or only afterward is not clear. His earlier accounts mentioned only the shells falling nearby that discouraged the tankers from crossing the bridge into town.

In any event, he walked across the bridge first, leading the tanks into the village. He said later that he did not believe the bridge was mined.

Still later: "No stage brigand ever moved more light footed or with greater caution than did Col Patton as he walked over it [the bridge] to see if the man [who had reported explosives ready to be detonated] was right—fortunately he was not."

Another version said: "we"—he was referring to himself—"walked over the bridge in a cat-like manner, expecting to be blown to heaven any moment, to our great relief we found that the bridge had not been tampered with."

"Some Germans came out of dug outs and surrendered to Gen McArthur . . .

"I walked behind [the tanks] and some boshe surrendered to me . . .

"I asked him [MacArthur] if I could go on and attack the next town Pannes. He said sure so I started. All the tanks but one ran out of gas."

The other tanks were "out of sight."

"The road from Essey to Pannes was rather a mess; a German

battery had apparently been caught by the American barrage and the road was strewn with dead men and horses."

"When we got to Pannes some two miles [away] the infantry would not go in so I told the sgt. commanding the tank to go in. He was nearvous at being alone so I said I will sit on the roof."

"I got on top of the tank to hearten the driver."

"This reasured him and we entered the town."

Another version had it: "Being very tired Colonel Patton, Lt. Knowles and one remaining runner mounted on the tank."

"Lt. Knowles and Sgt. Graham sat on the tail of the tank. I watched one side of the street and they the other."

"That was most exciting as there were plenty of boshe."

"Pretty soon we saw a Bosch who threw up his hands. I told Knowles & Graham to go get him and I went on out side the town towards Beney."

According to another version, as they reached the crossroads in the center of the town, Knowles and Graham dismounted to chase a German running into a house.

Using their pistols, Knowles and Graham took 30 Germans prisoner.

"On leaving the town [Pannes] I was still sitting sidewise on top of the tank with my legs hanging down on the left side when all at once I noticed all the paint start to chip off the other side and at the same time I noticed machine guns."

"I saw the paint fly off the side of the tank and heard machine guns so I jumped off and got in a shell hole. It was small and the bullets nocked all of the front edge in on me. Here I was nearvous."

After "I dismounted in haste and got in a shell hole which was none too large every time I started to get out the boshe shot at me."

"The tank had not seen me get off and was going on. The infantry was about 200 m. [meters] back of me and did not advance. One runner on my right got hit."

"I was on the point of getting scared as I was about a hundred yards ahead of the infantry and all alone in the field. If I went back [that is, returned toward the infantry] the infantry would think I was running and there was no reason [for me] to go forward alone."

"If I did not [rejoin the tank] they [the infantry] would not support the tank and it might get hurt. Besides m.g. [machine gun] bullets are unplesant to hear."

"All the time the infernal tank was going on alone as the men [inside] had not noticed my hurried departure. At last the bright thought occurred to me that I could move across the front in an oblique fashion and not appear [to the infantry] to run [from the enemy] yet at the same time get back [to the infantry]."

"Finally I decided that I could get back obliquely. So I started" —"listening for the machine guns with all my ears."

"As soon as the m.g.'s opened I would lay down and beat the bullets each time"—"laying down in a great hurry when I heard them, in this manner I hoped to beat the bullets to me. Some time I will figure the speed of sounds and bullets and see if I was right. It is the only use I know of that math has ever been to me."

After getting back to the infantry, "I found the Major of the infantry and asked him if he would come on after the tank. He would not [do so] as the next battalion on his left had not come up."

Another version had the infantry commander a captain, who said that the troops on his right had not advanced to his forward position.

"I asked him to send a runner to the tank to recall it. He said it was 'not his tank' "—"he was killed ten minutes later."

"Then I drew a long breath and went after the tank on foot as I could not let it be going against a whole town [Beney] alone. It is strange but quite true that at this time I was not the least scared, as I had the idea of getting the tank fixed in my head. I did not even fear the bullets though I could see the guns spitting at me, I did however run like Il——."

"I went and I burned the breaze too. So did the bullets. I kept the tank between me and the bullets as much as possible."

"On reaching the tank about four hundred yards out in the

field I tapped on the back door with my stick, and thank God it was a long one. The sgt looked out and saluted and said what do you want now Colonel, I told him to turn and come back. He was much depressed. I walked just ahead of him on the return trip and was quite safe."

A later and far less disjointed version that was supposed to be humorous:

> Colonel Patton, who was still sitting on the top of the tank, here had the most horrible experience; he could hear machine gun fire but could not locate them until glancing down the left side of the tank about six inches below his hand he saw the paint flying from the side of the tank as the result of numerous machine gun bullets striking against the tank. Owing to his heroic desire to make the tank a less enticing target he leaped from the tank and landed in a shell hole a great distance away. This shell hole however was exceedingly small and the Germans took an unpleasant delight in shooting at its upper rim so that the Colonel was greatly perturbed at finding [himself] covered with dirt. His embarrassment was enhanced by the fact that the tank unaware of this continued into the field, while the Infantry which had passed through the village was halted about 200 meters behind the Colonel. He was in a great state of perplexity as if he moved backwards and conducted a strategical withdrawal the Infantry would think a tank officer was running away; should he move forward he would become a distinct target of the four machine guns which he was now able to see about 500 meters to his front. He finally solved the problem by moving sideways until he regained the Infantry. During the course of this movement he was repeatedly forced to seek shelter in small shell holes. On reaching the Infantry he asked them if they would move forward. This they refused to do. He then asked them if they would send a runner to the tank which was cruising about in the field some 500 meters to the front. To this request the heroic Infantry made this reply "Hell no, It aint my tank." Colonel Patton was then faced with the unfortunate necessity of going to the tank himself. This he did in record time and without accident.

"By this time four more tanks had come up but there was no officer [with them]. I put Lt. Knowles . . . [on them and] asked the infantry if they would follow [the tanks]. They said yes so I started the tanks."

"We now . . . decided to attack the town [Beney]." He arranged the five tanks in line.

"While Col. Patton was arranging the attack on Beney, he handed his haversack to Sgt. Graham, who was guarding the twenty [or thirty] Germans. While the Sgt was capturing another German he saw in a house, the prisoners emptied the haversack and filled it with rocks. The loss was not discovered until hours later." It had contained his flask, razor, and tobacco.

"In the mean time some of our m.gs. had pushed out in front and one tank thought they were Bosch and began to shoot at them. I had no time to get some one so went out again [to stop the tank gunner from shooting]."

"A third time I went out as the tanks were keeping too far to the right but the last time was not bad as the [German] machine gunners were mostly dead or chased away by the tanks."

"The tanks went on to Beney but the infantry swerved off to the right and I sent a Lt. out to change the direction of the tanks. Then I followed the advance on foot but there was not much shooting. The tanks had scared the Bosch away."

"We took the town [and] 4 field guns and 16 machine guns."

Sometime during the foregoing, at 3 P.M., Patton sent his next recorded message to the IV Corps. He reported that he was 3 kilometers northwest of Pannes in what had formerly been no-man's-land. Five tanks had entered Pannes—perhaps he meant Beney—and were proceeding beyond. One tank had captured 30 prisoners in Pannes and had turned them over to the infantry. Some long-range machine gun fire was coming in, but no artillery fire was falling nearby.

"Then I walked along the battle front to see how the left battalion [Brett's] had gotten on. It was a very long way and I had had no sleep for four nights and no food all the day as I lost my sack chasing a boshe, I got some crackers off a dead one (they had not blood on them . . .) they were very good but I would have given a lot for a drink of the brandy I had had in my sack."

"I was very tired indeed and hungry as I had lost the sack with my rations and my flask of brandy . . . I found 25 Tanks. They had taken the town [Nonsard] and only lost 4 men & two officers but they were out of gas."

"The Major of the left battalion was crying because he had no more gas. He was very tired and had a bullet through his nose [it was a minor wound], I comforted him and started home alone to get some gas."

"All my runners were gone so I started back seven miles to tell them to get some gas [up forward]. That was the only bad part of the fight. I had had no sleep for two nights and nothing to eat since the night before except some crackers I got off a dead Bosch. I would have given a lot for a little brandy but even my water was gone."

"It was most interesting over the battlefield. Like the books but much less dramatic. The dead were about mostly hit in the head. There were a lot of our men stripping off buttons and other things but they always covered the face of the dead in a nice way."

"I saw one very amusing thing which I would have liked to have photographed. Right in the middle of a large field where there had never been a trench was a shell hole from a 9.7 gun. The hole was at least 8 feet deep and 15 across. On the edge of it was a dead rat, not a large healthy rat but a small field rat not over twice the size of a mouse. No wonder the war costs so much."

"When I got to . . . it had been raining two hours and the mud was bad. Here I met an officer sight seeing and he gave me a lift. This was luckey as the car got stuck in a jam and went slower than the men on foot and an air plane dropped a bomb on the road and killed two soldiers who had been walking just back of me.

"I got a motor cycle and got the gas and reported to the Corps."

"This is a very egotistical account of the affair full of 'I' but it will interest you.

"I at least proved to my own satisfaction that I have nerve. I was the only man on the front line except gen McArthur who never ducked a shell. I wanted to but it is foolish as it does no good. If they are going to hit you they will.

"I had in this action 144 tanks and 33 French Tanks quite a command."

Patton's report to the IV Corps of the action on September 12 read in part:

> . . . tanks with the 1st Division delayed in trenches. Attacked M.G. position in Bois Quart de Reserve with Inf. 7 leading tanks attacked and cleared Nonsard before arrival of Inf. Heavy work in trenches, used up gas faster than expected. Tanks were out of gas at 2 P.M. Spent . . . night 800 meters south [of] Nonsard. . . .
>
> American tanks with 42nd Division delayed in trenches. Tanks attacked Pannes with Inf. One tank attacked M.G. nest at Beney but Inf. was not up and tanks had to come back. But Germans stopped firing. 5 tanks attacked Beney at 12:45 P.M. but as Inf. had other objectives tanks withdrew after entering town. 1:30 7 [tanks] attacked Beney with Inf. and cleaned town. All gas exhausted at 3 P.M. Tanks spent night at Pannes. During night 12–13 [September] two tanks dragged up gas by sled from Bernecourt.

The French tanks with the 42d Division, he continued, found the mud so difficult that they followed the infantry to Maizerais. There they were stopped by trouble with their tracks.

Casualties, so far as Patton could determine, were 2 tanks put out of action by direct artillery hits, 3 by engine trouble, 2 French tanks by broken tracks. Forty tanks had become stuck in ditches or trenches but all were being cleared. Thirty were stalled because of lack of gas, but were being filled as gasoline arrived. Eighty U.S. and 25 French tanks were in operating condition for action on September 13.

Four men were reported killed, three officers and four men wounded, one severely.

The tankers had captured more than 150 German prisoners and had turned them over to the infantry for removal to the rear.

Afterward, when more accurate figures were available, the losses of the first day of action totaled 5 men killed, 4 officers and 15 men wounded. Of them, 2 were killed while inside tank, none was wounded there. Of the 174 tanks entering the battle, 3 were destroyed, 22 were ditched so badly that they were out of action all day, 14 had serious mechanical trouble.

The attack on September 12 had gone generally as planned against slight German resistance. The action was no real test of the ability of the tanks as fighting machines, but was interesting and valuable as an exploit in mechanics, driving, and endurance. Designed to cross trenches six feet wide, the tanks actually crossed ditches ten to fourteen feet wide, the first ones being pulled and hauled through by tankers, infantrymen, and engineers, later ones helped by cables that had been brought forward.

Brett had led the 326th Battalion with courage and coolness, walking in front of the tanks to guide them for several kilometers despite enemy machine gun fire, and setting a fine example for his men. His battalion reached its final objective, Nonsard, where Brett himself shot two German machine gunners out of the church steeple.

The French tanks had great difficulty crossing the trenches and never managed to pass through the infantry and lead the foot soldiers. Yet Chanoine's tanks remained close on the heels of the infantry and gave them invaluable support, in terms both of firepower and morale.

Compton's men encountered obstacles in the trenches east of St. Baussant, then entered Essey with the infantry, took Pannes, and, after some gasoline came forward, went on to take St. Benoit at 9 P.M.

All in all, Patton's tankers, known among themselves as the "Treat 'em Rough boys," had done an excellent job. In an initial encounter with the enemy, soldiers usually need at least a day to become familiar with and adjusted to the new and frightening sights and sounds of combat. Patton's tankers were so well prepared and so keyed up that they had performed like veterans.

The only real difficulty, and that was not the tankers' fault, was that the tanks had used up gasoline three times faster than had been expected because of the muddy ground, the large number of trenches and their broadness. Most of the tanks were out of gas by 3 P.M. Some additional fuel arrived by means of sleds dragged first by trucks to the trenches, then by tanks—originally in reserve—across the trenches and into no-man's-land.

All supplies were drawn from the main supply dump at Menil la Tour and brought forward by truck to advance dumps, where the combat units secured rations, ammunition, and other items.

Three trucks loaded with gasoline tried to move to Essey, but military policemen, who were regulating the badly congested traffic, stopped them and refused to let them continue. "This fact materially hampered the operations of the tanks on the morning of the 13th."

Diary

September 13 (Friday): "Saw Compton at 8 A.M. Sent [the rest of] his tanks to St. Benoit. Gen R[ockenbach] came up and we got gas to Brett who started for Vigneulles at 1 A.M."

"On the thirteenth we did nothing."

"The 13th of September was uneventful except that it marked a long struggle to obtain gasoline for the tanks and clearly showed the necessity for having large caterpillar tractors with each battalion to carry gasoline across country since the roads were so congested that it took thirty-two hours to move two trucks of gasoline fourteen (14) kilometers." Some gasoline trucks were on the road since 9 A.M. of the previous day.

Compton managed to get a few tanks from Pannes to St. Benoit during the morning. As a little gas became available, a few others moved to St. Benoit. There they were forced to remain immobile for lack of fuel. About 20 French tanks arrived nearby, and they too could go no farther.

Gasoline arrived for Brett's tanks in the early afternoon. After the tanks were replenished, they rolled through Nonsard to Vigneulles, where 50 were assembled by midnight.

Meanwhile, IV Corps Field Order 26, issued at 4:25 P.M., September 13, announced: "The enemy continues to retreat."

Diary

September 14 (Saturday): "Joined Brett at Vigneulles at 6 A.M. Went on. Passed St. Maurice all bound towards Woel. Here we found we were ahead of our infantry. Sent patrol to Woel. It was attacked. Lt. Grant took up 5 more tanks total 8 . . . I had heard show was over & stopped all tanks moving north. Reported to 1st Div & Corps. Got orders to pull out. Arranged to do so. Had a big row with Gen. R."

". . . on the fourteenth the left battalion personally conducted by me went to hunt for the enemy. We found the only place on the entire front where for the space half a mile there were no troops. We went through and were attacked by the boshe. We drove them six miles, took a town, Jonville, on the Hindenburg Line, [a] battery of field guns [and] 12 machine guns but no prisoners, then finding that we were eight miles ahead of our own line, and that all the canon in that part of Germany were shooting at us we withdrew with only four men hit. I was in at the start of this very fine feat of arms, but not at the finish as I was ordered back just after the tanks started and before we knew the boshe were there. We withdrew that night. Total loses 4 men killed 4 officers and 4 men wounded . . .

"This is a very egotistical letter but interesting as it shows that vanity is stronger than fear and that in war as now waged there is little of the element of fear, it is too well organized and too stupendous."

What had happened was that Brett's tankers on the morning of September 14 were unable to gain touch with the 1st Division headquarters. Impatient to move forward, Patton decided to move Brett's battalion through St. Maurice to Woel in the hope of finding infantrymen along the Woel-St. Benoit road, a logical consolidation line, for Compton's tanks working with the 42d Division were at St. Benoit.

Brett started forward shortly after 6 A.M. At 6:45, Patton sent a message to his adjutant, Captain Hebert, who was holding down the brigade command post, now quite far in the rear. He told Hebert to let the IV Corps headquarters and General Rockenbach know that Brett was pushing ahead with 51 tanks. "I will be back [to the CP] soon as possible wait for me." Then he rushed forward to join Brett's advance.

With Patton accompanying them, the tankers moved through St. Maurice against no opposition. They obtained from a partially burned and abandoned German warehouse some gasoline and a large quantity of cigars, hard bread, and blankets.

They reached the vicinity of Woel—about two kilometers short of the village—by 9 A.M. There, in an auto traveling from Woel Patton recognized Brigadier General Dennis E. Nolan, an original member of Pershing's staff. Nolan knew Patton well and stopped to chat. He asked where the tanks were going. Patton answered they were looking for a fight and for the 1st Division. Nolan informed him that the Germans had evacuated Woel, which was being held by about 20 French infantrymen. He had no idea where the American infantry was.

After telling Brett to conceal the tanks in the bushes and hedges along the road, Patton at 10 A.M. sent a message to the commanding generals of the IV Corps and 1st Division, also to Rockenbach, asking for instructions. He reminded them that the code name of his brigade was "Novelty" and that his headquarters could be reached by telephone through the exchange at "Orphans," no doubt the IV Corps. He hoped that Hebert at his command post would send a runner with any information or instructions that came through.

Patton also dispatched four officers mounted on captured German horses to try to locate some—any—American infantry troops in the neighboring forests.

While everyone was waiting for news from higher headquarters and for the return of the mounted patrol, three trucks filled with gasoline arrived. The trucks had been attacked by a hostile airplane and one soldier had been wounded by a bomb fragment that passed through his arm. The tanks were refueled and the men were given corned beef and coffee.

The officers on horseback returned and reported no infantrymen close by.

Still without word from corps, division, or Rockenbach at noon,

Patton sent a patrol of three tanks and five men on foot to Woel. He instructed the men to continue through Woel, then go down the road toward St. Benoit for two kilometers and see if they met any Americans.

The patrol found the town clear of enemy troops and no one on the St. Benoit road. While returning, the tanks encountered a German unit in close-order march, a column with eight machine guns and a battery of 77-mm. cannon. Sending a runner to Patton and Brett, the patrol commander reported that he was going to attack the Germans. Patton dispatched five tanks to assist him.

"These eight tanks unsupported by Infantry attacked the enemy and drove them to Jonville destroying five machine guns and driving the enemy away from the battery of 77's. In attempting to attach these guns to the rear of the tanks two officers and four men were wounded by shrapnel fire and the attempt to carry off the guns was abandoned."

Two tanks, disabled by mechanical trouble, were coupled to a third and towed to the battalion position just below Woel. The enemy began to register shells on the location of the battalion with 150-mm. howitzers, and "as the Commanding Officer had ascertained that he was at least two miles in front of the infantry line, it was decided to withdraw to St. Maurice."

From there Patton returned to his command post. He sent a report of the day's action and commended Brett for his gallantry and tactical sense.

At 9 P.M., he received word that all the tanks were to withdraw from the battlefield and concentrate in the Bois de la Hazelle, near the original jump-off positions. With the exception of three French and two American tanks, which were partially destroyed by direct hits, all the tanks, moving only during the hours of darkness, were in the assembly area by the night of September 18. According to Patton's humorous account:

The battle field abounded in large and deep shell holes. In those several tanks were lost but all were soon recovered except one. No trace of this could be found until some days later as an Engineer officer, walking over the field was accosted by a lean and hungry soldier who asked the authority of the officer for liberating his two pigeons. He and they were sticking by the lost tank to the last and while he cared little of his own suffering he hated to see the little birdies die. Why he was so secretive or failed to let us know by pigeon of his whereabouts is one of the unsolved mysteries of the war.

In Patton's severely military account of the operation:

Tactical Conclusions. Owing to the fact of the enemy's failure at serious resistance the full value of the tanks was not susceptible of demonstration. In spite of very serious obstacles of terrain the tanks were in a position to aid the Infantry and would have done so had such assistance been necessary. As it was, the tanks entered the towns of Nonsard, Pannes and Benney ahead of the Infantry and captured the town of Jonville unaided by any Infantry whatever.

To Beatrice:

All the losses were small, absurdly so. The great feat the tanks performed was getting through at all. The conditions could not have been worse. Only 40% did it the first day but we had 80% up by morning. The men were fine. Nearly all the officers led the tanks on foot.

This was quite different from the way the British worked it. General Elles, feeling that he had to establish a tank tradition, accompanied the tankers into combat at Cambrai while riding in the lead tank, which was marked with his battle flag and pennant. His chief of staff, Colonel Fuller, had remonstrated against this decision, but later admitted that he had been wrong, Elles right. Tankers belonged in tanks.

But, of course, the British heavies were large enough to accommodate General Elles. In contrast, the French Renaults were built to hold two crewmen. Although Patton—as well as Brett and Compton—might have driven a tank in the attack, he would have lacked the capacity to direct the action, for radio communications from and to tanks had yet to be developed.

Gen R. gave me hell for going up [with the forward elements] but it had to be done. At least I will not sit in a dug out and have my men out in the fighting.

I am feeling fine and just at present [he was writing on the 16th] I have little to do.

I saved my battle map for you as a souvenir. Here are some cap ornaments I got off a dead German. Personally I never fired a shot except to kill two poor horses with broken legs.

Rockenbach was angry over Patton's conduct during the battle. He believed that a tank brigade commander belonged at his headquarters or in close touch with it at all times. A lieutenant colonel in command of a brigade was not supposed to be running around the battlefield, where it was impossible for higher headquarters, meaning Rockenbach, to reach him—either to gain information or to transmit instructions.

A harsh letter from Rockenbach to Patton made these points: 1) the five light tanks of a platoon had to work together, had to be kept intact under its platoon commander, and not be allowed to split up; 2) when a tank brigade was allotted to a corps, the commander was to remain at the corps headquarters or be in close telephonic communications with it; 3) "I wish you would especially impress on your men that they are fighting [with] tanks, they are not Infantry, and any man who abandons his Tank will in the future be tried [by court-martial]. If a Tank is disabled one member of the crew must stay with the Tank while the other gets out and gets the necessary assistance."

This, of course, was contrary to Patton's instructions to his men who, he had made clear, were supposed to fight, tank or no tank.

Rockenbach was probably right. Tankers fought with tanks, they fought in organized units of tanks, and they fought as directed by a chain of command that needed every link to function properly and effectively. Hebert, left by Patton at his command post to answer the telephone and coordinate routine matters, was incapable of doing more than that. Rockenbach needed a responsive and responsible commander—Patton—at the tank brigade command post or headquarters. For without Patton to receive and transmit the instructions that came to Rockenbach from higher headquarters, without Patton to advise Rockenbach on the feasibility or impracticality of the orders issued by higher headquarters, without Patton at a central location where he could seize the initiative and take immediate advantage of the breaks, Rockenbach—or any other commander in his position—was helpless and lost. In short, by leaving his command post, Patton cut the Rockenbach–Patton chain of command, thereby nullifying Rockenbach's authority over the brigade and his responsibility to the First Army commander.

Patton, on the other hand, felt that too much depended on the performance of his tanks—the whole tank program, his entire training system, the overall meaning of tanks in warfare, the attack itself—for him to remain in the rear largely in the role of observer, reporter, coordinator, and detached director. His concept of leadership was more primitive and personal than Rockenbach's and more suited to an earlier age of warfare, when the melee of combat revolved essentially about the fearless behavior of the commander. Patton's type of commander inspired his men by example, by leading, by being in the thick of the action.

Had he placed Viner as his representative or deputy commander or chief of staff in his command post and had he been able to fashion a better system of communications between his CP and himself, he would have maintained the chain of command even as he personally led his men in battle.

Patton tried to mollify Rockenbach when he saw him on September 15. But by then there was no time to quibble over St. Mihiel. They were already immersed in plans for a new operation.

A day later, when Pershing sent a congratulatory letter to Rockenbach on the successful and important part played by the tanks in the St. Mihiel offensive, Rockenbach got over his pique. He forwarded Pershing's letter to Patton along with an expression of his own appreciation for the magnificent manner in which Patton's tankers had performed.

According to Lieutenant Julian K. Morrison, the tankers had operated with such élan because of the training they had received at Bourg:

Every day, some Sundays excepted, a fixed schedule was carried out from day light to dark and then for the officers school at night. The writer [Morrison] always got a great deal of encouragement from these lectures, usually given by Col Patton. He [Morrison] was made to understand by the Colonel that a Tank Officer was meant to die. His [Patton's] favorite message to his officers was "Go forward, go forward. If your tank breaks down go forward with the Infantry. There will be no excuse for your failure in this, and if I find any tank officer behind the front line of infantry I will —— [probably 'shoot him']." All Tank Officers know the rest. The result was that each officer left these lectures with the determination never to fall behind the front line of Infantry no matter what happened . . . This message of the Colonel's was passed on down by the officers to their men with the result that in the St. Mihiel drive Tankers could be seen any where from one to seven kilometers in front of the infantry. Everyone fought—cooks, company clerks, mess sergeants, runners and mechanics. So closely was the order carried out that the Tank Corps nearly starved for two or three days afterward. Needless to say before the next fight orders came out to the effect that anyone leaving the post assigned to him would be dealt with by Court Martial. The courage of the Tank Corps having been sufficiently proved.

More than the courage of the Tank Corps had been proved. The St. Mihiel offensive proved the success of Patton's methods of training for and commanding in combat. No troops had better morale, more desire to close with the enemy, a more consistent wish to go forward aggressively than Patton's tankers. They were anxious and eager to fight, and they were disappointed because they saw St. Mihiel as anything but a real battle, a real trial of their strength and mettle. The Germans gave way too easily. It was not much of a fight. The tankers would have preferred a real test because they felt they were ready to take on and to lick the best enemy troops in the world.

This was what distinguished Patton's leadership.

Without the least suspicion that her husband was in the thick of combat, Beatrice sent Pershing a letter on September 13 to wish him happiness on his birthday. "George writes in every letter," she added, "how happy he is in his work. He loves the tanks; and by our [news]papers, they seem to fulfil all his expectations."

Several days later she read an account of St. Mihiel cabled on September 16 by Junius B. Wood exclusively to the Los Angeles Evening *Express* and the Chicago Daily *News*. "Californian Perched on Tank During Battle," ran the headline on a story featuring Patton riding on the tail of a tank. Like a cavalryman.

CHAPTER 30

Meuse-Argonne

"I am reaping what I sewed."

Diary

September 15 (Sunday): "Got ready to move out [of the St. Mihiel sector] and arranged plans etc . . . saw Gen R[ockenbach] at Ligney and went over plans [for new operation] in a hurried way. Went to bed."

September 16: "Studied map [of the Meuse-Argonne sector] and made up plan. Bought a raincoat etc as I had lost mine."

The same tank organization that had operated at St. Mihiel—Brett's and Compton's battalions and Chanoine's 14th and 17th Groupes—would remain under Patton's command for the Meuse-Argonne offensive, but this time would work with the I Corps.

Patton drove to the new battle area and, dressed in a French uniform, inspected the front near Vauquois, making a careful reconnaissance of the ground.

Chanoine's tanks traveled by train to Clermont and detrained in the railway yard. They moved to a nearby place of concealment. The tankers started to work on their machines and prepare them for operational use. In the old area, Brett's and Compton's men, tucked away in a forest, were giving their tanks similar treatment.

Diary

September 18 (Wednesday): Got telephone connected and office and mess running. Expect to be shelled at 9:30 now 10:05 and nothing has happened but they [the Germans] are shelling Paris to the west.

September 19: "Went to Front line and found trenches not very wide. And ground rather better than I had expected."

Letter, GSP, Jr., to Beatrice, September 19, 1918

We are getting ready for another show and I am sitting in the only remaining house of a village. They have not shelled us yet but doubtless will shortly as Americans don't seem to be able to conceal them selves very well. I just got back from a reconnaissance where I was dressed like a Frenchman. I hope I did not get any bugs . . . I fancy our next show will be less easy than the first that is if the bosch fight and I think they will. The ground however is better for us being less of a swamp than the St. Mihiel salient proved to be. Still as it has been raining all the time it may get muddie here also. I just got through writing a report on the last action and recommended certain officers for gallantry. I hope they get something . . .

I must stop now and eat supper before it gets dark as we can have no lights. I will wire you after the next fight as I did this time. I am very well and love you with all my heart.

Diary

September 20 (Friday): "Went up to O.P. [observation post] in A.M. . . . Went to [railroad] station at 12 n. to unload . . . Unloading very badly handled. No plan at all. Much track trouble. Some shelling but all high."

Brett's battalion, now renamed the 344th, and Compton's battalion, now the 345th, detrained in Clermont and moved during the hours of darkness to wooded areas for concealment. While the tankers worked on their tanks in the general wooded area known as the Forêt de Facq, officers reconnoitered routes to their jump-off points.

. . .

The Meuse-Argonne attack, the second operation in which an American field army acted as an independent entity, was part of a larger Franco-American offensive. On September 26, along the front stretching from the Meuse River on the east (right) to the Suippes River on the west, the French Fourth Army on the left and the U. S. First Army on the right would attack generally to the north.

The American zone of attack lay between the Meuse and Aisne rivers and included the Argonne Forest, which was in the western part of the sector, near the Aisne.

Pershing assumed command of his front on September 22 and put three corps into the line, from right to left, the III, V, and I Corps. The I Corps had three divisions on line, from right to left, the 36th (Traub), the 28th (Muir), and the 77th (Alexander). Patton's tanks would operate with the 35th and 28th Divisions on the eastern fringes of the Argonne Forest.

Diary
September 21 (Saturday): "Went to Corps to see what they were doing. Got lost. Gen [Malin] Craig C[hief] of S[taff of I Corps] very nice to deal with . . . Was told to submit plan. Which I did. Have a fine elephant shelter Dug out and a good bed."

Patton's "Memorandum on Plan for the Use of Tanks" was a lengthy document that showed his usual thorough application to the job at hand. He opened by describing the terrain, which was less than favorable for tanks, for it was "an old battle-ground, heavily seamed with trenches and pitted with numerous shell-holes." Since, however, he had no choice, he would try to dispose the tanks in the way that promised success, even though this might not be "in accordance with most preconceived notions as to the proper use of tanks."

He felt that the correct way of using tanks was in depth that would permit a concentrated thrust. This offered the possibility of a relatively long-range penetration, and this in turn was to be followed by a pursuit. What he wished was to initiate a shock action followed by a cavalry-type maneuver.

Unfortunately, the terrain would inhibit this to some extent. There was

only one narrow opening which permits the employment of tanks. This opening is bounded on the west by the line of

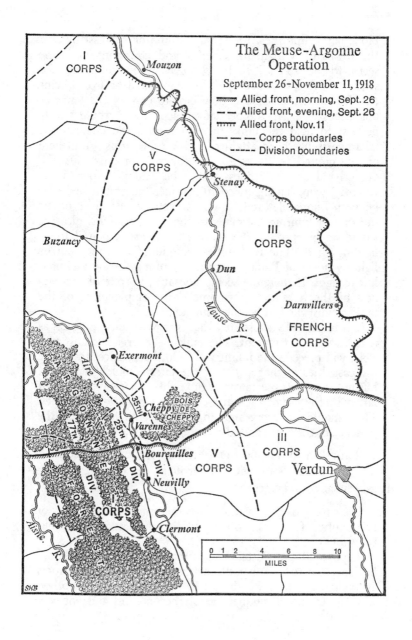

The Meuse-Argonne Operation
September 26–November 11, 1918

Allied front, morning, Sept. 26
Allied front, evening, Sept. 26
Allied front, Nov. 11
Corps boundaries
Division boundaries

bluffs paralleling the Aire River . . . and on the east by . . . the towns of Vaugquois, Cheppy and Exermont . . . The sector to the west . . . is too wooded and mountainous, the sector to the east is cut by deep ravines and by five streams . . . The question then is how best to employ the tanks at our disposal . . . to the best advantage. . . . it would clearly be best to hold the tanks in reserve until the line Baulny-Charpentry has been attained by the other arms. From here on the ground seems excellently adapted for tanks. On the other hand . . . selfishness would be exhibited toward the Infantry, who, having toiled to conquer the entrenched area between Boureuilles and Varennes, would be deprived of the pleasure of hunting Germans in the open, and this pleasure would be usurped by the tanks . . . There is bound to be fighting on the line Boureuilles-Vauquois. There may not be fighting north of Baulny, because there may be no Germans left to fight. It therefore seems advisable, in spite of the badness of the terrain, to recommend the employment of the tanks against the first hostile trenches . . .

It is respectfully submitted that infantry should progress as if tanks were not present. The tanks, whenever humanly possible, will precede the infantry and do their utmost to reduce the casualties in that arm . . . the latter should follow . . . but not simply as spectators of the fight, as has happened, but rather by the use of their arms, machine guns, 37's and rifles. They should do everything to intensify the fire which the presence of the tanks partially insures.

Patton asked for engineer and artillery support, "a special aeroplane" to communicate with the artillery. He discussed signals—flags, pennants, and pigeons.

The supply of gas for tanks is as important as the supply of ammunition for guns. Both revert to worthless junk without the supplies . . .

Regimental and Battalion Commanders of infantry should be requested to inform tanks acting near them of any orders as to change of plan which may be received by them, as otherwise the tanks will unquestionably become lost and not conform in the best way to changes which may arise.

Briefly, Patton envisaged using his tanks in a relatively narrow corridor, about three kilometers wide, between the Forêt d'Argonne and the Bois de Cheppy, where the ground was least difficult for tank operations. Normally, this opening would accommodate a single battalion. But the Aire River flowed through the length of the corridor and posed a complication. The river separated the zones of action of the 35th and 28th Divisions. Thus, it would make sense to put one tank battalion with one division and the other tank battalion with the other infantry division. But the 35th Division, east of the Aire, had room, that is open ground, suitable for committing two tank companies, while the 28th Division, on the west bank, had space for only one. This led Patton to decide to use a single tank battalion with both divisions even though the tankers on one side of the river would be unable to come to the aid of the others.

Brett was, in Patton's opinion, the more competent battalion commander, and his tanks had seen more action than Compton's at St. Mihiel. Consequently, Brett's tankers were more experienced, while his tanks were more worn and in worse condition.

Patton put Brett's battalion up front, with two of his companies working with the 35th Division and one company with the 28th. Immediately behind Brett would come Compton's men, with the companies deployed the same way across the front. Chanoine's Schneiders, inferior to the Renaults, would bring up the rear.

Although this deployment spread his units in line, that is laterally across the front, rather than in the preferred fashion, in column or depth, Patton sought nevertheless to attain sufficient push and thrust by means of his three waves. He hoped that Brett's battalion could start and sustain an advance to the first objective. There Brett's tanks would probably be mechanically exhausted or knocked out of action; they would be at the end of their usefulness. Patton would then pass Compton's tankers through Brett's for a drive to the next objective. There, where the ground was better for the heavier Schneider tanks, he would leapfrog Chanoine's French groupes through Compton's men for an advance as far as the tanks could go.

Craig, the I Corps chief of staff, approved Patton's plan, had Patton's lengthy memo reproduced, and furnished a copy to each division commander in the corps for information and guidance.

Diary

September 22 (Sunday): "345 Bn tanks not yet arrived. Am very mad. Got 20,000 gal gas sent to Langres for Pigeon baskets. Wrote memo on operation of Tanks. Still madder with Capt. Compton. He is an ass."

Letter, GSP, Jr., to Beatrice, September 22, 1918

Life is just one D—— thing after another. One whole Battalion has failed to show up and I cant find it. The Battalion Commander spent the day looking for a house instead of getting his Tanks. He is a fool but I a greater one to trust him.

Still I am reaping what I sewed. I spoon fed these hounds so much that they are helpless and run to me every time they ought to go to the W.C. to see if it is all right. Some times I think I am not such a great commander after all. Just a fighting animal. Still I will improve in time. At least if one learns by mistakes I ought to be wise. I have made all [the mistakes] there are.

I am getting on fine with the Corps & the Division which is a comfort as things ought to [be] right some where.

One fine example of efficiency nix has just happened. 100,-000 gallons of gas arrived in tank cars with no pump. Now we can't get it out except by dippers!!!

It is a good thing I have a cheerful disposition. I have inspite of certain lapses . . .

But I have got a rotten staff and no mistake. Probably my own fault. I have done too much for them. Well I will never do it again if I pull through this. But it is a big if. Hellish big.

Diary

September 23 (Monday): "Got all 345 Tanks unloaded by daylight under shell fire but no casualties. Got lot of mail from home. Five letters from B. Rained all day and a lot of shelling over us at Clermont. Cussed out Brett & Compton for carelessness etc."

September 24 (Tuesday): "Got Corps Plan. Wrote field order & annex. Gen R came up. Things are in pretty good shape but we are very short on men. The Bosch took pictures of us so I guess we shall be shelled or something to night. Wrote B & Mama."

Patton accumulated and stored 20,000 gallons of gasoline in reserve, stocks to be issued after the initial day's action. He ordered each tank moving into battle to carry two 2-liter cans full of gasoline on its tail even though this was dangerous—a bullet penetrating a can might turn the fuel into flame and burn the tank carrying it. But the risk, he decided, was preferable to having the tanks run out of gasoline prematurely as at St. Mihiel.

Patton issued his Field Order on September 24. After giving detailed instructions to each element of his command on routes and methods of advance, Patton gave orders on supply and liaison. The command post then established and the 321st Repair and Salvage Company were to remain at Camp Fourgons, where they were located in a quarry relatively safe from enemy bombardment.

Particularly for Rockenbach's benefit, although he was doing so for his units too, he indicated that he would establish an advance CP at the 35th Division advance headquarters at Les Côtes de Forimont. Then,

> After H plus 1 hour the Brigade Commander [Patton] will move forward along the line Route Nationale No. 46, and will be up with the leading tanks at H plus 3½ hours. He will be accompanied by a group of from 6 to 10 runners.

This large group of messengers would enable him to remain in contact with Rockenbach and vice versa.

In an annex to the field order, Patton took up repair-and-salvage efforts, motor transport, supply, administration, and intelligence.

Finally, he made three pungent observations:

> All Officers at the Brigade P.C. [command post] are charged with keeping the Corps Commander, the Chief of Tank Corps and the Brigade Commander fully informed as

to the state of affairs. By using every means to get information forward some may arrive.

The criminal waste of Government property is a fault of our Army. It will not occur in the 1st Brigade Tank Corps.

The attention of men not in the fight is called to the fact that they have often a more difficult and important part to play than if they were with the tanks. Their good work will not be forgotten.

Rockenbach's strictures over St. Mihiel were neither ignored nor overlooked.

Letter, GSP, Jr., to Beatrice, September 24, 1918

We had a very quiet day except that a shell took of[f] a mans foot for which I am sorry . . .

There is nothing of interest to report so I will go to bed as I shant have another sleep for some time.

Diary

September 25 (Wednesday): Inspected battalions at 9 A.M. 345th very dirty, ordered correction. 344th better but could stand improvement. Gen R called. Went to corps to get H-hour and D-day, also passes for gasoline trucks. Went to meeting at 35th Division. One of our trucks full of runners was hit by a shell 6:15 P.M. Near Neuvilly, no report yet. Had big dinner. Will start soon. Wrote B.

GSP, Jr., "Personal Glimpses of General Pershing," 1924

I personally know of one occasion when the presence of the Commander [Pershing] received a spontaneous tribute. Just at dark on September 25th many of us were lying in the ditches bordering the Flury-Varennes road, waiting for a German concentration [of artillery fire] to cease, when suddenly the big car with its 4 stars came up the road going to the front. Moved by a single impulse we all arose, and regardless of the shells, stood at salute until he had passed us.

On the night of September 25, the tankers moved to their departure positions. During this approach march, it was necessary for four tank companies—about 80 tanks—to cross a bridge at Neuville. As the leading tank arrived at the bridge, a German barrage opened, apparently aimed at the bridge. Some shells landed nearby and killed two military policemen who were directing traffic across the structure. The tanks halted. The moment the artillery ceased, one company rushed across the bridge. The Germans renewed their fire but only at regular intervals. Between these periodic shellings, the tanks raced across the structure without harm.

At their jump-off points, the men tried to catch a few hours' sleep. They knew they would be awakened at 2:30 A.M. by the start of a violent three-hour artillery preparation to be fired by American guns. At 5:30, they would attack.

Letter, GSP, Jr., to Beatrice, September 25, 1918
Just a word to you before I leave to play a little part in what promises to be the biggest battle of the war or world so far.

We kick off in the morning but this will not be mailed until after that . . .

I will have two Battalions and a group of French tanks in the show in all about 140 Tanks . . . I think that after this show we will have a rest. I hope so for the men are tired and all the tanks need over hauling . . .

I am always nearvous about this time just as at Polo or at Foot ball before the game starts but so far I have been all right after that. I hope I keep on that way it is more plesant.

Well if I wrote all night I could not tell you how much I love you and I had better eat a little first as I shant be able to for a few days.

. . .

The artillery opened its preparatory barrage on schedule, and at 5:30, September 26, in a heavy mist, American soldiers moved forward in attack. Some of the leading tanks encountered a mine field just beyond the American trenches, "but thanks to the courtesy of the Germans in leaving up warning signs the tanks avoided this danger."

As long as the mist lasted, the tanks advanced with little difficulty, for the enemy was unable to detect them. But in mid-morning, around ten o'clock, the fog suddenly lifted, and the German fires became intense and accurate. American infantrymen, particularly near Varennes and Cheppy, became somewhat confused, panicky, and disorganized.

Patton had said he would remain for at least an hour after the attack started in his advance CP—code-named "Bonehead," it was a dugout on the southern edge of some woods at Les Côtes de Forimont. But he became impatient. He could hear the tanks, the artillery, the machine guns, but the fog was so dense he could see nothing.

Sometime between 6 and 6:30, accompanied by Knowles, now a captain, an attached signal officer named Lieutenant Paul S. Edwards, and about twelve enlisted runners or messengers, some of them carrying telephones and wire, others pigeons in baskets, Patton left his CP and walked northward in the wake of the tanks operating on the eastern side of the Aire River. He and his party followed the tank tracks visible on the edge of the Clermont–Neuvilly–Boureuilles–Varennes road leading toward Cheppy. About halfway between Boureuilles and Varennes, they passed some French tanks, then Compton's support tanks.

Beyond a narrow-gauge railroad cut and near a crossroads just short of Cheppy, the group halted and sat down. Patton sent a message by pigeon, no doubt reporting his location.

Very little was happening in that vicinity. Infantry and tanks were out of sight. Shells were falling, Knowles later said, "to our front some considerable distance [away] probably at least one kilometer." It was desultory firing and difficult to judge how far off and exactly where it was because of the atmospheric conditions.

A handful of tanks came along, stopped for a few minutes to chat, then went on. After they had passed, some shells dropped nearby. Then machine gun bullets came close. Patton ordered everyone to take cover in the railroad cut. Once in the relative safety of that protection, Patton posted Corporal John G. Heming, who would later be commissioned, on the right front, and Private First Class Joseph T. Angelo, his orderly, on the left front. They were to give the alarm if the enemy attempted to advance on or to cut off the small command group.

Several disorganized groups of infantrymen, walking and running to the rear, came through. Patton stopped them and questioned them. The soldiers said they were separated from their units and commanders because of the fog and the machine gun fire. Patton told them to join his group. The shallow and short railroad cut soon became crowded.

As the enemy fire increased in volume and the machine guns began to shoot in short meaningful bursts, Patton led his now considerable number of men, perhaps as many as 100, back about 100 yards to the reverse slope of a small hill. Patton ordered everyone to spread out and lie down. The troops had just done so when machine gun fire began to sweep the area, seemingly from every direction.

About 125 yards to the rear and at the base of the slope, Patton noticed several of Compton's tanks. He sent Knowles down the hill with a message ordering them to come forward at once. Knowles discovered what was holding them up. Two enormous trenches, very deep and very wide, formerly held by the Germans, blocked progress. A French Schneider trying to cross them was bogged down and barring the only suitable crossing place. Some French tankers had started to dig away the banks with shovels, but when shells and bullets landed nearby, they abandoned their work and sat in the trench for protection.

Knowles passed on Patton's message to the American tankers, then continued to the rear to find Compton. He located Captain Williams and delivered Patton's order, then discovered Compton and repeated the instruction.

On the reverse slope of the hill, as time passed, Patton wondered why the tanks were not coming forward. He sent Lieutenant Edwards down the hill to get some action. He also dispatched Sergeant Edgar W. Fansler to find Compton and tell him to get moving.

Like Knowles, Edwards saw what was wrong. While Fansler proceeded to the rear in search of Compton, Edwards talked to the French crew and got no reaction. He walked to the group of five American tanks nearby and talked with Captain Math L. English, who was in command.

Growing increasingly angry because the tanks were still not moving, Patton started down the slope himself. He immediately saw that the infantrymen he had collected were preparing to abandon the hill in panic. If he left, they would flee. So he stopped. He called Angelo and sent him back to get the tanks moved up.

Angelo made little impression on the tankers, and when a volley of shells came in, he prudently jumped into a trench for shelter.

At this point Patton came down the hill himself. He immediately organized a concerted effort to get the tanks across the trenches. He set the French to work. He went over to the American tanks, which were being splattered with machine gun fire, removed the shovels and picks strapped to the tank sides, got the tankers out of their machines, handed them the tools, and put them to work tearing down the sides of the trenches.

All this time, enemy fire was sweeping the area, both artillery shells and machine gun bullets. A hostile plane flew over from time to time to direct the enemy gunners. Some of the men who were digging were hit.

Patton and English, despite repeated requests from Edwards and others to step into the trenches, remained in exposed positions on the parapet directing the work. Several times Patton shouted, "To Hell with them—they can't hit me."

When passages had been dug across the ditches, Patton and English chained several tanks together to get better traction in the mud. Then the two officers, still disdaining the shelter of the trenches, and now joined by Angelo, gave hand signals to help the drivers get across. Miraculously, they were not struck by the enemy fire.

Patton explained the successful crossing as "due to the coolness of the drivers who maneuvered with their doors open" at considerable personal risk.

As soon as English's five tanks were over the obstacles—the Schneider was hopelessly stuck—Patton sent them forward up the hill. Then gathering the men at the trenches together, he led them up the slope.

When the last of English's tanks crossed the crest of the knoll, Patton ordered all the men to spread out and follow him. Waving his large walking stick, which looked like a cane, over his head, he shouted, "Let's go get them, who's with me," and walked forward.

Enthusiastically, about 100 men jumped to their feet and started to follow Patton. Some of Patton's command group wanted to join their colonel, but they were unarmed. Sergeant William V. Curran was carrying a telephone and some wire, Sergeants L. T. Garlow and Lorenzo F. Ward were loaded down with pigeon baskets. Sergeant Harry M. Stokes was in a shell hole bandaging a wounded infantryman's leg.

Patton's force swept over the crest of the hill. They went no more than 50 or 75 yards when the incoming machine gun fire became terrific. Everyone, including Patton, flung himself on the ground and let the wave of bullets wash over the hillside.

It was probably at this moment that Patton had his vision.

GSP, Jr., "My Father," 1927
Once in the Argonne just before I was wounded I felt a great desire to run, I was trembling with fear when suddenly I thought of my progenitors and seemed to see them in a cloud over the German lines looking at me. I became calm at once and saying aloud "It is time for another Patton to die" called for volunteers and went forward to what I honestly believed to be certain death. Six men went with me; five were killed and I was wounded so I was not much in error.

When the noise of the firing abated, Patton picked himself up. Waving his stick and shouting "Let's go, let's go," he marched forward.

This time only six men accompanied him. Among them was Angelo. As they walked ahead in a miniature charge of the light brigade, Angelo noticed that the others were dropping to the ground as they were struck by enemy fire. Finally just he and Patton were left. "I told him they were all hit but us."

"We are alone," Angelo said.

"Come on anyway," Patton said.

Why? What did he hope to accomplish?

He and Angelo could certainly not hope to eradicate the hostile machine gun nests and stop the enemy fire. He himself was armed with his walking stick, although he wore a pistol in his holster. Angelo carried a rifle. Together in that hail of bullets they resembled Don Quixote and his faithful servant Sancho Panza.

Or did Patton believe that he and Angelo led charmed lives? They had, after all, both stood on the parapet at the trench below the other side of the hill and had urged the tanks across the ditches. Nothing had harmed them. Could they then pass safely through this rain of steel too and make their way up forward to the leading tanks where, surely, more work remained to be done?

Was Patton unwilling to admit defeat, to lose face with the others on the hillside, who were even now crawling frantically back across the crest to the relative safety of the reverse slope? Was he merely stubborn? Did he expect the men to see how easy it was to walk through the bullets? Did he think they would eventually join him?

Or was he seeking to be hit? Was he inviting the glory of death or injury on the field of battle? Was he fulfilling his destiny?

Or was it the thoughtlessness and mindlessness of battlefield madness, the pull and power of taut anger, barely controlled rage, overwhelming hatred—so strong that it makes a man tremble—that drove him toward the enemy?

"Come on anyway," he said.

No more than a few seconds passed when he felt the jolt of a bullet strike his leg. He took a few steps, struggled to maintain his equilibrium, kept going on nerve alone for several yards, and fell.

It was probably around 11:30 A.M. The place was a few hundred yards short of the village of Cheppy.

Angelo helped him into a small shell hole in the middle of an open field, cut his trousers, and bandaged his wound, which was bleeding freely. It was difficult and dangerous work, for there was little protection in that slight depression a shell had scooped out of the earth. Every time Patton or Angelo moved and exposed himself, German soldiers in a railroad cut about 40 yards away fired at them.

After a while that seemed like eternity, some tanks came by. They had crossed the trenches at the bottom of the slope, climbed the hill, and were following Captain English. The appearance of the tanks prompted a decline in the level of intensity of the enemy fire—no machine gunner in his right mind was going to expose his position to the tank guns. In that lull, Patton sent Angelo out to tell the tankers where the enemy gunners were located. Informed by Angelo of lucrative targets, the tankers departed.

More time went by. Sergeant Schemnitz, obviously looking for the colonel, came along. Angelo hailed him, and Schemnitz hurried over. Patton told him to carry the word back that he was wounded, that Major Brett was to take command of the brigade, and that no one was to come to carry Patton back because he would attract enemy fire.

Schemnitz ran back with these instructions. As he crossed the crest of the hill to the reverse slope, where Knowles, Edwards, and the runners were waiting, he shouted the news in great excitement—the colonel was wounded, Major Brett was in command, and nobody was to go near the colonel until the fire died down. He rushed off to find a stretcher.

Garlow released a pigeon with a message that Patton was wounded.

At the shell hole, a few more tanks passed nearby. Patton again sent Angelo to attract the tankers' attention and tell them where to go. Compton was in one of those tanks, and, following Angelo's directions, placed a few well-aimed shells and silenced a machine gun that had been harassing the two men in the hole. The tanks then continued on their way.

A medical aid soldier named John L. Close, who was working with the infantry, wandered through the field. He stopped, looked at Patton's wound, and changed the bandage. Patton thanked him courteously, and Close went on.

After about an hour or so—it was difficult to estimate the passage of time—the work of all the tanks in the area eliminated the machine gun fire. About 25 German machine gun nests were believed destroyed. The hostile artillery shelling became erratic as the gunners seemed to be ranging on the tanks up ahead.

Only then did Schemnitz, accompanied by Sergeant First Class

Ely and Corporal Heming, return to the shell hole with a stretcher. These three men and Angelo placed Patton on the litter and carried him back to the reverse slope of the hill.

Edwards went off toward the front in search of Brett, whom he found at 2 P.M.

Fansler relieved Angelo on one corner of the stretcher, and these five men took Patton three kilometers to the rear and delivered him to an ambulance company.

While the others returned to their duties, Angelo stayed with Patton. Before Patton would go to a hospital, he insisted on being taken to the 35th Division headquarters so he could report conditions on the front.

An ambulance drove him and Angelo there, and an officer came out and talked with Patton. Then he allowed himself to be moved to Evacuation Hospital Number 11. Angelo took his pistol and his money for safekeeping.

Diary

September 26 (Thursday): "Started forward at 6 A.M. H plus ½ hour. Heavy fog. Found men coming back and took them along with me. Heavy fire all around from m.g. Found mine field with Bosch notice on it. Got to R.R. cut near Cheppy sent pigeon message. Was fired on heavily and 35 Div came back on the run. Moved back about 200 m. [meters] Heavy m.g. [machine gun] & Art. [Artillery] fire. Lots of Dough Boys hit. [Captain] English & I got tanks forward. 20 men hit. Tried to make inft charge and got shot. Lay in shell hole an hour. Could hear bosch talk. Went to hospital and was operated on by Dr. Elliot of N.Y."

September 27 (Friday): "Woke up to find Capt Semmes on my right. Capt. Gilfillen on my left. Both wounded. Slept a lot. Wrote Beat. Tried to wire but could not."

Letter, GSP, Jr., to Beatrice, September 28, 1918

We went into our second fight on the morning of Sept. 26 at 5:30 A.M. It was terribly foggy and in addition they were shooting lots of smoke shells so we could not see ten feet. I started forward at 6:30 to see what was doing but could see little. Machine guns were going in every direction in front behind and on both sides. But no one could tell who they belonged to. I had six men—runners—with me and a compas so I collected all the soldiers I found who were lost and brought them along. At times I had several hundred.

About 9:30 we came to a town called Cheppy. I went passed the infantry as we were supposed to have taken the place. But all at once we got shot at from all sides.

With m.g. and shell also but still we could see nothing. Pretty soon some of our infantry came running back. So as none of my men had any rifles I went back with the inft. but stopped before they did. Also I stopped in a better place just back of a crest.

When we got here it [the weather] began to clear up and we were shot at to beat hell with shells and machine guns. Twice the inft started to run but we hollored at them and called them all sorts of names so they staied. But they were scared some and acted badly, some put on gas masks, some covered their face with their hands but none did a damed thing to kill Bosch. There were no officers there but me. So I decided to do business. Some of my reserve tanks were stuck by some trenches. So I went back and made some Americans hiding in the trenches dig a passage. I think I killed one man here. He would not work so I hit him over the head with a shovel. It was exciting for they shot at us all the time but I got mad and walked on the parapet. At last we got Five tanks accross and I started them forward and yelled and cussed and waved my stick and said come on. About 150 dough boys started but when we got to the crest of the hill the fire got fierce right along the ground. We all lay down I saw that we must go forward or back and I could not go back so I yelled who comes with me. A lot of dough boys yelled but only six of us started. My striker, me and 4 doughs. I hoped the rest would follow but they would not. Soon there were only three but we could see the machine guns right ahead so we yelled to keep up our courage and went on. Then the third man went down and I felt a blow in the leg but at first I could walk so went about 40 ft when my leg gave way. My striker the only man left yelled "oh god the colonels hit and there aint no one left." He helped me to a shell hoel and we lay down and the Bosch shot over the top as fast as he could. He was very close. The tanks began getting him and in about an hour it was fairly clear [of bullets].

Some of my men carried me out under fire which was not at all plesant.

Finally I got to a hospital at 3:30. I was hit at 11:15.

The bullet went into the front of my left leg and came out just at the crack of my bottom about two inches to the left of my rectum. It was fired at about 50 m[eters] so made a hole about the size of a [silver] dollar where it came out.

It has hurt very little and I have slepped fine. I will be out [of the hospital] in ten days.

Have tried to telegraph you but so far with out success.

CHAPTER 31

The End of the War

"I have always feared I was a coward at heart but I am beginning to doubt it."

Thomas M. Johnson, staff correspondent of the Evening Sun, with the American First Army at Verdun: "Col. Patton, Hero of the Tanks, Hit by Bullet—He Crawled into Shell Hole and Directed Monsters in Argonne Battle," October 8, 1918.

Lieutenant Colonel George F. Patten, Jr. [sic] of Pride's Crossing, Mass., one of the first officers of the American tank corps to be wounded, gave a splendid example of courage and self-sacrifice to the officers of this newest branch of the service which he did so much to build up.

At 11 o'clock in the morning of Sept. 26, Col. Patten was with a number of tanks south of Varennes in the Aire Valley. It was the first day of the Verdun attack and vitally important that the tanks get forward.

The mist, however, was so dense and the fog so thick that Col. Patten walked ahead of them choosing their route and also assembling some and leading forward infantrymen who had got lost.

The tanks were being heavily shelled and had also come within reach of the Hun machine guns. As Patten walked forward a bullet struck him in the right leg. He walked about forty yards further, and then crawled into a shell hole. His orderly, Joseph Anzelo [sic] of New York, bandaged the wound, whereupon Col. Patten lighted a cigarette and remained in the shell hole for some time, issuing orders to the tanks to spread out so as not to make so large a target.

He coolly looked about for the German machine guns, directing the tanks how to wipe them out. Finally the pain became intense and Patten at last consented to go to the rear.

Col Patten was one of the organizers of the tank corps, and had studied tanks on both the British and French fronts. He developed four new devices improving tanks which were adopted by the French and British. For some time he conducted the American tank service school where the corps now fighting so gloriously was developed.

Even though he was wounded and removed from the battlefield, he was surely present in the minds of his tankers, who carried out the precepts he had so firmly implanted in them. He would later write, "we broke the Prussian guard with the tanks," and his assessment was essentially correct. The tanks had helped the First Army gain a significant victory.

Although Patton had planned to commit his battalions in successive lines of attack in order to reach a series of objectives, serious German resistance, particularly near Cheppy and Varennes, made it necessary to bring all the tanks into action on the first day of the battle. The tanks on the western (left) side of the Aire River working with the 28th Division had run into strong concrete enemy pillboxes. It was the first time American tanks met this type of defenses, and the tankers mastered the obstacles and silenced the German gunners by employing a new technique—firing 37-mm. high explosive shells through the portholes of the bunkers. Tankers with the 35th Division helped materially in the capture of the strong position at Vauquois and the reduction of stubborn opposition at Cheppy. In the process, the brigade lost 43 tanks, some to enemy action, others to mechanical failure.

Brett, who would command the brigade for the remainder of the war, wrote:

> The entire 1st Brigade suffered that first day, for at the end we learned that the Brigade Commander, Colonel G. S. Patton, Jr. had been seriously wounded while heroically attempting to rally disorganized Infantry to attack a machine gun nest.

On the second day of battle, eleven tanks west of the Aire advanced along the edge of the Argonne Forest, knocking out machine guns and capturing their crews, which they turned over to the infantry. On the east bank, the tanks received repeated calls for help from the infantry, but no concerted effort was possible.

With only 83 tanks in operating condition on the third day, the brigade "took the town of Apresmont five times before the infantry would enter, consolidate and exploit the success." At the end of that day, Rockenbach withdrew the 14th and 17th Groupes because of the complete mechanical exhaustion of those tanks.

After a massive repair-and-salvage operation lasting all night, the two American battalions fielded 55 tanks for the fourth day of fighting. They helped the infantry establish a consolidated line, then withdrew from the battlefield and entered reserve positions, where they remained inactive for several days.

The men worked hard to get their machines in fighting condition, and on October 1, 89 tanks returned to combat. Fifty-nine were lost that day, and the tankers retired once more. On October 5, the brigade committed the remaining 30 tanks and lost almost half. With but 17 tanks left, Rockenbach called the brigade back.

A final action took place on October 16, when a provisional company, consisting of about 20 tanks, 10 officers, and 140 men, under Captain Courtenay Barnard, supported the 42d Division. Ten tanks reached their objectives, but—a familiar refrain in the Tank Corps—"The infantry did not follow and the tanks returned. Large bodies of the enemy were dispersed during this advance."

The excellent performance of the tankers, who had gone on until they had exhausted their machines, could be traced to the spirit and skill of Patton who had instructed them and inspired them, and their success was a reflection of his accomplishment.

. . .

Brigadier General C. D. Rhodes, who had been commandant of the Mounted Service School when the Pattons were at Fort Riley and who now commanded a field artillery brigade, tried for several days to ascertain how seriously Patton had been wounded. He finally learned from General Craig that Patton was all right.

Rhodes immediately wrote to Beatrice— "Dear Mrs. Georgie"—
and assured her that her husband's condition was good. Rhodes
had seen Patton the day before the battle:

> He looked well—hard and muscular—but his hair at the tem-
> ples has grown quite gray—and he said it was due to being so
> scared in the St. Mihiel drive—when the Huns, he alleged,
> knocked him off the top of the tanks . . . Now he's better off
> with a good honorable wound . . . and [he will] be the envy
> of everybody . . . I really envy Georgie that fine wound!

After spending three days at the evacuation hospital, Patton was
transferred to Base Hospital Number 49 in Allerey.

Diary
    September 30: "Was put on cattle train in rain and had a
rather bad night as the iron bars of the stretcher hurt my
back and I could not move."

On that day, Rockenbach recommended that Patton, Captain
English, and Lieutenant Edwards be awarded the Distinguished
Service Cross for gallantry and exceptional heroism in the Meuse-
Argonne offensive.

Diary
    October 1: "Breakfast on train consisted of bread and mo-
lasses. Got to Allerey at 11 A.M. was put in nice bed and felt
better. Dr. Greenbourg dressed my leg. A nice little Jew who
was careful not to hurt. Had two drains put in my leg. The
powder [in the bullet] burned my skin badly."

Letter, GSP, Jr., to Beatrice, October 2, 1918
    Here I am . . . missing half my bottom but other wise all
right.
    We staied at the evacuation hospital just back of the line
from the night of the 26 till the night of the 29. Then we left
by ambulance to the train. The train was box cars and we
were put in racks three high. I got a top. We were in stretch-
ers and they are not comfortable. We left in the freight
[cars] at 7 P.M. and got here at 11 A.M. on the 30th. It was a
pretty tiresome trip but as it was raining there was no dust.
They fed us once during the trip on coffee and molasses and

bread. It was good enough but not up to the pictures of red cross trains. This hospital is pretty nice but there are only two nurses for 50 officers. I got washed to day for the first time and I am the senior [officer in the hospital].

Still it might be worse though just how I cant see. The hole in my hip is about as big as a tea cup and they have to leave it open.

I just wrote to Boyd [one of Pershing's aides] to come and have a look at this place and get some books to the men and let them smoke . . .

One fellow died in the next bed to mine. His back was broken. It is strange that the "gentlemen" make less noise over their wounds than the others. But there is little howling even on the train I heard hardly any noise.

There is a fellow next to me with a smashed hip. He suffers a lot but jokes. I suffer none at all except when they dress the wounds.

I look as if I had just had a baby or was unwell . . .

This is a stupid letter but it is hard to write.

Letter, GSP, Jr., to Beatrice, October 4, 1918

I am getting on fine and will be sewed up in about a day or two. Now they spend their time taking "cultures" of my bottom to see if there are any bugs.

This is a rotten place with a cemetary just out side where they bury people all day long.

Also the food is very poor but I get on fine as I always do. And I am doing a lot of sleeping.

I think I am not very sensative by nature as I seem to suffer less than most people . . .

My scar wont ever show unless the styles change. I surely am a lucky fellow . . .

Will we have any money after the war so we can go on a Honcymoon. Lets us do it any how. We will have to get used to each other.

I love you.

I wired you on the 29th Sept. "Slightly wounded no danger love"

I love you George.

Letter, GSP, Jr., to Beatrice, October 10, 1918

I am sitting out in a wheeled chair in the sun smoking and it is quite nice and comfortable. We moved to a new ward yesterday and it is much better. There are more nurses and orderlies so all goes well. Also we are out of quarenteen for meningitis which makes it much nicer.

I had seven Captains two majors and my self in the fight. Of these all are hit but one capt and two majors . . . Capt. English was killed and Capt. Higgins got both eyes shot out. Two Lts. were killed and 15 wounded. But the tank corps established its reputation for not giving ground. They only went forward. And they are the only troops in the attack of whom that can be said.

I feel terribly to have missed all the fighting. It seems too bad but I had to go in when I did or the whole line might have been broken.

Perhaps I was mistaken but any way I believe I have been sited [cited] for decoration either the Medal of Honor or the military [Distinguished Service] cross. I hope I get one of them.

Letter, Pershing to Beatrice, October 10, 1918

George . . . was exceptionally gallant and was leading a body of men to attack a machine gun nest when he was shot in the leg; I think not very seriously. It was a gallant thing to do, and he has received all sorts of praise from those who know of the incident. You are to be congratulated and should be prouder of him than ever.

Letter, GSP, Jr., to Beatrice, October 12, 1918

Peace looks possible but I rather hope not for I would like to have a few more fights. They are awfully thrilling like steeple chasing only more so . . .

One of my men came to see me to day. He was a gunner in a tank and got his right thumb shot off. He did not know it until he went to pick up a shell and found he had no thumb.

I am getting on fine.

On October 13, Rockenbach recommended that Lieutenant Colonels Henry E. Mitchell, George S. Patton, Jr., and D. D. Pullen be promoted to Colonel.

Letter, GSP, Jr., to Beatrice, October 15, 1918

Your letter sent by [Lieutenant Elgin] Braine came to day and I was glad to get it. I have not seen Braine yet but will do so shortly I trust.

I think I told you that Rockie has recomended me for a Colonelcy. I would like it in a way but the more rank one gets the harder it is to get into a fight and fights certainly are fun. That is not a pose either. It is actually so and one of the few things I could enjoy. As you know I like most things solely for the results.

They took another culture of me to day. I hope they report no bugs . . .

I am feeling fine and do not suffer at all.

Letter, GSP, Jr., to Beatrice, October 16, 1918

My d—— wound is still full of bugs so they can't sew me up. It is most Provoking.

I have just been in to cuss out the surgeon but it does no good. As it is impossible to give special attention to any one here.

I am feeling fine and want to get out.

Letter, GSP, Jr., to Pershing, October 16, 1918

[Thanks for kind letter which came at right time and which Patton will treasure.] It is hard to have so much nice fighting going on and be in bed with a darned old hole that will not close as fast as I want it to. You see I was about thirty or forty yards from the gun that hit me and it natu-rally took out a lot of beef. I feel fine and eat too much. I re-spectfully request that you leave some Bosch to be beaten after I get out. With sincere thanks for your kindness and congratulations for your great victories.

On October 17, Patton was promoted to Colonel.

Letter, GSP, Jr., to Beatrice, October 17, 1918

What do you think of me. I just got my colonelcy over the wire and am not yet 33. That is not so bad is it. Of course I have class mates in the engineers who are colonels but none others. So I feel quite elated though as a matter of fact I don't believe I deserve it very much. I could have commanded just as well as a Lt. Col. well after the war the slump will be all the greater. [I will go] back to a captain.

Tell B & R.E. so they can be haughty while they have the chance. As "Je reviendra capataine apres la gare." [I will go back to captain after the war.]

I do hope I get the decoration. I would prefer it to the promotion.

Letter, Mr. Patton to Pershing, October 18, 1918

I want to thank you very much for all the family for your cable as to George's wound. Our first information was indirect through a New York newspaper followed by a notice from Washington reported him wounded "degree undetermined." So your cable came as a great relief to our anxiety.

Patton asked General Smith, commandant of the Army Schools, to try to get him transferred to Base Hospital Number 24 at Langres. Smith did so, and Patton was moved.

Diary

October 19 (Saturday): Spent the day at Bourg and played my new phonograph. Very nice. Felt tired.

Letter, GSP, Jr., to Aunt Nannie, October 19, 1918

I don't know whether I told you all in my last letter that I am a full colonel. Which is not bad for 32. Though I had always intended to be a general at 26. Of course I will probably drop back to captain after the war but that can't be helped.

Capt. Braine has just telephoned that he was coming to see me as he has just landed. I will get some late news. He saw B just before he sailed.

I have only 80 men out of 834 fit for duty in my T. Brig. Of course many are only wounded or sick but some are dead.

I am still unsewed up but hope to be soon.

Letter, GSP, Jr., to Beatrice, October 19, 1918

. . . to day I was worrying over what I would do after I get out [of the hospital]. And making all sorts of difficulties [for myself] when I remembered. What Gen R. [Rockenbach] once said namely that "most worries never happen." I guess I must have aged in apperance. All these doctors thought I was 45 but that is probably on account of not being able to shave every day and because I am thin.

I am a lot older in some things, for example when we were in Washington before we came over. Barnett told me about commanding a battalion of militia and I wondered at the time if I could have done it. Now I know that I could command a Division. Things realy are much easier than they appear. Hence why worry. C. D. Rhodes is a Maj. Gen. speaking of worrying.

I just got a telephone from Braine saying he was coming to see me, so I will get some first hand information.

Letter, GSP, Jr., to Beatrice, October 20, 1918
Braine got here at 10 P.M. last night and brought a lot of letters from you.

I asked him how you looked and if you had any gray hair. He said no. At least that you had fixed them . . . I always think of you as Undine so I don't want you to look 33, even if I do.

He said you wore a black dress like a neck tie. I could not tell whether he ment in texture or in size.

. . . I also am much relieved to know that you have that much money after all the taxes etc.

I must be getting about $400 a month now as a colonel . . .

We have a phonograph here to night and it plaied some of the songs you used to sing . . .

Your childish procilivites of which you boast do not interest me at all. I love you too much and I am jealous or something of children . . . Your only chance [to have another child] is accident or emaculate conception. You ought to be complimented but being pig headed I suppose you are not.

I love you too much.

. . .

Finally returned to France after his odysscy in the United States, Braine had fulfilled his role in the Tank Corps. Rockenbach sent him to Varennes on the Meuse-Argonne battlefield to inspect the disabled tanks still there. Braine analyzed the causes that had put them out of action, the mechanical reasons as well as the structural weaknesses in the armor protection. He then went to the 302d Tank Center for duty. The two American-built tanks he had brought reached Bourg on November 20.

Braine reorganized the mechanical and tank-driving courses at the school. He improved the efficiency of the tank-repair shed and machine shop. He created a central stockroom, established a salvage department, opened a central gas and oil station, and took charge of motor transportation.

He always felt that the Tank Corps had been cheated. It had "never had a seat at the [production] table and therefore did not get a fair showing" in the war.

Although he would reappear once or twice again, he gradually moved from the prominent place he had formerly occupied on the tank scene, and eventually he faded from sight. He was separated from the Army on June 30, 1919, and placed on the Emergency Officers' Retired List on July 31, 1928. A quiet man who had truly been one of the founders of the American Tank Corps, almost as important as Patton, Brett, Rockenbach, and Viner, Braine died in Columbus, Ohio, in May 1932 at the age of forty-four.

Letter, GSP, Jr., to Beatrice, October 23, 1918

I am back at a hospital in my "own home town" and my wound is nearly healed up.

I feel a lot better as I can see my officers and do a little work. I ought to be out in a few days.

I worked on one of my friends to get me transfered here, it is a better hospital and not so crowded . . .

My brigade . . . got a lot of nice letters from the division we fought with so we are feeling fine and are anxious to get at it again but I fear it will be a while yet.

Here is a nice letter I got from Maj. Brett who commanded after I was hit.

It is a very generous letter. He is mistaken as I still command the 1st Brig[ade] . . .

P.S. My dear classmates are reported as being very jealous of me. I don't blame them.

Letter, Sereno Brett to GSP, Jr., no date

Col Patton: Please allow me to congratulate you on your promotion, I'm damned sorry to see you leave the 1st Brigade, but happy to the same degree that you received a well-earned promotion.

Don't worry about the old Brigade. It fought them until we had no personnel left and then we organized the remnants into a Provisional Company and gave them another whirl for their money. Just now the company is laying back at Exermont waiting to tear into them again.

Was mighty sorry when your runner arrived announcing that you were wounded, but was not surprised at all. Its a miracle you weren't killed. Peculiar, but I was only about 100 meters to your right when the accident happened trying to corral a few tanks and send them forward. Of course, I didn't know you were there. But it was the hottest little hell I have ever burned in, and believe me I wouldn't have given three cents for my future pay vouchers for a while.

The Brigade has been mighty highly complimented by all around here, and I'm happy I can convey this appreciation to you as I know it will bring pleasure to learn that your work with the Brigade has been productive of such excellent results. I am sending you a copy of a letter the Brigade received from General Summerall, who [commanded the 1st Division and] is now commanding the 5th Corps.

Best of luck to you, Colonel, and I sincerely hope you will be out among 'em again by the time this reaches you.

Brett.

Letter, GSP, Jr., to Beatrice, October 24, 1918

I would never have gone forward when I got hit had I not thought of you and my ancestors. I felt that I could not be false to my "cast[e]" and your opinion. At the same time I did not realy think I would be hit. One has a sort of involuntary fear of the bullets but not a concrete fear of being hit. While I was waiting on the hill before I went back to get the tanks I remembered some story by Kipling where the officers smoked to reasure the men. So I smoked like a factory. We were then being shelled heavily from in front and were under rifle fire from both flanks and in front. But I kept saying to myself I am not to be hit I know it so I felt better but it was quite bad. Men were falling or rather being blown to bits all around.

Military education shows at such times. The hill in this section [of the front] was like this [drawing a hill in profile]. I put my men just back of the crest . . . there were no trenches there but I remembered Balastics [ballistics] and that a shell just clearing the top could not fall . . . [there] while they were falling at [the bottom] every second. Yet the foolish dough boys staied . . . [at the bottom of the hill]. None of my men were hit and at [the bottom] it was a regular shambles so I went down there and made the doughs move up. Then they got killed less.

One of my officers was in yesterday and told me during the fog we sat on the roof of a dug out that had a battalion of germans in it. We had only nine men. Some luck.

My wound is getting on fine and is nearly healed. The Dr. says that he can't see how the bullet went where it did with out crippeling me for life. He says he could not have run a probe without getting either the hip joint, the siatic nerve or the big artery yet none of these were touched. "Fate" again. I have never had any pain and can walk perfectly . . .

P.S. I was not altered by the gas as I was not gased. Some were, but none of my men as I made them all use the masks.

Letter, GSP, Jr., to Beatrice, October 26, 1918

Just one month to day I was hit and I was out walking just now and feel fine. They have decided not to sew me up but to let it fill up its self so I ought to be out in a few days . . .

I met a lot of my friends to day and they were all sore at me for getting promoted. It makes me mad.

If they had wanted to risk their skins in fighting instead of looking for staff jobs they might have been promoted too.

Letter, GSP, Jr., to Beatrice, October 26, 1918

Dear Beat: I just got your letter with a coppy of R[ockenbach]'s letter to you. It was a nice letter was it not. He is quite a poetical old cock . . .

I had four men recomended for the medal of honor and about 20 for the D.S.C. Two of them are dead.

I had a nice compliment from a Col. Keochlin-Swarts of the french army to day. He called on me and said "My dear Patton I am so glad you were wounded. For when you left I said to my wife that is the end of Patton he is one of those gallant fellows who always get killed."

Rather nice what. They all seem to think me quite a fellow for walking in front of the tanks. As a matter of fact it was the only thing to do. You say the Bosch will quit. Listen to this. One of my tanks was attacking a machine gun when the gun in the tank jammed so the men decided to run down the machine gun. The two Bosch fired to the last and the tank went over them. Next day they were found still holding their gun though dead.

There could be nothing finer in war. My men buried them and put up crosses. "Salute the brave" even bosch.

There are few d—— f—— [few] husbands who write twice a day to their wives even when their wives wear such low dresses as B [Jr.] says you do.

Please keep it till I get home or get a lower one. George.

Letter, GSP, Jr., to Nita, October 26, 1918

I have about forty letters from you to —— which I have not transmitted as I only got them. They had been following me from hospital to hospital . . .

I was out walking twice to day and feel fine. My wound is still open but only a little . . . It did not cripple me at all, the dr. said that it seemed impossible [not to]. . . . I was borne to be hung.

Had a [I] had a hemorage I would have bled to death as I was only 30 yds from the Bosch and every time I turned over to try to put on a dressing they shot at me. So I staied there for an hour with one of my tanks sitting by guarding me like a watch dog. That first Brigade [of tanks] was some bunch. Six captains out of seven were hit the first 3 days and 30 Lieutenants out of 35 also got hit, we ended up after 14 days with 80 men and 6 officers out of 800.

Of course not many were killed. Only 3 officers and 18 men so far.

I got a nice compliment from a french colonel. He . . . said "I am so glad you were only wounded. You are one of those gallant men who always get killed. But you will get it yet." I will not however . . .

One of my tanks broke their gun while they were attacking a Bosch Machine Gun. The Bosch held on to the last and we squashed them but even in death they were holding to their gun. My men burried them and put up a cross "To two brave men though S.O.B's." Quelle sentimente!

I will call and tell your friend about you.

Letter, GSP, Jr., to his father, October 28, 1918

Dear Papa: Your letter of Sept 28 has just reached me and as usual was most interesting. But instead of being in the fight as you thought I was in a hospital with a whole bath towel stuffed in my bottom and bleeding like a stuck pig. Still as usual at such times I slept which was the best thing to do.

I left the hospital to day and resumed command of my brigade or what is left of it. I am here in my own room and feeling fine though I can't walk much yet and lost about 30 pounds of weight which I will soon get back.

My letter written after St. Mihiel will have reached you by now. For once I out did the papers. I rode on top of the tank not on the tail and so riding I mopped up a town Pannes which the infantry would not enter later . . . I got shot off the top of it by the bosch but was not hurt, only scared.

Every one has been telling me what a heller I am for the Verdun-Argonne show that I am beginning to believe it. But if I had not thought of you and mama & B and my ancestors I would never have charged. That is I would not have started for it is hell to go into rifle fire so heavy that one fancies the air is thick like molases with it. After I got going it was easy but the start is like a cold bath.

Maj Brett who has been in all the while says that was the heaviest fight of the whole battle. There were 12 m.g. [machine guns] right in front of me at about 150 yds. backed by a battalion of guard infantry. While from fifty to 150 machine guns were firing at us from the flanks.

My "Guardian spirits" must have had a job to keep me from getting killed so one can't blame them for letting one slip by and hit me in the leg.

Gen Ellis of the British tanks said of it that it was "Splendid but not war." The same thing that was said of the Light

Brigade. However he was wrong. An officer is paid to attack not to direct after the battle starts.

You know I have always feared I was a coward at heart but I am beginning to doubt it.

Our education is at fault in picturing death as such a terrible thing. It is nothing and very easy to get.

That does not mean that I hunt for it but the fear of it does not—at least has not detured me from doing what appeared my duty.

My brigade will not be able to fight for a while yet so dont worry about me for a month after my birthday [November 11] . . .

My class mates are all soar as hell at me for getting promoted and probably lay it to Nita['s influence with Pershing] or some other hellish plot.

With much love to all your devoted son

George S Patton Jr. D. S. C.? Perhaps.

Col Tank Corps.

Commanding First Brig[ade]

. . .

Patton did not wait long after getting out of the hospital to make his presence known to his men. On the very next day he issued a formal order to the tankers in the units as well as the tankers in the training center. His subject: "Concerning dress, comportment and discipline of this command, most of which is extracted from Memoranda issued previously on the same subject." He wanted everyone to keep his shoes, leggings, and belts polished, his uniforms clean, his face shaved daily, and his hair cut short. Sweaters were not to be worn on top of but underneath the khaki shirt. Straw in the bedding in quarters was to be changed frequently. Military courtesy was to be observed at all times. And finally:

> There is a widespread and regrettable habit in our service of ducking the head to meet the hand in rendering a salute. This will not be tolerated. In rendering salutes the head will be held erect. The hand will be moved smartly to and from the head-dress or the forehead, if uncovered.

He also wrote a letter to Mrs. Math L. English, Fort Casey, Washington, whose husband was killed in battle. After confirming Captain English's death, Patton continued:

It may, however, help ameliorate your grief to realize in what very high esteem Captain English was held by all the officers and men with whom he came into contact. I believe that the Brigade is unanimous in attributing to him all the highest virtues of a man and officer . . . You and his children should always guard [the memory of his gallant action] as a perfect example of heroism and soldierly devotion to duty under the most trying circumstances . . . Please allow me, my dear Madam, to close in again assuring you of my heartfelt sympathy for you and my unbounded admiration for your gallant husband.

Patton sent a copy of this letter to Beatrice and added a handwritten note at the bottom: "This is a copy of letter I wrote Mrs English. He was a very fine man. He used to be a 1st Sgt. But was insured for $10 000. Still it would be nice if you wrote his wife. He had a litle boy I think GSP."

Letter, GSP, Jr., to Beatrice, October 29, 1918
Your two letters of Oct 10 & 11 came to day and I am dreadfully sorry to have shocked you so . . .
The account in the paper is correct except that I was carried off when they could get to me. The fire was so heavy for an hour that no one could come to me except the tanks. It did not take much nerve to direct them against the machine guns as that was what I was there for and there was nothing else to do. I could not walk as my leg would not work. I don't even limp now.
My orderly had two pigeons and it was funny when you think of it to be sending up "Doves of Peace" from a hole right under the nose of the Bosch.
My wound never hurt a bit but I have three boils that do . . .
Also I smoked a pipe not a cigaret.

On November 3, Patton sent a formal letter to Rockenbach recommending awards to members of the 1st Brigade, Tank

Corps, for gallantry in action. Recommended for the Medal of Honor were Captain Harry H. Semmes, whom Patton cited for two actions, Second Lieutenanat David M. Bowes, and Private First Class Joseph T. Angelo, whose citation read: "For dragging his wounded commanding officer into a shell hole at a range of about 40 metres from the German machine guns and for thereafter remaining with him under continued shell fire for over one hour, except when he twice left the shelter of the shell hole to carry orders to the tanks which were passing at a distance of about 50 metres."

Recommended for the Distinguished Service Cross were Commandant Chanoine, French Army (cited for two actions); Major Sereno E. Brett; Captain Newell P. Weed (with two citations), Captain Math L. English (Killed in Action and cited twice), Captains Harry H. Semmes and Dean M. Gilfillan; First Lieutenant Robert C. Llewellyn (Killed in Action), First Lieutenants Paul S. Edwards and Tom W. Saul; Second Lieutenants Julian K. Morrison, Darwin T. Phillips, and Edwin A. McClure; Sergeant Raymond C. Chisholm (Killed in Action) and Sergeant Charles C. Young; Corporal Harold W. Roberts (Killed in Action) and Corporal William E. Brophy.

.   .   .

About this time Patton wrote a paper entitled "German and Allied Theory of War." In it he sought to explain the course of World War I. Whether a lecture or a piece simply for his own meditation, it demonstrated his understanding of the tactical developments of the war.

When the French and Russians became allied, he wrote, Germany had to gain a prompt decision over one or the other in order to deal with the remaining one at some leisure. To that end, Germany concentrated military thought and training to produce an army "national in numbers and yet professional in ability." The end was to crush the French by a decisive battle or series of battles "likened to the knock-out blow of a pugilist and it obviously required great smash and driving force." This required "unlimited reserves at the point of impact," or forces massed in depth, and this policy contrasted with French and British theories of maneuver.

The tactics of the two combatants were equally at variance. The Allies looking on fire as a means of movement. That is, they fired only enough to permit them to close and finish with the bayonet. The Germans on the other hand looked to movement as a means of fire. That is, they moved their skirmish lines so that its withering flame might consume nearly all resistance and they looked to the bayonet simply as a means of giving the coup de grace . . .

Happily for the world their plans were brought to naught by 1st: The delay in Belgium. 2nd: The heroic value of the French and British Armies. 3rd: The fact that short maneuvers had taught the Germans to over-estimate the endurance of their men which consequently resulted in the over-marching of their command. 4th: Their error in converging their vast numbers in an attempt to reach Paris, consequently causing complication in supply.

Those causes coupled with the necessity of sending men to Russia made the German assault a failure and they were forced to assume the defensive on the Western Front which attitude they maintained with the exception of the 1916 Verdun Offensive until the beginning of the present year.

The ensuing developments made the struggle "the most futile form of war which history records." Allied efficiency diminished because of the large number of untrained men who had to be quickly trained as specialists. "These coarse creatures increased and multiplied . . . There were bombers who could not shoot and shooters who could not bomb and Staff Officers who could do neither. All of these claimed that they were the sole means to ending the war and that all others were useless and in the way." The result was the set-piece attack, the rigid rolling barrage, and the limited objective. Artillery pieces increased in numbers, the trench system kept pace, preparatory barrages were lengthened, shell expenditures grew, and combat became expensive.

Tanks were invented to relieve the intolerable situation "and to supply mobile firing power . . ." But the mechanical deficiencies of tanks and their scarcity in numbers made it necessary to continue the barrages before attacks, and warfare remained expensive and static.

The Germans, having disposed of Russia and Rumania and having checked Italy by the winter of 1917–18, had to end the war before the United States became the dominant factor. They therefore developed the tactic of surprise. They concentrated their attacking forces in a rear area so they could move toward any one of several attack points. When the decision was made on the point of attack, the troops moved there by night marches, padding the wheels of wagons and gun carriages with straw and taking extraordinary care to conceal their movements. With this, they launched their several successful surprise attacks, the first and greatest of which occurred on March 21, 1918.

"The old wrestling maxim that there is a block to every hold remains true however," and the Germans were blocked because "First that they did not realize the elasticity of the Allied defense and having made a hole of considerable depth they presumed the line to be broken and instead of pushing on until it was really broken they turned to the flanks to widen the wedge which they had punched. This gave the Allies time to close the nose of the salient . . . The second thing was . . . that" Allied artillery was able to concentrate shells in the path of the German attack and block them.

We will now consider how the tactics just described which were our own tactics when we assumed the offensive, may be used in future "Efforts to maintain Peace." A look at the map of the world makes it fair to assume that nowhere but in Europe will armies without flanks be encountered. Where this situation arises it will be possible by the uses of cavalry, armoured motor cars and light tanks to get behind the enemy and prevent the concentration of guns which have heretofore checked the successful advance of infantry. Also in wars in less civilized countries than Europe it will never be possible to have or move such quantities of artillery as now exists or to maintain the huge supply of ammunition which they daily consume. The same is true with machine guns and automatic rifle ammunition. Hence we will again revert to the Infantry skirmish line strengthened and made more deadly by automatic rifles and machine guns. Strategical maneuvers will return with the diminution of front[al] attacks but it will always be fire backed by the threat of bayonet which now as in the time of Gustavus Adolphus decided the fate of war.

Three pages of single-spaced typescript emerged from his machine on November 7. Entitled "Notes, Entraining and Detraining at Night," they were explicit and detailed instructions on how to get tanks on and off trains.

On the following day, he submitted a letter to the Assistant Chief of Staff G–5, the Training and Plans Officer at GHQ AEF, on the subject of "A suggested method of attack."

In suggesting the following form of attack it is not my purpose or desire to infringe upon the prerogatives of infantry or artillery officers. The plan as set forth is regarded from the point of view of a tank officer, and the changes recommended are those which my meagre experience in battle with tanks causes me to believe are perhaps useful to all arms concerned.

He went on to discuss the use of infantry working behind tanks, the method of advancing by rushes, and the proper application of overwhelming strength.

Two days later, in a paper entitled "Practical Training, Tank Platoon," he defined the duties of a tank platoon in combat when operating over broken ground.

Tanks must watch their infantry. If the latter is held up there is a reason; the tanks must go back and find out. They must also always watch for helmet and rifle signals from the infantry. It is perfectly useless for tanks to attack more than 200 M[eters] ahead of the Infantry. Tanks can take almost anything but they can hold practically nothing. Hence they MUST STAY WITH THE INFANTRY.

Ordering practice attacks to be held at the tank center, he wrote:

In all of this practice battle conditions will be supposed to exist. Officers must use signs and cover and not run about

with an heroic disregard of imaginary bullets. While it is not
the intention to make officers timid they must nevertheless
conserve their lives until the supreme moment. When as heretofore they will not hesitate to expose themselves [to enemy
fire].

. . .

It was all well meant but too late. The war came to an end. It
terminated on his thirty-third birthday. And that seemed like a
fitting date. Somehow it linked the war to his fate and destiny
and made the biggest conflict in the history of man a personal
event for him.

For Patton, the war had been a glorious experience. He had
established the Tank Corps in the U. S. Army and proved its combat value. He learned and saw much, grew a great deal, achieved
much, and earned both high honor and rapid advancement. He
organized men and shaped them and led them and did all this
expertly. He succeeded in his profession and passed the test of
battle.

Yet the war had been frustrating too. Despite all the dedicated
effort and the expended energy, all the thought and devotion he
had given to his job, all the problems he had overcome, he had
been in action less than five days. That was rather disappointing.

But surely there would be another war. There had to be if only
for his sake so that he could profit from the maturity and wisdom
he had accumulated and thereby fulfill his destiny or fate.

Diary
    November 11 (Monday): "Peace was signed and Langres
was very ex[c]ited. Many flags. Got rid of my bandage. Wrote
a poem on peace. Also one on Capt. English."

VIII

Postwar France

"I fear that laziness which ever pursued me is closing in on me at last."

CHAPTER 32

The Prize

"I realize that one is apt to attach too great importance to ones own exploits. If I am guilty, as is probable, of thinking too much of my self please forgive me."

Letter, GSP, Jr., to Beatrice, November 16, 1918

We are going on almost the same as usual [now with peace] but it is not so easy to get up in the morning as it used to be especially on saturday. I fear that laziness which ever pursued me is closing in on me at last. It will be funny [back in the United States] to command 74 men in a troop of cavalry after having commanded a thousand and more in battle and to be through by noon each day.

To avoid so far as possible the devil of idleness I am going to write a book. For in prose it is the pen which makes the sword great in peace. So if I write a good book I might get to be a general before the next war now. If I start the next [war] as a Brigadier General and hit the same pace I gained in this I will make three grades or end up as a full general. This is necessary to keep pace with Nita. Or at least her present hopes.

I inclose the chapters of the book with the subjects to be treated in each chapter. It ought to reach several volumes. Which no one will buy in all probability.

The idea of writing a book originated, no doubt, in a project he was working on with Brett. They were preparing a history of the 304th Tank Brigade operations in the Meuse-Argonne campaign. Patton knew the beginnings, Brett the later stages, and as Patton learned in detail what had occurred after he was wounded, he was impressed by what his men, the men whom he had formed and inspired, had accomplished during his absence.

The after-action report, issued on November 18, bore the unmistakable imprint of Patton's intelligence and style. Of 141 American tanks actually engaged with the enemy, 140 were accounted for—the one that was missing was swallowed up in an enormous shell hole or trench or lost in the underbrush of a forest, perhaps captured by the enemy. "The supplies of gasoline and equipment to the tanks and of rations to the troops"—the *sine qua non* of sustained operations—"was excellent, the chief difficulty arising out of the congestion of the traffic and the bad condition of the roads."

There were nine "Tactical Conclusions":

1. Infantry officers lacked understanding and appreciation of tank capabilities, for tanks needed infantry operating with them at all times to be successful—which subtly, probably unconsciously, foreshadowed a shift in doctrine from the use of tanks to support infantry to the contrary conclusion that infantry should be used to support tanks; but this idea would remain obscure until clarified with terrifying suddenness by the German blitzkrieg tactics in World War II.

2. A lack of liaison between tanks and infantry hampered efficient operations.

3. "Infantry should act as though tanks were not present and not expect tanks to overcome resistance and wait expecting tanks to attempt to consolidate a success."

4. Tanks were too valuable because of their strengths in firepower and mobility and too weak in mechanical reliability to be dissipated in reconnaissance missions.

5. The distance between readiness positions and the line of departure should be reduced, for "tanks cannot sustain a prolonged march without being overhauled and put in order."

6. A thorough preliminary reconnaissance on foot of the terrain to be used by tanks was absolutely indispensable.

7. "The enemy artillery is the dangerous adversary of the tanks."

Therefore, strong supporting artillery ready to deliver counter-battery fires, as well as screening smoke, was terribly important to insure tank success.

8. The value of tanks as attacking units and as a fighting arm had been demonstrated.

9. Some slight changes in tactical employment were necessary, those looking toward a better utilization of tanks in mass and in depth.

Letter, GSP, Jr., to Beatrice, November 17, 1918
Lininger was wearing his D.S.M. [Distinguished Service Medal] for [his service in] Mexico. He had just gotten it and it is a very pretty ribbon. I wish I had one for killing Cardanes. Perhaps I will get one. It is one degree lower than the D.S.C. [Distinguished Service Cross] but apparently I may not get that either though I think I will.

There are all sorts of Rumors about our going home very soon. I hope there is truth in them.

As to my needing money. I don't I have plenty as nothing has cost me much lately and I am getting on all right. And have a couple of thousand left. I may buy you a present?

The history of the tank brigade and Lininger's medal prompted Patton to make two requests.

Letter, GSP, Jr., to Pershing, November 17, 1918
In considering the two favors I am going to ask please treat me as a simple officer of the army. That is I do not want to presume on the fact that I have been on your staff. Nor do I wish to presume on your constant kindness to me.

First, if Pershing was satisfied with the performance and achievements of the tankers at St. Mihiel and the Meuse-Argonne, would he please write a letter of commendation that Patton could distribute to every man.

I realize however that most of your army are equally deserving and that perhaps I am selfish in asking so much of you.

The second favor is entirely personal and hence less deserving of your consideration. Lt. Col. Lininger . . . has been awarded the D.S.M. for his services in Mexico. I believe that my accidental encounter and killing of Col. Cardanes at San Miguel on May 16, 1916 might equally be considered as a service to the Government in that by good luck I was able to do in one morning with nine men what a whole regiment of cavalry . . . had failed to do in one week. I would not dare bother you with this were it not that it is only you and Gen. Cabel who know anything about it.

I realize that one is apt to attach too great importance to ones own exploits. If I am guilty, as is probable, of thinking too much of my self please forgive me.

Letter, GSP, Jr., to Beatrice, November 18, 1918

The most terrible thing has happened to me. I heard last night that I will not get the D.S.C.

Why I don't know as one is not even supposed to know that one has been recommended. I think that R. [Rockenbach] was in too big a hurry and put in [for the medal] with out sufficient data. Or else some one got me from behind. The worst part of it is that once rejected you cannot again be recomended. I woke up last night feeling that I was dying and then it would occur to me what had happened. I cannot realize it yet. It was the whole war to me. All I can ever get out of two years away from you.

But I will be G.D. if I am beat yet. I don't know what I will do but I will do something. If not I will resign and join the French army as a Captain or something. Gen. R. thinks my colonelcy is a compensation but it is nothing. I would rather be a second Lt. with the D.S.C. than a general with out it. It means more than an "A" [his West Point letter] and it would be of vast value in future.

I am sorry to bother you but I had to get it off my chest, onto yours even at long range by letter. I love you.

Letter, GSP, Jr., to Beatrice, November 18, 1918—"Night"

Darling Beat I wrote you such a desolate letter that I must hurry to tell you of what has just happened. It is not all I want but it is something. Gen Smith who has been commanding the schools is leaving so I called on him to say goodbye as he has been very nice to me. I also told him of my trouble and asked him what to do. It may work [yet]. Then just as I was leaving he said "It is against orders but I will tell you that I have to day recomended you for the D.S.M. for having had the finest spirit and discipline in your command that I have ever seen." Of course I may not get it either but then I may. And now I feel less alone in the world than I did. I just said my prayers for them both [both decorations]. I have a crude religion.

But an everlasting love for you. George.

Although the distinction was sometimes blurred between the Distinguished Service Cross and the Distinguished Service Medal, the former was generally awarded for gallantry in combat, that is, for action in direct contact with the enemy, the latter for distinction in a post of high responsibility.

Patton wanted both, but he wanted the Distinguished Service Cross more. He had distinguished himself on the battlefield against the enemy, and he therefore deserved the D.S.C. and the recognition and honor it bestowed. According to his values, those who aspired and who succeeded merited the tangible reward.

He had his wound and he proudly wore the wound stripe on his sleeve as his badge of sacrifice. He had his promotion and he proudly wore his eagles on his shoulders as his badge of excellence. Now he wanted the Distinguished Service Cross as his badge of courage.

It was characteristic of him that he wished not the highest decoration for heroism in combat, the Medal of Honor, which he never actively sought. He desired rather the second best, which was still a considerable honor. It resembled his quest at West Point for the position not of First Captain but rather of Adjutant, which still carried recognition. It was as though some innate sense of inferiority prevented him from seeking the highest place.

Perhaps he feared too much to be disappointed. Perhaps he had a clear and honest notion of his capacities. Perhaps he was too sensitive to risk unbearable hurt.

Diary

November 20: "Got letter from Nita in which she said Gen. P wrote her. 'I know of no one who has as much courage as George.'"

. . .

GSP, Jr., Lecture, "Tank Tactics," November 20, 1918

Historically the tank is in conception a very old idea. At the siege of Tire by Alexander the Great in 318? B.C. walls had already become so formidable an obstacle to the siege artillery of the time that it was necessary to devise some more efficient mechanical means for their reduction and the moving tower was invented.

The first year of this war again so enhanced the power of passive resistance capable of being offered by that inverted wall the trench that artillery again proved helpless to cope with it and the mind of man following the inevitable cycle of cause and effect reinvented the moving tower in the shape of the tank to cope with it.

Such at least in its inception was the purpose of the tank, but we shall show that like many other inventions it proved of vast utility in spheres of activity which its inventors never claimed for it . . .

The French . . . thought of it as a means of carrying infantry accross a relatively narrow Nomans-Land and then of dumping these soldiers like the Greeks from the Horse on the heads of the disgusted and demoralized Germans . . . To accomplish this end the tank evolved had no need to cross trenches and at the time of the origin of the idea Spring 1915 artillery was much less heavy than laterly so the shell craters to be encountered were negligable. Unfortunately the french plan was made abortive by two causes. First the British sprung their first attack with six tanks before the French were ready and second the artillery became so heavy that the French carriers could no longer negotiat the shell holes. They then were confronted with the necessity of converting their tanks into make shift fighting machines and of following as well as might be with these monstrocities the tactics of the British.

From the beginning the british had thought of the Tank

as a fighting machine and the more enthusiastic and less well educated from a military point of view went so far as to dream of mechanical armies. The first essay of the machine in battle proved the absurdity of such notions and the tactics of Tanks to meet the then existing conditions were at once evolved. With out going into minutee as to the drill formations of tanks I shall now explain to you the determinant factors in the evolution of tactics and call your attention to the steady changes in these factors with the corresponding change in tactics noting that nearly always the tactics lagged one stage behind the conditions they were destined to encounter.

When tanks first appeared upon the scene the defensive had outstripped the offensive. In spite of barrages so long drawn out and so terrific that the whole face of nature was changed there always remained some men some Machine guns and some wire which had escaped destruction and whose presence not only made attacks over the front trenches terribly costly in man and material but also so harrassed and shattered the morale and formation of the attacking troops that they were unable to reach the hostile gun positions where victory lies but were also easly victims to hostile counter attack. These counter attacks in turn were made possible by the notice of the impending attack given long in advance of D day by the mighty alarm bell rung in no uncertain terms by the Artillery preparation.

To recapitulate: At the moment of attack the infantry was always held up by some or all of the following obstacles and resistances. Wire, rifle fire, Machine Gun fire, counter attack and artillery. To facilitate the attack of the infantry then the Tanks had to do the following things. 1. They had to cut wire. 2. They had to help keep down the hostile fire from rifles and machine guns. 3. They had to help mop-up as doing this without them wasted too much time. 4. They had to repel counter attack. 5. They had to get into the hostile artillery positions and so disorganise them that they would be impotent to destroy the infantry while they were consolidating. But all these things they had to do as an AID to the inft. For now as in the time of Hanibal or as in the times to come

it is the infantry and only the infantry—the man on foot with
the hand arm—who wins the battle. This is true even and
perhaps more so since I who say it am first a cavalryman and
next a Tanker.

These duties of the tank were well understood from the
beginning but due to the fact that all new weapons are re-
guarded with suspicion not much credence was placed in the
power of the tank to accomplish its task.

This lack of faith was not very troublesome to the tank
except in that part of it which insisted on tremendious artillery preparations. These bombardments were very bad. They
cut up the ground to an almost unbelivable extent there by
ditching many tanks and so exhausting the infantry by causing them to walk for miles from crater to crater that they
were physically unable to progress the requisite 10,000 M.
[meters] to the hostile guns. Also they gave the alarm and
nice well arranged counter attacks were always waiting to
rebuf the few tanks and infantry which succeeded in surviving
the efforts of their own artillery as demonstrated in the con-
version of level fields into bogs and mine craters.

On Nov. 20 1917 the light dawned and Cambrae [Cam-
brai] was fought with out artillery preparation and from a
Tank standpoint was a great success.

One would think for a moment that the problem was
solved but it was not. Two things intervened. The brain of
the Bosch and the Trench mortar.

This latter animal began to appear in force and under various names about the time of cambrae or earlier. With his
nondelay fuse he was the answer to wire and hence to rigid
front line defense. His character needs no higher approval
than the German offensive in the spring of 1918. He was the
father begetting of Necessity the defense in depth . . .

Herretical as my statement may appear there is nothing
new at all in the machine gun. It is only the latest solution to
the age long riddle. Supremacy of fire. The men who invented
the sling beat those who threw stones by hand. Those of the
bow and arrow destroyed the javlen men. The transendent
genius who thought of the ballista which shot ten arrows at
a time was in his day the master of the world. So it goes down

the ages this incessant striving to have one man as effective as many men. And why? simply to reduce losses. Simply arithmetic. If one man can shoot as much as ten men and at the same time offeres one tenth the target down goes your losses. Here is the raison D'etre of the defense in depth. The front line can no longer be held on account of the belchings of that metal toad the T. M. [trench mortar]. If the defense were moved back just beyond T.M. range nothing would be gained as the toads though very awkward can hop a little and would soon be [moved forward] near enough to hit the line. Moreover a line in order to stop good troops must be dense even with machine guns and this causes losses also it eliminates surprise. Hence defense in depth. An area miles deep dotted with machine guns each mutually protecting every other. The front line while still held is only a rotting husk. The real line well to the rear is the place from which to launch counter attacks on troops disorganised and decimated by passing through the machine gun zone.

How did the tanks answer this question for answer it they did as the Peace [the Armistice] proves. Unfortunately they answered it not by subtily playing the game but rather by bulling through relying on their great margin of superiority over the machine guns but costing them selves and their infantry too dearly.

That lack of confidence or [that] conservatism which I have before alluded to made tanks think that because they had attacked held positions and cut wire at Cambrae and Himmel they should always do so, even when these trenches were no longer occupied and the wire had been blown to bits by trench mortars. They did this to the glory of God and the extreme satisfaction of the Hun. The result was that a large number [of tanks] were left stranded in the trenches which they could have easily crossed in column and the rest too weak in numbers arrived late to help the infantry and often with most of their gas exhausted. But this was not the end of the mistakes of the tanks. Having finally reached the infantry they were filled with a noble fire and hurried on to conquer the world. Forgetting the unvarying truth that tanks exist to help infantry. They cannot help a mile in front any more than a mile behind.

Now when the tanks went on with out the infantry the Germans often did not shoot at them [for the Germans were] waiting for the infantry. Tanks are at least 50% blind so many machine guns were not seen. Those that were were attacked and the [gun] crews killed or driven off. But the tanks often could not drive directly over the gun. When they had passed by the germans remanned the guns undestroyed; the guns unseen were still there and both sets opened up on the infantry. After some time possibly hours the tanks returned to help the infantry and this time having the infantry there to help point out the guns the attack was more successful but time had been lost. And something worse than time had been gained. The tanks in their first trip had attracted the notice of the Hun guns. These opened a barrage on the place where they had seen the tanks and when the tanks appeared proudly leading the infantry the latter caught hell from the barrage so kindly arranged for them by their tanks.

Now was it inevitable that these things should have happened? Yes it was since we are all poor weak mortals after all. Was it necessary? No.

Here is the French solution which not being my own I am at liberty to crytacise . . .

[He explained how time was lost and how bypassed enemy machine guns took attacking infantry in the flank. The French idea was to have tanks work with the reserve infantry battalions, those coming behind the assault elements to mop up.] Hence I say that this method of using the tanks while it has some virtue is not the correct method and hence I condemn it.

Here is the correct method. The answer to the [defensively] organised area and the way we would have attacked had the bosch given us the chance. I still hope he does . . .

[Patton's solution was to have infantry and tanks operate together, with infantry scouts ahead pointing out machine gun nests to be destroyed by tank fire or by tanks rolling over them. The best method was to get tanks across the few front lines of trenches so they could move into areas where few trenches existed. There the tanks could roam at will and demoralize the enemy.]

I will now point out to you a few of the more thrilling phases of tank tactics such as we will use in Mexico perhaps.

. . .

His lecture notes ended there, and from there, no doubt, he extemporized.

There was much of interest in what he said. He believed that the principles of war remained immutable and valid. Fundamentally, then, there was nothing new in the art of war. A military leader proved his genius or his lack of it by the way he adapted constantly emerging new weapons to the determining principles. How the combat leader organized his troops into formation and how he committed them to battle decided the outcome of warfare.

He still held the idea that the tank was a weapon designed to support the infantry. As one of his young captains would explain early in 1919, "Tanks are to assist the Infantry. If the Infantry needs no assistance don't employ tanks."

Although Patton was to cling rigidly to that principle, which would inhibit his military thought—preventing him in the end from breaking through to a new concept—there were already intimations in his thinking that tanks need not be tied always to the slow pace of riflemen on foot. This idea would remain undeveloped until the opening weeks of World War II, when the Germans—Guderian and others—displayed and demonstrated how tanks in conjunction with closely supporting airplanes, self-propelled artillery pieces, and motorized infantrymen could break defensive lines and roam at will through enemy rear areas, completely demoralizing outflanked and confused combat troops and command nerve centers.

Patton was also convinced that the likelihood of another war in western Europe, where good roads existed, was slight. He saw rather the prospect of war in underdeveloped regions of the world, for example, in Mexico, and there the close cooperation of tanks, cavalry, artillery, and infantry, he believed, would produce a type of warfare much like the somewhat primitive mechanized warfare in World War I.

These themes would characterize Patton's thinking throughout the two decades between the two world wars.

. . .

Letter, GSP, Jr., to Beatrice, November 20, 1918
    I am leaving in a few moments to see Gen Leroy Eltinge about a subject you can well imagine. I hope I get something out of it besides gigles. But I am . . . loosing faith in men . . . every one is your friend until you want something and then you have only your self for friend.
    Some of the T.C. [Tank Corps] is going home shortly but I doubt if it is my outfit. We will be held [for the occupation] I fear . . .
    Yesterday the big [heavy] tanks said they could beat the Renaults so they laid out a course. We followed and beat hell out of them.

The subject he discussed with Eltinge was the Distinguished Service Cross. What had happened, he explained, was this. Three days after Patton was wounded, Rockenbach hurriedly collected several certified statements and affidavits from those who had witnessed Patton's heroism. Knowles, Edwards, Angelo, and a few others contributed firsthand accounts that were quite generalized rather than specific and detailed. Attaching these as documentary proof of Patton's gallantry, Rockenbach wrote a proposed citation and recommended the award—all normal procedure. Rockenbach sent the papers on September 30 to the commanding general of the First Army, who was Pershing.

On the same day, Rockenbach placed in Patton's official file his assessment of his wounded subordinate. "This officer," Rockenbach wrote, "is recommended for the Distinguished Service Cross for conspicuous courage, coolness, energy and intelligence in handling troops in battle."

Four days later, Drum, the First Army chief of staff and a long-time friend of Patton, added his favorable recommendation to Rockenbach's and forwarded the papers to Pershing. As a routine matter, they went to the adjutant general who disapproved the recommendation, probably on the ground of inadequate documentary proof.

On October 24, Rockenbach resubmitted the papers to the First Army commander, who was now Hunter Liggett. Five days later, Liggett's adjutant general returned Rockenbach's recommendation with the statement "In view of the fact that this recommendation has been disapproved by the Commander in Chief, no further action will be taken in the premises." Presumably, "premises" meant the First Army headquarters.

That seemed like the end of the road.

Heartened by his conversation with his good friend Eltinge on November 20, Patton went immediately to see Rockenbach. He convinced Rockenbach that the recommendation might be approved if it traveled directly to the AEF adjutant general with fuller and better documentation of Patton's battlefield exploit. To expedite his request, Patton presented Rockenbach with a draft letter he had prepared for Rockenbach's use.

This letter read, in part, as follows:

> During the course of this opperation the progress of the Tanks was stopped by three lines of trenches. Colonel Patton reconnoitered a passage accross these trenches. He then supervised the work of digging a passage through them and during the course of this work encouraged the men first by starting to dig him self when the men showed fear at exposing them selves and later by mounting on the top of the parapet the better to give directions . . . It was necessary to get more shovles and as the men hesitated to leave the trenches in order to get the tools from the tanks against which the bullets could be plainly heard striking Col. Patton made three trips to the tanks each time bringing back shovles. During the whole course of this work he was exposed to rifle and machine gun fire which was effective as some twenty men who were engaged in the work were hit. His actions and encouragement to his men added materially to the success of the enterprise.

These facts were ascertained by Brigadier General S. D. Rockenbach, Chief of the Tank Corps U.S. Army from the statements of Capt. M. H. Knowles TC, 1Lt P.S. Edwards,

Signal Corps, Sgt. E. W. Fansler, Headquarters Section, 304th Tank Brigade, Pvt. J. T. Angelo, Headquarters Section. All eye witnesses of the affair . . .

I am of the opinion that Colonel George S. Patton, Jr. Tank Corps USA, has so destinguished him self by his extraordinary heroism in connection with the above military opperations that to an extent justify the award recommended.

signed, S. D. Rockenbach, etc.

Attached to this was his own memo to Rockenbach:

During the course of this opperation five tanks having crossed the trenches moved forward to the attack of Cheppy. About 300 men of the 35th division who were on the reverse slope of a hill at this point failed to accompany the tanks. Col. Patton urged them forward to the crest of the hill but here as the fire increased the men halted again. Col. Patton asked "Who will come with me" or words to that effect and started forward. Six men accompanied him. After advancing about fifty yards all the men were hit except Col. Patton and his orderly. At this time Col. Patton was shot through the upper part of the left thigh but continued to advance until his leg failed him and he fell about forty yards from the German position. And was dragged to a shell hole by his orderly.

Using this account by Patton as the basis for rewriting his recommendation, getting Knowles, Edwards, Angelo, and the others to redo their certificates and affidavits in fuller and more detailed form, and securing additional accounts from other members of Patton's command group, Rockenbach sent his request forward again. Attached were no less than eleven eyewitness reports of the battlefield incident.

Letter, GSP, Jr., to Beatrice, November 21, 1918
I inclose what purports to be copies of my citations [for the D.S.C.] at least they will be something like that. Of course do *not* let them get in any paper but you can show them to your friends if you want to. I do wish they would hurry up and give me something. If they dont I will see that John [Pershing] gets hold of it and does something as from a letter

of his of which I have seen a copy he is most nice about the affair.

We are working as hard as ever in order to keep the men interested but it is a hard job as war was the great stimulant and replaced to a degree the lack of inherent discipline from which we have always suffered.

As a matter of fact had it not been for the regular army officers we would have been in a very bad fix indeed . . .

I have bought my three stripe chevron for 18 months in France which I can put on the ninth of Dec. pretty soon now.

I hope you see me before I get a fourth stripe.

Letter, GSP, Jr., to Beatrice, November 22, 1918

To morrow I give a lecture to some generals followed by a demonstration of an attack with a battalion of tanks. One of Braines new American tanks will be there also to show that we did build them . . .

I wish you would get over this fool idea of war work. And attend only to your self. Your hair, your chin and your tummie. I have done plenty of war work for the family.

I don't know whether there will be a regular tank corps or not and if there is I don't know if I will stay in it. I would rather be a captain of cavalry than a major of Tanks but a Lt. Colonel of tanks might be different. Although tanks in peace time would be very much like coast artillery with a lot of machinery which never works. Still "Il faut voir" [we will see].

Patton's lecture at the Staff College to a group of general officers who had no specific assignments started as follows:

The amount of nerve required by a Captain [his Regular Army rank], even though camouflaged as a Col[onel] in attempting to lecture to so august an assembly is such that I respectfully suggest that someone of you recommend me for a medal for gallantry in lecture. However in the words of General Ellis at Cambrai, "I shall do my damndest."

Tanks, he continued, were the last word in shock troops, the modern equivalent of the Greek hoplite or Carthagenian elephant. He described the battle of Cambrai and British tank tactics. He indicated that the Americans had adopted, then adapted, the

British tactical methods. And he insisted that tanks must be used boldly.

Letter, GSP, Jr., to Beatrice, November 24, 1918

Yesterday I gave a lecture on Tanks to a bunch of Generals followed by a demonstration. It was a rotten affair as they all went to sleep. They were the culls and they looked it.

Tonight the 344 Battalion is giving a dinner & dance to which I am envited. The ladies will not be much class being telephone operators and nurses but still that is better than nothing . . .

We are getting up a football team here also. I am Captain [of the team] . . .

I got a letter from Col. J. E. Carberry Air Service. He was a year after me at West Point and is the only person around my time who has written to me. So if you see him be nice to him.

The weather remains fine and we could do lots with tanks if there was only a war on as the ground is hard and they can cross nearly any thing.

We tried out some American Renaults yesterday and they were O.K. faster than the French machines and better built.

If we could only have had a few hundred of them during the war it would have been something.

The following day he received a letter from Lieutenant Skinner, one of the British officers who had entertained him in the Tower of London, another from General Harbord, formerly Pershing's chief of staff, then commander of the Services of Supply. Patton felt better, less alone, to have these indications that friends thought of him and wanted to remain in touch with him.

Letter, GSP, Jr., to Aunt Nannie, November 24, 1918

My leg is much better. So well that I played foot ball yesterday and ran a nail in my foot but not far. As it was in my left foot I still limp on the same side.

We had a dinner last night and there were some Y.M.C.A. women and nurses at it. One of the former told me that the soldiers thought a lot of me because I walked accross a bridge at Essey to see if it was mined. I had forgotten the incident and was pretty sure it was not mined. Soldiers are funny.

. . . I just got a wire from Beat saying she had moved to Washington.

Letter, GSP, Jr., to Beatrice, November 25, 1918

We had a very nice time and danced until mid night with telephone girls, YMCA females and nurses. One of the Y.M.C.A. ladies sat next to me and told me that all the soldiers attatch great glory to me for something I forgot to mention. When we got to Essey we thought that the bridge was mined and the tanks stopped so I walked accross the bridge to see if it would blow up. It did not. So many more interesting things have happened since that I forgot to speak of it. I was pretty sure it was not mined. If it had been it would not have hurt me at all as there would have been nothing left to hurt. It is funny that this small thing should stick in the minds of the soldiers.

Letter, GSP, Jr., to Major S. E. Brett, commanding 344th Tank Battalion, November 25, 1918

My dear Major Brett: . . . I want to take this opportunity of putting in writing what I have long felt in my heart. I consider the enviable record of the 1st Brigade, Tank Corps, both in peace and war, has been due more to your earnest and constant efforts in training and valorous conduct in battle than to that of any other man or officer. Not only did you work here when we had nothing, not even hope, without a murmur, but, in battle you fought the Brigade until there was nothing left and even after that, you fought on. As far as I know no officer of the A.E.F. has given more faithful, loyal, and gallant service. Please accept my heartfelt congratulations and thanks.

Letter, GSP, Jr., to Beatrice, November 26, 1918

I took a long ride this morning and it did not hurt my tail much so I feel incouraged. Miss Green [his horse] wanted to jump all the mud holes she saw which was not very easy on my but[t]. She meant well . . .

I have been writing orders for a tank battalion attack all afternoon to use in a lecture I am going to give. I wish I had known as much when I was fighting as I do now but there was no one who knew and we had to learn by experience. I have been reading some German documents about tanks and they furnish the greatest compliments we could have received. They under estimated the tank and it cost them the war perhaps. At least it hurried the end.

I inclose copies of all the letters [of commendation] we [in the brigade] got as they are quite nice. Lots of them don't belong to me by right as I was out of it but I trained them and taught them all they know. Which is a satisfaction in a way. It was most interesting and very original. Realy it is almost as much fun working out manuvers as it [is] working out fights only the denouement is not so nice as in the case of a fight.

Well this is a hellish stupid world now and life has lost its zest . . . I think I will get fat lazy but I hope not. Don't you dare do so. I love you.

Diary

November 27: "Rode horseback and hurt my leg. So I do not feel very flip."

November 28: "Went on bore [boar] hunt . . . and killed a rabbit. Ate a huge dinner and felt very stuffed."

November 29: "Col Taylor came down to see about changing D.S.C.s to M Hs [Medals of Honor for] English, Morrison, Weed, Semmes, Corp Call and Lt. Boss. He also took some evidence about me. I hope I get it."

November 30: "Col Taylor left. Got Black male [blackmail] letter from a Mr. Whiting. Who in hell is he? Bill Reed says not to worry about it."

Letter, GSP, Jr., to Beatrice, November 30, 1918

I just had a great surprise. Some irate frenchman wrote me a letter accusing me of all sorts of things with respect to his wife. It was most interesting as I had never heard of the lady but he seems to have a lot of dope on me. . . . I was worried about it but Bill Reed said to pay no attention. To be insulted greatly one should at least be guilty . . .

I begin to think that I have a chance of getting the M.H. [Medal of Honor] after all. Some Col. Taylor who knows [knew] you and Nita at El Paso is president of the board now and seems very fair. All I want is fairness not partiality. I would surely like to have the blue ribbon with the white stars.

The appearance in draft form of a manual on tank tactics prompted him to indicate certain errors in the text:

> While the equation for tanks shows they can climb at 60% slope, no earth I have ever encountered will sustain the tracks at such an angle. Figure should read 40 to 50% . . .
>
> I believe that no wire entanglement can stop a Light Tank . . .
>
> The American Renault can also create a smoke barrage for defensive purposes by injection at will of a smoke producing substance into the hot muffler . . .
>
> Tank obstacles also consist of concrete walls burried, 1 to 2 meters high, 2 meters thick, with railroad iron embedded in the walls and sticking out in the direction from which the tanks will approach . . .
>
> While it is right and proper to place Tanks under Infantry Units the relation of the Tanks and Infantry must be clearly defined. Infantry Commanders may simply tell the tanks what to do and not how to do it. Also they should be prohibited in requesting Tanks to do Patrol and Guard Duty which is not one of their functions.

Diary

December 1: "Left with Maj. Brett at 6:45 A.M. for Varennes . . . Went over field South of Cheppy in P.M. Took pictures of my shell hole and trench where English was killed. Varennes is where Louis XVI was made prisoner when he tried to leave france. Little of it left now. Very bad mud."

December 2: "Went to Vauquois . . . most interesting and stupendus. More than 48000 French & Germans killed in fighting there. Went . . . to Landres-St. George & St. Georges which were the scenes of the last Tank attacks. The U.S. Barrage was most terrible. We went . . . to look at the Bosch positions and they had lost much material."

December 3: Went to Verdun and San Mihiel. Trench system is most interesting. French did more digging but Bosch better and they had better shelter for the men also better wire.

Patton and Brett returned to Bourg on December 4 just in time for Patton to learn he had won the prize. Someone, probably Rockenbach, no doubt telephoned from Chaumont to give him the good news.

Diary
December 4: "Got D.S.C. Wired Beat to that effect."

On the following day, confirmation came in writing:

Diary
December 5: Got letter saying I had D.S.C.

Letter, GSP, Jr., to Rockenbach, December 5, 1918
My dear General: Please accept my sincere thanks for the trouble you took in my behalf with reference to the D.S.C. I shall always prize it more than any thing I could have gotten in the war. My gratitude to you is based on the fact that with out your earnest effort I should not have gotten it. Thank you again . . .
With renewed thanks I am most sincerely, G. S. Patton, Jr.

Diary
December 6: "Left for Paris on 2:18 train [for one week of leave, rest and vacation]. Gen. R. let me wear my D.S.C. Ribbon."

CHAPTER 33

The Wait

"Generals are made—by themselves . . . by a life of ceaseless effort at the military profession."

Soon after Patton, wearing his D.S.C. ribbon, left for Paris, Rockenbach rated him. "This officer is very efficient, but youthful. He will, I believe, sober into one of highest value."

The process of sobering an exuberant young man into an officer of highest caliber was already at work. It could be seen in Patton's serious application to his professional duties.

He lectured regularly at the General Staff College. He gave formal talks to his own officers and men. He assiduously collected British and French training notes, and he would continue to add to his collection of materials, operations reports, and after-action histories, to expand his knowledge of tank warfare. He gathered —and apparently studied in fascination—citations awarding soldiers decorations for bravery in combat. He continued to be interested in technological improvements. He frequently directed exercises at the tank center.

Diary

December 5 (the day before he left for Paris): Gave lecture to General Staff College. They asked to have it printed. Had manuver in P.M. quite successful. Wireless tanks worked for first time; sent and received messages while in motion. Staff very inattentive due to end of war probably.

For his presentation at the Staff College, Patton wrote two lectures on the subject of "Light Tanks in Exploitation." One was a draft lecture, the other he actually delivered. Each was interesting in its own right.

The draft lecture notes—later marked by Patton, "This was not given as here shown. GSP"—advanced his thoughts on tank doctrine almost to the blitzkrieg concept. His proposal or thesis: once the tanks and infantry, working together, crossed the line of trenches composing the forward enemy defenses, thereby breaking the hostile defensive positions, the tanks ought to take advantage of their mobility and exploit the victory.

Exploitation signifies that the situation is such as to at least justify the hope that there is something to exploit. In other words that the crust has been broken and we are about to eat the pie. This occurs when the Infantry and Tanks have passed the first organized positions and are rushing headlong on the harrassed and fleeing enemy . . .

Before proceeding further to tell of these thrilling exploits, it may be well to try to picture as vividly as possible the actual position of the defeated enemy as seen close up.

Above our heads the constant roar of our barrage fills the air and we hope kills the enemy. Unfortunately I have yet to see our own shells bursting. As after the first hour of progression, our barrage has invariably been from two to four miles ahead of us.

As to the enemy, he is only represented by a few shells falling in unpopulated fields. For the rest, the country is empty and uninteresting dotted with clumps of trees, ruined houses and perhaps a camouflage bordered road. The tanks and Infantry advance. The latter in platoon columns; the former in skirmish lines. Finally the Tanks gain sufficient distance (150 meters) ahead of the Infantry, deploy and then proceed to form there a grotesque line. All is progressing as on the drill field when suddenly the hostile shells become more numerous and inquisitive and then from several places at once the put put put of the Boche machine guns.

The defeated and demoralized enemy has been run to earth; we are upon him; it only remains to finish him; but where in hell is he. He is apparently all around and for once appearances are not deceptive. He is not in those dense waves of surging green humanity so vividly depicted by newspaper reporters and other fiction writers, but scattered in groups of a few men armed with one, two or 4 machine guns

or automatic rifles admirably placed and almost totally concealed.

This is the form of battle called Exploitation or at least the
first phase of Exploitation. The name is apt . . .

Having thus sketched in my most charming style the toute
ensemble of the scene, I will attempt by the use of the black-
board to show how all around fire above referred to is arranged. If I have appeared frivolous, it is because being a
graduate of this institution I know that the [student] . . .
prefers amusement to instructions and a lecturer who would
not have his voice drowned in a barrage of snores must try to
amuse for at least the first five minutes.

. . . Four to eight Kilometers back of this [front] line is
the real defended position, usually a naturally strong line enhanced by skilfully prepared trenches linking together well
organized villages and backed by a numerous artillery and
well placed machine guns, but in the area between the first
line and this second one is the organized zone where we must
make our first essay in exploitation . . .

These men [on the defensive] are often described as being
in "Checkerboard" formation. To me this term is misleading
as it presupposes regularity of distribution. There is no regularity. The guns are arranged solely to attain two things. First:
concealment so as to avoid discovery and destruction. Second: mutual support . . . nearly always the forward ones are
on reverse slopes with a short field of fire to the front and
relatively longer ones to one or both flanks. Each gun position has been selected with the greatest care . . . The guns
are placed in a position to kill or be killed. When first the
Tanks advance through this area preceding the infantry these
guns do not fire but . . . fire only on Infantry targets after
the passage of the Tanks. For this reason it has often happened that tanks have gone forward meeting no resistance
from machine gun fire while the Infantry following them have
been decimated by a tempest of machine gun bullets.

. . . this solitary advance of the tanks while apparently a
very useful operation is in reality a perfectly futile one. Tanks
can take nearly anything. They can hold absolutely nothing.
Furthermore the visibility from within a Tank is not over
40%. Hence at least 50% of the machine guns remain un-

seen by the Tank . . . if the Infantry and Tanks enter the
fight firmly impressed with the fact that they are mutually
necessary one to the other and take proper steps to maintain
contact, the problem of the organized area is solved.

The Tank is the answer to the machine gun but like any
other solution it must be rightly applied . . . the tanks must
see more than they now do. This can be accomplished by
placing a line of Infantry scouts from 100 to 150 meters
ahead of the tanks . . . the infantry taking a hostile machine
gun should act as a catcher behind the bat. He makes all preparations to catch the ball and does catch it unless the bat, in
this case the tank, interposes . . . if the tank is successful the
infantry which has been lying supine has lost distance and
distance in war means time and time means victory.

The above are the tactics of the first phase of exploitation
of the Light Tank. Proceeding in this manner the tanks and
infantry arrive at the main line of resistance . . .

If the tanks have been successful in quickly reducing machine gun resistance, this main line of defence will have lost
much of its virtue because it is constituted not to resist vigorous attack of unbroken troops but rather to check the strag-
gling assault of troops wearied and weakened by the machine
gun infested area in front of it. Hence it too will fall to the
vigorous attack of the Tanks aided by the infantry using all
its arms, which means an overwhelming fire of rifles, machine
guns, automatic rifles and 37's concentrated with the aid of
the tanks upon certain strategic points of the second line of
resistance.

Assuming then that we have successfully negotiated the
organized area and the line of resistance, we arrive at a second organized area, but a much less highly developed one
. . . and there should be no difficulty in continuing the same
methods to maintain the continuity of our progression.

Finally we have reached we will say the corps objective, but
night is falling. It appears injudicious to attack at night so
we must use the night as a means of preparation for renewing
activities at dawn. From the tank standpoint these preparations consist of refilling the tanks with gasolene, oil and ammunition. This is the most difficult task as anyone who has
ever seen an axial road must admit but upon the solution

of this question the next day's operations of the tanks wholly depends. It never yet has been fully solved because the mechanical means to the solution have been absent. If we had had ten ton munition tractors capable of carrying sufficient gasolene, etc. and negotiating the fields on either side of the road, the solution would have been easy. These tractors should move forward as soon as the hostile fire permits and should arrive at the tanks before midnight. With them should come sufficient extra men and company mechanics to thoroughly groom and refill the tanks while tank crews snatch a few hours sleep.

When morning comes the exploitations of our dreams has perhaps arrived. The enemy's artillery positions have been passed. Any fire he may direct upon us is not based upon carefully prepared firing data but is either direct over the sights which is futile or is indirect based on very insufficient information. We may then push rapidly forward along the roads. It is impossible for his infantry or artillery to stop tanks under such circumstances but it is futile for the tanks to advance faster than their infantry can follow them. If then during the night new infantry has arrived to proceed forward say at two miles an hour behind the tanks we may progress indefinitely . . .

The hostile infantry deprived of the support of the artillery is powerless against the tanks even if they fortify themselves in the upper stories of the houses of villages. They will be cut off by the infantry, who is pressing forward on either side, need only leave a party of moppers-up and may continue their march with practically no delay.

The only thing that will stop this progression will be a river without bridges or a Hindenburg Line or an artillery resistance where the guns have been placed long before and have accurate firing data for all approaches by which the Tanks could menace them.

The vision emerging inevitably out of this prospect was to use tanks in long-range thrusts of exploitation through the enemy rear areas. It was a thrilling view, for the tanks could advance indefinitely until they reached an impassable barrier. If the obstacle was a river, bridge-laying engineers accompanying the tanks could

get the machines across in quick time; if a concrete wall, engineers
could demolish it.

One unsolved problem burst the bubble of using tanks as long-
range instruments of mobility and shock. That was how to refuel
the tanks so they could continue to advance with only short and
few halts. The difficulty would be overcome only in World War II.

In 1918, the notion of a deep penetration by tanks was too radical for general acceptance, and Patton decided to give as his lecture a more conventional presentation. He used an earlier talk,
which stressed the employment of tanks as supporting weapons
for the infantry. The more original thought, that infantry could
support tanks in long-range thrusts, was merely intimated.

*Letter, GSP, Jr. (Hotel Lotti, 7 & 9 rue de Castiglione), to
Beatrice, December 8, 1918*

. . . this is the only place I could get a room. Paris is terribly crowded with every sort of people. You should see how
the civilian clothes have blossomed since the Peace . . .

The most melancholy thing I have ever tried is amusing
my self alone. I doubt if I stay the entire seven days [of
leave] I have coming . . .

I called on the Boyds [Colonel Carl Boyd was an aide to
Pershing] this morning and Anne is quite cute . . . She is a
very nice little girl and quite a relief being American.

I am going to Zig-Zag at the Follies to night. It is all in
english and they say it is good. I had to pay 18F for a little
folding seat.

Diary

December 11: Semmes, Weed, and Castle came to tell me
good by. They are all on the way to the States.

Letter, GSP, Jr., to Beatrice, December 11, 1918

[Bought a police dog named Char for $200; he has a long
pedigree.] Since marrying you I have never been satisfied with
any thing but the best . . . I also bought you a little present
a folding cigarette holder in gold. It is very chick and
pretty . . .

Paris is terribly expensive. A lunch for one with beer costs
50F. at any good resteraunt . . .

I lunched with John [Pershing] . . . and had a very nice talk with him. He says we shall all be home in less than a year.

Diary

December 14: Went to Place de la Concorde to see the President. There was a large crowd but little noise. Gen. P. was in fifth or sixth carriage. "Pres [Wilson] looked fine and very much a man."

Woodrow Wilson had sailed from the United States to take part in the peace talks. He would remain in France until mid-February, 1919, then return home. After less than two weeks in the United States, he would come again to France early in March, this time staying until the end of June.

Letter, GSP, Jr. (Hotel Plaza Athénée, 25 avenue Montaigne), to Beatrice, December 14, 1918

Darling Beat: I have just seen the deflade [défilade] of Le President Wilson. It was quite interesting but very little yelling. I was on the street in the crowd and the smell of bad tobacco was fierce . . .

The crowd is funny as it is made up of people one never sees usually. It reminds me of Kiplings story of the earth god's at sea where all the funny creatures were thrown up.

. . .

War Department General Orders No. 133, December 16, 1918

By direction of the President, under the provisions of the act of Congress . . . the distinguished-service cross was awarded by the commanding general, American Expeditionary Forces, for extraordinary heroism in action in France to the following-named officers and enlisted men:

George S. Patton, jr., colonel, Tank Corps. For extraordinary heroism in action near Cheppy, France, September 26, 1918. He displayed conspicuous courage, coolness, energy, and intelligence in directing the advance of his brigade down the valley of the Aire. Later he rallied a force of disorganized infantry and led it forward behind tanks under heavy machine-gun and artillery fire until he was wounded. Unable to advance farther, he continued to direct the operations of his unit until all arrangements for turning over the command were completed.

GHQ—Tank Corps, AEF, General Orders 24, December 17, 1918

[The Commander in Chief, AEF] in the name of the President has awarded the Distinguished Service Cross to the following Officers and Enlisted Men of the Tank Corps, U.S. Army, for the acts of extraordinary heroism described after their names:

Colonel George S. Patton, Jr., Tank Corps, No. 1391. For extraordinary heroism in action near Cheppy, France, September 26, 1918.

Colonel Patton displayed conspicuous courage, coolness, energy and intelligence in directing . . .

By command of Brigadier General Rockenbach.

At the tank grounds at Bourg, now known as Camp Chamberlain, all the troops of the 304th (1st) Brigade, Tank Corps, and of the 302d Tank Center were present at a review held on December 17. They honored seventeen officers and seven enlisted men who were decorated with the medal.

Diary

December 19: Battalion manuver; "it went very well and showed possibilities of Light Tanks in bad country in open war."

Letter, GSP, Jr., to his father, December 20, 1918

I mailed you under seperate cover a copy of one of the lectures on Tanks which is quite good I do not read my lectures but deliver them and amplify the text. They are all thought to be very good and I am perfectly at ease lecturing to any old thing that comes up to major generals. I must inherit your "gift of gab." It is quite a gift.

I am sending one company of tanks for a review which is to be held for the president of the Republic on the 25th. I hope it does well. I inclose a copy of my citation order also a D.S.C. ribbon as a Christmas present for you all. I could get hold of nothing else worth sending.

Diary

December 20: "Gave lecture to a bunch of artillery officers. They were all most interested and it was a pleasure to talk to them. Had demonstration in P.M. which was not well staged as the tanks bunched too much."

December 22: "Went to Chaumont to have uniforms tried on. Had to wait two hours there was such a crowd."

December 24: Braine and I talked over our last Christmas eve. I read a Book B gave me "The Kingdom of the Blind."

December 25: "Ate [Christmas] dinner here [at Bourg] at one. Went to Gen P's for dinner at eight . . . Got some nice presents . . . Left at 12:30 A.M. in snow storm. Char [dog] had eaten my shoes."

Letter, GSP, Jr., to Aunt Nannie, December 29, 1918

My Xmas box came on the 27th and all the presents were very nice and in good shape. I also got a lot of Presents at the Generals house. Last Christmas I was the only one who gave presents so this year I decided not to and every one else did.

I got a cigarette case, a pocket book and cigars and handkerchiefs in profusion also a nice scarf from J.J.P. We had a lot of fun at the dinner. The generals nephew and I were the only out siders and we had a lot of fun. We shook dice and danced after dinner . . . I ate so much plumb pudding that the general ordered the waiter to give me no more there by saving my life.

The General had on most of his ribbons and they made three and a half rows on him and looked fine. I was the only D.S.C. there so was well pleased with my self.

Quekemeyer gave me two guard Corps Bosch helmets brand new. They are very fine. There are all sorts of rumors about our going home soon. I hope they are correct as I would like to rest up a while before the next war when ever it may be.

I hope I do as well next time as I did this. I ought to get the D.S.M. and [the] two stars [of a major general]. I surely am some soldier if I say so my self, and my shape is a great help.

Diary

December 31: "End of a fine year full of interest. I hope it will be the only one in which I am away from B. for such a long time. Sat up until 12 reading French history from 1814 to 1914. Got letter from Frenchman again accusing me of all sorts of vice and saying he would write Gen. P. I hope he does."

Rockenbach assessed Patton as an officer "believed to possess ability to render good service in any position." General H. A. Smith, former school commandant in Langres, called Patton "A strong forceful active young officer. One of our very best."

Diary

January 3: Order to be ready to leave (for the United States) on short notice.

January 6: Started infantry training in "gang" attack tactics.

Letter, Maj. Gen. André W. Brewster, Inspector General, AEF, to GSP, Jr., January 6, 1919

Thank you for your letter of the thirtieth with the inclosures, which I have taken the liberty of having copied; if you have any objection to this I shall destroy them. I needed no certificates of witnesses to establish in my mind the fact of your gallant conduct both before St. Mihiel and in the Argonne. It was the talk of the men of the different divisions with which your brigade was serving and it caused me no surprise. I was very happy to see you get your decoration, both from the point of view of an Inspector who likes to see justice done, and, personally to see a friend get a decoration which he had so gallantly won.

I wish in turn a very Happy New Year for you and yours, and I hope that you will receive earned promotion.

Sincerely your friend.

Letter, GSP, Jr., to his father, January 8, 1919

So far the question of my returning to the united states is very uncertain. The Tank Troops are to return and in fact are now under orders but there is a general order to the effect that regular officers will turn over their commands at the port of embarcation and be given other duty in France. Gen. Rockenbach is trying to have an exception made in our case so the chances are about fifty fifty that we come home. I hope we do.

I am sending you in two seperate packages A bosch 105 shell case arranged as a tobacco jar. I hope you will like it. I also sent you a knife with a silver blade in it to eat oranges with. The handle is ivory and the steel very famous.

I hear that the tanks which were shot up in the fighting are to be shipped to America and that various cities are to get them as trophies. The cities will have to pay the cost of shipment. I suggest that the Los Angeles Chamber of Commerce at once ask for one. As I may be clamed as a citizen and I commanded the American Tanks in the first two actions in which they fought and in the only actions in which light tanks participated. A bronze plate with some such screed on it should be attached to the Tank by my grateful fellow citizens. If they want one they had best apply to the chief of Ordnance at once and specify RENAULT TANK.

All the troops in France were paraded at 3:00 P.M. to day and held in parade rest for Twenty one minutes while the 21 minute guns were fired in honor of the death of President [Theodore] Roosevelt.

. . . I am very busy writing a book on war and also a Tank Manual both at the same time . . .

I think that in six months we will have to go to Russia for a war. So I hope I can be back [home] for a little while any way. Then I must come back [to Russia] so as to get the Medal of Honor which I missed getting this time on account of all the witnesses getting killed or being Bosch.

Patton was enormously pleased when Beatrice sent her reaction to his D.S.C. citation and to his crossing of the supposedly mined bridge at Essey:

As I read the letters & citation & your own about the "little affair of the Essey bridge" which you say you "forgot to mention," I am [struck] dumb—if you were only near enough for me to whisper it to you.

> Georgie, you are the fulfillment of all the ideals of manli-
> ness and high courage & bravery I have always held for you,
> ever since I have known you. And I have expected more of you
> than any one else in the world ever has or will.

He copied the last paragraph into his diary, adding, "I am glad
she likes me."

Diary
> January 15: Started writing lecture on German Tactics.
> Gen. Eltinge told me I was to be inspector of Military police
> 3 army (Third Army in the Occupation). Col. Grubbs said I
> was going home.

Trying to keep busy, Patton read British, French, and German
tactical papers and reports of all kinds, avidly studying the art of
war. He received from Mitchell, now Rockenbach's chief of staff,
a training note written by Fuller for the British tanks; Mitchell
had scrawled across the bottom: "Patton here is some thing that
may amuse you for a while. Mitchell. Keep it if you want to." Patton read it and put it into his files, recognizing the soundness of
Fuller's views. Fuller was the tactical brains of the British tank
service; he would continue his tank work and teaching after the
war and would eventually be regarded as the father of tank doctrine.

Diary
> January 16: Went to manuver with Tanks and 82 Div. (In-
> fantry). Men took no interest and showed no idea of what
> they were doing.

Patton and Mitchell left on January 17 for the Second U. S.
Army headquarters at Toul and a visit with units to give lectures
and demonstrations on the functions of tanks. In their travels
they were with the 35th Division at Commercy, the IX Corps
headquarters at St. Mihiel, the 88th Division at Gondrecourt, the
79th Division at Souilly, and Patton became familiar with the terrain of that part of France, ground over which he, as an Army
commander, would lead his troops 25 years later.

Letter, Colonels H. E. Mitchell and G. S. Patton, Jr., to Second Army G–3, January 24, 1919, subject: Notes on Tanks
. . . The tank, in other words, is the answer to the machine gun. Tanks are then a separate weapon as truly new and original as the aeroplane. They are not mechanical cavalry, neither are they artillery or armed infantry . . .

[Tanks, like Stokes mortars, and] other abnormal weapons, have a debilitating effect on the infantry soldier, who, seeing himself supported and propped up by numerous auxiliary arms, loses pride in himself . . .

Success in the attack of tanks on infantry depends chiefly on three factors: 1st—determination and dash on the part of both tanks and infantry, 2nd—tanks keeping in touch with their infantry. To do this the tanks must get on the Infantry skirmish line, and not vice versa. 3rd—Infantry must maneuver promptly and boldly, so as to take immediate advantage of the opportunities created by the tanks . . . Like all other phases of war, success in the operation of tanks with infantry depends on teamwork.

At the bottom of this paper, Patton wrote some years later: "Col. Mitchell signed but did not write this report. GSP."

Continuing his trip, Patton, presumably still accompanied by Mitchell, drove through Pont-à-Mousson, Metz, Thionville ("the cleanest town I have seen"), Esch, Diekirch ("a very nice town as are all in Luxembourg much like America"), and Luxembourg City, all of which would figure prominently in his 1944–45 campaign.

Diary
January 28: Went to Trier. Went to the theater. A very nice town like an American [town]. Some fine Roman ruins.

Letter, GSP, Jr., to his father, January 28, 1919
Right now I am in the north end of Luxembourg. It is a very rich country and has also many mines. The people speak German and look it. You know my feelings toward the Germans before the war. Well they are more so now . . .

This whole country looks cleaner, more modern, and more like America than any other place I have been since I left home.

I am billeted with an old lady whose son in law commands the Luxembourg army. He is a major. He said it was very hard on him as last week all his soldiers went on strike and were discharged so now he has nothing to command except the policemen.

This is the first country in the world to have no army. It is a horrible example of what not to do.

Returned to Bourg, Patton received word that he was about to be relieved from duty with the Tank Corps and sent to Germany for the Occupation.

Rockenbach asked the AEF chief of staff to hold up Patton's reassignment for at least a month and explained the reason for his request. There were 1355 men in the tank brigade and only four Regular officers.

This is not a sufficient number of officers to enable me to enforce discipline to keep the men exercised, entertained, and in a sanitary condition. As you know Colonel Patton exercises a great deal of influence not only in his own Brigade, but also in the Tank Center, which I estimate, will have for approximately one month a total of nearly 5000 men.

The chief of staff agreed with the cogency of Rockenbach's statement. If Patton had not already complied with orders to proceed to Treves for duty, he could remain with the tank brigade until the tankers departed for the United States. At that time, Patton would go to Germany.

This information reached Patton as he was leaving on another round of conferences. He wrote in his diary: "Just before starting found that I would have to go to Treves after Brigade goes home. God-Dam."

He was in a foul mood during his trip. "Officers in billet were drunk and kept me awake." The officers in the billet were drunk again the following night. Officers were uninterested in their work. This officer was "a dead one," another was "dead and a fool." The weather was cold, and his wound "hurt like the duce."

Letter, GSP, Jr., to Beatrice, February 7, 1919
I have not had a chance to write for the last couple of days

as I have been on the go all the time and have slepped in places with no lights.

Letter, GSP, Jr., to Beatrice, February 7, 1919
I wrote you a brief note this morning from Toul . . .

You poor thing you surely have a hell of a time. [Beatrice had been ill.] Please die your hair. I am going to [do the same] . . .

I just heard the French translation of Y.M.C.A. "Ilya moyen coucher avec." [They can be slept with.] That shows the way they are thought of here . . .

As to J. and Nita. It is possible that the game is up. You see he could get anyone in the world and they are after him. Ambition is a great thing and without soul. I have no reason for knowing this but ??? "C'est possible."

It is a good thing you and I are safely married??—Other wise I would have to have proposed to you all over again for having seen the world I have yet to see your equal. I love you.

The book Patton worked on between November 1918 and March 1919 grew to 26 single-spaced, typewritten sheets on the subject of "War As She Is," which was very close to the title of the book his wife would publish shortly after his death, *War as I Knew It*.

The incomplete manuscript contained Patton's deeply held beliefs on patriotism and warfare. Much of it was trite, much synthetic. What was based on his experiences revealed originality of thought and expression.

GSP, Jr., "War As She Is," Bourg, France, spring 1919

Foreword
War, to quote Clausewitz, "is but the continuation of policy by other means." Hence logic demands of us that in approaching our subject we consider these other means; namely the soldiers and officers which are the molicules forming the Body Military.

Having dealt with these we must consider War in general and finally the duties of the various arms which combine to produce the only admissible result—VICTORY.

It thus appears that we have set ourselves a task of no mean proportion and one which would tax the ability of a far more learned author. Therefore, we hasten to disavow any attempt at a full exposition and purpose simply to set down some thoughts on this vast subject which our limited experience and reading has taught us to regard as specially important.

It is hoped that our modest effort will perhaps find approval in the eyes of that large class of readers, who while not soldiers, yet take a patriotic interest in our means of national perpetuity—the ARMY.

Chapter I. The Soldier.

The success of armies and consequently the existence of states depend upon the caliber of the individual soldier. Therefore it seems self evident that soldiers should come from the people, the whole people and nothing but the people.

To entrust our most sacred possession—National Existence —to any one class is as foolish as to entrust our legislature to a class of men who legislate for personal profit not for national benefit . . .

Thus far our professional hired army has held untarnished the highest traditions of American manhood and patriotism. But the cycles of history are inexorable; the day will come when due to unjust prejudice and small pay the class of our enlisted will fall . . . When that day arrives a second [battle of] Zama will write a crimson "FINIS" to all our proud hopes and noble ideals . . .

With wars on the present scale there is no nation rich enough to pay the vast masses of men necessary to maintain an active army and competent reserve adequate to its defense . . . for national health the army must be composed of all the able bodied citizens whose age and physique permits to them the privilege of bearing arms . . . What manner of man is it who when insulted, hires another to shoulder his responsibility? Even the despised jackall protects its young personally and not through the interposition of some more courageous animal hired by the offer of some choice bit of carrion.

. . . there must be a uniform and fundamental belief that the highest privilege of man is to perpetuate his native land even at the forfeit of his own life. The soldier in the service must be actuated by this belief else he prostitutes his high office and goes to battle an unwilling slave . . .

. . . the man who has served his country for a year [in training] with sweat and some discomfort feels truly that he has a part in his country . . . and he is a Patriot . . .

The boy who has served his time as a soldier has stood on his own feet . . . He has seen rich and poor doing just what he is doing. He is considerate for the democracy of the squad room . . . and the man who carelessly disturbs his sleeping comrades by a late and noisy entrance will gain a most valuable lesson as to the rights of others in the form of a well aimed marching shoe. These things bring a realization of the fact that liberty means equality for all, not license for one . . .

. . . the man who serves his country serves also himself. But to get the maximum results presupposes two things. First the willingness to serve, bred of early training in patriotism and second disciplined instruction . . .

Discipline may be defined as "Prompt, cheerful and AUTOMATIC obedience." . . . if each man of a company of 250 delayed thirty seconds in finding his place it would take two hours to form the company . . .

. . . the training of the soldier must be absolutely uniform . . . Interchangeability of working parts of industrial machines has long been recognized as an economic necessity. Men are the working parts of an army.

. . . one of the salient reasons for a national army is the prohibitive expense of a hired one. Neither we nor any other nation can afford to pay men enough to make them willing to die . . . Men so venial as to deliberately barter their lives would be equally open to similar offers from the enemy. This statement would seem to cast disparagement on our present regular army but such is not the case. The men of our regular army serve from a spirit of adventure and a genuine liking for the service. The pay to them is incidental. It seems highly improbable that a decided increase in pay would in any way effect the number of enlistments . . .

Since we cannot pay enough to secure soldiers we must resort to compulsion and rely on a general improvement in patriotic education to make that service less grudgingly rendered and trust to the final educational influences of the army itself to insure the cheerful giving of life itself if the need arises . . .

. . . The soldier, being a citizen, owes the country service and whatever he gets in return is a gift, pure and simple . . .

All pensions and bonuses voted soldiers . . . are most detrimental to public morality and national thrift . . . [They are] bribary . . .

This does not apply to pensions or support tendered soldiers actually incapacitated while in line of duty . . .

The above sentiments will doubtless be unintelligible to those who regard the nation as a convenience to the individuals . . . The nation is the one common possession of all the citizens and as such they are all bound to insure its maintenance—not it, theirs.

. . . The nation owes all an equal chance but is not responsible for the faults and follies of those who fail to avail themselves of these opportunities.

Chapter II. The Line Officer.

. . . The officer's sense of patriotism, discipline and self-sacrifice must be no cosmus incoherent shape, but clear and vital so that its lambent flame may distill that most vital of all his attributes—a sense of OBLIGATION . . . [which] is inseparably connected with discipline . . . [which] is made up of so many tiny and apparently trivial things. In essence however, it consists in doing the task set, however small, absolutely, perfectly, and better than it was ever done before. Here is the heart of the whole matter—a perfect performance . . . perfect also in the light of your own conscience . . .

. . . leniency to self . . . is inimical to duty, hence to victory.

. . . In war there are no individuals and consequently their feelings as such do not exist. The least and the most that is required of an officer is a perfect performance of his duty. Not excuses, or failures, but results must be forthcoming. In doing his utmost, even to death, the officer is not conferring a favor, he is privileged to be able to give that much for his country . . .

. . . man is a poor thing at best and loves his little span [of life] better than he will usually admit. The word fearless is a misnomer; all men fear, some show it less than others, hence when we say that officers must be brave we mean they must show fear less—be more stoical. And this too may be

developed . . . we must make officers so proud of their calling that the fear of disgracing their cloth shall be more potent
than that of the animal shrinking from imminent dissolution . . .

Each year a sufficient number of soldiers who have completed their service and who desire to further serve their
country as officers should be sent to military academies similar to West Point. The idea in this requirement is to insure
complete democracy among officers and to produce a thorough understanding [among officers] of the viewpoint of
soldiers . . .

Upon graduation these cadets will . . . for at least two
years serve as officers . . .

. . . [Then] those desiring to, should return to civil life
and be given preference for employment in all branches of
state and Federal government. (Average age 24). Those who
remain in the service should be promoted or retired according to their deserts. But all who leave the service should . . .
be available to return to the colors . . . in cases of emergency.

. . . [Some people] insist that a few weeks training makes
them competent to command in war . . .

Suppose some eminent broker has surgery for a hobby and
reads it two evenings a week and attends several clinics during the year. Which one of you with an inflamed appendix
will select such a man as your surgeon? If there is any such,
our definition of Courage will have to be revised along with
our estimate of his sanity . . .

This is no reflection on the thousands of gallant officers
who led our armies in the World War. On a desert island . . .
one layman may, and must, operate upon another . . .

It seems incredible that in America the land of specialists,
trained men are demanded for every occupation but that of
officers. Yet only in the army is lack of trained specialists
paid for with the blood of our first born and the tears of our
people . . .

The road to high command leads through a long path
called the "History of War." Like all long roads the scenery is
not always interesting; there are desert stretches of prosaic
facts, but now and again the traveler reaches eminences where
he sees the most sublime panoramas ever vouch safed to

mortal—the deathless deeds of the great who have passed to that Valhalla which is death but not oblivion.

To be useful in battle, military knowledge, like discipline, must be subconscious. The memorizing of concrete examples is futile for in battle the mind does not work well enough to make memory trustworthy. The officer must be so soaked in military lore that he does the military thing automatically. The study of history will go far towards producing this result; the study of mathematics will not.

But the above study must continue after entry into the service and last until the day of retirement . . .

Here it is well to call attention to the possibility of falling into an age old error. Namely that of presuming that all future wars will be an exact replica of the most recent past war . . . when the foam of freak expedients has been blown away by the sterile breath of retrospection, war settles back to the same old bitter draft, the ingredients of which, have been, are, and ever shall be—DISCIPLINE, SIMPLICITY and BOLDNESS.

Strategy and tactics do not change, the means only of applying them differ. A sound and profound historical education should have as its end an absolute grounding in the immutable principles of war comprehended so that they are sufficiently flexible to permit of having implaced on them the transitory expedients which evolution from time to time produces. The uncontrolled specialist is one of the greatest menaces to an army . . .

While it is a patriotic duty and privilege to be an officer we are all human and if the path to glory is beset with its normal hardships coupled to poverty, the temptation to let some other patriot wear the shoulder straps [of an officer] will remove many a good officer from the service.

Chapter III. Staff Officers.

The Staff Officer, as a class, is probably the object of more criticism than any other officer in the service. This criticism is partially justified and partially the result of misunderstanding . . .

Like Line Officers, staff officers should first be soldiers, next officers, and finally, as the result of special training and aptitude, staff officers . . .

To be efficient and avoid criticism the general qualifications of the Tactical Staff are as follows, arranged in order of importance:

a) A personal knowledge of troops, learned by actual command . . .

b) . . . loyalty to the chief they serve. Nothing is so subversive of discipline as criticism of superiors by juniors . . .

c) . . . TACT . . . to give direction or instructions to officers of superior rank . . . The sight of a bumptious Staff Major airing his views to a General of Division is one of the most nauseating of spectacles . . .

d) . . . they must stick absolutely to facts, unadorned by anamus, sympathy, or enthusiasm.

e) The following pun always elicited great applause in the World War: "If bread is the Staff of Life, what is the Life of the Staff?—One long loaf." . . . Staff Officers should constantly visit the troops to keep in first hand touch with the situation . . . The presence of Staff Officers in the field has both a real and a physological [psychological] influence. The information so gained is reliable, the difficulties of the soldier are realized and the actual sight of the Staff Officer makes the soldier more trustful of him. The Staff Officer is the Servant of the Line . . . he must see all and then while others rest he must translate the information gained by his eyes into orders by his brain. This task ought to be the more willingly performed since though the hours of work for the staff are longer the surroundings of that work are more pleasant.

THE CHIEF OF STAFF . . . The Commanding General should be relieved by his general staff of all vexatious details in the working out of any project . . . In the exercise of his function as coordinator, the Chief of Staff must often act with repression upon many brilliant schemes, excellent in themselves, but not well balanced as viewed from his general point of vantage . . . the Chief of Staff must guard against the habit of becoming too repressive. The habit of constant negation is an insidious disease and if allowed to florish unhindered may do more harm than good.

. . . the Commanding General should be required to spend a minimum of time in his office and hence have much leisure to personally inspect and supervise the training and marching of his soldiers. It is only by such personal contact that he may instill confidence and devotion in them—hence fulfill his duties as a General. . . .

ASSISTANT CHIEF OF STAFF G–1 . . . The services are created to serve the troops. Battles are won by troops, not by services. It is the duty of G–1 to see that the troops are served . . .

ASSISTANT CHIEF OF STAFF G–2 . . . it would be useless to plan the most splendid cavalry raid in country which G–2 knows to be waterless . . .

ADVISORY STAFF OFFICERS . . . Chaplain, charged with fighting the Devil. (Usually unsuccessful.)

Chapter IV. Generals.

. . . an attempt to define what have appeared to us the leading characteristics in varying degrees and combinations of American Generals with whom we have had the honor to be associated.

. . . first impressions are of vast importance . . . a general [must] have a soldierly bearing and typify in his person as well [as] possess in his mind the highest qualities of a soldier . . .

To this soldierly bearing should be added that indescribable something which we call Personal Magnetism. Men admired Wellington but they worshipped Lee.

Tact . . . [but not] that cheap and disgusting fawning on the men practised by some, to their own ruin, for the men are the first to perceive and ridicule such procedure . . .

Finally . . . Impartial Justice . . .

. . . actuated by the highest ideals as to life, patriotism and duty . . . final decision as his final responsibility is for him alone and not to be taken by a vote of advisers like a club election. Clive said he had only called one council of war and fortunately had not abided by its decision.

. . . utmost fixity of purpose . . .

Health . . .

A desire to fight . . .

A trained military mind soaked with the theory and practise of war by daily study and environment so that no matter what the circumstance, the mind will think in a military way, automatically.

. . . Generals are made—by themselves.

. . . they acquired them [the above virtues], not at birth, but by a life of ceaseless effort at the military profession.

Chapter V. War.

. . . we are not concerned with the causes of war for these are provided by statesmen . . . and are always just . . . From the time Paris stole Helen to the time William [of Germany] tried to steal the world, the peoples at issue have believed implicitly in the justice of their cause. Nothing but this in-hereent idea of the justice of their cause can explain the sacrifices made throughout the ages by all peoples. The fact that half these assumptions must have been wrong in order to have the other half right in no way detracts from the fact.

. . . On the decision and courage of a Boy Lieutenant hangs the success or failure of the General's plan. But . . . during battle the General is powerless to direct this Boy. He is, however, none the less responsible, for he should have trained his Lieutenants to do the right thing . . . as a result of habit.

First in importance of these vital habits comes the automatic instinct of forward movement . . . Men who think only of going on, will be victorious or killed. They will be victorious more often than killed.

. . . It is the failure to do something offensive instantly, whether right or wrong, that has lost more battles than any other one fault and this failure is due to just two things: lack of courage and lack of habit . . .

Victory alone will come through the will to conquer relentlessly and automatically applied in battle.

Note on Chapter VI. Combat General.

In spite of the kaleidoscopic changes in the outward semblance of war, it in fact remains the same in principle and these principles are—have been—and ever shall be the following:

First—getting the largest force of the right sort to the right place at the right time. We must however, be careful in our definition of force. It is not of necessity numbers . . .

. . . force in the form of fire, must so discomfort opposed forces in the same form that it [the latter] gives back and that this recession must be followed by numerical force, killing and bluffing other opposed numerical force . . . inaccurate fire of whatever nature is not force but noise—useless—impotent.

. . . Our moving force in fire and flesh [in the offensive] advances over the enemy's front positions but in his back positions we are met by concealed fire beyond the range of our own concealed fire [artillery] and we must overcome this force also before we can get to the place where we may overrun the enemy by a display and use of stone-age brawn.

In trench war the solution of this difficulty was usually sought by the use of limited objects. Such attacks failed because the undisturbed concealed fire in the back area was superior to ours and we were slaughtered while consolidating. This form of attack failed also because limited objectives disregard psychology in omitting the ultimate threat of beef [more numbers of men].

. . . In wars without such flankless lines penetrations or encircling movements by cavalry and tanks will, I believe, be sufficient to break up to a large degree the great gun concentrations and thus permit moving fire and force to gain decisive results.

In other words, cavalry and tanks would restore mobility to the battlefield. The next conflict would be unlike the trench warfare in France. If Patton saw clearly into the future, and certainly if he had his way, the next war would be a war of movement.

CHAPTER 34

Going Home

"I will get a M.H. [Medal of Honor] in the next war. I hope."

WRITING A DETAILED INSTRUCTION—eight typed pages, single spaced—for his troops on how to prepare for their return to the United States made Patton feel blue and depressed. He wanted to go home too. Yet he was scheduled to be part of the forces occupying Germany.

He traveled to Chaumont to deliver to Pershing some shells his men had turned into tobacco and cigar boxes for presentation to President Wilson. Arrived at the AEF headquarters, he was invited to attend a luncheon Pershing was giving to the men who had been awarded the Medal of Honor. He accepted, of course. He had a chance to chat for a few minutes in private with Pershing who "talked to me of Nita and I wrote a letter advising her to enter YMCA." He also decided to write a letter to his friend General McAndrew, Pershing's chief of staff, "about my going home."

Letter, GSP, Jr., to Commander in Chief, AEF (through channels), February 10, 1919, subject: Return to United States of America

Request that instead of being detailed on Provost Marshal duty at Treves, as at present ordered, I be allowed to return to the United States with the Tank Corps troops, and that Col H. E. Mitchell, TC, be given my detail as he desires to remain in Europe.

REASONS: I have been in France since June 18th, 1917. During this time my wife has lost both her father and mother and is at present in very poor health. Prior to coming to Europe I had been in the Mexican Punitive Expedition from beginning to end so that with the exception of about three weeks I have not seen my family for more than 2½ years. I have been in the Tank Corps since its inception and would feel great pride in being allowed to accompany it to the United States.

For the above reasons request my application be given consideration.

Letter, GSP, Jr., to Beatrice, February 10, 1919

I had a most interesting day. I went up to the generals house to take him some shell cases . . . When I got there I found that all the medal of honor men had been invited to a boufet lunch. Besides [the Medal of Honor recipients] there were present Gen P., Gen Bullard, Gen Ligget, Gen Summeral . . . Corps commanders and a lot of staff generals. The generals helped serve the M.H. men all of whom were soldiers or lieutenants. I helped also. All of them were young except one captain and one corporal. The rest were just boys but all had fine clear eyes. It struck me as a splendid contrast the Brains of the army and the brawn . . . One of mine [that is, a tanker] was there Lt. Call. The other [who was awarded the Medal of Honor] is dead. Gen Summerall asked me to present Call to him and I did. The general was very nice to Call who is a fine looking youngster. I wish I had gotten an M.H. but one can't have you and every other good thing too. At least not all at once. I will get a M.H. in the next war. I hope.

I have just wired you "Have Nita stay with you till letter arrives, Love All. Patton."

I talked to the General and he said wives could not come over. He also said that he would be here until late next fall.

Then he said "Why can't Anne come over in the Y.M.C.A.? I want her and I could arrange her coming so that no one would know I had." I said "General she can't come unless it is known [because] she belongs to a distinguished family in her state and it would cause remark. That is why she has not come. Out of consideration for you." He said "I think she could come from Washington all right and all those rumors are dead any how." I said "you are wrong but I don't

think any thing can hurt you. Shall I write?" he said "Yes do."
I am.

This seems to me to settle the facts of the case so far as his
continued affection is concerned. Now this is what I think.
You may not like it but here it is.

Nita loves him and he her (or she). It might be unpleasant
for her to come but it would be more unpleasant for her to
loose him. He is great and much sought after. One more year
of seperation might ruin two lives and loves. It is better for
her pride to suffer a little than for her to loose such a Great
man. Therefore I say tell her to come. One word from her
and he can fix it. This is my best judgment in the matter. If
she comes they will be married here. I am sure or nearly so. If
she does not [come] who can say what may not happen.

I inclose a letter I just wrote [to General McAndrew] trying to get home. It is the only chance. No leaves will be
granted and there is no other way. Consider what I have said
[about Nita] from your *head* not from *sentiment*.

I love you.

Letter, GSP, Jr., to Beatrice, February 11, 1919

In addition to writing you last night I also wrote Mama. I
am still of the same opinion as when I wrote.

I wrote a personal letter to Gen. McAndrew the Chief of
Staff asking him to consider my official letter favorably and I
hope and trust that he will.

Bowditch [one of Pershing's aides] just called up saying
that the Prince of Wales would be dining with Gen. Pershing
on Thursday and asking if I could come and bring some of my
minstrels to entertain H.R.H. . . .

One of my men is an artist and he is going to make a picture of me . . . I must stop now and pose.

Letter, GSP, Jr., to Beatrice, February 12, 1919

. . . if I get to go I ought to be home in a month. It seems
too good to be possible but I hope it is just the same. If I
learn anything definate I shall wire you at once which ever
way it is.

We had a dinner last night to the original officers of the
304 (1) Brigade and to the other officers who were here prior
to August 21, 1918.

There were numerous speeches etc. I made every one pay 3 francs and I paid the difference to the amount of 900 francs.

We also got up a souvenir book which we will print. My picture is the frontice piece.

As there is nothing much to do now I am getting worthless the same as I got in Mexico. I hate to feel this way.

Patton was one of six American officers invited to a reception for the young Prince of Wales, future King Edward VIII, who would abdicate his throne to marry the woman he loved. The Prince's evening with Pershing and his staff was postponed several days because of a sad occurrence.

Diary

February 13: Bowditch telephoned that Carl Boyd [one of Pershing's aides] died last night and for me to come up and go to Paris with them for the funeral. Sent B. my picture drawn by Corp. Land. Had dinner with Gen. and got on the Special train at 10:30. About 25 officers were on it all going to funeral.

February 14: Arrived Paris 9 A.M. Went to Generals House 73 Rue de Varenne. Went to Hammonds & got my Blouse also a regulation Over coat. Lunched at house. Went to church at 1:30. Went to cemetery. Cars stuck on the hill. We pushed them up. Mrs. Boyd did well at funeral. I spent the evening with them, Ann sat in my lap and cried about 2 hours. Asked Gen McAndrew if I could go home. he agreed.

February 15: Took Ann for walk in morning. Called on Gen. Rhodes. He is a fright to look at. Gen. [F.C.] Marshall came also. Saw Floyd Gibbons. Queck and I went to the Boyds and I told stories for 3 hours and got them to laugh. Got on train at 11:30. The H.R.H. [Prince of Wales] had not yet arrived. He was at a dance.

February 16: Met Prince of Wailes and his aid Capt. Sir Claud Hamilton Cloudstream Guards as they left the train. Saw Gen. R[ockenbach] at his office. Lt. Col. Bowdich and I took the Prince to lunch with Gen. H. T. Allen 8 Corps. Saw some good [prize?] fights. I rode back with Prince. A very nice fellow. Reception at Gen P's house. Dinner at 8 P.M. I had the itch.

February 17: Gen. P. the Prince, Capt. Hamilton, Queck, Bowditch and I went to Commercy to review the 35th Division. Had lunch with Gen. Dargan Division Commander. Rode around Division. Then inspected on foot. All [men] were in fine shape and perfectly equiped. On way back rode with Gen P. for 2½ hours. He talked all the time and told me a lot of recent history. I asked him if I could go home. He said Haugh [a grunt or something equally noncommital]. Returned to Bourg.

Letter, GSP, Jr., to Pershing, February 18, 1919
Please allow me to thank you for letting me have the sorrowful pleasure of attending the funeral of poor Boyd and the honor of having met the Prince of Wailes. I talked so much about my self yesterday that I think I had better reinforce my statements. Besides I like to appear well in your eyes. For both these reasons I am inclosing the statements of two men [Angelo and Edwards] who were with me on the 26th of September. Some day if you have time I should appreciate it if you would read them.

Letter, GSP, Jr., to Nita, February 18, 1919
I have been having a very historic time. Col. Boyd died of pneumonia on Wednesday and Gen. P. asked me to go up with him on his special train thursday night . . . The funeral was on Friday and I spent the rest of the day consoling Mrs. Boyd and Ann. Next day I called on Gen. Rhodes who fell out of an Airplane and lost most of his nose. He is a sight . . . Then I took Ann for a walk and later told stories to her and her mother until eleven P.M. when I had to walk most of the way to get the special train. The Prince of Wales and his aid Sir Claude Hamilton were on the train.

Sunday when we got to Chaumont Col. Bowditch and I took the H.R.H. over to the 8th Corps . . . for lunch . . . On the way back I rode with the Prince and he told me a lot of stories supposed to be bad. Some were. He said "Bein a dashed prince rather cramps one style What?" There was a reception and later a dinner. After the dinner the prince and several of us danced to a phonograph and then he wanted to play poker but none of us knew how so we shot craps sitting on the floor. The H.R.H. got a hundred and fifty of my francs and then went to bed. He did not have much money and had to borrow to start the game. I stayed at the house all night and the next day we left for Commercy to inspect the 35th Div. There were twenty thousand men in ranks and we walked about seven miles to inspect every man. Every one with a wound stripe was talked to by the Gen. and the Prince . . . On the way back I rode in the Machine with J. and we talked for about three hours. He told me all sorts of secret history . . .

When I left after dinner the Prince said "I should like awfully to nock about with you in america on the border." He possibly says that to every one. J. made a fine speech to the Division and the P. said a few words.

I am inclosing for you all a couple of copies of the statements of two men who were with me when I was hit. Dont loose them.

I realy think it would be a fine idea if you would come over here in the Red Cross or the Y.M.C.A. . . .

I dont know yet whether I am going home or not. If I do I shall leave here a week from to day. But that would not interfere with your coming and might make it easier for you to leave Pa and Ma. In fact that is a good idea. You might write some one and then he would send me home. I still have the itch but otherwise am well.

Much love to all your devoted brother

Diary

February 19: 305th Tank Brigade, commanded by Col. H. E. Mitchell, left this morning for home.

Letter, Mr. Patton to GSP, Jr., February 20, 1919

My dear Son—When your cable came—asking Nita to wait a letter—we all decided to stay [in the East]—& hope your letter will arrive now any day—

Nannie is sick in N.Y. & Mama & Nita are with her and I am here with B & the babies. I hope . . . you are coming home—or that B can join you soon—leaving the children with us.

. . . Among other things I have been worrying for fear that the "gift of gab" you have developed may get you in trouble—unless restrained such a gift is always dangerous The temptation to say smart or striking things is hard to resist—and it is only next day—that cold reason condemns. You are now 34—and a Col and the dignity going with your rank invests what you say with more importance so I hope in your speeches you will be very careful & self restrained—for your own good & for your future—Another gift you have developed I really regret—and that is the ability to write verse upon vulgar & smutty subjects. That is very dangerous. The very men to whom you read & recite such stuff as your last one will laugh—and apparently enjoy it—but you have really lowered yourself in their eyes—above all it lacks *dignity*—and you need to cultivate that especially in view of your rank.

All my life I have known such instances—and never has it failed in my experience—that the Club wit—who indulges in smutty stuff hurts himself. You may some day want to enter public life—but you must couple with your talent . . . great self restraint & sense of dignity—Most men have no real sense of humor—& fail to distinguish little matters of this sort—from realities & judge one accordingly. All the really big men I have known—abstained from repeating vulgar stories —and all who were facile in speech—cultivated great reserve —or if they sometimes forgot themselves—always suffered for the lapse. I dont want to preach and will say no more but I am sure your own judgment—upon reflection will agree with mine—

B is much improved & if you could come to her or she go to you, I think she will be as good as ever . . .

February 21: Request to go home with brigade disapproved by Lt. Col. Obrien.

February 22: Went to Chaumont about going Home. No one there. Heard that Gen. McAndrew would return at 8 P.M. Telephoned him. He said I could go but that Mitchell would Stay. I told him Mitchell had already gone and he said it was o.k. anyhow. Wired B.

February 23: Inspection of all Property to be taken home.
The rest to be turned in. Heard definately that I was to return to the U.S. Heard dogs not allowed on boat.

Letter, GSP, Jr., to Pershing, February 23, 1919
Thanks to your permission I am leaving France with My
Brigade . . . [and thanks also for] all your kindness and con-
sideration . . .

I have attempted in a small way to model my self on you
and what ever success I have had has been due to you as an
inspiration . . .

[Is not quitting Pershing's service, but] I beg that you will
permit me to count my self as one of yours . . .

[Regrets Pershing's absence from Chaumont making it impossible for Patton to say goodbye in person; hoping to serve
again under Pershing] in America or else where.

Diary
February 24: Wrote letters to Gens. Summerall, Burtt,
Brewster, Conner, Harbord. Lt. Colonels Collins Reed Shal-
lenberger. Gen. Nolan. Gen. Rockey [Rockenbach].

February 25: Finished packing and got out Train order.
Hope this is my last night at Bourg. Gave Maj. L. K. Davis
blank check on Morgan-Harjes bank to close my account.
Had my hair cut so I will look neat when I land. Will have to
be up at 4:45 A.M.

Patton specified the regulations to govern the conduct of the
brigade and of the attached units and casuals en route to the port
of embarkation. All men, formed in units, were to be at the train
siding at Bourg at certain designated hours. Uniform for officers
was to consist of overseas cap, overcoat or trench coat, side arms
(pistol) on Sam Browne belt, gas mask, trench helmet, and hand
baggage. Uniform for enlisted men was to be overseas cap, overcoat, field equipment, trench helmet on pack, gas mask. Guards
were to be posted to keep the men on the train. There would be
four kitchen cars and three days' travel rations. Men were not to
ride on the roofs of the railroad cars or sit in the doors with their
feet hanging out. All personnel were to maintain a soldierly appearance

and will not appear at the doors or windows of cars or on the station platform unless their uniforms are buttoned throughout. The efficiency of the Command is judged by its soldierly appearance. All men and Officers will make special efforts to remain clean and neat. Military courtesies will be strictly observed. No liquor of any kind, including beers and light wines will be allowed on the train . . . All men must be instructed to guard against Venereal Desease by abstinence and when they have failed to do so by prompt use of the Government Propholaxis.

Diary

February 26: Got word at 4 A.M. that train would not be in until 8 A.M. Notified battalions. Train got in at 11 A.M. Morale very bad. Got loaded and left at 1:45 P.M. Two cars jumped track and it took 3 hours to put them on. Fed men. Got to Langres at 6 P.M. put on second coach. 30 officers 1470 men. 37 baggage cars, 36 American 1 French. Two 2d class coaches for officers.

February 27: On train all day. Two men missed train. Passed Lyons. Everything nice. Men very well behaved. Good food. Made men keep buttoned up and neat. Ate sandwitches and had a nice time. Weather fine and rather clear.

February 28: Arrived Marseille at 12:30 P.M. Met at once by R.T.O. [Railroad Transportation Officer] who told us just what to do. Found that we were to sail on S.S. Patria next day. Held vermin and I.G. [Inspector General] inspection of men at once finishing at 8 P.M. Adjutants worked on rolls all night. I went to bed at 4:30 A.M. and got up at 6:00 A.M.

Telegram, Harbord to GSP, Jr. (at Marseilles), February 27, 1919

Letter received good bye good luck go to see Mrs. Harbord at sixteen sixteen twenty first street Washington.

The authorities at Base Number 6 were efficient and polite. They directed officers and men to proceed to the Marseilles Breakwater in a column of twos on March 1 for embarkation aboard the SS *Patria*—65 officers and 1475 men of the 304th Tank Brigade, plus five casual companies, totaling altogether 71 officers and 2010 men. Barracks and tents vacated were to be thoroughly policed and cleaned one hour before departure.

A board of officers convened by the base commander inspected the *Patria*, due to sail March 1 from Marseilles via Gibraltar with a crew of 200. It had a capacity for 150 officers in first class, 204 enlisted men in second class, and 1749 in third class—2103 in all. Patton was designated the commanding officer of all the troops sailing and would be responsible for discipline aboard ship and for compliance with regulations.

Diary

March 1 (Saturday): Went to Boat with Lt. Bowes & Simmons at 7:45. Went over entire boat and found it very clean and well appointed. Quarters for men excellent. Mix up on state room. I lost mine to Mr. Moore a Mason 33°. Supposed to sail at 6 P.M. failed to do so account of strike of crew. Tried to get mess Sgt. Allenby on board but could not do it account passport.

The men were aboard ship by 10 A.M., a record, for they had been at the base camp only fourteen hours. The base commander told Patton that his contingent was the best disciplined unit he had seen pass through.

Although Patton would not know it until much later, he was awarded the Distinguished Service Medal that General Smith had recommended—for

exceptionally meritorious and distinguished services . . . energy and sound judgment . . . very valuable service in his organization and direction of the Tank Center at the Army Schools at Langres. In the employment of Tank Corps troops in combat, he displayed high military attainments, zeal and marked adaptibility in a form of warfare comparatively new to the American Army.

Diary

March 2: Captain told me we would know at noon when we could sail. Put one man on shore with fever 103°. Arranged bed space for men and had a lot of bother account of worthless officers. Food for men good.

March 3: Had a good deal of difficulty getting men straightened out in quarters. Boat very steady and comfortable. Sea perfectly quiet and weather warm.

March 4: Reached Gibraltar at 8:30. Let most of officers and 150 men go on shore. Lot of Bum boats came and sold brandy. Men got drunk and we had pretty bad time. Found over 40 quarts on board. Some officers arranged to go to Tangier on mail boat.

While the ship took on coal, Spanish entrepreneurs sold the soldiers bottles of brandy hidden in baskets of oranges. Eight men became very drunk.

Letter, Beatrice to Mr. Patton, March 4, 1919
Here are the two letters from Georgie for which we have been waiting [with respect to Nita and General Pershing]. Don't worry, we are not going to do anything about it at all until this Roman business is settled [there was a possibility of Mr. Patton's becoming ambassador to Italy], as it doubtless will be soon, one way or the other. *Don't* write Nita to break it off.

I have just seen Mr. Hammond & this is the situation. [Thomas Nelson] Page is anxious to get out as soon as he can & the question of the appointment will presumably be settled as soon as Wilson lands on the other side. Vance McCormick, now in Italy is believed not to want it. Your only chance *not* to get it is that [Colonel Edward M.] House may have committed himself to another man. If not, you are sure to get it. Walsh is doing all he can & Mr. H[ammond] all *he* can & he says your being here [in Washington] would make no difference at all. If you are offered the job you will have to decide at once & you may get the offer *quite* soon. Mr. H. has been through the figuring end of it exhaustively with one of the secretaries of the last three ambassadors (Page inc[luded]) & he says that, to live as you would want to you would spend about $30,000 yearly outside your salary. Now this would be for 2 years only. Mr. H. says that, at this period of the world's history he would think it worth while to make great sacrifices to take the position.

Now, if you go to Rome: it will be: 1) The best thing the

country could do for itself. 2) Great for Italy. 3) Just what you deserve. 4) Would make Aunt Ruth [Mrs. Patton] proud & glad. 5) Might make a difference in G's whole future. 6) G. & I would see one another a lot & I would love it. 7) Just what I've always wanted for the babies. 8) Last & most important right now—the most dignified way for Nita to go abroad & the only thing extraordinary enough to put her back on her feet if the worst should happen. *And* would make *some* impression on John [Pershing].

You will have to decide quickly when you get the offer & I hope for all our sakes that you will take it.

I should not mention the financial side if I did not feel that that would do much to decide you. But it would be only fair for us to halve the bills & it would *not* be fair for you to turn it down for that reason. Its all in the family & I would like to have some fun of that sort & may never have another chance. And it would make a difference in G's whole future.

As for Nita—you can see by these letters what it would mean to her: a dignified, suitable way of seeing John again, or a great diversion if she doesn't marry. Uncle George, you *couldn't* turn it down? & it would make us all so happy . . .

[P.S.] I asked Mr. H. what "sacrifices" he would be willing to make in your shoes. He said "*any* sacrifice of personal wishes or comfort for the time being. I would borrow money on my securities."

Diary

March 5: I went on shore [at Gibraltar] and called on Naval C.O. Went up rock. Place could be taken by Synide [cyanide] shells shot on face of cliff so that drainage could poison water. Command of sea would be necessary. Nothing in town to see or buy. Maj. Benson shot at Bum boats to keep them off. I will throw coal at them in the morning.

He explained later: "we fired at the water near them [the Spanish sellers of brandy] and they left. It was safe to fire as they had no recourse at law being without license [to sell fruits]."

March 6: Let 172 men go on shore and got very nearvous for fear that they would not come back. All returned. 3 men got mumps. We left Gibraltar at 7 P.M. I hope nothing stops

us until we get in. Hardly any young officers can be trusted
to obey orders.

March 7: Weather very rough and nearly all the men sick.
I had to leave the table at noon and was sick but got up at
3:30 and inspected the ship. About half the men were able to
eat supper. I was very nearvous and tired when we left Gib
and drank a quart of claret for supper. This I think upset my
stomach. Also I got up too late for breakfast and ate candy
instead.

March 8: Weather fine and bright. Had fire drill that is
boat drill at 2:30. The crowding is such that in case of a real
alarm there would be trouble. Saw soldier eating a huge sand-
witch at 9 A.M. Asked him if he had had breakfast. He said
yes but not yesterday. Got Wireless that one man had been
left at Gib. Felt strange not to have to write B a letter daily.

March 10: men sick on food in 3d class but believe it
due to fact that they are not hungry as they do no work.

March 12: Found worms in the beans of the men.

March 13: Felt very worthless all day until 4:30 when I
did some exercises and climbed a stay on the smoke stack.
This made me feel better.

March 15: Mens meat full of worms so we had to stop it.
Some of men were mad. Menu has been Meat-maceroni,
bread, coffee & jam or marmelaid. I would like to know what
is in the future and where I will be ordered. This will be the
10th time I have had to start fresh.

Typed Statement, aboard S.S. Patria, March 16, 1919
A testimonial of personal affection for Colonel Patton for
his energy, his leadership, his courage, his constant attention
to the welfare of his officers and men, his understanding and
foresight, his sterling sense of justice and fair-play.
[signed by Major Sereno E. Brett, Major C. C. Benson,
and 48 other officers.]

Diary
March 16 (Sunday): All work on reports completed at
noon. Passed fire Island light ship at 3:30 P.M. Ambrose

Channel at 6 P.M. Capt. Murray came on board with instructions. The end of a perfect war. Fini.

The ship docked on March 17, a misty day, at the foot of 31st Street, Brooklyn. Welcoming boats had dignitaries and bands of music.

Form letter, 2d Captain S.S. Patria *to Commanding Officer of Troops (Patton), March 17, 1919*
    This is to certify that this ship has been left in proper state of police [cleanliness].

The return home of the tankers created a minor sensation, and there were many news stories about the men and their machines.
    There was also a somewhat unpleasant incident, an expression of dissidence among some members of Patton's contingent. According to the New York *Tribune's* headline: "Troops Spurn Hylan-Hearst Welcome Body—Protest Signed by 500 on the Patria Tossed to Committee on Police Boat—'Take That to Mayor' [Hylan]—Returning Tank Fighters Silent as City Officials Greet them with Gifts."
    The story read:

Soon after the midday meal was finished on Saturday, when the troopship Patria, from Marseilles, was some five hundred miles east of Sandy Hook, 40 officers and 450 men of the homecoming 304th Brigade of Heavy Tanks got together and prepared resolutions on William Randolph Hearst.
    This tank organization, which had "treated 'em rough" throughout their assault on the Hindenburg Line, had had many informal discussions during the voyage concerning the position Mr. Hearst occupies on the reception committee. They decided that they would express their indignation to Mayor Hylan as soon as the brigade came ashore . . .
    [The resolution drafted and signed aboard the *Patria* read] We the undersigned officers, noncommissioned officers and enlisted men registered our unqualified disapproval of the designation of William Randolph Hearst as a member of a committee formed for the purpose of welcoming members of the American expeditionary force returning to the United

States. The protest is registered because of the conviction that he has proved himself to be un-American, pro-German and inhumanitarian, and therefore totally unfit for membership on a committee of the above character.

. . . Colonel George Smith Patton, jr., an officer of the regular army, whose home is in San Gabriel, California, did not sign the document. It was said that as an army officer in command of troops he did not feel that it was proper for him to align himself with any factional protest.

This was not what he wrote Pershing about a week later. Unknown to Patton, he told Pershing, some men had composed a round-robin letter which they threw into one of the boats. The message said that they wanted no welcome from Mr. Hearst. "I knew nothing of it until I saw it in the papers next day. I was very worried but so far I have not been tried [by court-martial] or any thing."

He was still upset when he wrote to his father on April 1.

I was very much worried about that foolish round robin about Mr. Hearst which some of my men sent.

I knew nothing about it until I read it in the papers. Of course had I had any idea what they were [up] to I would have prevented it. It was most uncalled for and ungrateful. My idea is that it was gotten up by a small minority of the men who had it in for me on account of my severe discipline and who took that means of getting even.

None of the regular officers on the ship had heard a word of it.

I heard some reserve officers talking about Hearst and I told them that what ever their opinion they ought to be gentlemen enough to appreciate what Hearst was now doing for the returning soldiers and not critacize him. They said they would do nothing and I thought no more about it, but as I said some fools must have heard them and done it to get me in trouble.

As to the poem I don't know where it came from.

I hope I don't get hit for something of which I was perfectly inoscent.

The poem to which he referred was doggerel, several verses, each ending with the line "For the hand that shook Bernstorff's [the former German ambassador to the United States] will never shake mine."

By then the affair was all but forgotten. What everyone remembered was the delight to be home. What everyone recalled was the joy on the faces of those who welcomed them.

Patton was surrounded by newspaper reporters, and he loved the attention. The New York Evening *Mail* quoted him as having said: "The tank is only used in extreme cases of stubborn resistance. They are the natural answer to the machine gun, and as far as warfare is concerned, have come to stay just as much as the airplanes have."

The New York *World* quoted Patton as saying: "I was wounded on Sept. 26 in the Argonne, while on foot with the tanks. Lying there, helpless, I was picked up bodily by Private Joseph Angelo of Camden, New Jersey, who dropped me into a shell hole. He stuck by me for two hours while I continued to direct operations from that shell hole."

The New York Morning *Sun*, after telling how Patton chained three tanks together and brought them out of a shell hole where they had been embedded, quoted him as saying that tanks "have come to stay on land just as the airplane has come to stay in the clouds and below them."

The New York *Herald* ran a story headlined "Colonel Patton Tells How Big Machines by Hundreds Attacked the Germans" devoted more than half of the coverage to him, featured his photograph, described his battlefield exploit, mentioned the Distinguished Service Cross, and noted that he had "also been cited by the French for the Croix de Guerre."

The Washington *Post* gave Patton prominence. The Los Angeles *Times* reported: "Southland Man is Back a Hero. Col. Patton Wounded in Tank Action in Argonne. San Gabriel Officer's Gallantry Wins Recognition." The Los Angeles *Herald*: "Victory of Tanks is Described by Patton—L.A. Colonel Tells How Argonne and St. Mihiel Battles were Won." Patton had supposedly said: "The American soldiers were the best equipped and best rationed in Europe, and, while other nations may produce as good fighters, they are not superior." The Richmond *Times-Dispatch* told all of its story in the headline: "Returned Officer Tells of Exploits of Tanks—Col George Smith Patton on Foot Led Huge Juggernauts Through Argonne Forest. Has D.S.C. and Wound Stripe—Believes Steel Machines will Prove as Useful as Airplanes in Future Wars."

The marvelous publicity culminated in a letter Patton received several days later:

> Dear Sir—I shall greatly appreciate it if you will permit me to have your photograph together with the details of the exploits which won you citations, for the Sunset Magazine [which had a large circulation among Californians]. They take excellent care of photographs and it will be returned to you in good condition.
>
> Thanking you for the courtesy of an early reply, I am, Very truly yours.

Telegram, Aunt Nannie (New York) to Mr. Patton (Pasadena), March 17, 1919
George landed today at noon Gone to Camp Mills for few days Beatrice met him and says he looks well and happy.

IX

The Immediate
Postwar Years

"People seem to be trying to put the army on the bum as hard as they can."

CHAPTER 35

Camp Meade

"War is the only place where a man realy lives."

THE SPRING AND SUMMER of 1919 were a time of transition and adjustment for Patton. The war and the glory were behind him, although there would be moments when he relived the past. The peacetime army posed problems for his own future career—what would the role of tanks be in the postwar military establishment and should he remain with the Tank Corps or return to the cavalry?

After a week at Camp Mills, Long Island, Patton traveled with the tank brigade to Camp George G. Meade, Maryland. Located between Baltimore and Washington and close to both cities, the camp was particularly convenient for the Pattons, for Beatrice had established a home in Washington.

At the Benjamin Franklin Cantonment, which was the tank part of the post, troops were demobilized. The AEF Tank Corps, drastically reduced in size, was then merged with its U.S. counterpart, including elements moved from Camp Colt, Pennsylvania, to Camp Meade.

With Rockenbach remaining in France, the tankers came under Colonel Welborn, who had offices in Washington, and Colonel W. H. Clopton, Jr., the post commander who acted as Welborn's deputy. Next in rank to them was Mitchell, who commanded the heavy tanks. Then in order of seniority came Patton, who commanded the light tanks.

Writing to Pershing and warning him "there is nothing important in the letter so don't bother to read it unless you have time," Patton passed along some observations of how Americans regarded

Pershing. "Your picture and statues of you—all very bad—are in the store windowes." At the Hippodrome Theater in New York, moving pictures showed Theodore Roosevelt, President Wilson, and Pershing. "T.R. got most applause," Patton candidly reported, "you next, and Mr. W [was] a poor third." St. Mihiel had "made you solid with the people." His mother and sister were coming that afternoon to see Patton for the first time. "Please excuse the frankness of this letter. It is designed to show you how things are here . . . so far no other man in the sense you were a man had yet been born."

A few days later, after repeating his injunction—"There is nothing important in this letter, so dont read it if you are busy"— Patton talked about a combined recruiting and Liberty Loan drive that he found "a most week kneed performance." "A lot of flannel mouthed officers" had sought to sell re-enlistment on the advantages of travel, vocational training, and fun in the peacetime Army. "The whole thing was peculiarly norsiating to me as I believe in compulsory service as a national duty." He assured Pershing that "every one I have seen has it in for Gen. M. [Peyton March]," who was Pershing's arch rival. Patton was concerned about the development of a split between Regular officers who had served abroad during the war and those who were kept at home. He liked the new mathematical rating scale for officers.

And finally, he had been to West Point and talked with the Superintendent, who mentioned public pressure to shorten the course at the Military Academy. Patton hoped that could be resisted.

> What West Point makes is a soul. We the graduates are efficient because we can't help it. We dont run away because we are a lot more afraid of our own conscience than we are of the enemy. The Soul cannot be built in on[e] or two years. It would be much better to have several West Points [if the Army needed more Regular officers].

He added that his mother and sister were staying with him and were quite well, then concluded:

I went to a war Play last night and the noise of the shells and the machine guns made me feel very homesick. War is the only place where a man realy lives.

Probably stimulated by his remark that he believed in "compulsory service as a national duty," Patton wrote a paper headed "Notes on the Desirability of Universal Service." Perhaps he delivered it as a talk to officers on post or to townspeople near Camp Meade. It stated in part:

It is the common experience of mankind that in moments of great excitement the conscious mental processes of the brain no longer operate. All actions are subconscious—the result of habits. Troops whose training and discipline depend on conscious thought become helpless crowds in battle. To send forth such men is murder. Hence, in creating an Army, we must strive at the production of soldiers so trained that in the midst of battle they will still function . . .

[A soldier] is in the midst of thousands of shells and hundreds of corpses . . . He is tired, in a strange environment, hungry and for days has been working himself up more or less to a nervous state in the expectation of battle and possible death. The training which will produce habit and that will operate under such circumstances must assuredly be longer and more intense than the practice necessary to you as a motorist . . .

He may learn his multifarious duties in three or four months . . . but it takes innumerable repetitions, or soaking in the idea for a long time, at least a year, before he can perform them without thought. Since he can not think in the midst of battle he is worthless as a soldier until he has reached this state . . .

The salute . . . is the mark of brotherhood, the cryptic hand shake exchanged between members of the most patriotic of societies—the Army . . .

The soldier at attention, saluting, is putting himself in the same frame of mind as the [football] player—alert, on his toes, receptive.

In battle the officers are the quarterbacks, the men the disciplined team on their toes, with that lightning response to orders which means victory, and the lack of which means death and defeat, which is worse.

Now we come to the greatest of all reasons for universal service, namely, the fact that it makes patriots . . . The man who has served a year with sweat and some discomfort feels that truly he has a part in his country, that of a truth it is his —and he is a patriot. . . .

At the end of his year of service the boy emerges a man, courteous, considerate, healthy, and moral. To get these results in a democratic way service must be absolutely universal. There is some phase in the vast mechanism of the Army where all may serve; the lame, the halt, the weak, and even the blind . . . the year he serves his country and renders it great and sound . . . can only be looked upon as a year well spent.

Letter, GSP, Jr., to his father, April 1, 1919

I am very much ashamed not to have written before, but being in America has upset my habits to such an extent that I have neglected to do so. I have thought of you all the time and am most anxious to see you . . .

Mama and Nita seem fine. Beatrice is much better. I hope to get a leave soon but things are so upset that I can't fix a date.

With much love your devoted son.

Letter, GSP, Jr., to his father, April 1, 1919

I am in favor of Nita's going to england as that will finally settle the matter one way or another.

For the present I shall stay in the Tank Corps as I will thus probably keep my rank and besides I owe it to the Corps. Also if I went to the cavalry now I should find my self on the border at once. As I have no friends over here.

There is a good chance of my getting detailed in Washington to write a Tank Drill regulations. This would be fine for Beat and for me. Also I have been away from the "flesh pots" so long that I rather yearn for a bath tub and warm water to shave.

I bought a Pierce Arrow automobile as I can afford it and believe in enjoying my self between wars.

Camp Mead[e] is only an hour and a quarter from Washington by trolley or auto so even if I stay here it is not bad.

If I get the Detail on the Drill regulations I shall not be able to take a leave until that is over. If I don't I might get a leave pretty soon but things are too unsettled to say yet.

Patton was flattered to receive a letter from a board of officers in France who canvassed his opinions on cavalry tactics, armament, and organization, and its future role in warfare. He replied at once, explaining: "This paper did not reach me until I had returned to the U.S. As I am deeply interested, I am taking the liberty of answering."

His response was oriented toward the use of cavalry in a future war in Mexico and concerned with gaining "great fire power and mobility." He recommended that the newly developed air-cooled machine gun replace the water-cooled barrel, that the number of automatic rifles in a cavalry division be increased drastically, that the Stokes mortar be added to cavalry squadrons, and that the saber be retained to stimulate "morale and dash. It is worth its weight." He hoped that cavalry would concentrate its operations in terrain impassable to armored cars and tanks and that the troop (or company) would be expanded

to 5 officers and 150 men so as to ensure getting 100 men into battle . . . Our pre-war theories were correct but more emphasis must be placed on daring and reckless bravery . . . Cavalry must attack always and not dig in and howl for help. Cavalry is an arm of bluff and must make that bluff good . . . The [mounted] attack must be delivered with more emphasis on speed and violence than on cohesion. . . .

The killing or wounding of a few men and officers at drill [or training] should not be regarded as a national calamity . . .

In my opinion the prompt decision is the essence of training, for more losses will occur while seeking a perfect solution than will occur by using an inferior solution promptly.

Somewhat significantly, for it betrayed his indecision over his own future place in the Army, he signed his paper "Col. Tank Corps (Maj. Cav.)."

While still in France, Patton had filled out a card to indicate: 1) the branch of service in which he preferred to serve, and 2) the special duty he desired within that branch. Somewhat boyishly, he had put down: 1) "Tank Corps," 2) "Fighting."

Now he filled out a more detailed "Personal Report" to set forth his professional qualifications and his wishes for future duties. He indicated that he spoke French fluently and Spanish slightly, read French rapidly and Spanish slowly. He had special knowledge of the sword, horsemanship, gas engines, and tractors (tanks). He was a graduate of the Army General Staff College at Langres, France. He was 6 feet 1 inch in height and 170 pounds in weight. He had achieved expert rating in the rifle and pistol in 1913—"No oppertunity to fire [for scores] since."

Perhaps to avoid the necessity of choosing between the tanks and the cavalry, he said he preferred duty as a military attaché in London or, even more, as a student at the Army School of the Line at Leavenworth, Kansas.

. . .

Sometime in April Patton drove, probably in his new Pierce-Arrow, to Camden, New Jersey, where Joe Angelo lived, and listened without interrupting, no doubt amused but not daring to show it, as Angelo told newsmen in his hometown how Angelo had won the Distinguished Service Cross. The newspaper featured the story under the headlines "Camden Soldier Called Bravest Man in the Army—Tank Commander Lauds Boy who Saved His Life when Wounded."

Angelo's recollections were somewhat hazy. He said he had gone over the top at 6:30 with Patton and 15 men and 2 first lieutenants, along with 150 tanks moving through a dense fog. Angelo walked beside Patton until they reached a crossroads, where Patton told him to watch for Germans.

Two American infantrymen came along, and Angelo asked what they were doing.

"Just mopping up," they answered.

"Well," Angelo said, "if you don't get out of here, you will get mopped up. The Germans are pouring plenty of lead over our way."

The infantrymen took shelter in a shack nearby. Moments later, a shell struck the building and blew it to "atoms."

Angelo saw two German machine gunners behind a bush. They fired at him. He returned the fire and killed one. "The other one," he said, "beat it."

Patton had gone ahead, and he reappeared on top of a knoll and shouted, "Joe, is that you shooting down there?"

Almost immediately, Angelo "thought sure hell had broken loose." Bullets were flying all around.

"Come on," Patton yelled, "we'll clean out those nests."

Angelo followed him up the hill. Patton was sore because the infantry had not taken care of the enemy machine guns. It was their job.

Then Patton saw that several tanks were not moving. He sent Angelo to see Captain English and find out why. Angelo discovered that the tanks were stuck in the mud.

Patton went to the tanks, almost hub deep in the mud, grabbed a shovel, and began digging the tanks free. Other men and Angelo began to dig. German fire started to fall in, but they got the tanks moving and over the hill.

When Patton found some infantrymen wandering around without officers, he rounded them up. He told Angelo to take about 15 riflemen and clear out the machine guns.

Angelo did so but soon returned. "They have all been killed," he told Patton.

"My God!" Patton said. "They are not all gone?"

Yes, Angelo said, they were all killed by machine gun fire.

We'll clean out the machine gun nests ourselves, Patton said.

"I thought the Colonel had gone mad and grabbed him. He grabbed me by the hair and shook me to my senses. Then I followed him. We went about 20 yards and the colonel fell with a bullet in his thigh."

Angelo assisted Patton into a shell hole and bandaged his wound.

Patton passed out. He revived two hours later. He told Angelo to find Major Sereno Brett and tell him to assume command of the Tank Corps. Angelo did so, then returned to Patton.

Two American tanks and a French tank came up and camped about 20 yards from their hole.

"Jump out there," Patton ordered Angelo, "and scatter those tanks or they will be blown up."

Angelo rushed out and told them to do so. The American tanks got away, but the French tank was shot to pieces.

Patton told Angelo to take a tank and wipe out the machine gun nests. Angelo did so.

Then he ordered four infantrymen passing by to carry Patton to the rear.

Angelo, the newspaper stated, had been employed at the Du Pont powder works before the war.

In mid-April, together with Lieutenant Colonel James E. Ware and Majors Viner and Sasse, Patton reported to Welborn in Washington to formulate tank regulations and prepare a drill manual and a course of instruction for the tankers. Taking Patton's place as commander of the Tank Corps at Camp Meade until Clopton returned from leave was Lieutenant Colonel Dwight D. Eisenhower.

The Tank Board worked for a month in Washington on the basic doctrine that would shape the training and employment of tank units. Then, augmented by Mitchell, the board members proceeded to the Rock Island Arsenal, Illinois, and to the Springfield Armory, Massachusetts, to inspect Tank Corps matériel in development and production.

Letter, GSP, Jr. (Hotel Blackhawk, Davenport, Iowa), to his father, June 2, 1919

I am out here with the rest of the Board looking at the Mark VIII Tank. It works much better than we thought. I went to Peoria, Ill. Saturday to see the Holt factory and had a nice time though I felt sick all the time. When I got here I went to a Dr. and he told me I had Chicken Pox. I was delighted to find that I was still young enough to have it. He says that I am practically over it but had best stay here a day

or two to get looking decent again. I am all swelled up
now . . .
   Nita must be over [in England] by this time and things
always come out for the best. Even the Pox is giving me a
good rest.

*GSP, Jr., Poem, "Written while I had the chicken pox, Daven
port, Iowa, 1919"*

A Soldiers Burial

Not midst the chanting of the Requiem Hymn
Nor with the solemn ritual of prayer
'Neath misty shadows from the oriel glass
And dreamy perfume of the incensed air
Was he interred.

But in the subtle stillness after fight,
In the half light between the night and day,
We dragged his body, all besmeared with mud,
And dropped it, clod-like, back into the clay.

Yet who shall say that he was not content,
Or missed the priest, or drone of chanting choir,
He, who had heard all day the Battle Hymn
Sung on all sides by thousand throats of fire?

What painted glass can lovelier shadows cast
Than those the Western skys shall ever shed,
While mingled with its light, Red Battle's Sun
Completes in magic colors o'er our dead
The flag for which they died.

   Later that month Patton wrote Pershing to suggest that he
consider running for President. Patton had recently been in Chicago, where Leonard Wood was being boomed for the presidency
on the basis of his great organizational ability. What about you?
Patton asked. How about Pershing's great organizational ability
as demonstrated in the Philippines, in Mexico, and in France?
"The last time I was with you I told you that you did not advertise
[yourself] enough. I respectfully repeat that statement. There are
too many others who are using it to hurt you."
   Pershing was, obviously, pleased by Patton's remarks. When he

replied, he said he thought that all presidential booms were premature. It was better, he believed, to wait and see what the people wanted, better too because the Army required a complete reorganization in terms of the lessons of the Great War, and this Pershing intended to carry out.

He informed Patton that he had seen his sister Ann in England recently at the Keith Merrills', Beatrice's sister and her husband. They had all had a pleasant visit. Nita was very keen on her work, though perhaps somewhat lonesome. Her plans, Pershing said, were indefinite, and so were his.

The Holt Manufacturing Company of Peoria, Illinois, proudly advised Patton that a five-ton caterpillar tractor had gained the summit of Pike's Peak despite fifteen-foot snow drifts during the last two hours of its climb.

Perhaps stirred by this feat, which foreshadowed remarkable improvements in automotive and tank designs, Patton wrote a formal letter asking to be sent as a student to the School of the Line at Fort Leavenworth that September.

Welborn endorsed his request favorably, saying that he considered Patton especially fitted for the course of study. He was one of the best informed officers on the operations of tanks, and he would prove particularly valuable in helping to formulate the general course of instruction.

No action was taken.

Early in July, Patton showed his concern over former noncommissioned officers who had been commissioned during the war, who were known as Class III officers, and who were about to be discharged from the Army. Patton was indignant because separation from the Army would "work an injustice on many efficient men and at the same time result in a great loss to the service." The former enlisted Regulars had proved their merit as instructors in peace and as commanders in battle, had learned no other profession, had families for whom they had provided by "blood and sweat." Now that the war was won, they were given solely the opportunity to re-enlist as privates or noncoms if they wished to practice their profession. Many would probably depart the military service altogether, and that would be a real loss to the Army, for they were all well disciplined and highly trained, and all of them had performed

> always in a most efficient and loyal manner . . . This letter is submitted in the hope that it will aid in calling attention to the condition of so many fine officers and that something may be done to hold them as temporary officers, perhaps with the loss of one grade each, until such time as a definite policy may properly place them.

He wrote much the same thing informally to Harbord, who was again Pershing's chief of staff. Patton hoped that Pershing could do something to safeguard the commissioned grades of former noncommissioned officers until legislation could provide some way for them to remain on duty.

Patton told Harbord that he had gone to the War Department and visited seven offices. Each passed the buck until someone in the seventh office referred him to the office where he had started—

> and I blew up. On this they said that they would consider it [Patton's suggestion] . . . I talk like I was a class three officer My self but it is only due to the old dictom that the good soldier should look out for his horses and men.

Harbord passed Patton's letter to Pershing, but nothing could be done. The country was interested in retrenchment and economy after the exertion and expense of the war.

Soon after Patton's departure from France, Rockenbach had rated him according to the new mathematical scale and in July Patton's new superiors did so. His capacities and performances were scored as follows:

	Physical Condition	Intelligence	Leadership	Character	General Value to Service	Total
Rockenbach	12	12	15	14	32	85
Welborn	14	12	15	14	32	87
Clopton	13	14	14	15	35	91

The perfect officer, theoretically nonexistent, would accumu-late 15 points in the four personal categories and 40 for general value, giving a total of 100.

Requesting leave for 45 days, Patton listed these reasons to justify the fifteen days beyond the normal leave period: first, while he had been in France, Catalina Island, of which he was part owner, was sold; his share of the sale, "which is a fair sum," had never been invested, and he wished to do so; second, in 1915, he had started a farm in California to raise thoroughbred horses; he now had nineteen, many of which he had never seen. One month's leave, of which ten days would be consumed by travel, would give him insufficient time for these concerns.

Welborn approved Patton's request, and so did the Adjutant General.

Letter, GSP, Jr., to Aunt Nannie, July 11, 1919
Everyone will be back to their old rank on or before Sept. 30, 1919. So if I want to show off as a colonel I had best get home before that time . . .

It is very stupid sitting around. Doing nothing. I hope Ma does not break her neck in her Electric [auto] as that would be a sad fate. Monday Beatrice ran into a truck with the Frank-lin and busted Off the lights and the bumper but did no other harm. It made her very mad especially as it was her own fault but it might have been much worse.

Writing Rockenbach about the men who had been recom-mended for awards but who had failed to receive them because their exploits were deemed insufficiently meritorious for the the decoration, Patton said:

I do not believe however that any officer of the Brigade would recommend men unless they had shown merit above the ordinary. It has therefore occurred to Major Brett and myself that it might be possible for you to get out a general order from Headquarters Tank Corps, mentioning these men by name and saying something about their meritorious serv-ice, the idea being that the possession of such an order would enable each man specifically named therein to wear one silver star on his victory medal. I believe that you will agree with me that this is the least that can be done for these men. Major Brett just at present is taking the trip across the continent with some motor trucks trying to recruit men for the TC.

Letter, GSP, Jr., to his father, July 12, 1919

I just received a letter from Gen. H. A. Smith saying that he had just heard that I had been given the D.S.M. for which he had recommended me last August. If he is correctly informed as must be the case I am delighted as the number of people with both [D.S.C. and D.S.M.] medals is very limited.

I am inclosing a draft for $1500.00 which is the rest of the amount I owe you on that Benson loan. I got it from the sale of the Packard to the Government in France.

I got the tickets today to leave here on the night of Friday the 18th. we should arrive [in Los Angeles] 22 or 23 I don't know which. We leave Chicago on the limited Santa Fe Saturday night.

I was only able to get a months leave but Col. Welborne is letting me fudge about six days three each way. Besides I shall telegraph for an extension. Still a month is better than nothing . . .

Beatrice is having her Picture Painted so is having a fine time.

Letter, GSP, Jr., to his father, July 17, 1919

Inclosed is a copy of my citation for the D.S.M. So far as I know the only other man with the two decorations is Gen. McArthur, of course there are probably others but in a very limited quantity.

I inclose also two poems which I wrote at speed but which have the unusual merit so far as my poems are concerned of being short.

We leave tomorrow evening [for California].

The citation, issued by GHQ AEF on June 16, 1919, read as follows:

Under the provisions of Cablegram No. 2830, received from the War Department, March 1st, 1919, the Commander-in-Chief, in the name of the President, has awarded the *Distinguished Service Medal* to you for exceptionally meritorious and distinguished service . . .

He later wrote:

Col Patton was awarded the D.S.M., and it is common knowledge that it was never earned by him but was the result of the generous and splendid manner in which the Tank Corps carried out the orders as to dress and deportment. They won the medal, fortune pinned it on him.

GSP, Jr., "My Father," 1927
Beatrice, the girls and I came home on leave in June [July] 1919. Papa and I had long talks about the war. He had followed it carefully and was a delight to talk with. He insisted that I have my picture taken . . . He was so proud of me that he embarrassed me. When he presented me to his friends he always said: "Mr. so and so you remember my son Colonel Patton."

Neither he nor mama ever made an actual fuss. The nearest I can recall is when one day Mama called me "Her hero son."

The Pasadena *Star-News* welcomed Patton home with a spread featuring the headline "U. S. Tank Leader is Home with High Army Honors," and showing a photograph of him standing beside a tank; the caption read: "Col. G. S. Patton Jr. Who Led First American Tanks into Battle Is Visiting Parents at their Home in San Marino." He had arrived in Pasadena accompanied by Mrs. Patton, and with his German war dog, Char.

The Los Angeles *Times* ran a big story headlined: "Col. Patton Designing American Super-Tank—Pasadena Hero who had Iron Cavalry in France Says Warfare with Mobile Forts is Yet in Infancy," and showed Patton standing in front of a tank. He was quoted as saying that tanks were as far behind the times as planes had been ten years earlier. He said too that he had acted as aide to the Prince of Wales who was "a very democratic young man . . . I also met King George and found him to be democratic."

He spent quite a bit of time during his vacation fishing off Santa Catalina Island.

Returning east on the train, the Santa Fe Limited, Patton wrote a poem while riding through Kansas:

Marching in Mexico

The column winds on snake like,
Through blistering, treeless spaces;
The hovering gray-black dustclouds
Tint in ghoulish shades our faces.

The sweat in muddied bubbles,
Trickles down the horses rumps;
The saddles creak, the gunboots chafe,
The swinging holster bumps.

At last the "Halt" is sounded.
The outpost trots away;
The lines of tattered pup-tents rise,—
We've marched another day.

The rolling horses raise more dust,
While from the copper skies
Like vultures, stopping on the slain,
Come multitudes of flies.

The irate cooks their rites perform
Like pixies round the blaze,
The smoking greasewood stings our eyes,
Sunscorched for countless days.

The sun dips past the western ridge,
The thin dry air grows cold.
We shiver through the freezing night,
In one thin blanket rolled.

The night wind stirs the cactus,
And sifts the sand o'er all,
The horses squeal, the sentries curse,
The lean coyotes call.

Back at Camp Meade, Patton discovered that Rockenbach was in the United States and was the new Chief of the Tank Corps, U. S. Army, replacing Welborn, who became his deputy.

A concerted effort was made throughout the Army to get official files in good order, and several of Patton's superiors submitted reports on his past performance.

Clopton, who had earlier that year cited Patton as having worked "excellently," called him "an excellent energetic ambitious officer. His only fault is his impatience when unable to pursue his work along his desired lines, thus failing to appreciate the details of team work." Clopton nevertheless judged Patton "average" in judgment and common sense, and "above average" in physical energy and endurance, attention to duty, initiative, organizational ability, and capacity for command.

Welborn, who had said that Patton's work as a board member in Washington "was well performed," wrote: "This officer is enthusiastic about any work he has to do and will accomplish results." He marked Patton "superior" in energy and endurance, as well as initiative, "above average" in his attention to duty and capacity for command, "average" in judgment, common sense, and organizational ability.

Rockenbach characterized him as "intelligent, active, and gallant. Possessing great dash and courage." He scored Patton "superior" in all categories except judgment and common sense, which were "above average." Patton had performed his duties "most excellent and gallantly," and was fitted for either staff or command assignments.

Major General J. W. McAndrew, who as commandant of schools in Langres had been Patton's superior, wrote: "Colonel Patton is an exceptionally fine soldier and has demonstrated his ability in the field. He is an unusually efficient leader of men in action, and his great usefulness lies in that direction rather than in General Staff work." McAndrew thought him "above average" in physical energy and endurance, judgment and common sense, "superior" in all other qualities. He added that Patton was best fitted for service with troops or tanks, duties he had performed "exceptionally well. The Army Tank School of the A.E.F. owes the greater part of its success to Colonel Patton Jr."

Brigadier General Harry A. Smith, who had succeeded McAndrew at Langres, wrote: "One of the strongest most active and forceful officers in the service . . . Organized and directed the Tank School in a superior manner." He gave Patton "superior" in all categories. He added, "One of the strong officers in the Army." Pershing marked him as "an able officer especially adapted for active field work." Patton was "superior" in physical energy and endurance, attention to duty, initiative, organizational ability, and capacity for command; "above average" in judgment and common sense.

These testimonials were flattering and merited, but they seemed to belong to a bygone age, for, in September 1919, Patton was appointed a member of a board of officers, headed by Mitchell, to investigate into and report upon ordnance equipment for tanks. It was hardly thrilling work, but Patton, as usual, threw himself wholeheartedly into it. The language of the board's proceedings, findings, and conclusions indicated that Patton took a lively part in and probably dominated the discussions.

At one meeting, for example, the board suggested putting a lock on tanks, changing the type of grease cup on the pump, shortening the handle of the gearshift by six inches; also "Modify gear shift mechanism so that gears can be shifted into proper place without driver looking at them."

If this was tedious, it was necessary, for Patton was convinced that the tanks had to be brought out of their mechanical infancy and fashioned into reliable and hard-hitting instruments of warfare.

Occasionally, there were interesting exercises. For example:

Letter, GSP, Jr., Commanding Officer, 304th Tank Brigade, to the Chief of the Tank Corps, September 20, 1919
The recent operation, conducted by this Brigade, of moving 27 tanks by trailer from Campe Meade to Washington and return has I believe finally demonstrated the unsuitability of this form of transportation.

The move was 31 miles each way, 23 miles of this distance was over concrete boulevard and city streets. The shortest time for either leg of the trip was six hours. The longest was fourteen hours going and twenty-three hours returning.

There were seven accidents of a serious nature. Two cupling poles were broken. Three trucks were ditched or wrecked by the trailers running into their rear ends. Two trailers were badly ditched from side slipping. These accidents accounted for the long duration of the trip in the case of the slowest trucks and also sent two men to the hospital with serious injuries in the form of broken legs . . .

[During this march, as well as in recruiting marches, especially good roads were selected and used only by day.] In war necessity not desirability dictates the roades to be used. In my experience the roades are always bad and crowded and the marches must be made at night. Both these facts will militate still further against the efficiency of trailer transportation . . .

I desire to go on record as believing that neither truck nor trailer transportation for tanks will prove efficient except over metaled roades. For long halls or where dirt roades are to be expected railroad transportation is the only solution.

Letter, GSP, Jr., to Aunt Nannie, September 20, 1919

I was in the parade in charge of the tanks and we made a pretty good show except that one tank just missed taking down the triumphul arch . . .

We saw in the paper that Pa. had been recomended for secretary of commerce along with two other men. I do hope he gets it and accepts the job. It would be fine for him and not for long enough [meaning only until the end of the Wilson administration] to make him sick.

Beatrice and I are having a party at the Chevy Chase club to night for her cousin Beatrice Banning who is a very nice girl and quite pretty. Gen. R. [Rockenbach] is going to party and will stay all night with us.

Col. Collins is back at the war colledge as captain and I am delighted.

I am inclosing a copy of a new poem which I have written.

Letter, GSP, Jr., to the Secretary, Naval War College (through channels), September 24, 1919, subject: Naval Tactics

[It is possible that in the future tanks will combat each other.] In my opinion such an engagement will partake somewhat of the nature of a sea fight with much diminished ranges . . .

If possible I request information as to suitable maneuvers and formations for attacking a line of hostile tanks in similar original formation. Assuming that at the beginning of the fight it was known that hostile tanks were to be encountered request information as to the best original formation for the approach and for subsequent maneuvers.

How to improve the tank and how to employ it successfully in battle would occupy much of Patton's time between the two world wars. He would read a great deal, write much, and think even more. But his activities would, for the most part, be somewhat hidden. They were off-duty interests for much of the period.

While his quest for professional knowledge, his search for military perception, his desire to learn better his trade as a soldier would continue unabated, he would suffer the disappointment of frustration and even the bitterness of what must have seemed like betrayal. The Army in the 1920s and 1930s would be moribund. This would appear to him as a kind of rejection of himself and of his contributions to the art of tank warfare in the World War. Yet he never explicitly complained.

In compensation for the inertia in the Army, he would find other outlets for his energy, ambition, and drive. His fate or his destiny, he must often have thought, had deserted him. Yet he had to move on in pursuit of glory, for if that eluded him, what else would remain?

CHAPTER 36

Camp Meade: Goodbye to Tanks

"Our calling is most ancient and like all other old things it has amassed through the ages certain customs and traditions which decorate and enoble it, which render beautiful the otherwise prosaic occupation of being professional men-at-arms: killers."

VERY ACTIVE in his thinking, writing, and lecturing on tanks in the fall of 1919 and the first half of 1920, Patton was trying to establish a doctrine or methodology for their employment. He never quite managed to systematize a coherent theory, in part because he was unable to resolve satisfactorily some of the basic questions, in part because the Army failed to solve some of the fundamental problems.

If tanks were auxiliaries designed primarily to help the infantry, their functions could be classed with those of the artillery. If tanks were a separate and distinct arm capable of independent missions, they required a life of their own. If they were the mechanical equivalent of cavalry, they would best be joined to that branch of the service.

These issues, which provoked discussion among a very small coterie of American officers during the next twenty years, were never properly worked out for the U. S. Army before World War II. As a consequence, Americans made few advances in tank warfare. Even their machines—in a country where the automobile became king—remained rudimentary and primitive, primarily because the appropriations furnished by Congress for research and development were small.

In grappling with the problems of using tanks, Patton came close to creating a new and convincing technique. Despite his ardor and perception, in the end he failed—in large part because he grew persuaded that lack of funds and interest would block an imaginative approach to tank warfare and rob the Army of its capacity to advance.

Unlike Billy Mitchell in the Air Force, he was unwilling to risk his career for an idea. Unlike J. F. C. Fuller in England, whose dogged work and stringent logic, despite the discouraging obstacles thrown up by the conventional military leaders, produced tank principles that were publicized by Liddell Hart and eventually brought to life by Guderian in Germany, Patton lacked patience and forbearance. His self-discipline generated quick action and decisive movement rather than intellectual rumination and wide-ranging thought. What sharpened his insights was actually working with formations of men on the drill field and maneuver ground, as at the tank center in Bourg.

The Army between the wars would fail to provide machines and soldiers in sufficient quantity and quality to permit experimentation. Held back by the inertia around him, finding little stimulus and, finally, little reason for creative solutions, he would turn increasingly aside from the problems and look elsewhere, concealing his disappointment and frustration in a life of physical exertion.

His papers and lectures showed how near he came to enunciating an original view of tank tactics.

In September 1919, speaking on "The History, Employment and Tactics of Light Tanks," probably at Camp Meade, Patton described

> briefly the latest views on the imployment of tanks in the various phases of war. These ideas are not final as they are ever subject to changes imposed by improvements in the tanks themselves and in the means of combatting them.

Tanks could be used in purely offensive operations or in defensive warfare for counterattacks. They were simply an auxiliary arm to assist the advance of infantry. Suffering more from wear and tear than from hostile fire, they could and should be employed sparingly and only when necessary, only in decisive moments.

Tanks like all other arms must be deployed in depth . . . [to] insure the constant and uniform feeling of the front line and at the same time to have forces available to exploit to the front and flank and to repel counterattacks.

Against hostile tanks, he postulated, tanks provided the best defense. He visualized combat between machines as resembling a naval battle.

Tanks are not motorised cavalry, or armoured infantry or accompanying guns; they are tanks—a new auxiliary arm whose purpose is ever and always to facilitate the advance of that master arm the Infantry on the field of battle.

Thus, he saw tanks primarily as supporting weapons designed to assist the infantry—the mission they had performed in the World War.

A lecture entitled "The Effect of Tanks in Future Wars" took a somewhat different course.

In view of the prevalent opinion in America, that soldiers are, of all persons, the least capable of discussing military matters and that their years of special training are as naught compared to the innate military knowledge of lawyers, doctors and preachers; I am probably guilty of a great heresy in daring to discuss tanks from the viewpoint of a tank officer. I am emboldened to make the attempt, however, not from a bigoted belief in the infallibility of my own opinions, but rather in the hope that others will assail my views and that the discussion engendered will in a measure remove the tanks from the position of innocuous desuetude to which they appear to have been relegated by the general public.

The specific reasons for the present paper are that during the time which has elapsed since November 1918, I have heard not a few experienced officers poo poo the idea that tanks will ever again be used, or that if used they will have any material effect. Admitting that my intimate relation with tanks may perhaps cause me to be over sanguine as to their future, it still appears to me that to utterly disregard them is a very serious error . . .

CAMP MEADE: GOODBYE TO TANKS

The infantry are peculiarly susceptible to the attack of tanks, and are perfectly impotent to withstand them, except insofar as they are assisted by the accompanying gun. The discovery of other means for combatting tanks appears, then, to be vital to the infantry; and in view of the improved tank which we shall discuss, to the cavalry also. Artillery, while less likely to suffer from tanks, is equally interested in their development, because artillery is the weapon most dangerous to tanks, hence best adapted to combatting them.

I have neither the ability nor the desire to point out to the arms above mentioned, tactical improvements designed to assist or combat tanks. My purpose is simply to call their attention to what appears to be a lack of effort in that direction; to show some of the causes which have led to this lassitude, and to suggest, in a very sketchy manner, certain tactical uses to which tanks will be set in future wars.

. . . the lack of interest in the future employment of tanks is due primarily to the following: Comparitively few American units operated with tanks. The tank of 1918—a war production—had many grave mechanical defects. Tank warfare, the necessities of which caused the invention and construction of the tank is, never the less, peculiarly ill adapted to tank combat . . . the great mass of people are totally unaware of the great improvements made, and [in the] making, in the tank. Only those of us who doctored and nursed the grotesque warbabies of 1918 through the innumerable inherent ills of premature birth know how bad they really were, and by virtue of that same intimate association, are capable of judging how much better they are now, and how surely they will continue to improve.

. . . tanks now exist in several countries, capable of a speed across country of from twelve to fifteen miles per hour, and, on the road, up to twenty miles. They are impervious to small arms bullets, and shell fragments. They can cross trenches up to twelve feet. They have fine interior visibility, and all around fire from both cannon and machine guns, and finally they have a radius of action of more than two hundred miles, without resupply of any sort. Such machines exist, and others will surpass them. It is futile to ignore the dreadful killing capacity of such arms . . .

[Tanks] are laboring . . . from unimaginative conceptions
as to future wars. Too many people vainly fancy that future
unpleasantness will follow as sealed patterns of the World
War. With trenches, barriers and plasticine maps. With air
photographers so accurate that the latest activities of some
careless rabbit are easily discernable. Wars of preparations,
concentrations . . . of air raids, welfare workers and Big
Berthas. . . . wars with endless intrenchments and flankless
armies.

They forget that not in Asia, Africa, or America, can such
a war be staged. Because all the above luxuries depend upon
two things. First, ROADS—hundreds of good metalled roads
to carry the limitless supplies. Second, FRONTS short
enough to be continuously occupied . . .

In the continents just mentioned the scanty network of
inferior roads precludes the first; and their vast size prevents
the second . . . In such regions the fragile line of rails, . . .
the Placenta of the army, harrassed by aerial bombardment,
cavalry raids, and the vassitudes [vicissitudes] of weather will
prove inadequate to the double task of feeding the maw of
the guns and the bellies of the troops.

. . . there is strong presumption that the possible loci of
some, possibly most, future operations, will be continents
which only admit of the use of the various arms in something
very closely approximating their pre World War proportions
. . . battles will be gained by rifle, automatic rifle, and machine gun fire, unaided by artillery to any marked degree . . .
surprise and uncertainty will prevail to a degree unknown in
the World War. To guard infantry and supply columns from
the unsupported raids of fast tanks accompanying guns will
have to be distributed at short distances along the columns,
reconnaissance will have to be wide and completely new
tactics will have to be evolved and tanks will be necessary . . .

There is no belief on the part of any tank officer that the
tank has replaced in the least degree any one of the existing
arms. It is distinctly a new instrument added to the full
chorus of the Military Band. But having appeared the new
pieces composed by future generals will demand the peculiar
tone of the tank instrument for the proper rendition of their
compositions.

The tank is new and for the fulfillment of its destiny, it must remain independent. Not desiring or attempting to supplant infantry, cavalry, or artillery, it has no appetite to be absorbed by any of them . . . Absorbed . . . we become the stepchild of that arm and the incompetent assistant of either of the others . . .

The great expense of tanks precludes the possibility of their being equally distributed to all units of the other arms. Hence their hyphenation with any such arm will lead to an unequal distribution.

The [Tank] corps should be kept, as was the case among all armies in the World War, a separate entity and be assigned [in battle] by higher authority to that unit where their presence will add the most to the general good. Like the air service they are destined for a separate existance. The Tank corps grafted on Infantry, cavalry, artillery, or engineers will be like the third leg to a duck, worthless for control, for combat impotent.

As he urged the continued independence of the Tank Corps despite his view that tanks supported infantry and perhaps even cavalry, he realized that the primary problem underlying all questions of tank warfare was how to get machines that were mechanically reliable and operable for longer periods of time. Despite their size, frightening appearance, and steel construction, they were fragile creatures, breaking down at the slightest hint of trouble; and their guns were merely adaptations of infantry weapons.

Patton therefore threw himself with zeal into the deliberations and study of the Tank Corps Technical Board of Officers selected in September to consider how to improve tanks. Late that month, the board—Patton, Mitchell, Grubbs, and Sasse—traveled to Aberdeen, Maryland, and inspected ordnance equipment of various sorts, including guns specifically suitable for tanks. A few days afterward, the board recommended that the Browning tank machine gun be equipped with special ammunition designed to increase the tank's firepower.

The board met frequently in Washington through the final

months of 1919 and the early months of 1920, looking into such items as periscopes, fan belts, a handrail for the engine compartment, a bracket wheel for the sun pinion, how to prevent a clutch from sticking, the radiator, exhaust manifold, brake drum, speedometer cable, and other essential items. The members visited repair shops, studied preventive maintenance, recommended changes in the ammunition storage system, the driver's location, the engine, the eye-slits, the foot accelerator, the ground clearance of the axles, the movable roof, the pistol ports, the antiaircraft protection, the seat suspension, the small-arms ammunition racks, and the placement of tools.

Letter, GSP, Jr., to his father, September 29, 1919

What do you think of my new [writing] paper? [The sheets were headed "Colonel George S. Patton, Jr., Commanding 304th Brigade, Tank Corps."] I got it too late as the latest news is that we will all be busted on the 31 of October and repromoted according to length of commissioned service. That will make me a junior or more probably a senior captain. I believe that I shall still command the brigade but according to the latest dope that will be a skeleton. In fact people seem to be trying to put the army on the bum as hard as they can. A congressman shook his fist in the face of an officer the other day and in every way they are trying to lower our authority and reduce the discipline of the men. I told John Rogers that if he did not look out the army would strike and if they do that is the end. He had never thought of that, none of them have. But it is true just the same.

Senator Phelan Gave B and I a dinner with the Secretary Of War and two assistant secretaries of state present also two senators. It was very nice of him but we did not know till next day that we were the guests of honor.

. . . you cant make a gentleman in one generation . . .

I am inclosing for your benefit a copy of a lecture I wrote. It is the best I have written so far. Also a copy of a poem. B has sent most of my poems to a publisher to see if he thinks them worth publishing.

They will not appear under my name . . .

B and I will meet Nita [returning from Europe] so you need not worry about that.

He collected about 30 poems for publication and prefaced his work with the following disclaimer:

> Preface. These rhymes were written (over a period of years) for his own amusement by a man who having seen something of war is more impressed with the manly virtues it engenders than with the necessary and much exaggerated horrors attendant upon it. They are offered to the public in the hope that they may counteract to a degree the melancholy viewpoint so freely expatiated upon by most writers. If such slush is left unanswered it is feared that it will have a detrimental influence on the spirit of our youth, who in the cause of freedom, may again be called on to battle for the right.

When he mentioned "the right," he was hardly thinking in the political terms that owed their origin to the way the parties were seated on the right and left of the French Chamber of Deputies. He meant the moral right—God, liberty, and the United States. Yet the leaders of what came to be the parties of the right would unconsciously echo his words. Mussolini in Italy and Hitler in Germany would shout that war was the noblest activity of man. Although Patton had interest in neither their politics nor their social and economic panaceas, he agreed with this aspect of their thought and propaganda.

A typical poem in Patton's collection was entitled "Fear."

> I am that dreadful, blighting thing
> Like rat-holes to the flood
> Like rust that gnaws the faultless blade
> Like microbes to the blood.

There were several verses, all in the same vein.

Having sent off his poems—no publisher would accept them—Patton composed a series of eleven lectures for delivery to the officers of his tank brigade. "The Obligation of Being an Officer," dated October 1, revealed his thoughts on the profession of soldiering and, rather gently for Patton, laid down some ground rules prescribing conduct and etiquette, for example, what was expected of a young officer in the matters of social calls and invitations at an Army post.

. . . we, as officers of the army, are not only members of the oldest of honorable professions, but are also the modern representatives of the demi-gods and heroes of antiquity.

Back of us stretches a line of men whose acts of valor, of self-sacrifice and of service have been the theme of song and story since long before recorded history began . . .

In the days of chivalry—the golden age of our profession—knights-officers were noted as well for courtesy and gentleness of behavior, as for death-defying courage . . . From their acts of courtesy and benevolence was derived the word, now pronounced as one, Gentle Man . . . Let us be GENTLE. That is, courteous and considerate of the rights of others. Let us be MEN. That is, fearless and untiring in doing our duty as we see it.

. . . our calling is most ancient and like all other old things it has amassed through the ages certain customs and traditions which decorate and enoble it, which render beautiful the otherwise prosaic occupation of being professional men-at-arms: Killers.

. . . Some of the more common and most frequently neglected [customs] are the following.

MESSES. Officers should behave in as polite a manner at mess as they would if dining at home with the ladies of their family. They should not tell smutty stories, or swear, or pick their teeth. Above all it is the height of bad manners to refer to any lady by name at mess . . .

QUARTERS. Officers should live in a neat way, their rooms should . . . not look like the cells in an insane asylum . . .

GOSSIP. Gentlemen do not gossip. It never does any good and is unfair; many men who would never think of hitting a man from behind will nevertheless stike a deadly blow at his character from behind his back . . . It is the lowest form of sin no matter what cause prompts it.

GROWLING AND CRITICISM. The man who always whines about what he has to do usually is incapable of doing anything. The man who criticises his superior in the presence of soldiers or junior officers is disloyal to his oath as an officer and is doing more than a bolshevic to destroy discipline.

DRINKING . . . never taking a drink when on duty, or about to enter on any duty. Officers of different grades should not drink in company. . . .

MONEY MATTERS. Too much emphasis cannot be laid on the sacred nature of Government money . . . If you must borrow money go to a bank . . .

MILITARY COURTESY. . . . Toothpicks like tooth brushes are for private use. To sport one in the mouth in public smacks very much of the idea that the officer so doing is proud of being able to have bought a meal. . . . Such acts [as saluting, standing at attention, and the like] show that you are a soldier, not simply a uniformed person.

PROMPTNESS. This is always referred to as a military virtue. But like the buffalo it appears to be becoming extinct . . .

EXAMPLE . . . You have no idea how men watch you. If you grow a beard half the company will have beards . . . if you curse so will they . . .

DRESS . . . No one respects a tramp and soldiers will not respect a dirty officer. The rougher the work especially in the field the more inspiring to the men is the sight of a clean, well-shaved officer.

EDUCATION . . . Do you imagine that the successful broker spends his evenings studying the progress of the National League? Hardly. He studies the market . . . Few are born Napoleons, but any of us can be good company commanders if we study. When we are that [company commanders], try for the Battalion and so on, for Four Stars. Hence read military history and books on tactics. I am making out a list of such which I will give you and some of which we will study together. But I earnestly advise you all to read military subjects 3½ hours a week . . .

DON'TS. Don't try to gain success by "Pull" or accuse others of doing so. The man with the alledged pull usually has the goods too.

So far as I know the above remarks do not apply to any one here, but we are none of us perfect . . .

Telegram, GSP, Jr., to his father, October 13, 1919

Ship two horses by express to Camp Meade Maryland valuation two hundred a piece. See that horses have necessary medical certificates also that they will be fed enroute. Wire date of shipment and whether collect or prepaid. All well.

Letter, GSP, Jr., to his father, October 15, 1919

Inclosed is check [for $672] for shipment of horses if you have prepaid them . . . I was sorry to miss Nita and Mama but could not get to Washington [he meant New York] before 6:05 P.M. and they left at 6:00 P.M. I will write as soon as I get time. Love

Letter, GSP, Jr., to Nita, October 18, 1919

Dear Anne: I am very sorry that I did not get the chance to see you in New York and also that I have been so long in writing to bid you welcome home. The earliest train that I could catch landed me in New York at 6:05 P.M. just too late to see you. I of course had no Idea you would get accomidations so soon. I hope that you take a good rest after you get home for the sort of work you have been doing is more trying on a person than they always realize at the time. Then if you feel full of energy I would get into business. Real business. I would suggest the Blankinhorne-Hunter Company. You have shown that you possess ability and the best way to stay contented is to use that ability.

The United States in general and the army in particular is in a hell of a mess and there seems to be no end to it. We are like people in a boat floating down the beautiful river of fictitious prosperity and thinking that the moaning of the none too distant waterfall—which is going to ingulf us—is but the song of the wind in the trees.

We disreguard the lessons of History—The red fate of Carthage; the Rome of shame under the Pretorian guard—and we go on reguardless of the VITAL necessity of trained patriotism—HIRING an army. Some day it too will strike and then the end. FINIS written in letters of Blood on the map of North America. Even the most enlightened of our politicians are blind and mad with self delusion. They believe what they wish may occur not what history teaches will happen.

We dined with John Rogers last night. He said that my
views were interesting but impossible. What gets me is the
fact that I being a loyal fool will be among the first to
decorate with my highly intelligent head the arch of Triumph
of some future COMMUNE. What a pitty that such a splendid receptical of Military knowledge should be doomed to
putrify in such a place.

We are loosing all hardihood! To day at the races I saw a
jockey killed. A large healthy man near me shuddered and
said that steeplechasing was so dangerous that it should be
abolished. Such squemishness is fatal to any race.

I have been very busy lately trying to teach military art to
my officers. The only one that is profiting is my self. Still it
makes time pass rapidly.

I hope Aunt Nannie is still improving and that the rest of
you are well. Some one stole Char so I am desolate.

When Rockenbach asked Patton his opinion on certain procedures at Camp Meade—duty hours, the number of officers required on post, administrative practices—Patton replied in his
usual manner, with zeal and thoroughness. Many officers would
have regarded the subject as rather trivial, especially after combat
service in France, and if asked would have answered quickly and
effortlessly. Was Patton then unable to differentiate between important and relatively unimportant matters? It would appear that
whatever distinctions he might have made, he regarded all his
obligations as requiring his best, his utmost. This, of course, contributed on occasion to a useless expenditure of energy, but he
had more than enough vigor for all his activities.

He sent out a barrage of technical papers, sometimes in reply to
a request, other times without prior request, bombarding the
Chief of the Tank Corps with suggestions on how to improve not
only the mechanical aspects of the fighting machine but also the
effectiveness of tank formations. For example, he recommended
changes in the eye-slits in tanks for increased visibility and a better
method of assigning renovated tanks to the tank battalions.

Patton also pondered the question of how best to keep tanks
supplied in battle.

The most striking example of the necessity for direct action by the tank corps in obtaining supplies not delivered by normal channels is the case of ammunition for this brigade at the beginning of the St. Mihiel operation. Ammunition estimated as necessary . . . was requisitioned some weeks in advance. On Sept. 9, 1918 this ammunition was not on hand and could not be traced. In order that we might enter the battle [on the 12th] it was necessary for the chief of Tank Corps to send his adjutant to Paris to obtain the ammunition from the French and deliver it by truck to the Brigade. It arrived if my memory is correct on the morning of the eleventh. Had normal channels been resorted to in this case we should have entered the battle with less than half the necessary ammunition and no case shot at all. Similar situations are bound to recur in war . . .

Just before the St. Mihiel operation the Brigade commander . . . made a personal reconnaissance of the sector . . . He found that to move in the very greasy ground each tank would have to be equipped with 16 steel "Grousers." Had it not been for the fact that the Chief of Ordnance A.E.F. turned over the entire machine shops at Is-sur-Tille to the tank corps for the making of these "Grousers" the 2304 "Grousers" necessary for the success of the operation would not have been made. This prompt action was only possible by use of the telephone and prompt support from the Chief of Ordnance. Normal channels would not have worked. A workshop under the Chief of Tank Corps would have removed the danger of a hitch.

Tanks are so new in war that special arrangements will constantly be necessary; the work thus required can only be obtained from shops under the Chief of Tank Corps.

Absolute liaison with the G–2 and G–4 of the units with which the tanks are operating is vital to remove misunderstandings as to use of roads, priority of supplies etc. In the St. Mihiel lack of such liaison delayed our resupply of gas for more than thirty two hours.

Liaison with the signal corps is necessary to prevent the tanks [from] destroying the ground wires.

Genuinely interested in perfecting the tank, Patton struggled with the fact that the Ordnance Department, rather than the Tank Corps, produced tanks, delivering these and other equipment to the Tank Corps. Ordnance demands for safety, versatility, and structural solidity in tanks were often in conflict with the requirements or wishes of the tankers, who wanted instant modification of features that took months of lead time to produce, even when sufficient funds were on hand for research, development, production, and purchase. The Congress would be penurious toward the Army in general and the Tank Corps in particular.

Sometimes the tankers themselves were unable to agree on certain aspects of matériel. For example, the Technical Board approved new tables of allowances at one meeting, decided that the subject of gasoline capacity needed further research, and clashed over the best kind of gun to mount on a tank.

This meeting apparently prompted Patton to write a paper on the "Desirable features in Proposed Tank." He listed certain basic desiderata under five categories: armament, hull, suspension, motor, and speed.

The armament, he believed, should be a single cannon, preferably a model similar to that used by either the infantry or artillery in order to "simplify the ammunition supply." A tank should also have two heavy Browning machine guns much like those currently in use.

The hull, he wrote,

requires the most careful study. Heretofore it has been made to conform to the motive power. This is an error. The Hull should be designed: first from a tactical view point, i.e. it should afford the greatest facility for the use of the arms and for control and visibility; second: from a balestic [ballistic] and weight standpoint, i.e. it should afford as fiew straight surfaces susceptable of normal impact to hostil projectiles as possible . . . in the next war antitank weapons of heavier calaber than the rifle will surely be encountered. The only answer to such weapons is the construction of a body which precludes normal impact. If it were attempted to thicken the armour as a counter to such weapons the weight of the Tank will become prohibative . . .

My own experience and observation leads me to the firm conviction that the turret mount is the only one admissable for tank guns . . .

It is my firm conviction that the cannon and one of the machine guns on the Proposed tank should be mounted on the same trunions and operated by the same gunner using one sight—preferably telescopic—with ranges for the cannon on one side of the vertical hair and ranges for the machine gun on the other . . . tanks rarely have more than one target at the same moment . . . [if] both [guns] are always on the target the gunner has but to choose which class of fire will be the most effective. Further this method of mounting will eliminate one machine gunner . . . The second machine gun should be in a seperate turret and have . . . the duty of firing at targets not covered by the other guns and further be so located as to be able to sweep with its fire the top of the tank to repel assault. It should be at the rear of the tank and the gunner should be also charged with keeping liaison with the infantry. Both turrets should be provided with perescopic sights for both observation and firing under intense hostile fire.

The problem of suspension required further study and experiment.

The motor, Patton felt, should be of a heavy type with reliability for a minimum of 500 hours of "unskilled driving with out the need of readjustment. The Best tank is but a pile of junk when the motor stops . . ." A tank motor needed a self-starter. The tank also needed an internal lighting system. Shaft drives, he believed, were superior to chain.

As for speed, a tank should be able to run on wheels as well as on tracks. Road travel on wheels or special tracks should offer the possibility of running at 20 miles per hour. Cross-country driving should have the same maximum speed, "if attainable."

The Army would adopt the idea of a single gunner controlling both the tank cannon and one machine gun, and the American tank in World War II would embody this feature.

Probably the most significant development in tank design between the wars occurred on October 30, 1919, when Patton, Benson, Brett, Captain Barnard, and Lieutenant Hahn made a thorough investigation of a new type of tank known as the Christie gun mount. In a report dated the same day, their recommendations and remarks were enthusiastically favorable.

The Christie gun mount is, so far as we know, the first attempt in the field of self-propelled mounts or tanks where the entire machine and each component part there of has been designed and constructed solely from the military standpoint. In other words it is a production job, not an assembly job. This fact is noteworthy . . .

The power plant is unique in three particulars: First: it is set in across the length of the machine, thus saving much space and also the necessities of diverting the power through a right angle by the use of beveled gears. Second: the power plant is completely equipped with large ballbearings at all points of friction. Third: the motor and transmission are mounted on a sub-frame or chasse [chassis] and are not bolted to the armor . . . The transmission is separate for each track: running through two separate sets of gears situated one at each length of the crack [crank] shaft . . .

The christie arrangement gives added simplicity by doing away with one clutch and two trains of reduction gears, and adding one transmission. The saving in space is obvious.

Further, this machine gives four speeds forward and four reverse, by the simple addition of one idle gear . . .

The control is effected very simply by two combined clutch and steering levers, one gear shifting lever and one reverse lever . . . The entire motor and transmission which are combined in one crank case may be taken out as a whole by the simple removal of one of the side plates. This is very important from a tank point of view.

Suspension. Six of the eight wheels or track rollers . . . have independent spring action on the spiral springs . . . the Christie machine obviates both these difficulties [the problem of friction and the condition of having axles too close to the ground—by having better track rollers and also rubber tires on the wheels]. The ability which the Christie machine possesses of running on tracks or wheels is interesting, but

from the tank point of view, hardly essential . . . [This may
have been a sop to the Ordnance Department.]

Recommendation. The board is of the opinion that much
good will be accomplished if Mr. Christie is empowered to
design and construct a tank combining the mechanical features and masterly construction of his present mount with
the tactical ideas of the Chief of the Tank Corps.

Impressed with the Tank Corps enthusiasm, the Ordnance Department prepared to award a contract to Walter Christie of the
Front Drive Motor Company of Hoboken, New Jersey, who was
to construct a tank with a combination wheel and track mechanism, that is, a vehicle that could run either on wheels or on
tracks, which were interchangeable and could quickly be alter-
nated even in the field. Before final approval was given and the
contract was signed, the Ordnance Department had some second
thoughts. In a memo from the Tank, Track, and Trailer Division
to the Chief of the Tank Corps Tactical Staff, the Ordnance Department pointed out that several features and specifications of
the Christie tank failed to meet Ordnance standards. Would the
Tank Corps take these under consideration?

The memo came to Patton who replied at once. He stressed the
excellence of Christie's basic design. Even though the Christie
tank failed to meet, exactly and rigidly, the specifications of the
Tank Corps, as well as of the Ordnance Department, it was nevertheless worth pursuing. Once the machine was built, it could be
improved and perfected. It could also be altered to conform with
the specific Ordnance requirements.

Reinforcing Patton's statement was a memo, prepared by Sasse
and signed by Rockenbach, that the Tank Corps was favorably
impressed by the Christie tank primarily because it represented a
novel and promising departure from the tanks then in existence.
Even though "it is believed that the Tank Corps has been required
to answer questions involving technical details, which have always
been a function of the Ordnance Department," the Tank Corps
saw the Christie tank as the best approach to tank development
quite apart from compliance with "technical details." The Tank
Corps hoped that the Ordnance Department would go ahead.

Learning that the Ordnance Department was still worried about the specifications on the Christie tank—Ordnance had too little money for adequate research and experimentation and had to be careful with its funds—Patton sent a strong letter of encouragement about a month later.

On June 15, 1920, the contract between Walter Christie and the U. S. Army, represented by the Ordnance Department, was finally executed. The contracting officer certified that he was satisfied with the value of the rights and services the contractor proposed to furnish and also with the terms of payment, which he deemed fair and just. Letters of patent had been granted to Christie on April 6 for a tractor and gearing transmission. Now Christie was to build what might become a prototype for an altogether new American tank.

Patton was elated by the letting of the contract. But by then, he was no longer directly involved with tank development.

Letter, GSP, Jr., to his father, October 29, 1919
The horses and boxes arrived here in fine shape last night. Apparently they had a perfect trip. I rode Bouvard from the station to the stable a distance of about two miles and he went perfectly fine. I went to Boston Saturday night and returned Sunday night. B and I spent the day in going over the 395 Commonwealth house and selecting things. I am going up again Friday night to be at some races that Freddie [Beatrice's brother] is riding in on Saturday.

There is considerable unrest here over the Labor situation and we are doing a little extra work [in anti-riot training] on some [tank] crews in case of necessity. That is Private . . . It is funny that it is impossible to arouse any of the Congressmen to the Gravity of the situation. Also the business men think nothing will happen simply because it would be so bad for them if it did.

Patton presented the American Legion Post #19 (Tank Corps) in Washington, D.C., with its colors. On that occasion, where Semmes and other friends who had been in the brigade were gathered, Patton's remarks to the veterans included the following statements:

Discipline which is but mutual trust and confidence is the key to all success in Peace or War . . .

The Flag is to the Patriot what the Cross is to the Christian.

Letter, GSP, Jr., to his mother, November 6, 1919

Dear Mama: I have been pretty bad about writing lately but realy I have been flying around so much that I have some excuse. I have been to boston the last two Saturdays and was at Long Island the week before that. Last week at Freddies we had a fine time. First there was a race meeting in which Fred won the heavy weight steeplechase then there was a hunt in which I rode and then a Hunt Breakfast at which I made a speech and finally a dance. At the Breakfast and dance I was pursued by a man in a Pink coat who wept bitterly and protested that I was the Goddamdest Officer he had ever met and the only one whom God had endowed with Braines equal to his own. He would then wipe his eye with the tail of his coat and take another drein from a cutglass bottle about two feet long which he carried in the tail of his coat. He said he had heard me lecture in Langres at the [staff] college and had then and there decided to moddle himself on me which he was doing at the time . . .

We have had great luck in tanks lately. A man who is an inventer came here and after he got our ideas as to what was necessary from a fighting viewpoint he designed what I think will be the greatest machine in the world. It is far ahead of the old tanks as day is from night. And for a wonder there is lots of room in it . . .

Newtie the Cootie [Secretary of War Newton D. Baker] pins the D.S.M. on me officially tomorrow at 3:30 P.M.

Letter, Major General C. P. Summerall (Commanding the 1st Division, Camp Zachary Taylor, Kentucky) to GSP, Jr., November 8, 1919

My dear Patton: I am very glad to receive your letter of November fifth, in which you have recommended for citation Major Brett and Captain Barnard. It gives me great pleasure to enclose the citations requested, and I beg that you will deliver them with the assurance of my deep appreciation of the services which they rendered the First Division and the 5th Corps. I am also enclosing a citation which I consider that you richly deserve in the operations which resulted in the reduction of the St. Mihiel Salient.

Very sincerely yours.

The citation naming Patton for gallantry in action and devotion to duty read as follows:

An officer of superior courage, dominant leadership and technical skill. During the operations of the First Division in the attack on the St. Mihiel Salient September 12th 1918, he commanded the Tank Unit assigned to the Division. By his gallantry, his superior organizing ability and his determination he overcame great difficulties and contributed effectively to the success of the Division in crossing the enemy's trenches and wire and in giving protection to the advancing Infantry while bridging and crossing a difficult stream.

Colonel Walter H. Gordon of the Inspector General's Department rated the efficiency of officers on duty at Camp Meade above the grade of major and gave Patton "Very Good."

The Pattons had a nice Thanksgiving. Beatrice and Beatrice Junior came to dinner at the mess and later all three went riding. He obtained a three-day pass to go to the Army-Navy football game. When he returned, he and Beatrice had General and Mrs. Harbord, General and Mrs. Fox Conner, and Mr. John Hays Hammond to dinner.

Early in December, when a brief flurry of trouble arose on the border, Patton suggested a method of recruiting tank soldiers. "In view of the, not unlikely, commencement of Hostilities with Mexico," he wrote, letters should be sent to the old members of the brigade offering re-enlistment in their former units. He was sure that 60 percent of the enlisted men and 80 percent of the officers with the brigade in France would return. Those who volunteered could come directly to Camp Meade for refresher training. "This would enable us to put at least nine companies in the field with in two weeks of the declaration of war."

There was, of course, no war.

Mitchell rated Patton as having performed his duties "Excellently." He was a "very well informed; capable, energetic; very high type of officer and gentleman. Known [him] intimately for 10 years." Patton was "superior" in military neatness and bearing and in general value to the service; "above average" in physical energy and endurance, judgment and common sense, attention to duty, intelligence, professional knowledge, leadership, force, initiative, handling men, performing field duties, instructing, training troops, handling troops tactically, equitation, topography, map reading, machine guns, army regulations, and military intelligence; "average" in tact, administration, and executive duties.

Christmas was a painful time for Patton. Three days before, according to the doctor's report, "While riding horse on target-range, Tank Corps, Camp Meade, Md. . . . the animal 'bucked,' and the officer [Patton] was thrown forward on the pommel of the saddle and sustained injuries to his testicles." The condition resulting was called "Orchitis, bi-lateral" and it was "moderately severe." Even though "The disability: Incapacitates officer for all duty," the doctor was certain that "With proper treatment and absolute rest in bed . . . the condition is entirely curable." Patton received a month's leave of absence.

In the spring of 1920, Patton's parents visited in the East. He and Beatrice and his mother and father and sister drove "to Winchester and saw the Grave [of his grandfather]. I was still a Colonel and had my Picture taken by the side of the two other Patton Colonels [his grandfather and his Uncle Tazewell, Colonel, 7th Virginia, killed at Gettysburg]." They went to Gettysburg, to Fredericksburg, and to Richmond "and looked at the many graves of our ancestors there and at the statue of General Mercer . . . I have always regreted that we did not go to Lexington."

Letter, Leonard Wood (written on train en route to Cleveland) to GSP, Jr., April 1, 1920

Dear Colonel Patton: Thank you for your letter of the twenty-second. I can hardly imagine their taking the saber away from the Cavalry. From present indications, there is little or no attention paid to outside recommendations. Things are run not in accord with the views of the majority of those in the service, but quite otherwise. I will do what I can for the saber. Sincerely yours,

This was Patton's last direct contact with Wood, who sought the presidential nomination of the Republican Party that year and came close to getting it. Appointed Governor General of the Philippines by President Harding, Wood remained in the islands until his death in 1927.

Tanks in the Great War, a book by Colonel J. F. C. Fuller, impressed Patton to such an extent that his notes, made from his close and careful reading, covered seven pages typed single-space. The salient points that appealed to him were diverse.

He found it funny but true that some soldiers welcomed the end of the war because they could now get back to *real* soldiering in peacetime, with its spit and polish. To those officers lacking imagination or the warrior frame of mind, war was an aberration. To the dedicated professionals, on the other hand, the main problem of war was how to strike blows against the enemy without receiving them. Patton remarked:

Gun powder rendered armour carried by men useless but it took from the end of the 12th to the beginning of the 14th century for this fact to perculate. Will it take a similar period to show the futility of unarmoured men against armoured machines? Probably.

Leonardo da Vinci in 1482 had described imaginary covered and invulnerable armed chariots, which forced large armies to retreat, thus allowing infantry to advance in safety and without opposition. "The motive power is not staited [by Leonardo] but it is a clear description of a tank written 350 years before the first appearance of the successful TANK."

When Napoleon was elected to the French Institute, he selected as his subject for the initial paper he delivered "The automobil in war." In October 1914, Swinton proposed "catapilar drawn machines. The Tanks developed from this idea were first used Sept. 15, '16. The british tanks from this date to end of war fought 85 actions."

Tank tactics, Patton wrote,

> may be summarized as "Penetration with security." Due to present machanical defects tanks should be used in Groups not smaller than two. After penetration tanks must widen hole by opening out to one or both flanks. If the defense is in depth reserves of tanks must be used for this opening out further in [the enemy positions].

This was, in essence, the "expanding torrent" concept made popular by B. H. Liddell Hart, and it became the basic tactical principle of German blitzkrieg in World War II.

Still drawing from his reading of Fuller, Patton said that the considerations affecting a battle between tanks were suitable ground, enemy guns, smoke, minor objectives, appropriate departure positions, and surprise. "No well planned tank attack has ever failed. Each has brought in more prisoners of war than the casualties to the attacker."

Staff preparations required for a tank offensive included reconnaissance, movement, secrecy, supply, communications, assembly of forces, tactics and training with infantry, reorganization. The tank staff had to be on the field before and during the action to ascertain and report actual conditions and results. Airplanes and tanks had always to work together for information, protection, and, possibly, supply.

This too became a fundamental part of blitzkrieg warfare.

In World War I,

> The German [antitank] methods tipify lack of forethought. They never imagined the consequences of possible improvements in the type of tank . . . This same lack of imagination is the besetting sin of our army with respect to tanks and means of aiding or combatting them at the present time . . . Slowness of american construction of tanks is shown by the fact the time which it took to get twenty american renaults to France was longer than the time it took from the first drawing

of the British Mark I in February 1915 to its apperance in France in August 1916.

As for armored cars—"They can do nothing that a tank cannot do and they cannot do many things a Tank CAN DO."

Yet an armored car was less expensive than a tank, and in the 1920s and 1930s, the U. S. Army would have to make do with armored cars, and Patton would become a vigorous exponent of using armored cars as an adjunct of cavalry action.

In summary, Patton wrote:

> He [Fuller] goes on to elaborate on the use of tanks in what is doubtless a possible but at present impractical extent, because Nations of sufficient wealth and resources to provide such mechanic armies are by the very nature of their wealth those nations [which] are incapable of looking on war in a serious manner and are willing to devote to it only their minimum effort. His ideas as to the use of tanks in small wars are less chimerical but his entire views are extreme and though sound will not be realised in our generation. The lesson to be drawn from his book is the necessity of using our imagination in an effort to combine mechanical with muscular means of combat. Tanks Gas and Automatic weapons are all in their infancy. In planning their future use we must be guided less by what they have done than by what they reasonably will do. And above all we must remember that the will to win is the basic element of victory and that this will must be DISCIPLINED to be useful. A mechanic[al] army manned by mechanics who were not at the same time soldiers would be a MESS.

Patton was delighted when Summerall wanted a tank company as a demonstration unit to show infantry men of his 1st Division how tanks worked. Always interested in promoting tank-infantry coordination, Patton personally selected Captain Barnard as the most suitable young officer for the detached service.

Letter, Major General C. P. Summerall to GSP, Jr., April 14, 1920
    My dear Patton: I am greatly pleased by the receipt of your letter of April 10th, and I beg to assure you of my deep ap-

preciation of your congratulations upon my permanent appointment [as a major general]. My chief reward lies in the
approval and the good will of my old friends, and I especially prize the sentiments that have ever existed between us.

We are extremely glad to have Captain Barnard and his
Company, and I hope that they will be happy with us.

Mrs. Summerall joins me in regards to you and Mrs. Patton
and the children.

Faithfully yours,

A welcome break in Patton's routine occurred in April when, as
a member of an Army team, he went to New York City and took
part in a Duelling Sword Competition.

The May issues of the *Infantry Journal* and of the *Cavalry
Journal*—the magazines exchanged articles because of a paucity of
material being written and offered—carried Patton's article on
"Tanks in Future Wars." The ideas were drawn from papers and
lectures he had previously prepared, but he was pleased to see
them in print, together with his name, pleased to have his
thoughts recorded and disseminated throughout the Army for the
benefit of the relatively few officers who read professional journals
and discussed developments in warfare.

The situation in the country became even more discouraging
for serious career officers. Money appropriated by Congress for
the military services was scarce and so was public interest. A
training exercise held at Camp Meade on May 14 illustrated the
Army's difficulties. The mock order of attack, which gave unit
objectives and boundaries and provided the other information
needed for the maneuver, observed: "NOTE: Due to lack of troops,
only [the] first assault line will be indicated by infantry."

As though that was hardly bad enough, a heavy rain almost
washed out the practice. Four radios, the Technical Board later
reported, "were entirely put out of action, due to the rain storm
which came up shortly after the maneuver began, and it was several hours before the apparatus could be dried sufficiently for further operation." Instead of recommending the development of a
waterproof radio, one that would work effectively in damp

weather, which would be an expensive endeavor, the board contented itself with an expedient and cheaper solution, suggesting that a cover be provided for the tank radio to prevent water that leaked into the tank from short-circuiting the radio.

It was perhaps a sense of discouragement that led Patton to consider seriously whether he ought to leave the Tank Corps. A "Personal Report and Statement of Preferences" he filled out late in April indicated his continuing wish to be the military attaché in England or a student at the School of the Line at Leavenworth, Kansas. Perhaps it was hardly surprising that he wrote: "When returned to Cavalry," he hoped to be assigned, in the following order of preference, to Fort Myer, Monterey, California, or Fort Riley.

Lieutenant Colonel E. G. Beurat of the Inspector General's Department investigated the efficiency of officers at Camp Meade. Patton, he reported, was regarded by his commanding officer as "An efficient officer." Beurat's evaluation: "Efficient; keenly interested in the development of tanks. I consider him average."

Toward the end of May, Patton took seven days of leave and went fishing at Fort Myers, Florida. He needed some time to think, some leisure to ponder the future of the Army and the future of his own career. For things were about to happen that would abruptly change the course of both.

On June 2, Congress passed the National Defense Act of 1920, one of the most important laws in American military history. Among other provisions, the legislation established the Air Service, the Chemical Warfare Service, and the Finance Department as new branches; it abolished the Tank Corps. Tank units and personnel were assigned to the infantry. From now on, tankers would be designated as belonging to the "Infantry (Tanks)." Rockenbach's position as Chief of the Tank Corps was eliminated, and he moved to Camp Meade to become the post commander and de facto chief of a branch of the service that was no longer independent.

The law created several new positions, among them a Chief of Cavalry, who would serve at the War Department as principal adviser on cavalry matters to the General Staff; and a Chief of Infantry.

The act instituted the postwar military reorganization.

Teams of doctors examined all officers on active duty to determine their fitness for retention and promotion. Patton was certified as being physically qualified to hold any grade.

At the end of June, he was discharged as a Colonel in the Tank Corps, National Army; he reverted to his basic Regular Army grade of Captain of Cavalry. Late in August, he would be promoted to major, with rank from July 1, together with 44 other officers, among them his classmates Devers, Baehr, and Philoon.

After the reductions in rank, Rockenbach showed great consideration for Patton. He retained Patton, now a mere captain, in command of the 304th Brigade, while Mitchell, reduced to major, remained in command of the 305th Brigade. What Rockenbach did was to assign the majors to his own headquarters or to Mitchell. Otherwise, that is, if a major had been placed in Patton's brigade, he would have outranked Patton and would have had to receive command of the unit. Therefore, Rockenbach assigned Majors R. L. Collins, D. C. T. Grubbs, and C. P. Chancler to his own General Tank Corps Headquarters; and Major Daniel W. Colhoun to Mitchell's brigade. The result was that Rockenbach, a colonel, had 3 majors, 3 captains, and 2 first lieutenants in his headquarters; the 305th Brigade had 2 majors, 7 captains (among them Eisenhower), and 12 lieutenants; the 304th, headed by Patton, had 9 captains (including Benson and Floyd L. Parks) and 16 lieutenants. The arrangement was a thoughtful kindness on the part of Rockenbach.

Detailed to a board meeting at Camp Meade to determine the temporary officers to be retained on active duty and those to be released, Patton informed Pershing, who was now in Washington, that it was "Hard and nasty work especially as I am recorder and the president of the board is an old man who has been dead for years." His main reason for writing was to congratulate Pershing on the "fact that so many of your old men [like Summerall, Harbord, and Conner] have been definately recognised [by promotions]. It certainly is fine." Patton was living at Camp

Meade, which he liked better than staying in Washington. Beatrice and the children were in California for the summer. Would Pershing care to come out some day and ride over the lovely Maryland countryside with Patton?

Letter, Pershing to GSP, Jr., August 3, 1920
My dear Patton: I have your very kind letter of July 16th and am glad that the list of promotions meets with the approval of the Army in general, which I think is really the fact —although many of the older set naturally feel disgruntled. However, there is little doubt that in time all those who deserve promotion will be recognized.

Nothing would give me more pleasure than to go to Camp Meade and have a days trip somewhere out in the country with a Troop of Cavalry, or a ride over the hills in that vicinity . . . but I am very busy myself with various Boards and have been held down to the vicinity of Washington almost all summer.

With very many thanks for your letter, and with affectionate regards to Beatrice and the children, I remain, as always, Sincerely yours,

Early in August Patton suggested to Rockenbach that he try to secure a unit citation for the 304th Tank Brigade for its wartime service. This award would honor all who had served in combat.

Having thereby symbolically discharged his debt to his brigade and his men, Patton wrote a formal letter through channels to the Adjutant General on August 15. He asked to be relieved as soon as possible from his present assignment with tanks and returned to duty with the cavalry. He gave the following reasons 1) The Tank Corps was now part of the infantry, and Patton had no wish to transfer to that branch. 2) Having wanted to return to the cavalry as early as September 1919, he had refrained from applying for a transfer because the 304th Tank Brigade had been in the process of reorganization, and he had believed it his duty to assist; since then, the brigade had been built up by recruitment from one company to its full strength of thirteen companies, and therefore his obligation was complete. 3) He had been with the Tank Corps nearly three years; to remain longer, he believed, would benefit the tankers little and himself less, for he would lose all touch with the cavalry. If he could be useful to the tankers because of his experience in the war, he would be happy to act as an instructor delivering courses of lectures and directing or judging tank demonstrations—as a matter of fact, he would like very much to do so.

. . .

What really motivated his desire to return to the cavalry? The niggardly funds appropriated by Congress for the Army in general and for tank development in particular disturbed him. The War Department decision to put the Tank Corps under the infantry upset him.

Was his resentment on both counts evidence that he was divesting himself of the idea that tanks had to be tied to infantrymen? Or was he concerned because he knew relatively few infantrymen, particularly those who were important and could help him advance in his career? Perhaps he felt that cavalrymen would have better chances for promotion and advancement as soon as Pershing became Army Chief of Staff, a post he would assume in 1921.

There was something else. The Tank Corps loss of its independent status negated Patton's standing as one of the few high-ranking and experienced tank officers who could reasonably hope for promotion into the general officer ranks. Disappointed, he preferred to go "home" to the cavalry, where he could play polo, participate in horse shows, and hunt. Being a cavalry officer would facilitate these pursuits in a way that service with the infantry would not, for cavalrymen were expected to be prominent horsemen.

Furthermore, he and Beatrice liked Washington, nearby Fort Myer was a cavalry post, and they knew enough leading people in the capital to have a fine and exciting social life.

To a large extent Patton was intuitively inclined toward the cavalry. The tanks were far from being reliable machines. Until they were perfected, they would remain relatively fragile mech-

Lieutenant Colonel Patton in France, July 1918

Major Patton, Fort Riley, May 1923

The Patton family, 1929. Major and Mrs. Patton, daughters
Beatrice and Ruth Ellen, and son George IV

Presentation of the Argentine Polo Cup to the War Department "Whites," winners of the 1931 tournament. Left to right: Major John Eager, Lieutenant Gordon B. Rogers, Major George S. Patton, Jr., and Major Jacob L. Devers

Master of Foxhounds,
Cobbler Hunt, Virginia,
1932

Sailor and navigator,
aboard the *Arcturus*

Father of the bride, daughter Beatrice's wedding, 1934

Commanding Officer, 5th Cavalry, Fort Clark, Texas, 1938

Fort Myer Horse Show, benefit for infantile paralysis fund, January 1939. Left to right: Colonel Patton, commanding officer, Fort Myer, President Franklin D. Roosevelt, and Colonel Edwin M. Watson, White House Military Aide

Colonel Patton and members of his staff, Fort Myer, June 1940

Fort Myer review, June 1940

anisms, unable to take to the field to fight anywhere, any time, and under any conditions.

In contrast, horses could go everywhere. Unrestricted by terrain and weather, they were dependable. The cavalry was mobile. And he expected the next war to take place in primitive areas of the world, where the absence of roads, while hampering tanks, would restore the cavalry to importance. In particular he kept anticipating an outbreak of hostilities with Mexico, perhaps because he had first enjoyed combat and glory there.

In the tanks, a man was tied to engines and gasoline and oil, to masses of troops and machines, to careful coordination, planning, and protective maintenance—as in France. In the cavalry, a man on horseback was an individual, relatively free, able to charge recklessly and mordantly while waving a saber—as in Mexico.

If Patton had hoped that the tanks might be transferred to the cavalry instead of to the infantry, he had only himself to blame. To a large extent, his papers and lectures had helped persuade the Army that the proper role of tanks was as auxiliaries to assist the infantry. Although the field artillery played that role, it managed to retain its independent status as a separate branch of the service. In contrast, the tanks were new; they lacked the traditions that might have argued successfully for independent status.

Absorbed into the infantry, the tanks were there regarded as "armored infantry" and as "accompanying guns." And thus they tended to lose their mobility. Had they instead gone to the cavalry, they might have developed the mobility that had characterized Patton's thinking in the World War and that would characterize the German blitzkrieg.

Had the tanks been shifted to the cavalry, Patton might well have remained a tanker. Instead, like most cavalrymen, he became tied to the horse and associated with those who were obsessed by the horse cavalry.

To Patton's request for transfer to the cavalry, Rockenbach added his approval on the first indorsement. He recommended that the change take place on October 1. The letter traveled to the Adjutant General, and from that office went to the Chief of

Cavalry, who also approved the transfer. His executive officer consulted with the Chief of Infantry, who had no objection to Patton's transfer from the infantry (Tanks). The Adjutant General then issued orders on September 4, 1920, assigning Patton to the 3d Cavalry at Fort Myer.

Letter, GSP, Jr., to Quartermaster General, September 15, 1920

When I left the Mounted Service School, Ft. Riley Kan. in 1915, I expected to go to the Philippines and shipped some of my furnature at my own expense to Topeka Kan. for storage. It is still there.

After returning from Mexico I was on duty at Camp Stewart Tex. While on Leave from that station I received telegraphic orders about May 18, 1917 to Report to Gen. Pershing for duty—Copy of telegram is lost. I accompanied him to europe and my wife shipped my furnature from El Paso to my fathers home at San Gabriel California on private B.L.

Since returning to the U.S. in March 1919 I have been on duty in the field and have had no property shipped.

I am now ordered for duty to Fort Myer Va. . . .

Request authority to have furniture etc weighing about 4500 lbs shipped on Government B.L. From Pasadena California to Ft. Myer Va. And for a shipment of similar property to the weight of about 2500 lbs shipped on Government B.L. from Topeka Kansas to Fort Myer Va.

Should the weights of these shipments exceed my allowance of 7200 Lbs I will pay the difference.

Letter, GSP, Jr., to Aunt Nannie, September 19, 1920

We started to get ready to move yesterday and expect to be moved by the second or third [of October] depending on when I get back from the Bryn Mawr Horseshow which starts on the 29 and lasts till the second.

We will probably have the same house we had as lieutenants. It is not as large as we could wish but will have to do.

Becoming interested in whether tanks could be used to advantage in street fighting, particularly in Latin American cities, Patton wrote:

Owing to the peculiar conditions and general lack of preparedness which exist in Latin-American countries, it will be
possible in the use of light tanks to have them depart from
the general principle of avoiding main streets because antitank cannon and tank traps will probably not be found.
Hence, unless Intelligence reports clearly point to the presence of the above named tank defences, the tanks should cooperate with the Infantry Street and Roof Detachments.

His methodology for operating on broad and narrow streets, as
well as "In the attack of churches and public buildings surrounded
by plazas," was concerned only with fulfilling the mission; it
paid no attention to the possible destruction of lives and property.
He advised:

You will find that in Guerrilla warfare or riots that the
average street-fighting does not force you to contend with
much real military preparation or Artillery . . . [Tanks were
to] form a bulwark for the Infantry advance and shield the
Infantry from hostile fire from the front.

Letter, GSP, Jr., to Pershing, September 24, 1920
I trust that you will excuse the personal vanity which emboldens me to intrude this upon your valuable time. But as I
am one of the few officers who has ever registered hits on a
human target I am very anxious to have that fact on my
record.

In short, he would consider it a great honor to have a statement
from Pershing placed in his official file on the Rubio affair in Mexico. Would Pershing please write to the Adjutant General? To
stimulate Pershing's memory, Patton sent an account of the Rubio
ranch action. He said that it came from his diary, but it was a
recapitulation of his letters to his father and to Beatrice at the
time.

There are quite a few references to me in the above but
then it was my diary. I trust that after the Great War you
will not consider me too childish in mentioning this matter
to you.

I trust that when I get to Fort Myer I shall be able to see you and perhaps take you for a ride [on horseback].

Pershing was nice enough to have an aide look up his own report of the fight. He then sent a quoted paragraph for inclusion in Patton's file. This formed the basis for the award, which Patton later received, of the Silver Star decoration.

Letter, GSP, Jr., to Rockenbach, September 28, 1920
My dear General: It is rather hard to tell you goodbye and express to you my sincere appreciation of your long suffering and great kindness to me during the past three years. While serving under you I have had the most vivid and interesting experiences of my life and shall always remember your considerate treatment of me and my various vageries.

I believe I have learned much of value and what ever I have learned has been due to the latitude and councils and example you have given me.

I hope to continue along the lines I have learned from you. Please believe that I shall ever remain most grateful to you for the oppertunities you have [give]n me and for the support you have ever been ready to tender.

With best wishes to you and the Tank Corps, I am
Affectionately,

GSP, Jr., Parting Speech to 304th Brigade, September 28, 1920
I could not deny myself this oppertunity of seeing you all once more, for though you probably think me the meanest man in the world I assure you that you exagurate. I have a great pride and sincere affection for the brigade and the men and officers composing it. Neither now nor at any other time have I thought it necessary to apologize for my acts since what ever I have done has been the result of an honest effort to perform my duty as I saw it. When I have cussed out or corrected any of you, men or officers it has been because according to my lights you were wrong, but I have never remembered it against you. I have never asked any of you to Brace more, work more, or fight more, than I have been willing to do my self; with the result that in keeping up to you in France I had to get shot. You have always responded and con-

sequently where ever the brigade or any part of it has served it has been an example of discipline, courage and efficiency. In consequence of the splendid work of the Brigade in France I was given the Distinguished Service Medal, but be sure that I realise it was the Brigade not I who won it. For the future you have only to mould your conduct on the past. If you do so, and I am sure you will, the members of the Brigade, dead or departed will have nothing more to ask and our pride at having been of you will ever increase. God bless the 304th Brigade.

Letter, Beatrice to Aunt Nannie, September 29, 1920

Your idea about moving to Washington is o.k. We expect to be there two years & I wish any or all of you w'd come . . .

They have some fine pictures of G's last review here. I am having prints made for you all. It was very impressive; &, on the night of the 27th there was a big hop for Col. Mitchell & us. The 305 Brigade officers gave Col. M. a silver vase . . . & the adjutant of our Brigade made a speech saying that G. & I were to have a present, delivered at Myer on Nov. 11th! & then gave me a huge bunch of roses!! We nearly died. Also, I had to lead the grand march with Gen. Rockenbach!!

Next day, G. assembled all his men—700—and made a very touching farewell speech. (He will send you a copy.) Then the headquarters Sgt. Maj. & 2 others advanced and presented me with a beautiful cup. About a foot high, solid & very heavy. On one side was etched a light tank. On the other was "To Colonel & Mrs. George S. Patton, Jr. from the enlisted personnel of the 304th Brigade." I made a little speech, & we all cried some, especially G & me & the Sgt. Major. . . . It was very touching.

This A.M. I went to the hospital & thanked all the sick men for their share in the cup . . . They certainly do appreciate G. . . .

G. went to Philadelphia last night & I certainly am glad, I hope he'll have lots of fun & we'll be all settled when he lands [in Washington] Sunday. If he had to move us all up, after the emotional strain he's been under this last week I w'd be sorry. The horse-show [in Philadelphia] seems heaven-sent. And I don't even have to clean the house, so many are helping us.

Everyone wants to help. And bags of apples sweet potatoes & pears & eggs & chickens are pouring in . . . to go on the truck tomorrow.

It was quite a wrench for Patton to authorize the publication of General Order 9, Headquarters 304th Brigade, Tank Corps, Franklin Cantonment, Camp Meade, September 30, 1920, in which he relinquished command of the brigade. To the formal order he added a sentence that was somewhat unconventional. "In leaving the Brigade with which he has been associated since it's existence, his regret at parting is only exceeded by his pride at having commanded such a unit."

CHAPTER 37

Fort Myer Again

*"Insist on . . . BOLDNESS . . . THE ENEMY IS
AS IGNORANT AS YOU . . . BE BOLD . . .
YOU ARE NOT BEATEN UNTIL YOU ADMIT
IT, Hence DON'T . . . The 'Fog of war' works both
ways. The enemy is as much in the dark as you are.
BE BOLD!!!!! . . . War means fighting—fighting
means killing, not digging trenches . . . YOU
MUST HAVE A DEFINATE PURPOSE . . . Try
to make fenatics of your men. It is the only way to
get great sacrefices."*

It took Patton less than a month to make the transition between
tank training and cavalry drill. After returning from the Bryn
Mawr horseshow on October 3, 1920, Patton relieved Lieutenant
Colonel Harry N. Cootes in command of the 3d Squadron (or
Battalion) of the 3d Cavalry, and he and his family moved into
quarters #5 at Fort Myer. Three weeks later he was instructing
his officers and men on the art of warfare and the practice of
soldiering with the same enthusiasm and flair he had demonstrated to his tankers.

His goals were to inculcate respect for standardization and uniformity and to stimulate desire for imagination and initiative
among his troops. His program would show careful attention to
the progressive feature of Pershing's training in Mexico, an orderly sequence from the smaller to the larger units. His method of
imparting knowledge was by example and practice, and he would
insist that his officers be clear in their explanations to the men
and thorough in their supervision of the exercises.

Patton started with the essentials of platoon combat, the mutual support required between a base of fire and a maneuvering element.

Offensive combat consists of FIRE and MOVEMENT. The purpose of FIRE is to permit MOVEMENT. When a group of a rifle platoon is rushing [forward in the attack] the fire produced by rifles is diminished despite the fact that the portion of the line not rushing should increase its rate of fire. To maintain or augment the intensity of fire at such times the Automatic Rifles should be used in full force. Hence they must not rush at the same time the riflemen rush. They must be in position and firing during rushes . . . [to keep] the enemy's heads down [and] thus facilitate the advance of their comrades . . .

The foregoing applies to an attack against an enemy in line in open country; where the hostile resistence consists of isolated groups or in closed country an automatic rifle may steal forward . . . and by taking the enemy in enfelade [enfilade] may facilitate the advance of the whole line . . . more brilliant and complicated methods cannot be specified but are up to the initiative of the officer on the spot. Mention is made of them here to awaken inventive interest.

He told his officers to "Explain Par[agraph]s. 2 and 4 to the men. I will question some of them to assure myself that this has been done."

Dissatisfied with the appearance of his squadron, Patton specified in detail how personal gear and equipment were to be packed and precisely what items a cavalryman carried.

Having determined the strengths and weaknesses of his unit, he opened a school for his officers and scheduled 22 lectures and lessons for a single month. He delivered 16 himself—on hippology, marches, stable management, parts of the horse, shoeing, orders for the attack, military hygiene, orders for the advance, the rules of land warfare, outposts, riot duty, division attack, and advance and rear guards.

Next followed troop (or company) instruction, including the proper methods of fighting on horseback and dismounted. His exposition on how to make the approach march, how to conduct a reconnaissance, how to select objectives, how to attack, how to deploy and commit the reserve was thorough.

These words to his officers were typical:

Take all the time you want but attend to these details. Read C.D.R. [Cavalry Drill Regulations] Pars. 650 to 670 inc, and Pars. 716 to 735 incl. Also I.D.R. [Infantry Drill Regulations] Provisional 1919. Pars 358 to 360 and 361 to 371 inc. Explain to the men what you are trying to do.

Throughout his training program, Patton avoided blind conformance with the regulations. He insisted always on the thoughtful consideration of problems, each of which was unique and had its own solution. For example:

Now while column of fours may occasionally be used as an approach formation its use will be exceptional because if Cavalry has gained, as it should have, a suitable position before dismounting it will be too near the enemy to justify column of fours . . .

Since the duty of the cavalry is to retain mobility by means of a quick decision and since conversely its mobility should enable it to select a point of attack where a quick decision is possible, the approach march for cavalry will ordinarily be shortest [shorter] than that for infantry . . .

Of course this is a violation of the principle to avoid normal formations, on the other hand men must have something to go on or they can never improvise an attack.

After discussing "fan wise" formations, "maximum useful density" on the firing line, and other technical matters, he directed his subordinates to "Read the Paragraphs in the manuals referred to above and get the idea in your head. Now apply it"—in exercises and maneuvers.

After the charge assemble the men and explain to them what has been done and why. If you have time repeat problem on way home. If you carry out this exercise slowly and with attention to detail men will learn it in one trial.

During the first three months of 1921, Patton put his squadron through a series of problems and exercises. He invented mock situations, supervised the maneuvers, and criticized the solutions his subordinate officers offered. These theoretical situations— worked out near Merriefield, Dunn Loring, Gallows Road, Annandale Road, Bailey's Crossroads, and Holmes Run—forced his officers, as well as himself, to think about the art of command, to learn the art of war, and to reflect on the art of leadership.

In a game played on January 16:

> if things go badly Gen. D. must ride up and rally his men personally. In the event of a panic he should show the greatest resolution and if necessary get killed. If his men should break in the withdrawal which is more than possible Gen. D. SHOULD NOT SURVIVE IT. THERE IS NOTHING MORE PATHETIC AND FUTILE THAN A GENERAL WHO LIVES LONG TO EXPLAIN A DEFEAT.

A problem game a month later, this one on how to prevent or delay the capture of Alexandria, Virginia, involved making certain estimates—of the situation, friendly forces, morale on both sides, the terrain, and alternative courses of action—all of which were preparatory to reaching a decision. According to Patton:

> The plan adopted is that of a desperate man and is only justified by desperate conditions and a will to fight. The placing of the guns is particularly faulty but if they hold out till run over they will enfelade [enfilade] at rifle range any attack on his right which is his weak flank and will give his line the appearance of great length.

Instructions for another:

> We must approach the consideration of this problem by the admittance of one unalterable fact and the acceptance of one arbitrary assumption. Troops moving at night are confined to roads.

At the conclusion of his three-month course in tactics, Patton examined his officers. After questioning them on the problems and the exercises, he then presented several supplementary lectures and lessons to correct the deficiencies uncovered by the tests.

Somewhat later, he issued a squadron-training schedule for four consecutive weeks. Its purpose was dual—to comply with training requirements imposed by higher headquarters and to train his junior officers to develop individual initiative. His troop commanders were to turn in weekly reports showing their compliance with the drills specified by Patton and indicating those exercises they had personally devised for the remaining and unallotted time.

Patton's final maneuver, called a tactical ride, set up a theoretical situation in which the Potomac River separated two hostile states at war. Assigning Troop A the task of covering the Ballston–Halls Hill–Chain Bridge Road against an attack launched by the rest of the squadron proceeding via Upton Hill to the Leesburg Pike, Patton wrote a scenario that posed problems not covered in the drill regulations. For example, you meet a civilian in an automobile; what do you do? Stop him? Interrogate him? Pay no attention to him? The object was to test officers in situations likely to be met that could be handled only on the basis of alertness, imagination, and common sense.

. . .

Colonel W. C. Rivers, the regimental commander of the 3d Cavalry and Patton's immediate superior, rated Patton at the end of 1920 "below average" in tact, "average" and "above average" in most characteristics, and "superior" in general value to the Army. Feeling that his evaluation somehow did less than full justice to Patton's capacities, Rivers added another category of his own invention, "mental energy," and in that he graded Patton "superior."

Patton was, according to Rivers,

An officer of more than usual power mental and physical. I estimate him to be of good habits—pleasing personality—has many attributes of a natural soldier and is much interested in his profession. Good type of officer to have in a command—gets good results and aids in keeping things on a good general plane of efficiency. Keen on both athletics and on military work—a desirable and not too frequent combination—has power and push.

On March 4, 1921, the troops at Fort Myer took part in the Inaugural Parade. A newspaper photograph showed Patton riding a horse beside the automobile carrying Presidents Wilson and Harding to the White House.

Later that month, Rockenbach returned to Patton a manuscript that Patton and Brett had written on the history of the 304th Tank Brigade. Rockenbach wanted two additional points incorporated into a revised narrative. First, it was Rockenbach who had taken Patton around to become acquainted with the British tank school system, not the reverse. Second, after Patton was wounded, it was Rockenbach who personally directed Brett's operations.

Your paper illustrates one of the most important considerations to be used in handling soldiers, that is, to keep them thinking they are the whole show, but I think it is an error if the impression is made that the Tank movements were not all carefully planned and given the necessary direction. I think it is quite important to emphasize the fact that, due to throwing everything in that we had and using it to exhaustion, we had to get additional mechanical assistance and from necessity, I was able to get mechanical reinforcement of one motor mechanic company.

In other words, Rockenbach wanted to make sure that his role in the combat employment of tanks was neither slighted nor overlooked in favor of those who commanded the troops on the battlefield.

Mitchell, who had also returned to the cavalry and was assigned to Fort Myer, rated Patton "superior" in equitation, "above average" in all the other categories except tact, which was "average." Patton was "a very well informed, gallant, loyal officer."

Major H. H. Pritchett of the Inspector General's Department made a three-day examination of Fort Myer, and his report carried this observation:

Particularly deserving of commendation was the orderly and clean condition of quarters, store rooms, kitchens, stables and equipment of the troops composing the 3d Cavalry [Squadron], commanded by Major G. S. Patton, Jr.

A notebook Patton maintained in 1921–22 recorded some of his thoughts on warfare. "Success in war," he wrote, "depends upon the Golden Rule of War. Speed-Simplicity-Boldness."

He listed the personal equipment he carried as a cavalryman. On his belt, a pistol, four clips of ammunition, a knife, wire cutter, and first aid pouch. Around his neck his identification tags, a compass, and field glasses. In his right pommel pocket a mirror, "raisor, sharpner, shaving brush, tooth brush, tooth powder, nail brush, match box, hair brush, listerine." In his left pommel pocket long silk drawers, socks, clothes brush, handkerchiefs, flashlight, candle, coffee, salt, "sacerine," saddle soap, sponge. In his dispatch case maps, pencils, map measurer, message book, notebook, Field Service Regulations, Cavalry Drill Regulations, and small camera. In his bedding roll 1 shirt, 1 blouse, 1 sweater, 1 pair of breeches, 1 pair of long silk drawers, 1 wool undershirt, 1 bath towel, 1 sleeping bag, 1 extra blanket, 1 small pillow, 1 canvas bucket, 1 rubber basin, 2 shoe laces, 1 pair of shoes, 1 pair of leggings, 1 "housewife" (probably a sewing kit), handkerchiefs, hay fever "medicin, asparin, laxatives, toilet paper, stamped envevelopes, writing paper, large flash light, extra battery, army regulations, manual [of] courts martial, 1 flask brandy." In his pockets a knife with can opener and hoof pick, a mechanical pencil and fountain pen, toilet paper, "$100 preferably gold." On his right wrist a whistle. On his left wrist a watch.

He wrote instructions to himself:

Insist on: Maximum distances; BOLDNESS; Prompt and accurate reports. Speed is more important than the lives of the [men at the] point. THE ENEMY IS AS IGNORANT AS YOU. Do not halt on the near side of a river below a hight . . . You must not be delayed by blufs. Bluf your self . . . BE BOLD. Camps unless screened by trees are sure to be noted by enemy airplanes. They will then be bommed.

BILLITS for this reason are preferable. . . . YOU ARE
NOT BEATEN UNTIL YOU ADMIT IT, Hence DON'T
. . . The "Fog of war" works both ways. The enemy is as
much in the dark as you are. BE BOLD!!!!! . . . War means
fighting—fighting means killing, not digging trenches . . .
YOU MUST HAVE A DEFINATE PURPOSE . . . "THE
ROAD TO THE BAYONET IS PAVED BY FIRE SU-
PERIORITY" Patton. . . . Remember that the information
you get is for instant use not for history. . . . Try to make
fenatics of your men. It is the only way to get great sacrefices.
. . . OFFICERS MUST BE MADE TO CARE for their
men. That is the sole Duty of All Officers.

Rivers judged Patton in June 1921 as "superior" and "above average." Patton was "physically and mentally a powerful officer:
good habits and pleasing personality: a superior type of officer.
Excellent both on mental and physical side of an officer's development; keenly interested in riding and polo, but also progressive
in tactics and in studies."

Patton played on an Army team that participated in the polo
tournament at Meadowbrook, Long Island, that summer. He was
one of nine officers authorized to participate in the American
Junior Polo Championship Tournament at Philadelphia. The performance of the Army team was disappointing.

In order to improve the caliber of the Army's polo, the players
were solicited for suggestions that might make the Army a con-
tender for the championships next year.

*Letter, GSP, Jr. to Colonel J. R. Lindsey, October 10, 1921,
subject: Polo*

I have played polo in a humble sort of way since the Spring
of 1905 when I began it at the Military Academy. Due to
good luck I have usually been on the first team and have always had to work hard to stay on it. Still as a result of the
above I had come to entertain the belief that I knew something of Polo.

But subsequent to my brief acquaintance with REAL Polo
my golden illusions have been shattered and I KNOW—not
think—that I know nothing of Polo.

Admitting than that I am probably the only polo "AT-TEMPTER" in the Army who has grasped none of the following self evident truths I yet take the liberty of recounting them to you with the belief or perhaps hope that you may see fit to call them to the attention of others who while they probably think they already know them have none the less never in my observation practised any of them.

Before starting however, I desire to place my self on record as one who recounts the exploits of others and in no way poses as a performer of similar merit.

RIDING OFF. There is a wide spread falicy among us that . . . we [Army officers who play polo] are rough. Compared to good players we are as lambs to raging lions . . .

Instead of so maneuvering as to come into a man at an angle sufficient to give him a bump which will loosen his fillings we come up parallel and try to "Two Track" him off the ball . . .

We do not start at top speed, whip and spur, to catch the loose man, unless he is easily caught. We simply follow him trusting that an ever merciful God will cause him to miss; unfortunately God is seldom on the job . . .

SPEED. In polo we never realize what a football coach once told us: "You don't have to hurry, you have to run like hell" . . .

STARTING . . . We must learn to start at full speed. It will be objected that our horses are not up to this. True they usually are not because we do not require it of them . . .

DISCIPLINE. Strange as it seems the average Army team has less discipline than the average good civilian team . . .

MYSELF. I have never done correctly one of the things for which I criticise others. I just have hopes.

The remedy for the above is fast polo on good fields by as large a number of Army players as possible, drawn from as many sources and localities as possible . . . We have the ponies now . . . We have the physique. We have in undeveloped form the mental quickness. To date we have not the practice.

Next summer two or three teams with substitutes, men and horses, should be sent to Meadowbrook, put in camp and placed under training conditions as to early hours and prompt attendance. In addition to polo ability the men selected should be responsible and earnest. For the simple purpose of winning the Junior next year one team would probably be all who should compete. But from the broader and more important standpoint of developing polo and more teams that enter, the better for the Army.

Horse shows occupied much of Patton's time. In September he rode at Syracuse, in November in Madison Square Garden, New York. He won cups and ribbons. He also fell with his mount, injured his hip, and was forced to withdraw from the competition.

The rotogravure section of a New York newspaper showed "A Who's Who in the Kingdom of the Horse Scene at the Annual National Horse Show Breakfast" held at the Hotel Biltmore. Gathered about a horseshoe-shaped table and a miniature tan-bark ring was "Practically Everybody Who is Anybody in the Exhibition of Horse Flesh in the United States." Patton was there.

A letter from Beatrice informed Pershing that the Pattons were busy with horse shows and "collecting cups."

The Pattons attended—he was on duty—and were moved by the ceremonies on November 11 for the Unknown Soldier, whose tomb was established at the amphitheater in the Arlington National Cemetery.

Letter, Chief of Cavalry to Commanding Officer, 3d Squadron, 3d Cavalry, November 18, 1921, subject: Appearance of Command at Ceremonies

. . . noted with appreciation the excellent reports concerning the appearance and conduct of your command during the ceremonies incident to the Burial of the Unknown Soldier at Arlington and the meeting of the Limitation of Armaments Conference.

Letter, Brigadier General H. H. Bandholtz, Commanding General, Headquarters District of Washington, to Commanding Officer, 3d Squadron, 3d Cavalry, November 14, 1921

. . . appearance and marching of the third Squadron, 3d Cavalry, under your command on November 9th and 11th, 1921, were in every respect most satisfactory . . . I am highly pleased with their snap and military bearing, and that I have received many favorable comments from officers on the appearance of the men, horses, and equipment.

Rivers indorsed both letters and transmitted them to Patton with his own commendation.

GSP, Jr., Lecture, "The Cavalryman," 1921
[The superior cavalry officer had to] possess a combination of qualities not often found in one individual.

He must have a passion—not simply a liking—for horses, for nothing short of an absorbing passion can make him take the necessary interest in his mount . . .

He must be a veterinarian in theory and practice; a farrier and a horseshoer better than any man in his troop, a stable sergeant and horse trainer, a saddler. Above all he must possess a sense of obligation to his mount, which, with the whip of a remorseless conscience makes him—him personally—seek the welfare of his horses above his own.

No one acquires these qualities at teas or card parties, or by slapping his leg with his whip.

Such knowledge can only be acquired by reading books on horse diseases, on horse management, on conditioning and training. By association with horsemen of all sorts and conditions wherever met . . .

But . . . he is neither a stable sergeant, nor a horseshoer, nor a veterinarian; such arts are but means. The end is to become a cavalry officer who will be a success in war.

. . . why?

Because success in war depends on getting to the right place at the right time . . . Nearly all the remediable failures of the world result from being LATE.

. . . affection for the horse; tenacity of purpose; a studious mind; a feeling of obligation and a sense of time . . .

A thorough knowledge of war by reading histories, lives of cavalry men, by the study of the tactics of his arm and by the constant working of problems . . .

He must train himself into the possession of a GAMBLER'S Courage.

. . . the successful cavalryman must educate himself to say

"CHARGE." I say educate himself, for the man is not born who can say it out of hand . . .

Civilization has affected us; we abhor personal encounter. Many a man will risk his life, with an easy mind, in a burning house who recoils from having his face punched. We have been taught to restrain our emotions, to look upon anger as low, until many of us have never experienced the God sent ecstasy of unbridled wrath. We have never felt our eyes screw up, our temples throb and had the red mist gather in our sight.

And we expect that a man . . . shall, in an instant, the twinkling of an eye, direct [divest] himself of all restraint of all caution and hurl himself on the enemy, a frenzied beast, lusting to probe his foeman's guts with three feet of steel or shatter his brains with a bullet. Gentlemen, it cannot be done—not without mental practice . . .

Therefore, you must school yourself to savagry. You must imagine how it will feel when your sword hilt crashes into the breast bone of your enemy. You must picture the wild exaltation of the mounted charge when the lips draw back in a snarl and the voice cracks with passion . . .

When you have acquired the ability to develop on necessity, momentary and calculated savagry, you can keep your twentieth century clarity of vision with which to calculate the chances of whether to charge or fight on foot, and having decided on the former, the magic word will transform you temporarily into a frenzied brute . . .

To sum up then, you must be: a horse master; a scholar; a high minded gentleman; a cold blooded hero; a hot blooded savage. At one and the same time you must be a wise man and a fool. You must not get fat or mentally old, and you must be a personal LEADER.

A paper entitled "Tactical Tendencies," dated November 26, 1921, stated a significant point in Patton's thought, his belief in the inherent superiority of tactics over strategy.

. . . while Strategy needs occupy the minds only of the more exalted of the stellar officers; tactics is the daily lot of all. Splendid strategy may be made abortive by poor tactics, while good tactics may retrieve the most blundering strategy.

Tactical officers had little choice in selecting their forces, but they would, in time of war, be responsible for using them. Predominant force of the right sort applied in the correct way at the proper place at the right time was the basis of all military success. "A mistake of yards or minutes . . . may blight our career and butcher our men."

While I do not hold with those who consider the World War as the sealed pattern of all future efforts to maintain peace, it is nevertheless, our most recent source of information, and the tactical tendencies shown by its last phases will most certainly color to a considerable degree our initial efforts in the next war.

As soon as the first battle of the Marne was won, the World War became a special case, due principally, in my opinion, to two reasons.

Fixed flanks which prevented maneuver; and the splendid rail and road [system] on both sides which permitted a very heavy concentration of men and a relatively easy ammunition supply. Without these good roads and short hauls it would have been impossible to have fed and supplied the vast armies and the war would have taken a different course . . .

The restricted area, long deadlock, and vast resources, permitted the employment of masses of guns and ammunition which probably during our life time cannot be duplicated, certainly not in any other theater of operations. The great results apparent and real accomplished by these guns has so impressed the majority of people that they talk of future wars as Gun wars. To me, all that is necessary to dispell such dreams, or at least limit their sites to western Europe, is a ten mile drive along country roads in any state of the Union except perhaps a favored half dozen along the coasts.

Tactics then based on a crushing artillery are impossible except in one place [Western Europe]. But even where roads permit its use in mass, the effect of artillery alone is negative, so far as offensive victory is concerned . . . all the artillery ever built cannot defeat an enemy unaided . . . Little as it may please our self love to admit it [in the Cavalry], the "Dough Boy" wins the battle. Hence, if we aspire to high command we must know his tactics.

The Guns are the greatest auxiliary—but only that . . .

Another feature resulting from the war and which also has left its mark is the evolution of the SPECIALIST.

His birth is the result of an unholy union between trench warfare and quick training . . .

Our own men, thanks to the genius of General Pershing, were less troubled by the specialist disease . . . but due to lack of time many of ours were not and could not have been well rounded open war soldiers . . .

The outstanding Tactical features of all these great battles [in 1918] were First, Open War methods, and second, Surprise made possible by secrecy and deception. Notice that all three of these features are as old as war . . .

Yet even with the locking of armies in the west and the total absence of flanks, there were chances for cavalry . . .

In Russia and under Allenby, Cavalry was as important as ever in its history . . .

A general survey of the Tactical tendencies at the close of the World War seems to me to point to greater and not lessened usefulness and importance for Cavalry.

The necessity, due to air observation, for more marches of concentration being made at night adds vastly to the destructive power of the mounted man, for charges with the saber or pistol or surprise fire by machine rifles will be terribly effective and most difficult to prevent.

The importance of airplanes in war was bound to increase, and consequently, wooded country was bound to become the best terrain for cavalry action, as well as for the action of infantry. Thus, cavalry tactics would probably be one of the following: delaying or harassing action against infantry; attacks against flanks or thinly held sectors; actions against enemy cavalry, "ALWAYS OFFENSIVE"—"the cavalry man who dismounts in the face of a mounted opponent gives his birthright for a mess of potage"; action against enemy lines of communication; against strong positions where cover or obstacles prevented maneuver.

The charge itself is simply the blind stampede of furious and exhausted men initiated on the spot by a few brave spirits who start going and are followed pell mell by the rest. And unless the enemy is so situated that he cannot get away he departs before the Bayonets ever reach him. At least that is how I have pictured it, how I have heard it described, how I once saw it enacted by about twenty Americans against a group of machine guns and how it felt when I was in one— which failed to arrive as all were hit . . .

The Bayonet Charge and the Saber Charge are the highest physical demonstrations of moral victory. The fierce frenzy of hate and determination flashing from bloodshot eyes squinting behind the glittering steel is what wins. Get as close as you can to the objective, unseen or helped by covering fire and then CHARGE in line in column or in mass it makes no difference.

At the end of 1921, Rivers judged Patton "superior" as a squadron commander, "above average" in field duties, and "average" in tact. In addition to being a "loyal type," Patton was

An officer of superior mental and physical qualities, [a] high class man devoted to his profession. Very capable all round man; while he is known as an exceptional horseman and swordsman he is also keen on military studies and keeps well abreast of the times by intelligent industry. Studious man fond of study and reading; yet Major Patton can take a horse, or a saber, or a rifle, or a pistol and equal or surpass any man—officer or N.C.O. or [enlisted] man—in his squadron with either or all.

General Bandholtz, the District of Columbia military commander, added his indorsement: "I concur in above report. An unusually accomplished and capable officer."

Letter, GSP, Jr., to the Chief of Cavalry, subject: Machine Rifle Pack, January 22, 1922

I have the honor to inclose a description and pictures of an improvised Pack for the Machine Rifle. So far as I know no such pack exists. The one submitted is cheap and easily made and might be of use to the service.

While at the New York Horse Show I talked with Major A. R. Chaffee and he asked me to send him some description of this pack which I had described to him. I am inclosing three copies and request that if the idea of the Pack meets with your approval your office send Major Chaffee one set of Pictures with description as it seems to me such information should first pass through your hands.

Col. W. C. Rivers has often examined the pack and has authorized its use in this Squadron of his regiment as an experiment.

I have two additional sets of Pictures should you desire them for the Cavalry Journal or the Cavalry School.

Automatic Rifle Carrier, Improvised.

Since each Troop of Cavalry is now supplied with four Automatic Rifles, and has a separate Platoon designated to use them, some method of carrying these weapons is necessary.

Up to the Present Time no Ordnance Pack for this purpose has been issued, hence the following improvised Pack has been designed.

About a year ago one such pack, and one similar, except with more complicated ammunition Packs was constructed at Fort Myer, Va. These two Packs were given a test of daily use at drill on the same horses for a period of three months, no sore backs resulted. As a result of this test the troops of the 2nd Sqdn., 3rd Cavalry, at Fort Myer, Va., are now equipped with four such packs each.

The cost of construction of the packs is *nothing* as they are made of expendable issue articles throughout, except the iron straps forming the forks, the iron for this purpose was "SECURED" free of cost. The saddles used are not hurt in any way.

. . . any average troop saddler and horseshoer can make the packs, at least they were so made at this post.

It is not claimed that the pack is perfect . . . Above all they COST NOTHING . . .

This carrier was designed by Major Patton, Sqdn. Sgt. Maj. Negus and 1st Sgt. McCormick, all Third Cavalry.

On January 26 and 27, Patton suffered a temporary shock and cardiac weakness from an allergic reaction—probably from eating shellfish. The doctors called it a "protein sensitization manifested by swelling of loose areolar tissue of face and of mucous membranes of mouth and respiratory passages." He was puffed up and had difficulty breathing, but the condition soon passed.

Although he was still shaky, he worked throughout the following night of January 28, when the Knickerbocker Theater disaster occurred.

More than two feet of snow had fallen on Washington, and at 9 P.M. that Saturday, the overburdened roof of the Knickerbocker movie house gave way and fell on the audience, killing nearly one hundred persons and injuring many more. Pershing came to the scene of the catastrophe about an hour later and, seeing the urgent need of help, telephoned General Bandholtz and directed him to order out all available troops. Soldiers, sailors, airmen, and marines came promptly from Fort Myer, the Washington Barracks, Bolling Field, the Navy Yard, and elsewhere to assist the police and firemen in clearing the debris and removing the dead and the injured.

Letter, Brigadier General H. H. Bandholtz to GSP, Jr., January 31, 1922

It affords me great pleasure to send this letter of appreciation of your highly efficient services during the rescue work following the Knickerbocker Theater disaster. All reports indicate that the work of yourself and of the officers and men under your command, was of the highest order, and that without it many of the injured would have died. It is the cause of much gratification to me, as it must be to you, to feel that the Army, in such a disaster, carried out the best traditions of the service.

1st Indorsement, February 2, 1922

Transmitted with the commendation of the post commander, Rivers.

Patton sent Pershing a book entitled *The Desert Mounted Corps* because it reminded him "of you and your methods in Mexico and France. It is the greatest military book I have ever read and believe should be a text book at Riley." He had marked parts of the book for Pershing, especially "all the thirty three

Mounted Charges with the SABER." Mailing, he said, a great cavalry book to a great cavalryman,

> I am also impelled by the desire to emphasize the importance of CAVALRY; for western Europe is very small and in all the rest of the world there will be fine chance, to stick the enemy from the horse.

Letter, Pershing to GSP, Jr., February 14, 1922
> My dear Major Patton: . . . I heartily agree with you that it is a very interesting book. It especially appeals to those of us who have learned by experience that the saber is a valuable part of cavalry equipment.

Letter, GSP, Jr., to Beatrice, April 16, 1922
> Darling Beat: I went to the Cat & the Canary [a play] with May and Dick, it was fine and I enjoyed it very much. The people were very much keyed up and a little girl in front of me screamed several times.
>
> I . . . went to the tank corps where I had a very dull time. All they want to do is to talk of their passed life which is far from exciting.
>
> I hid the [Easter] eggs down in the gulley. B found hers and put them in a pile while she went for a basket. Tank [the dog] found the pile and took a good "hark" on it. So she fed him the eggs.
>
> I saw Mrs. Harbord and she said she was very sorry you had to go [Beatrice went abroad because her sister Kay was ill] . . .
>
> You behaved fine [when she left] and I never saw you look prettier.

Patton played his first polo game of the season at Fort Myer. He informed Mrs. Charles Dawes, wife of the future vice president, who had asked Beatrice to lunch, of Beatrice's absence. The children went to the egg roll at the White House but there was such a crowd they all came away at once. "I escort Jofre [Marshal Joffre] on Wednesday so will have to put up a good show."

Letter, General H. A. Smith (Commandant, Army War College, Washington) to GSP, Jr., May 11, 1922
> I hope with you that in the next war we may again serve

together. If I could have had a few more officers like you in France, the schools at Langres would have been much more of a success.

Letter, GSP, Jr., to Beatrice, May 15, 1922
Darling Beat: I had a better day to day getting three ribbons and a cup.

Ball Room got second in Local Saddle horses being beaten by that same black mare that beat him last winter.

In the military jumping eight 4 foot jump both Allahmande and Dragon went perfectly clean.

Allahmande made a really wonderful performance. He changed his gate [gait] the whole way and took every jump in his stride. Several people left the stand to congratulate he and I.

Dragon went almost as well. He got too close to the wall but got over it. I lost in the polo class . . . Still I feel less depressed. I think I put up a very fine ride.

I am well, hope Kay is better
I love you.

Commendation [by Inspector General's Office, July 19, 1922]
Major George S. Patton, Jr., 3rd Cavalry, is to be commended for the excellent condition of equipment, fine appearance of men and animals, and cleanliness and orderliness of Barracks and stables.

That summer Patton was one of eight officers, together with enlisted personnel, mounts, and equipment, ordered to Mitchel Field, New York, to train with an Army team for the Junior Championship Polo Tournament to be held at Narragansett Pier in August. In charge of the group was Major C. L. Scott, who would command the 2d Armored Division in the opening years of World War II.

Letter, GSP, Jr., to Beatrice, July 4, 1922
I have been dining and lunching with Belmonts, Harrimans, Penn Smiths, Stoddards, Brice Wings, etc to a great extent. These are the nicest very rich people I have ever seen. Their houses are very simple and they drive Fords and

Dodges with out chauffeurs. All the women do something to their hair to keep it from getting gray. Other wise they don't make up except their lips . . .

I have gotten nice and thin and only weigh 165 in my polo clothes. But I am perfectly well.

Letter, GSP, Jr., to Beatrice, July 5, 1922

Booker [Pershing's orderly in Mexico and France, now working for the Pattons] told me with great pride that he had sent you an account of Newman's death. I had not intended you to see it. The fact that a man is now and then killed at polo makes it no more dangerous. Further the accidents always happen in the slow games with the bad ponies. I am playing in fast games on splendid ponies so don't worry.

Letter, GSP, Jr., to Beatrice, July 7, 1922

I hope I put up a fair game and am not self conscious. I will hope for the best any way.

I think it is perfectly certain that I will not go to Riley until December.

Letter, GSP, Jr., to Beatrice, July 24, 1922

It was fine practice to play with or against the greatest Players in the world. I got cussed less often than I had feared.

Letter, GSP, Jr., to Beatrice, July 28, 1922

I mailed your letter to Mrs. Newman. I am glad you have so much sense about Polo. I am being very careful.

Letter, GSP, Jr. (from Washington), to Beatrice, July 30, 1922

Every thing was so nice and the post so pretty and green that I realy felt most depressed at the thought of having to leave in January. I think we are established better here than any where we have ever been and I have enjoyed it very much.

G. S. Patton, Paper, "Polo in the Army," autumn 1922

In retrospect it seems a far cry from polo as we first knew it on the ten dollar ponies and skinned fields of the western garrisons to the polo of the Army Team at Point Judith which won the Junior Championship in 1922.

. . . There is little or no similarity in American Polo opportunities and that obtained in the British Army with whom we are so often disparagingly compared.

The vast distances which separate our posts make inter-regimental matches difficult or impossible. The constant changes of personnel in these same regiments prevents the development of teams of men used to one another's play . . . Further the majority of our mounted troops are of necessity stationed far from the centers where good civilian polo is played and hence we lack high class competition.

The above drawbacks are indigenous and cannot be overcome . . . But there are also other facts which have retarded our development . . .

Most of our officers do not take the game seriously . . .

Now from the standpoint of the Army officer, polo is not simply a game; it is a vital professional asset . . . it is the nearest approach to mounted combat which can be secured in peace . . .

Further there are constant and real physical hazards in polo and talk as we will of the necessity for cold judgment in combat it is none the less a fact that no man can stay cool in battle unless he is habituated to the exhilerating sense of physical peril. No sport save possibly hunting and football is so good a school in this respect as polo.

War also demands quick decision while engaged in rapid movement under the disconcerting influence of profuse perspiration resulting from vigorous exercise. Such practice is not acquired behind the steering wheel, at golf or while riding at a walk.

. . . The officer who . . . trains and conditions his horses acquires more knowledge of present and future value to his Government through the actual practice of polo than from the study of a hundred easily forgotten treateses on horse management.

An officer's efficiency is measured by his activity and as he is an investment by his useful life . . .

The War Department, then, in encouraging polo is doing a very economical thing. The civilian polo player by helping and supporting the Army in the same line is not only doing a very sporty thing but is also of vast assistance in rendering more efficient a body of men, on whom should war recur, the honor of his country will depend.

GSP, Jr., Paper, "Army Polo. (No. 2)," autumn 1922

. . . The great improvement in the play [of the Army team] was due chiefly to three things. The assistance of the War Department in permitting the assembling of selected players. The efforts of the American Remount Association in producing and making available more suitable horses for polo and for war. The generous support of civilian players in helping and playing with the Army Team . . .

This element of personal risk is not a drawback but a decided advantage. No matter how brave a man may be he is none the less a creature of habit. If his most lethal experience prior to battle has consisted in dodging automobiles on city streets the insinuating whisper of bullets about his sacred person will have more disquieting influence on him than would be the case had his same person received a few cuts and broken bones on the polo fields.

This last statement seems a trifle harsh but such is the nature of truth.

After visiting her sister in England and touring the battlefields in France, Beatrice returned home at the end of August. Patton took a three-day leave of absence and met her in New York.

Letter, Major General C. J. Baily, Third Corps Area commander (Baltimore) to GSP, Jr., December 3, 1922

[Deep appreciation of] the splendid appearance which they [Patton's men] made in the parade in this city on Army Day, December second, and in the formation in the Stadium. I realize that this command had to be put to considerable trouble and personal effort in marching over to Baltimore in order to appear mounted in the parade. I need hardly say that the appearance of the squadron was a distinct feature of interest to all concerned, and especially so on account of its well-known record for fighting in all the wars of our country since it was first organized prior to the Mexican War.

In December, Rivers judged Patton "superior" as a squadron commander, and an officer of good habits and agreeable personality, and of superior mental and physical powers, superior type of officer. Keenly interested in and superior in riding, polo, etc; and also a hard student of his profession—devotes himself assiduously to military studies in winter season. Have had to get after him about supervising troop paper work and troop fund books better occasionally. Minor deficiencies called to his attention [from] time to time: immediate improvement resulted.

Bandholtz concurred in his endorsement.

In mid-December, the Pattons, together with their children, left Washington to spend Christmas in California. Early in January 1923, the family traveled to Fort Riley, Kansas, where Patton enrolled in the Advanced or Field Officers' Course at the Cavalry School.

Attendance at the Cavalry School indicated that he was once again integrated into his basic branch. His work at Fort Myer had been recognized and approved, and his selection for schooling meant that he was marked for advancement.

Letter, Beatrice (303 N. Jefferson Street, Junction City, Kansas) to Pershing, January 22, 1923

Georgie is getting well started at the school. He has been at work a week today, and is sitting opposite me as I write [studying a map and], coloring rivers in purple.

X

The Middle
Years

---

*"I am an enthusiastic if not a good Cavalryman
. . . success . . . hinges on the taking of calculated risks."*

CHAPTER 38

Riley, Leavenworth, Boston, Hawaii

"Sad to say, it [my photograph] is not so fierce as I had hoped though it has a more or less Prussian expression."

IF THE FIRST THREE DECADES of Patton's professional life consisted of an apprenticeship for high command, if his career before World War II was preparation for his unique leadership, the 1920s expanded his horizons despite the confining nature of his work. His schooling and staff assignments restrained and tempered his natural inclinations, at the same time disciplined his character and intellect without destroying his ebullience. Perhaps it was his physical exertions, his hard play on the polo field, that permitted him to maintain the patience required for the sedentary tasks imposed on him.

He attended the Cavalry School at Fort Riley, Kansas, during the first five months of 1923, and completed the Advanced Course. The single paper remaining from that experience was the draft of a lecture he delivered to his fellow students.

I am going to talk about Napoleon's marshals. In this school we deal with great plans and projects, theories and organizations, and I have taken this subject lest we forget that in war the personal element is most important.

After recommending *The Three Musketeers*, that highly romanticized account of combat, as proper reading background to understand the marshals, he showed pictures of Napoleon in 1796, 1809, and 1815. To explain why Napoleon was less than at his best during the last three years of his active career, Patton suggested:

that large protuberance about the waist line . . . may be becoming and not at all harmful to a lawyer, a doctor, a banker or a chief justice, but to a military man it is ruinous. When you see one gradually coming upon you two measures are necessary; eat less, exercise more.

Taking the marshals in turn, Patton characterized their special gifts. Berthier had "the ability to present in a simple manner the most complicated situations." Murat had no intellectual capacity, understood nothing of strategy, but could maneuver 20,000 cavalrymen in the field to perfection. Having discussed them all, Patton concluded that their fathers' occupations had had no influence on their attainments—"a great leader may be inherited from a notary or a noble, a mason or a manufacturer, a lawyer or a landowner and . . . no walk of life has a monopoly on military talents." Nor was formal education necessary for military leadership, except in staff duty.

The great danger in military schools is that they will become narrow, too much concerned with teaching . . .

The personal element is given too little consideration in peace time training and in schools, yet it is the most important element in war and no where in history is this better exemplified than in Napoleon and his marshals.

Nowhere would this be better exemplified than in the case of Patton himself.

Upon Patton's graduation, Brigadier General Malin Craig, the commandant, rated Patton:

Very energetic, enthusiastic and versatile officer. Does everything exceptionally well. This report is the combined opinion of 28 Instructors, 4 Directors [of courses] and the Commandant.

Colonel Guy V. Henry, the assistant commandant, certified to Patton's "marked proficiency" in tactics, marksmanship, map reading, sketching, and field fortifications.

His high standing in his class led to his selection to attend what had been called the School of the Line, was then named the General Service Schools, and would become known as the Command and General Staff College, at Fort Leavenworth, Kansas.

Before reporting to Leavenworth early in September, Patton spent three months of leave in Massachusetts, where he and Beatrice performed a heroic act. They were sailing off Little Mission rocks near Salem in a twelve-foot catboat when a sudden squall almost swamped them. As they turned and headed for shore, they heard cries and saw three boys—two were sixteen years old, the other was ten—whose boat had capsized, struggling in the water. The youngsters had managed to turn their dory over and, about three-quarters of a mile from land, were standing in the boat in water to their waists, waving their oars and shouting.

The Pattons went to their aid. The wind was so uneven and uncertain that they had to go past the boys, then tack back. They took the youngsters aboard with great difficulty and at some personal danger, then brought them and their boat to land. "Their deed, especially Mr. Patton's," one of the boys later stated, "was one of fine skill in handling the boat in such weather and also one of courage and of almost self-sacrifice."

Beatrice had affidavits drawn up and signed by the rescued boys, each of whom gave his version of the incident. Then she transmitted the documents to the Secretary of the Treasury, who awarded Life Saving Medals. Her own narrative stressed the bravery of her husband, who, she knew, was fond of decorations, recognition, and fame.

No more was heard of the occurrence for some time.

Beatrice, who was expecting their third child, remained in Massachusetts when Patton traveled to Leavenworth.

Letter, GSP, Jr., to Beatrice, October 7, 1923
If you come here you will be very lonely for a while as I go to school at 8:30 usually get out at 12:00. Go back at 1:00 P.M. and get back at 5:00 and then have to ride or play tennis to get exercise. Except of course on Saturday and Sunday when there is nothing to do.

I am not telling you this to discourage you but simply as a warning.

He had their house at Leavenworth painted so it would "be less of a shock to you than would other wise be the case. I even got them to make the bath room all white."

Letter, GSP, Jr., to Pershing, October 23, 1923

As I have frequently told you I am an enthusiastic if not a good CAVALRYMAN and this fact together with the knowledge that I am not grinding any personal axe emboldens me to write you about the next chief of CAVALRY. I have talked the matter over with Quek [Quekemeyer, a former aide to Pershing in France] and we both think that *if* Gen CRAIG is not available that Col Henry would be *next* best. The only thing I can see against Col Henry is that he is too cold. It seems to me that we want a good soldier and also a good mixer for the next chief. To my mind General Craig is both. Of course I know that it is none of my business and that my opinion will not divert you from what you think best but I think that all cavalry men owe it to them selves to get the best chief possible.

I am getting on fairly well here and DONT like it a bit but suppose it is a necessary disease like measles.

Letter, Pershing to GSP, Jr., November 27, 1923

. . . you are not only a very enthusiastic but a very good cavalryman, remembering one particular instance . . . when you brought in 2 important Mexican dead strapped on to the front of your automobile . . .

Craig seems to be the general choice, and if things work out as I think possible, he will probably be selected. Of course, all this is confidential—only for you and Quekemeyer —but you know I have the interests of Cavalry at heart and shall always do everything possible for my old branch of the service.

Patton bought his daughter Ruth Ellen a police dog five weeks old. "When I let him out to look at him he left the others and bit a cow in the leg. The cow kicked him over and instead of howling he growled and bit her again: this decided me that he must be a good dog."

Beatrice arranged by mail with Patton's manservant Booker to give Patton a surprise party on his birthday.

Letter, GSP, Jr., to Beatrice, November 11, 1923
I got enough candy from Cal[ifornia] to keep me sick until Christmas . . . It is after 12 [midnight] as I was reading so I must stop. I think you were fine to arrange for the party. Inspite of my advanced age I still love you.

Letter, GSP, Jr., to Beatrice [November 1923]
Darling Beat: I have just mailed you by seperate package one of my recent Photos. Sad to say it is not as fierce as I had hoped though it has a more or less Prussian expression.

He wrote to General Hines, the Deputy Chief of Staff of the Army who would soon succeed Pershing as Army Chief of Staff, asking to be detailed, upon the completion of the course at Leavenworth, as military attaché in England. In a quite long and friendly letter, Hines replied that someone else had already been promised the job.

He had Thanksgiving dinner with John Lucas and his family. Lucas would command the VI Corps in Italy during World War II and be relieved at Anzio.

Letter, GSP, Jr., to Beatrice, November 26, 1923
I have the usual unthankful feeling of having vastly over eaten and not had much exercise . . . I hate to write such a stupid letter but don't seem to have many ideas. I do however think I have a lot to be thankful for and hope that I am properly grateful . . . The most thankful thing I have is that you love me.

In December, Patton sent Beatrice a letter of congratulation he had received from Pershing on the impending birth of the new Patton baby. "You ought to keep it for 'it,'" he wrote, "(notice avoidance of gender)."

Gen. [Malin] Craig wrote me that he was after the job as chief of cavalry. So if you see Gen Brewster talk him up. Of course it is secret. I hope he gets the job. So far I have done pretty well [at Leavenworth] but the marks are so close that one may slip at any moment.

He spent Christmas vacation with Beatrice, who gave birth on December 24 to a boy, George S. Patton IV.

Mr. and Mrs. Patton, Nita, and Aunt Nannie were there, and Mr. Patton "insisted on having George IV baptized at once. This was done in the house. Papa wrote some nice things in the baptismal book but it was burned."

Letter, GSP, Jr. (Leavenworth), to Beatrice, January 1, 1924

I enjoyed my Christmas very much and am especially glad that you had so little trouble [with the delivery of young George].

Patton worked hard on his studies, and he mentioned his efforts in almost every letter to Beatrice.

So far I have done better than I have expected on almost all the problems though I doubt if I stand as high relatively as I did at Riley. Still I hope to improve and I think some of the others will crack—I hope so . . . Gen Smith [the commandant] gave us another lecture to day about not worrying. I have not done so yet and I hope I shant.

Again:

I certainly busted all my rules about studying to day. I studied from 2:30 P.M. to 6:00 P.M. and from 7:15 to 11:45 and have [seven] or eight hours in all but I know the subject so it is all right and don't happen often.

Once more:

I have been getting "A" again so feel much more mental than I did though I can still stand to improve. However I am not taking it at all seriously . . .

Had a nice letter from [Ralph] Sasse today full of advice. He is some soldier and ended up with real emotion saying that I was the only man who could speak his language.

Later: "I have been studying to beat hell."

Finally:

I never seem to get through any more. It is now 11:30 and I have just finished. Either I study harder or the lessons are harder. We had our physical exam to day. I was perfect as usual.

Letter, Joseph J. Angelo (2415 Sherman Ave., Camden, New Jersey) to GSP, Jr., February 3, 1924
Dear Col. P. We received your letter and sure thank you for your check as it helped us a lot. As it put us on our feet. Hoping I can some day return you a favor. Am sending the other letter [attesting to Angelo's character and recommending him for a job] to the fire dep't. Am very glad to hear that you have a son and hope he will some day be an officer like his father . . . I will let you know if I get in the Fire Dept and I am looking for a job every day willing to take everything. I know you are working hard in that school as I remember how hard we worked in the tank school . . . Bettey is doing nicely outside of a cold. With Best wishes for all I remain Your Friend always Joe.

General Frank Parker, commandant of the Army War College, wrote and thanked Patton for his kind and complimentary letter of congratulations on Parker's promotion. "I especially appreciate your letter," Parker said, "as it comes from a man for whom I have a very high regard personally and professionally."

Letter, Rockenbach to GSP, Jr., February 5, 1924
My dear Patton: I am very much pleased to see that school has not dulled your capacity to estimate the situation correctly, for I was wondering why I had not heard from you and I assure you that your congratulations, though much belated, are highly valued. [Rockenbach had been promoted to Brigadier General.]

I have gotten my promotion, as some of my stupid friends inform me, in spite of the Tanks, but I believe in Tanks, I believe that the machines that we have in manufacture at the present time are going to win many of our opponents and are going to force you, cavalrymen, to adopt them. Consequently, I believe that my promotion is connected with the Tanks and will make others think more of them. I have delayed going to Washington, with a view to letting the Army get accustomed to the fact that a Brigadier-General is a suitable officer for the command of the Tank School.

I am wearing the first stars which you gave me and also the Tank insignia.

Don't let it get into your crazy head that I don't need the approval and sympathy of my juniors. I often felt in my long period of waiting [for promotion and for recognition of the tanks], that had they [his juniors] known the amount of scrapping I did to get them what I consider their well-merited reward, at a time when there was a mad rush to grasp the decorations, they would have realized that all the time I was behind them, looking after them, and ready to get into a fisty cuff with any one who was derogatory in his remarks.

I shall leave here probably next Monday but there are two things that I want your active assistance in: the first is, to keep alive the interest in Tanks and the other is to get up a suitable memorial in Arlington [Cemetery] for our men who died in France . . .

Let me know what your plans are on leaving the School there. There are a good many things in the District of Washington that will have to get more snap and pep into them and assuming that the various schools you have gone to have had a beneficial exterior effect on you, without curbing your Napoleonic spirit when the fight is on, I may have to call on you.

With regards to Mrs. Patton and yourself. Sincerely yours,

In September, Rockenbach would be appointed commanding general of the District of Washington. He would retire from the Army in 1933. Until his death in May 1952, he was convinced that Patton was his protégé and had gained fame because of what Rockenbach had taught him.

Patton was an honor graduate of the 1923–24 class at the Command and General Staff College, standing 25 of 248 students, with an average overall grade of 88.948. This high mark placed him in the General Staff Corps, a status much sought after. Colonel Charles M. Bundel, the Director of Instruction, judged him to be "a superior officer of marked ability." In his endorsement, the commandant, Brigadier General Harry A. Smith, concurred, adding, "In my opinion he is one of the ablest and best officers of his grade in the service."

Malin Craig, the new Chief of Cavalry, congratulated Patton, saying:

> . . . you have added additional prestige to our branch of the service.
>
> I consider it the duty of every Cavalry officer to take advantage of the courses of instruction made available to them—a matter of duty to the Cavalry service. Furthermore, I firmly believe that lasting individual honor and preferment are gained only through individual effort to improve the efficiency of the service at large.

Shortly before Patton's graduation, Smith had written in behalf of "one of our best students," Patton, to Major General Robert L. Howze who commanded the 1st Cavalry Division at Fort Bliss, Texas. Smith wanted to keep Patton at Leavenworth as an instructor, but the War Department had decided instead to assign him to duty as a General Staff officer. Smith recommended that Howze request Patton as his G–3 or operations officer because he believed that Patton would be valuable and

> because I am very fond of him personally; second, he was one of the best subordinate officers I had in France and one of the most outstanding; third, he is a high class student here and has demonstrated that he understands the theory, as well as the practice, of war. He is a fine man to have around, aside from his military ability, and I regret exceedingly that I cannot keep him here.

The War Department would transfer Patton to the I Corps Area headquarters in Boston. As soon as he heard of his assignment, he wrote to the corps commander, his friend Major General André W. Brewster, who had been a member of Pershing's staff.

Letter, Brewster to GSP, Jr., May 27, 1924

Dear George Patton. Thanks for your letter. I am expecting to see your order [assigning Patton to the I Corps Area] very shortly and shall be glad to have you by my side. We have taken the old Proctor house at Prides and Fred Ayer told me last Sunday that he had got the Brown "Mansion" nearby for you. It has a fine swimming pool. I am glad that you are all pleased with the detail [to the I Corps Area]. Give our love to Mrs. Patton and the children.

In Boston, Patton became the G–1 officer concerned with personnel and manpower management, including plans to control the mobilization of all the reserve units and installations in the New England area.

When Pershing retired from the Army on his sixty-fourth birthday in September 1924, an editorial in the Boston *Transcript* marked with lavish praise his distinguished career.

Letter, GSP, Jr., to Pershing, September 22, 1924

At the request of the paper I wrote the editorial . . . I tried to express in a very restrained manner my enthusiastic admiration for you as the Greatest American Soldier. The restrictions of publication however prevented me saying all I feel. In my opinion the greatest honor a soldier can have is to have been privaleged to serve under you as I was allowed to do. While you were on the active list I did not tell you my feelings as I did not want to be thought guilty of bootlicking for my own benefit . . . With renewed expressions of my sincere admiration, I am Very respectfully.

Letter, Pershing to GSP, Jr., September 30, 1924

. . . it is particularly pleasant and somewhat rare to hear such good things of oneself while still alive. In this connection, I cannot let this opportunity pass to repeat my warm congratulations on your own splendid services to the Army and the country, and I want you to know that I am particularly grateful for the very loyal and efficient support you have always given me.

Having established firmly his sense of belonging to the cavalry, Patton began to look again toward the tanks. Perhaps he was stirred by Rockenbach's promotion and letter. Perhaps he always felt that machines of one sort or another could hardly be excluded from warfare in the future.

A paper he wrote sometime that year and published in the *Cavalry Journal* on "Armoured Cars with Cavalry" opened with a futuristic fantasy. He described Major General Alonza G. Gasoline sitting in his command car, gas-proofed against chemical agents, watching the screen of a radio motion picture projector. The film was being photographed by a camera on an observation helicopter hovering over a battlefield. Close support planes were flying low and squirting liquid fire—an aerial flamethrower of the equivalent of the more modern napalm. Many tanks were meeting in head-on combat.

These visionary events led him to his main question: How could the Army adapt and use the numerous mechanical inventions due to appear, he was certain, in the near future?

Waging war depended on the existence of roads, and roads were restrictive. If Grant had had all the trucks in the AEF, he could not have supplied an army in the Wilderness campaign much larger than the one he actually had and kept supplied with wagons. Wheeled transportation was no better than the available roads.

What released a field army from its bondage to roads were caterpillar tracks, and

the time may conceivably come when in the immutable cycle of military endeavor we shall see small professional armies of highly trained mechanical soldiers operating simple yet powerful machines again dominate the battle field as did their prototypes the heavy cavalry of the armies of Belesarius and Narses. Or again we may see the roadless machine with all its apparent potentialities sink to a position analogous to that occupied by the submarine which but a few years since was so touted as the future mistress of the sea.

He was, he said, confining his comments to armored cars working with the cavalry, for "Regretfully . . . at the present time there is no tank AVAILABLE FOR ISSUE in this country which can keep up with any unit of cavalry." Neither could the armored car, but it could be easily and cheaply constructed from existing motor vehicles with limited armor plate and with existing machine guns—an "assembly [line] proposition, not one of [individual] manufacture."

What he hoped for was an armored car built on a stock chassis, that is, a commercial two-ton truck, which would insure an abundant supply of spare parts. He would accept pneumatic tires and the absence of a roof and a protective floor. He would dispense with anything that impeded mobility. And this the developers of new weapons failed to understand. "Unfortunately," he remarked sarcastically, "inventors don't have to fight [with] the things they make." What they failed to realize was that every ounce of extra weight on an armored car or tank reduced its fighting strength.

The important quality was mobility. "A quail is not doomed to death because he has no armour, neither is a Destroyer. An armoured car with cavalry is a land Destroyer." Men who fought in tanks would willingly dispense with 50 percent of protection in order to gain 5 percent of mobility. "To be useful in any of the above capacities the car must be mobile practical and simple of repair; not a costly hypothetical monstrosity."

This was one side of his ambivalent feelings. Showing his versatility, he displayed the other when he lectured in Boston on "Cavalry Patrols." According to General Grant, he said, war was very simple; it consisted of locating the enemy, then hitting him as hard as possible, and continuing to push him. In this context, cavalry and the air service—"In bad weather [only] the cavalry" —were responsible for finding the enemy, and this the cavalry did by patrols.

Cautioning his listeners against being unduly influenced by the Great War, he said they were unlikely to find

a situation in which when conflict is imminent a courteous G–2 will hand us a large scale map artistically marked out in red and blue and accompanied by fifty pages of mimeograph information as to the exact location of the enemy's latest efforts in the line of new latrines or machine gun emplacements. When such *modern conveniences* exist cavalry reconnoissance will be as useless as it will be impossible.

Only in western Europe were "such refinements" possible, for elsewhere in the world the opposing forces would be separated by mountains or forests, by deserts or prairies, by farm lands or swamps. And in this rough terrain lacking good roads and railways, the cavalry would have the task of learning where the enemy was and in what strength.

Patton touched humorously upon some common errors made by patrols. "Because these defects are mentioned in lighter vein," he warned, "is no reason for their being so regarded."

When you set out to find the enemy . . . remember that he is as much lost in the Fog of War as you are. He has no ghostly scouts to penetrate unseen the trackless woods and lurking in every cover to instantly report your slightest move. His men get just as tired and hot and dusty or cold and wet and stiff as do yours. His patrols as yours will follow the easiest way—the ROADS and it is there that you will find him.

Further remember that maneuvers [in peacetime] to the contrary notwithstanding—a man does not die every time a gun goes off—not by several thousand rounds . . .

Remember success with cavalry hinges on the taking of calculated risks. History proves that such risks may be great— "FORTUNE FAVORS THE BOLD" . . .

Patroling is both physically and nervously exhausting, neither men nor horses can remain on it indefinitely so we must provide reliefs for mind you, a reconnoitering detachment will be out days, not hours . . .

It is a cardinal principle that tactical unity must be preserved . . .

Attention is here called to the fact that eye sight is a God given sense intended to be used and that the Signal Corps has aided the Almighty by the issue of field glasses. Take every good occasion to follow the advice so freely displayed at railroad crossings: "Stop-look-listen"; and when you so stop remember to cover the patrol with a modified form of march outpost . . .

If the enemy is so strong that you cannot charge him it is folly to fight him on foot . . . If you are not destroyed you will surely be made useless for information is not gained by shooting competitions. WHEN A CAVALRY PATROL IN SEARCH OF INFORMATION CANNOT CHARGE IT MUST RUN . . .

A patrol is not working for an historical society. Most of the information it gets while priceless today will be worthless tomorrow . . .

During the battle of Custozza in June 1866, 104 Austrian Cavalry met a column of 10 000 Italian infantry on a wood road. The meeting was a surprise and the Austrians charged instantly in column of fours. In thirty minutes they had ridden through the column and back and still had sixteen men in the saddle . . .

And finally, what was to become one of the Patton bywords in World War II: "get around if you can't get through . . . IT IS THE DUTY OF CAVALRY AND SHOULD BE ITS PRIDE TO BE BOLD AND DASHING."

His tour of duty at Boston lasted only eight months. He expected to be sent to the War Department General Staff in Washington, but late in January 1925, he was abruptly ordered to sail in March to the Hawaiian Islands. Beatrice was not feeling well, and he would travel alone.

His annual physical examination disclosed a long and impressive history of injury: 1905—fractures of the radius and ulna at heads, just below the right elbow joint; fractured nose; 1906—dislocation of the left ankle; 1907—fracture of the left radius; fractured nose; fractured sixth left rib; 1910—fracture of the third right metacarpal; 1911—prepatellar bursitis; 1912—lacerated wound, five inches long, sagittal suture region, 16 sutures; 1914—concussion with partial paralysis of the right arm; 1915—lacerated wound, head, 5 sutures; 1916—lacerated wound, left eyebrow, 3 sutures; second-degree burn of head and neck, third-degree burn of ears; 1917—lacerated wound right side of neck and over right eye; 1918—penetrating gunshot wound, left thigh; 1920—left hydrocele cord tapped; 1921—fracture of arch of pubis, left; 1922 —lacerated wound, head, 2 sutures; lacerated wound, penetrating,

upper lip; 1924—fractures of eighth and nint.
wound, head, 3 sutures; severe sprain, left knee.
The physicians discovered that he had a long tu.
over the ascending arch of the left pubic bone, prob.
by injuries received from a horse, which had fallen on him
resulting in a probable fracture and massive callus formation.
He had mild myopic astigmatism, which was corrected
glasses, stood 72½ inches tall, weighed 179 pounds.

Letter, GSP, Jr., to Beatrice, February 17, 1925
I suppose you are about ready to leave the Hospital and
hope that you wont be too strenious . . .
It hardly seems six years since I got back from France and
we stayed in Moose's house at Mitchell Field but such is the
case. We are well Preserved considering the time.

Colonel C. D. Roberts, chief of staff of the I Corps Area, rated
Patton as a "superior" officer, "an experienced, well educated, ac-
complished officer. Excellently fitted for General Staff work or
high command."
This first mention of his qualification for high command re-
flected the rigorous schooling he had successfully completed at
Fort Leavenworth. A graduate of that esteemed institution was,
per se, capable of assuming high command.
Patton boarded the ship *Château-Thierry* in New York on
March 4.

Letter, GSP, Jr. (from Panama), to Beatrice, March 11, 1925
Mrs. Simonds and Tracy Pope came to meet me (they
thought you were along too). We had dinner and drove
around. It is perfectly beautiful and most attractive. I almost
want to be stationed here. If Hawaii is better it must be
fine . . .
It is lovely beyond words and very different to what I had
pictured. I saw an aligator. Have your opera glasses repaired
as they will be useful. Cameras are useless as things are on
too large a scale.

Letter, GSP, Jr., to Beatrice, March 15, 1925
Every one on board is Bridge crazy and Play all day. Several
of the ladies have fights and the children holler all the

time . . . It is foolish to write when the letter wont be mailed for a week however as I think of you all the time it is well to write once in a while.

Patton debarked at San Francisco and made a quick trip to see his parents, sister, and aunt—"Papa and I drove a lot together" —then returned to board the army transport *Grant*.

Letter, GSP, Jr., to Beatrice, March 27, 1925

When I woke up yesterday I found the ship stopped and on going on deck found much smoke pouring from the after hatch and learned that she was on fire. There were four hose lines into the hold. On inspecting after breakfast we found about eight feet of water in the hold with two automobiles and your Pianow floating happily around. All the rest of our things are drenched with water but were not floating. It is hard to say how much they are hurt but unquestionably they are all damaged to a degree. There is no need to worry about it as nothing can be done. They are drying out the place as much as possible. I am not sure that the books were in that hatch as I could not find them nor could I locate the chests of Blankets. If on opening the stuff I find that some things are permanently ruined I will write you. We were luckey on the Packard. It was so big that it could not be put in the hatch so was on deck and not hurt any by the fire. I radioed Fred [Ayer, Beatrice's brother] for information asto the name of the company in which we are insured and for information of what to do and to send me papers. I am sorry to write you such bad news but thought you would want to hear and would be excited over the Radio to Fred . . . The ship is nice and I have a room and bath so am very comfortable.

Letter, GSP, Jr., to Beatrice, March 29, 1925

The men who dared this ocean must have been great fellows and fine seamen. At least one of the book boxes was burned all to pieces but I think that the water did less harm than I at first thought.

The passengers sighted land on the afternoon of March 31. Patton smelled Hawaii's fragrance six miles offshore. To him, it looked like Catalina Island, but with heavier surf. It was dusk by the time the ship docked, and the lights of the city were on. He was met by a friend who had a wreath—a lei—for him and an automobile and who said that Patton was detailed to Schofield Barracks, where the headquarters of the Hawaiian Division was located. The headquarters of the overall command, the Hawaiian Department, was at Fort Shafter.

Schofield Barracks was on a big flat with high mountains on each side. The post was constructed along loops, but a single loop was as big as all of Fort Sheridan. The verdure resembled that of southern California, that is, southern California with rain. Honolulu was not quite so good as El Paso; it was 21 miles from camp on a concrete road. Waikiki beach was much smaller than he had imagined.

Letter, GSP, Jr., to Beatrice, April 2, 1925
The climate while seeming cool is very sweaty. If you walk seven or eight blocks you are very wet like a melon in an ice box . . .

Asto coming here: I think it was not the intention of the W.D. [War Department] but was some inside politics of the island. The man I am replacing who goes to the [War] Department as G–4 (the place I was to have had) is supposed to be the meanest man in the Army. I think it was a scheme to get rid of him. The official family here seems to me to be much too large and in a sort of cat fight. We get a new Chief of Staff soon which may help though all of them except me are ex Coast Artillery men. While I was not supposed to come here I think it was the luckiest thing in the world that we did as it is cooler and in all ways nicer [than Washington] except asto houses . . .

I have made this rather long as I doubt if you get any more mailed to Boston. However I shall write one or two more there and then write to California. I am well and hope you will like this place.

After he rode around half the island, he thought the scenery looked like Mexico and Florida. The beaches were excellent for swimming. There were all sorts of places to "picknick and even I might be tempted to do it. There is a valley full of burial caves where chiefs in their armor were buried. No one seems to go there." Hawaii was "a swell place and I am sure we shall have a good time." The polo was not much. "I am well and not over worked."

Letter, GSP, Jr., to Beatrice, April 7, 1925
. . . as distance removes sorrow to a degree I had just as well tell you [after uncrating the furniture] that practically every thing is ruined. Water was still seaping out of the linen and blanket chests. There is mildew on about a third of the things rust on some and die off hangings and pictures frames on some. About half the linen is so stained I sent it to the French laundry just now . . . I had to stretch string in five rooms and hang up every single thing to day in the house as it is raining steadily out side. The big mahoginy table is busted all to little pieces. My shaving [stand] and bureau are busted we may be able to save one by using part of the other. The graflex [camera] and typewriter are junk. The gold frame mirrors are no more. The two big screnes are not worth repairing. The backs are off 75% of the books and they swelled so much that most of the book boxes are burst open. Your bureau and the one with brass handles are not hurt. Your sewing cabinet is all right. The two sets of nested tables are all right. So is the oval table with the glass tray top. All the chairs including my leather one seem all right. The Daven-port is not hurt much. The Hoover and all the electric irons are ruined but perhaps can be rewired. The highboy is not hurt much. Neither are the mattresses or pillows. All the clothes I sent and all the hangings you sent have been soaking in salt water for two weeks but may recover. I can't tell till they dry. However we have still more than enough furnature to get on with or we can buy it here. The insurance appraiser seemed to me very broad minded and I think we will get 2500.00 or 3000 damages which will realy replace every thing. I am doing the best I can to fix up what is left so you may find things better than this letter indicates. I told you all the horrors as distance will soften them and you may find that time and a good carpenter has repaired some damages.

He added that Schofield Barracks was quite a military place, with no less than eight marching bands in existence, and with 13,000 men in ranks for a division review. He had no servants in his house, but was taking his meals at the officers' mess, which was close by and quite good. "I don't think much of the C.O. nor of the chief of staff but they might be worse. I should like very much to be detailed as G–3 [operations officer] and may manage to work it as the present one leaves soon." He added a postscript: "The Bed is not *hurt at all.*"

Patton was fortunate to be transferred to Hawaii. In the continental United States, the Army was dispersed in small detachments across the country. Training major units such as regiments, brigades, and divisions was consequently impossible. In contrast, the Army posts in Panama, the Philippines, and Hawaii were relatively large and accommodated sizable numbers of troops. Exercises of the important formations were periodically undertaken. Even though the weapons used were left over from the World War and were becoming increasingly obsolete, even though there was little opportunity to test new equipment and doctrine, training was feasible.

Patton arrived in time to observe the large-scale maneuver held annually by the Hawaiian Division.

Lieutenant Colonel J. B. Murphy rated him as a "superior" officer, then continued:

Major Patton served as my assistant during the Grand Joint Army and Navy Exercises April 1925. I had an excellent opportunity to observe the manner in which he performed his duties as a general staff officer. His tactical judgment is superior, he is well balanced, and he is a quick and enthusiastic worker. Major Patton is well educated along tactical lines and he would be a superior Chief of Staff, G–2 or G–3 of a Corps during combat. While I have had no opportunity to observe him in command of troops, it is my opinion, based on general observation, that he would be an excellent commander of combat troops during war.

Patton sent General H. A. Smith, under whom he had served in Langres and Leavenworth, an informal report of the exercises, together with photographs and documents, plus some desultory thoughts about the next war.

Smith replied and said that he was about to depart Leavenworth regretfully for Washington. "I dislike the War Department very much and if my choice friend, General Hines [the Chief of Staff], were not there, it would be still more distasteful." But he hoped to land at the Army War College and, further, to welcome Patton to the course. He warned Patton somewhat jokingly but with an undertone of seriousness not to become so accomplished a staff officer that he would get only that kind of duty in the future. "I note with a great deal of pleasure what you say about the next war and I hope that you are a good prophet. If I get either one of those jobs [you predicted] you will command the First Division."

Meanwhile, Patton was appointed Acting G–1 (personnel officer) and G–2 (intelligence officer) of the Hawaiian Division, positions that kept him working with papers of one sort or another but left him enough time for riding, polo, and other strenuous exercise.

Colonel Howard L. Laubach, acting chief of staff, cautiously rated Patton's work as "above average." Several months later, when Laubach knew him better, he considered Patton an "average" G–1 and G–2, but thought him to be

> an upstanding gentleman of courteous, well-bred demeanor. Very loyal and dependable. A student of his profession. This officer is a man of energy and action and in my opinion is better qualified for active duty than the routine of office work.

In November, Patton was placed on detached service with the Hawaiian Department, where he remained as acting or temporary G–1 for almost a year.

In a lecture at Schofield Barracks, "On Leadership," Patton categorically fixed the foremost trait of a military leader as

> the possession of a superiority complex. . . .

. . . what other traits are necessary [?] . . .

Perhaps the attributes he should possess are best illustrated by a comparison to the ignition system of a gasoline motor. No matter how carefully designed and accurately machined and assembled it may be, the motor is but iron sloshed with oil until fired to powerful and harmonious activity by the electric spark—the soul of the leader.

For this reason the vigorous possession of a self confident combative instinct is more important to the commander of any army than to the commander of a squad for in the former case the voltage must be higher in order to overcome the resistance of inertia in the mighty mass whose functioning is dependent on his vitalising power.

The wires which, so to speak, conduct this energy are five fold: Habit, Personality, Example, Fear, and Reward . . . In practice they are inexorably commingled and mutually dependent.

Habit, he said, induced a sense of responsibility in the leader and made it "impossible to fail in the discharge of his trust." He cited as an example the high proportion of officer casualties when compared to that of soldiers.

Personality, an intangible quality, consisted of

charm, reserve, tact, consideration and aggressiveness in combat. It enables its possessor to be in but not of a group; it produces an aura of authority . . .

The lifelong habit of command and responsibility, produces in the better sort, a command personality. Since we cannot breed our leaders, our efforts must be bent towards the fullest possible development of this trait . . .

The leader must demonstrate his superiority in the technique of combat. He must be a better rider, shot, scout, cook, etc. than any of his men . . .

. . . the ability to make quick and correct tactical decisions, producing thereby a self confidence which battle may reduce but cannot destroy [is fostered by solving problems in service schools and makes for] a sense of demonstrated ability . . .

The battlefield alone offers him [a leader] the opportunity

to make a reputation for dauntless courage without which it is impossible to obtain the uttermost from his men. For despite the calming influence of excessive civilization, the human animal still retains his age old admiration for heroism, seeing that in the dark beginnings of our race it was the one prerequisite to success in the stark battle for existence.

Few men are by nature devoid of physical fear. The blistering heat of battle withers many a budding reputation when the poor shrinking flesh fails to sustain the soul midst the myriad forms of dissolution in which the reaper seems to stalk the field. To combat this it behooves us to develop an antitoxin to fear and with it to inoculate our men. The best virus is a mixture of race consciousness, a mind saturated with former deeds of heroism, an abundant sense of obligation and an insatiable desire for present distinction and posthumous celebrity, so that in the fateful hour he may subdue his weaker self with that mighty potion—fear of fear.

Like a cold bath the first plunge is the hardest. Later, if he live, custom, fatigue, fatalism and pride will make him master of his emotions, for devoid of fear no normal man can ever become. Once on the morning of battle an officer asked Turenne if his knees shook from the cold and the veteran replied: "No my friend they shake from fear but if they knew where I shall this day take them they would tremble more."

Opportunities for reputation are not prevalent in the dug-out, nor do they flock to the leader with the reserve. Glory and death are brothers and their abiding place is the front line. The man who would qualify as a leader must lead—lead not by the cold incandescence of his super-refined intellect but by the fiery passion of his blazing manhood—a very king of beasts . . .

We do not stress enough the necessity for personal exposure and rash boldness on the part of our officers. Man loves life and too often yields to the sophistry of the subtile demon Fear, when he whispers, oh! so temptingly: "Your men need you, you must save your self for them" forgetting that the inspiration of an heroic act will carry men to victory . . . forgetful too that the blood of heroes like the dragons teeth will sprout new leaders to replace his loss.

War is elemental in its physical aspect and responds alone to psychology based on physical means . . .

There is no inspiration in the squeaking voice made dim and quavering by a mile of [telephone] wire nor can the most impressive personality accompany the wiggling atoms of a six hundred meter radio wave through the dreary wastes of interstellar space . . .

Courage as in the day of our neolithic ancestors is the greatest and most prized of virtues; lacking it, a shoulder full of stars is impotent to make a leader.

The recruit, in a new and strange environment, sought an ideal to copy and he looked to his officers. Courtesy, smartness, and promptness—"in a word discipline"—were best indoctrinated by example, but courage above all evoked imitation. Therefore, the leader must

never deviate from the role of a perfect soldier. He is always on parade. His orderly will report the number of his baths and the cleanliness of his undershirt. The mess waiter will recount the shinyness of his leather at meals and so on; while ten thousand men will hear and see and copy.

There was only one way to handle fear, and that was by prompt and public punishment, linked with ignominy and ridicule. "Punishment is not for the benefit of the sinner but for the salvation of his comrades." And this Patton would act on in the summer of 1943 in Sicily, where he slapped two soldiers in public for what he believed was cowardice on their part.

And finally, speaking of reward, Patton said:

The vital influence on morale and hence on leadership inherent in decorations cannot be overstated. Nor does the person exist to whom these baubles are repugnant. Our service has never realized nor capitalized [on] this fact . . . if a dime's worth of ribbon will make a hero of a craven it is the best investment in the world.

This does not mean that we would cheapen the decorations but it does mean that we should be more prompt and generous in their distribution; have more of them if need be . . .

Deterred by the fear that one coward will benefit, we let a hundred heroes starve of their due, the inspiration of their lives, their half inch of ribbon.

Patton spent the Christmas holidays with Beatrice and the children at his parents' home. "Papa and [young] George had great fun together."

Soon after Patton returned to Hawaii in January 1926, he replied to a memo circulated by the G–2, who proposed that a school be organized in order to qualify selected junior officers in foreign languages. Patton had two main objections. First, "Personal experience in the study of two foreign languages convinces me that no useful working knowledge can be received save by residence in the Country concerned and the absolute separation from all English speaking companions." Second, junior officers were already overburdened with administrative and school duties requiring excessive indoor or clerical work. Enlarging on the latter point:

wars are won by the physical courage, energy and initiative of junior officers and . . . such qualities are only engendered in the young male animal . . . by much recreation and violent physical exercise. The previous enviable record of our Army is in my opinion largely due to the fact that prior to the World War, young officers were less confined and by leisure stored up a reserve supply of energy and enthusiasm which enabled them to conquer in battle.

Beatrice and the children were now in Hawaii with Patton and life was more than pleasant for all of them. "We are going to a big dance at the opening of the new Royal Hawaiian Hotel tomorrow night," he wrote his father, "and will stay at Walter Dillinghams for the night." But if Patton was playing polo and frequently sailing with Beatrice, he was also reading and studying and occasionally giving lectures. He talked to a group of artillery officers on the "History and Employment of Light Tanks," a lecture he had originally written in 1919. It had then consisted for the most part of history, plus a few general principles of employment. He now had something more to say.

. . . the notion [is] too prevalent, among military men, that the last war no matter where fought is the final word, the sealed pattern of all future conflicts . . . and [it] has infected to an alarming degree both our tactics and our organization . . . [We are] seeking so hard for an approved solution that will avoid the odious task of thinking . . . The characteristics of the next war are as insoluable as are those of an unborn babe. From his parents we can deduce his probable color. For the next war we can alone be certain that it will consist of wounds, death and destruction. How the baby will think, or how the war will be fought are veiled. But as surely as we know the child will have hands so are we certain that the war will have tanks . . . Whether the tank shall precede or follow the infantry or even be associated with it is irrelivant. When the next war comes some of us, God willing, will have the Tank ready to our hands as one of the instruments with which to inflict wounds, death and destruction. As Forrest well put it: "War means fighting and fighting means killing." Let your best thought and keenest ingenuity based on principles and untrammeled by all labored memory of past *tactical details* be bent to the employment of the instruments of combat; infantry, cavalry, artillery, air service and TANKS in the best way most suitable to kill the enemy.

This was the idea of the combined arms, the combined use of all the weapons in the Army to make war on the battlefield, and it would characterize the operations in World War II.

The Treasury Department transmitted to Patton in February a silver Life Saving Medal of Honor—"in recognition of the gallant conduct displayed by you in bravely rescuing three boys from drowning in Salem Harbor, Massachusetts, August 21, 1923." Major General Edward M. Lewis, who commanded the Hawaiian Division, ceremoniously pinned the decoration on Patton, in the presence of a host of friends and a regimental infantry band.

Walter F. Dillingham, a resident of Hawaii, a polo player who had become one of the Pattons' best friends, wrote to congratulate Patton and to tell of his delight in what he called the merited recognition to Patton and his heroic wife. "I am prepared to decorate the whole family for bravery on general principles, but I had always thought of your special forte as being one of killing rather than saving lives. It must be a fine sensation to know that one is a well rounded hero."

CHAPTER 39

Hawaii: Schofield Barracks

*"There are probably as many ways of winning a war
as there are of skinning a cat."*

GSP, Jr., Lecture, "The Secret of Victory," March 26, 1926

Despite the years of thought and oceans of ink which have
been devoted to the elucidation of war its secrets still remain shrouded in mystery.

Indeed it is due largely to the very volume of available information that the veil is so thick.

War is an art and as such is not susceptible of explanation
by fixed formulae. Yet from the earliest time there has been
an unending effort to subject its complex and emotional
structure to dissection, to enunciate rules for its waging, to
make tangible its intangibility. As well strive to isolate the
soul by the dissection of the cadaver as to seek the essence
of war by the analysis of its records.

Yet despite the impossibility of physically detecting the
soul its existence is proven by its tangible reflection in acts
and thoughts.

So with war, beyond its physical aspect of armed hosts
there hovers an impalpable something which on occasion so
dominates the material as to induce victory under circumstances quite inexplicable.

To understand this something we . . . shall perchance find
it in the reflexes produced by the acts of the Great Captains . . .

Not in the musty tomes of voluminous reports or censored
recollections wherein they strove to immortalize and conceal
their achievements. Nor yet in the countless histories where
lesser wormish men have sought to snare their parted ghosts.

The great warriors were too busy and often too inapt to

write contemporaneously of their exploits save in the form of propaganda reports . . . biographies were retrospects colored by their vain striving for enhanced fame, or by political conditions then confronting them.

War [is] . . . violent simplicity in execution [and] . . . pale and uninspired on paper. . . .

The white-hot energy of youth which saw in obstacles but inspirations and in the enemy but the gage to battle, becomes to complacent and retrospective age the result of mathematical calculation and metophysical erudition; of knowledge he never had and plans he never made . . .

Colored by self deception, shaded by scholarly book worms our soldiers stand before us as devoid of life as the toothless portraits of Washington which adorn the walls of half our school rooms . . .

Disregarding wholly the personality of Frederick [the Great] we attribute his victories to a tactical expedient, the oblique order of battle . . . accounts of valor mellow with age . . .

Yet . . . the history of war is the history of warriors; few in number, mighty in influence.

Alexander, not Macedonia conquered the world. Scipio, not Rome destroyed Carthage. Marlborough not the allies defeated France. Cromwell, not the roundheads dethroned Charles . . .

. . . the tendency . . . to consider the most recent past war as the last word, the sealed pattern of all future contests to insure peace . . . all unconscious of personal bias we of necessity base our conceptions of the future on our experience of the past.

. . . personal knowledge is a fine thing but unfortunately it is too intimate . . . So with war experiences . . . [we forget that] it was the roads and consequent abundant mechanical transportation PECULIAR to western Europe which permitted the accumulation of enough gas shells to do the strangling . . .

Due either to superabundant egotism and uncontrolled enthusiasm or else to limited powers of observation . . . [the specialists] advocate in the most fluent and uncompromising manner the vast FUTURE potentialities of their own weapon. In the next war, so they say, all the enemy will be crushed, gassed, bombed or otherwise speedily exterminated, depending for the method of his death upon whether the person declaiming belongs to the tank, gas, air or other special service.

. . . many of them possess considerable histrionic ability and much verbosity [and] they attract public attention. The appeal of their statements is further strengthened because . . . they deal invariably in mechanical devices which intrigue the simple imagination . . . [and their schemes have] a strong news interest which insures their notice by the press . . .

. . . [newspapers have a] tendency to exploit the bizarre . . .

To . . . [pacifists] the history of the race from the fierce struggles in primordial slime to the present day is a blank . . . the lion loses his appetite and the lamb his fear, avarice and ambition, honor and patriotism are no more, all merge in a supine state of impossible toleration. The millions who have nobly perished for an ideal are fools, and a sexless creature too debased to care and too indolent to strive is held up for emulation . . .

There is an incessant change of means [in warfare] . . . [but] the unchanging ends have been, are and probably ever shall be, the securing of predominating force, of the right sort, at the right place, at the right time.

. . . High academic performance [in the study of war] demands infinite knowledge of details and the qualities requisite to such attainments often inhabit bodies lacking in personality. Also the striving for such knowledge often engenders the falacious notion that capacity depends on the power to acquire such details not the ability to apply them . . .

. . . no soldiers ever sought more diligently [than the Germans] for prewar perfection. They builded and tested and adjusted their mighty machine and became so engrossed in its visible perfection, in the accuracy of its bearing and the compression of its cylinders that they neglected the battery till when the moment came their masterpiece proved inefficient through lack of the divine afflatus, the soul of a leader . . .

We require and must demand all possible thoughtful preparation and studious effort possible . . . Our purpose is not to discourage such preparation but simply to call attention to certain defects in its pursuit . . .

In acquiring erudition we must live on not in our studies. We must guard against becoming so engrossed in the specific nature of the roots and bark of the trees of knowledge as to miss the meaning and grandeur of the forests they compose . . .

All down the immortal line of mighty warriors . . . [they] were deeply imbued with the whole knowledge of war as practised at their several epochs. But also, and mark this, so were many of their defeated opponents; for . . . the secret of victory lies not wholly in knowledge. It lurks invisible in that vitalising spark, intangible, yet as evident as the lightning— the warrior soul . . .

Dry knowledge like dry rot destroys the soundest fiber. A constant search for soulless fundamentals, the effort to regularise the irregular, to make complex the simple, to assume perfect men, perfect material and perfect terrain as the prerequisites to war has the same effect on the soldier student . . .

War is conflict, fighting an elemental exposition of the age-old effort to survive. It is the cold glitter of the attacker's eye not the point of the questing bayonet that breaks the line. It is the fierce determination of the driver to close with the enemy, not the mechanical perfection of a Mark VIII tank that conquers the trench. It is the cataclysmic ecstasy of conflict in the flier not the perfection of his machine gun which drops the enemy in flaming ruin . . .

. . . Hooker's plan at Chancerlorsville was masterly, its execution cost him the battle. The converse was true [with Napoleon] at Marengo . . .

Staff systems and mechanical communications are valuable but above and beyond them must be the commander; not as a disembodied brain linked to his men by lines of wire and waves of ether; but as a living presence, an all pervading visible personality . . .

. . . Napoleon Bonaparte and Stonewall Jackson stand preeminent in their use of . . . time . . .

In war tomorrow we shall be dealing with men subject to the same emotions as were the soldiers of Alexander; with men but little changed . . . from the starving shoeless Frenchmen of 1796. With men similar save in their arms to those who the inspiring powers of a Greek or a Corsican changed at a breath to bands of heroes all enduring and all capable . . .

There are certainly born leaders but the soldier may also overcome his natal defects by unremitting effort and practice . . .

Loyalty is frequently only considered as faithfulness from the bottom up. It has another and equally important application, that is from the top down. One of the most frequently noted characteristics of the great who remained great is . . . loyalty to their subordinates. It is this characteristic which binds with hoops of iron their juniors to them.

A man who is truly and unselfishly loyal to his superiors is of necessity so to his juniors and they to him . . .

A man of diffident manner will never inspire confidence. A cold reserve cannot beget enthusiasm . . . there must be an outward and visible sign of the inward and spiritual grace.

It then appears that the leader must be an actor and he certainly must be. But with him as with his bewigged counterpart he is unconvincing unless he lives his part . . .

The fixed determination to acquire the warrior soul and having acquired it to conquer or perish with honor is the secret of victory.

These sentiments, expressed publicly, burned within him. The deeds of derring-do he dreamed of contrasted with the routine duties he performed as a staff officer, a G–1, who was concerned with matters of personnel and administration. Sitting at a desk was anathema to him and to his vision of the warrior. Yet accompanying his drive for battlefield greatness was his loyalty to the Army and to his superiors that gave him the patience to endure. As he wrote to Aunt Nannie, "The present indications are that I shall be kept on this down town job for another three months which is a great nusance but there is no help for it." With as much good grace as he could muster, he performed the functions required of him.

He did, of course, a great deal more. He led an extensive social life. "Gen and Mrs. Howze are over here visiting their daughter and we are giving them a party on Saturday with all the rank in the army coming." He was president of a riding club. He devoted a great deal of time to polo, not merely to playing the game but also to the details connected with arranging the matches.

He continued his professional reading. Annotating Swinton's *Study of War*, Patton commented: to live meant to fight tenaciously, disarmament was disastrous to nations, and countries had constantly to prepare for war.

Patton reviewed for the *Cavalry Journal* Captain B. H. Liddell Hart's *The Remaking of Modern Armies*, saying in part:

> . . . many of its ideas are radical. In other words, their thoughts must be chewed to be digested, for if swallowed whole, like patented foods, their nutritive qualities will either fail to develop or else they will overstimulate and produce mental colic . . .
>
> We are informed that "Sudden and overwhelming blows from the air—could destroy Essen or Berlin in a matter of hours." Having learned by experience and by reading, the difficulty of destroying anything and the obstacles incident to the production of overwhelming instruments, one is tempted to suggest [that] . . . a steam roller . . . would be as useful and as attainable . . .
>
> The question he asks as to the future of the French Army might, with some limitations, be asked of our own. The answer is fraught with great moment.

In the same issue of the *Cavalry Journal*, Patton reviewed with great charm and literary facility a biography of Major General Sir Frederick Maurice, soldier, artist, and sportsman.

Of Major B. C. Deming's *The Future of the British Army*, he wrote:

> There are probably as many ways of winning a war as there are of skinning a cat. Some of us pin our faith on an accurate use of commas, others on grease or gas, on footease or saddle

soap, and in the ardor of our enthusiasm for our especial panacea forget that the way to skin a cat is to remove his hide, and the way to win a war is to beat the enemy. Whether or not we belong to those who pin their faith on grease, and mechanization as the surest means to future victory is, however, immaterial to the fact that any soldier will be benefited and interested by reading [the book under review].

. . . our future triumphs or disasters depend on whether or not we are able to compromise, to select the virtues of the new and add them to the merits of the old—to mix grease with footease.

The last was a subtle reference to the place of the gasoline engine in warfare. Still interested in machines, Patton could not afford to be altogether outspoken in his advocacy of mechanization if he wished advancement in the cavalry.

The Hawaiian Division commander signed a letter prepared by his G-1, Patton, recommending a revision in an Army Regulation to prevent "an unduly rapid flow of promotions among reserve officers, thereby doing an injustice to them by making them eligible for commands in war for which their training does not qualify them. And at the same time militating against public interest by the placing of the lives of our soldiers in untrained hands." At the bottom of the paper in Patton's handwriting was the notation: "Form proposed and written by GSP Jr. Approved with minor modifications." He may have disliked staff work, but he took pride in his minor triumphs.

Colonel A. G. Lott, chief of staff of the Hawaiian Division, rated Patton as "above average"—"an officer with 'a punch' who is better suited for duty with Cavalry than for peacetime administrative details."

Early in 1926, Patton learned that the Commandant of Cadets at the Military Academy was soon to be transferred. He immediately sought the post. He telegraphed three influential friends, Generals Harbord, H. A. Smith, and Malin Craig, asking them for help.

Harbord regretfully said that he had already committed himself to support another officer, for it had not occurred to him that

Patton wanted the assignment. Otherwise, Harbord would have been for him. Quekemeyer, he informed Patton, had been selected but had died very suddenly of pneumonia.

Smith wrote to the Superintendent of the Military Academy and recommended Patton without reservation. Patton, he said, was "one of the best informed officers in his profession that I know." He was a hard worker and extremely loyal, had a fine personality and a delightful family.

Smith also talked with Fox Conner, the new Deputy Chief of Staff—"He is for you, as you know I am, and we will do whatever we can for you."

Telegram, Malin Craig (Fort Riley) to Major General Robert C. Davis (War Department), March 4, 1926
Following cable received from Honolulu Quote Please recommend me for commandant of cadets signed Patton Unquote You know Patton so foregoing is for your consideration.

Letter, Malin Craig (Washington) to GSP, Jr., March 16, 1926
My dear George: Your cable reached me at Fort Riley where I was making an inspection. All I could do was to transmit it by wire to Davis with the necessary recommendation. I regret I was not here, as I would have gone to General Pershing, though of course Davis [a member of Pershing's staff in France] knows you. As you know, the detail has gone to a man named [Major Campbell B.] Hodges of the Infantry, who, I understand, was the personal selection of General Stewart [the Superintendent]. I regret very much that circumstances existed as they did as you are one fellow for whom I am always ready to go to the bat. When the next thing comes off I would naturally like a little more time as it is astonishing how details are prepared for and sewed up in advance.

Letter, Major General Fox Conner to GSP, Jr., June 15, 1926
My Dear Georgie . . . I am afraid the poor old Regular is in for hard sledding . . . As a matter of fact our whole trouble is one of money. I think we have ourselves largely to blame for we have, in the past at least, wasted a H— of a lot of money . . . I notice that the French Air Service have not

yet knocked the Riffs out [in Morocco, where natives were in revolt]. Something must be wrong. Perhaps they [the Riffs] refused to be anchored! [He was referring to their mobility.] As far as I can make out China is the place to be now. Drop me a line on how you size up the maneuvers [in Hawaii]. Much love to the family.

Letter, GSP, Jr., to Eisenhower, July 9, 1926
Dear Ike: Your letter [following Eisenhower's graduation from the C&GS College] delighted me more that [than] I can say. As soon as I saw the list I wrote you congratulating you on being honor[ed] but I had no idea that in addition you were no [number] ONE. That certainly is fine.

It shows that leavenworth is a good school if a HE man can come out one [in his class].

You are very kind to think that my notes helped you though I feel sure that you would have done as well with out them. If a man thinks war long enough it is bound to effect him in a good way.

I am convinced that as good as leavenworth is it is still only a means not an end and that we must keep on. I have worked all the problems of the two years since I graduated and shall continue to do so. However I dont try for approved solutions any more but rather to do what I will do in war. This applies both to formations and to verbage of the order. Orders in battle must be written wholly by the general him self not by a committee of his staff. Hence they must be short. Further in battle par 3 not par 2 is the important point.

As for par 4 let them live off the country and in par 5 state that the CP is the head of the maine blow. [He was speaking of the paragraphs of the standard field order.]

You know that we talk a hell of a lot about tactics and such and we never get to brass tacks. Namely what it is that makes the Poor S.O.B. who constitutes the casualtie lists fight and in what formation is he going to fight. The answer to the first is Leadership that to the second—I don't know. But this I do know that the present Infantry T.R. based on super trained heroes is bull. The solitary son of a bitch alone with God is going to skulk as he always has and our advancing waves will not advance unless we have such superior artillery that all they have to do is to walk.

First Read Battle Studies by Du Pique (you can get it at Leavenworth) then put your mind to a solution. The victor in the next war will depend on EXECUTION not PLANS and the execution will depend on some means of making the infantry move under fire. I have a solution for the Artillery and cavalry but only a tentative one for the infantry. After you tell me what you can make of it I will send you mine.

You did not say in your letter where you were going? I think probably an instructor ship is the best. The G.S. [General Staff] is punk. You and I will never have a G.S. [assignment] at least not as now invisioned.

With renewed congratulations and best wishes, I am

Most Sincerely, G S Patton Jr.

P.S. I gave you the last copy of my notes. Since they have been so useful I should like to get hold of a copy. Do you think you can locate one for me. If so I would like it. GSP

Letter, GSP, Jr., to Major Jack W. Heard (Cavalry Board, Fort Riley), August 12, 1926

I have made rather profound studies on the subject of Saber and Bayonet charges and it is my opinion based on history that the cases where two lines will meet will be VERY exceptional. One side will loose its nerve and run. In the rare instance when the lines meet, it will be at a very reduced pace or at a halt as the big majority of horses will refuse the shock. In either case, then a light handy saber will be more useful than a long awkward one. The above remarks in no way imply that I have lost faith in the saber. I have however decided that it is the enemies soul rather than his body which is defeated. For the same reason the formation which a charge is executed is immaterial; determination and speed are the only requisite. *The leader must be in front.* It is interesting to remember that the mounted bowmen never closed nor did the pistol fighters of Maurice of Nassau—Reason—the weapons they used could be discharged at a distance. In both cases they were put out of business by the charge with the steel NOT because the steel was more *deadly* but because the determination to use it, being of a higher order, broke the spirit of the enemy. Pistol fire, if effective, would kill more enemy than the saber. Rifle fire from the hip would kill more enemy than the bayonet but man, being what he is, will never close to effective range unless he knows that his weapon is useless at any other. It is the apparent menace of death rather than actual death which wins battles. The vicious saber charge wins long before the lines touch; and having won, anything is sufficient to stick the enemy in the back. Sincerely yours,

The last point came directly from the writings of Ardant du Picq, military thinker and writer who fathered the idea of élan, the spirit of the charge, who died during the Franco-Prussian War, and whose concept was adopted and fostered by Grandcamp and Foch—so that at the beginning of World War I, the professional French officers, convinced of the superiority of men over machines and of the necessity of the offensive, threw away thousands of soldiers against the machine guns that mowed them down.

And yet, who could deny that one of two opposing lines usually broke and ran. The steady—meaning Regular—troops of the French and British employed in far-off lands and romanticized in the 1920s and 1930s by such novels as *Beau Geste*, always withstood the howling mobs attacking them and sent them streaming back in confusion and defeat before physical contact was made.

Patton's letter to Heard was probably his clearest exposition of this point of view.

Colonel Lott rated Patton as "above average"—"an enthusiastic soldier with a 'punch,' and a serious student of his profession, exceptionally well fitted for duty with troops of his arm (cavalry)."

The polo was splendid during the summer of 1926, and Patton's Army team defeated the two civilian teams in competition and captured the Island championship. To the senior officers in Hawaii, the games were not merely amusement but rather a "creditable exhibition of fine sportsmanship, leadership, and team play, qualities essential to success in the military profession."

Letter, H. A. Smith to GSP, Jr., October 26, 1926
I enjoyed your letter very much, and when I read Mrs. Smith the sentence, "May we soon have a war so that you can exercise command" she said, "You needn't read any more. I know George Patton wrote that." However, maybe

we can kick up a good war. I am thinking some of starting a filibustering expedition to one of the Central American States. How would you like to go along on that?

Smith was only joking.

Letter, GSP, Jr., to Beatrice (visiting in Massachusetts), November 2, 1926

I have always hoped that as the result of a great war I would secure supreme command and such fame that after the war I would be able to become President or dictator by the ballot or by force. In that case we would not have needed a house for we would have persuaded a grateful people to build us a marble Palace at the flag pole at Fort Myer. However as I approach [the age of] 41 and there is no war I almost doubt the Palace and fear that I shall live to retire a useless soldier. In which case as we could still hunt it would be nice to have a place in the hunting country. As inspite of polo ponies, boats and Squash Courts you don't spend ¼ of your income I think the house might be fine and certainly no extravagance.

Letter, C. P. Summerall to GSP, Jr., November 4, 1926

My dear Patton: I deeply appreciate your very good letter congratulating me upon my appointment as Chief of Staff. It has been one of my peculiar privileges to serve with you under varying circumstances and difficulties, and I have always felt the most sincere appreciation of your loyalty and admiration for your efficiency. Indeed, it is to you and to the officers and soldiers with whom I have served that I owe whatever success may have come to my efforts. I can only place my reliance upon you for the support and cooperation that I shall need in my future tasks.

Letter, GSP, Jr., to Beatrice, November 16, 1926

Darling Beat: I got three letters from you to day one with the clippings about the Riley Races. What is the matter with your eyes [in one of the photographs], are they crossed?

Beatrice and young Bea traveled from Massachusetts, Patton, Ruth Ellen, and young George came from Hawaii, and all met in southern California for Christmas.

GSP, Jr., "My Father," 1927

In the spring of 1926 Papa Mama and Nita visited us at Schofield. Papa was very feeble and his tongue used to get black and we would joke him about it. He suffered a lot with constipation. One day he went swimming with us and once he and I took a ride of about an hour. It was his last ride. We drove all over Oahu. Papa had a little Oakland Coupe which we rented for him.

After they left for home in July, Papa wrote me much less often and his writing was much less firm and clear. Mama wrote that she was much worried about him. He went to the hospital and was cured of his constipation but his bladder became inflamed and he underwent a thorough physical examination. In November he wrote me that he hoped we would all come home "so that we could have one more Christmas together."

While we were home last Christmas [in 1926] he seemed to improve. Still he was very weak and worried about trivial details. He and [young] george used to walk in the Cannon gorge with a pop gun and they would pretend to kill lions as I had once done. Papa took me with him when ever he could always asking me to drive to the Post Office with him for the mail. One day I was lazy and did not go. The sorrow in his voice when he said "All right son never mind I will be right back" Haunts me.

In 1922 Papa [had] bought himself a Hup Roadster. He used to write me about it and took a lot of interest in it. So far as I know this was about the only present he had ever bought just for him self. He and Mama drove all over the country in it especially on Sunday Morning when they would most frequently drive towards Duarte. In 1926 it was old and stiff so Beatrice and I made him turn it in and we got him a new Hup Eight. Papa protested violently that his old car was good enough for him but I shall never forget the pleasure of his smile when the new one came and he walked around it poking the tires with his stick and saying "it is a gentleman's car." He liked it a lot and used to tell mama that it was the best sort of car. He and I took several drives in it, once to Duarte, but at the time of his death he had driven it less than a thousand miles. The memory of his pleasure at it is a great happiness to me . . .

The morning after we arrived Christmas morning 1926, papa took me to his office and told me that the examination he had taken disclosed the fact that he had T.B. in his left kidney. He asked me not to tell any of the family as it would worry them. I went to see the doctors and after consulting with them and with Nita and Beatrice we decided that it was better not to operate as we feared he would fret so in the hospital that it would kill him; besides some of them said that sun baths might arrest or cure the disease.

At this time he was more interested in affairs than he had been for some time. He wanted to make a trade with Mr. Huntington so as to get the bottom of the Cannon [canyon] back of the house especially as it would improve Nita's place. And he was again interested in the Pyramids and their significance and had several new books on them which he read in connection with Biblical prophecies.

He had always expressed to me his belief that the very fortunate career I had had in the army was Fate and that I was being specially prepared for some special work. He and Mr Gaffey felt that the end of our Civilization was at hand and that war was sure. When I used to bemoan the fact that wars were getting scarce and that all the time I had spent getting ready would be wasted for lack of opportunity he used to assure me with the greatest confidence that I would yet be in the biggest war in history. He was most convincing and I believed him, particularly as I have always felt the same thing concerning my self . . .

This same Christmas period he took me to his office and showed me the relics he had about his father and family.

One evening when the rest had gone to bed he said to me wistfully "Son you had more experiences and saw more of life in two years in France than I have in all my seventy years." He was not bitter or complaining, only wistful. He had a romantic and venturesome spirit which had been curbed by circumstances and a sense of duty to those he loved. I am sure he felt that death was the only adventure left for him and yearned for it with out fear and with great curiosity and an-

ticipation being only deterred from so expressing such feelings by his love for his family and his fear of wounding them.

One evening I made him dictate to me all his memories of
the civil war as he saw it as a boy. I have this at schofield [Bar-
racks] and will type it and file it with this.

After we left Papa became much worse and suffered intensely . . .

Letter, GSP, Jr., to his father, February 6, 1927

As I wrote you the other day I can arrange to get off any
time and come home either to go east with you or to be present if you have an operation. I have already gotten the permission from General Smith . . . I cannot urge too strongly
my earnest hope that you realy exercise your will power to
take care of your self. You are such a good arguer that it is
too easy for you to reason your self out of doing things that
are a nusance. And you are then perfectly convinced that you
are doing the right thing when in fact it is not so. When you
were a cadet [at VMI] you did what you were ordered with
out question. Cant you ORDER YOUR SELF to take a regular course of treatment what ever it may be and then TAKE
IT. The surest way in my opinion is to set aside a certain
hour and then arrange things so that in spite of hell or high
water you can do it. There are too many people who love you
for you to disreguard their wishes and kill your self by carless-
ness. I hope you will forgive my preaching and do your duty
to your self.

Long-distance admonition from son to father had little effect,
and sometime in February, Mr. Patton wrote and asked George
to come home if he could. Unknown to Mr. Patton, Nita wired
the same to her brother. A few days later, feeling he was incon-
veniencing his son far too much, Mr. Patton wired him not to
come. George disregarded his father's telegram.

When Patton reached the family home at Lake Vineyard, he
found things better than he had expected. All the doctors consulted or in attendance favored an operation.

Thin, weak, and suffering from pain, Mr. Patton, according to
his son writing to Beatrice,

has gotten over his idea that the family is financially ruined
. . . He thinks he is not eating but so far to day has eaten
more than I have . . .

After he sent me the wire not to come he was terribly worried for fear I would pay attention to it so, as usual, you were
right in telling me to come. He does not know that Nita
wired me to come and thinks that I did it in response to a
letter [from him]. I am certainly glad I came as it seems
to have done them all good. I think that Pa has a very good
chance for recovery. If not it would be better for him to die
than to suffer, or think he suffers, the way he does.

GSP, Jr., "My Father," 1927

I was in the room with him when the attendants came to
wheel him to the operating room. I kissed him and as he went
out the door he waved his thin brown hand at me and smil-
ing said "Aurez War [Au revoir] Son." The courage of that
act would have won the Medal of Honor on any field of battle. He was seventy, had never been operated on, so dreaded
it, and he was very weak; yet going to what he thought was
death he tried to cheer me with out thought of self.

Mr. Patton came through the operation nicely and slept quietly
immediately afterward. Mrs. Patton was in good spirits "and did
not show any excitement." Patton had a room next door to his
father's in the hospital.

After a bad night, Mr. Patton improved.

GSP, Jr., "My Father," 1927

I stayed with him every day till the thirteenth when I left
for San Francisco. He suffered a lot the first five days but
then seemed much better. The last afternoon I was with him
I was smoking and he asked me to fill his favorite pipe for
him and we smoked together. That night I kissed him for the
last time and said good by. He smiled and said he would take
care of him self. Next day I called him on the long distance
from San Francisco. The last words I ever heard him say
were: "Good by Old Man take care of yourself."

*Letter, GSP, Jr. (on the Dollar Steamship Line steamer S.S.
President Polk) to his father, March 17, 1927*

I have read two books and written some notes on the defense of columns against Air Planes. I hated to leave before you were completely well . . . I never saw one go out to die with as much calmness and assurance as you did. When they wheeled you out of the room you waved your hand to me and said "Aurey vois" with a smile and in a perfectly natural voice. Now please as a favor to all of us use that same high courage to get well and strong so that you can enjoy life and we can enjoy having you.

Letter, GSP, Jr. (in Honolulu) to his father, March 21, 1927
You ought to be like me and not worry. In getting off the steamer a friend offered me a bottle of whiskey so I put it in my overcoat pocket and was arrested on the dock. I was very polite and all that happened was that it cost me five dollars no publicity or any thing. Beatrice did not even know that it had happened nor does she yet for that matter for she is like you and would have at once started to picture the penetentiary court martial etc. Worrying does not help any thing and hurts every thing. STOP IT . . . Everyone seemed glad to see me back and my new assistant is a very good officer and seems willing to do all the work while I get what glory there is.

Letter, GSP, Jr., to his father, April 22, 1927
I hear that you have got your self on your mind and dont eat etc. Of course if you want to die that is the best way to secure the end desired. You will now say that I dont understand you and that you cant help it. You can if you will. With all the people who love you and want you to live it is selfish and poor sportsmanship to act as you are doing.

He invited his father to come for a visit and promised he would not ask him to ride or to swim or to do anything but sit in the sun. He had just returned from the island of Hawaii, where he had spent eight days buying horses for the post. He had purchased 66 animals and had had a nice time staying with Mr. Alfred Carter who ran the Parker ranch of 500,000 acres, quite a "fudal" place.

He wrote again on April 27, telling his father that he and Beatrice had sailed in two races on Saturday and Sunday and had finished third and fourth in a field of eleven boats. The 66 horses he had purchased had arrived, "and every one thinks that I am a famous horse buyer . . . The longer we stay here the more we like it and hate the thought of leaving. We have not yet decided whether or not to ask for a fourth year."

Letter, GSP, Jr., to his father, May 24, 1927
I am sorry that you had such an awful trip [here last year] for when you are well [and can come for another visit] you will like it here. Right now it is lovley.

Mr. Patton died early in June, and his son went home, too late for the funeral.

GSP, Jr., "My Father," 1927
The morning I arrived I wore my uniform and went alone to his grave. The whole lot was covered with flowers all of which had wilted save the pall of red roses over the spot where he lay. These to me seemed fresh, vivified by the great soul of him who lay beneath them.

For an hour I stood there and the knowledge came to me that the grave no more held Papa than does one of his discarded suits hanging in a closet. Suddenly I seemed to see him in the road werring his checked overcoat and with his stick which he waved at me as he had been used to do when he was impatient and wanted to go some where.

I knelt and kissed the ground then put on my cap and saluted not Papa, but the last resting place of that beautiful body I had loved. His soul was with me and but for the density of my fleshly eyes I could have seen and talked with him.

As I write this in his office where we talked and smoked so often he is here. I like to remember not the symbol of his gallant spirit which I saluted in the church yard but Rather Papa as he was wheeled out to die perhaps, and to think of his words so true of our present temporary seperation when he smiled at me and said "Aurevoir Son."

Oh! darling Papa. I never called you that in life as both of us were too self contained but you were and are my darling. I have often thought that life for me was too easy but the loss of you has gone far [to] even my count with those whom before I have pitied.

God grant that you see and appreciate my very piteous attempt to show here your lovely life. I never did much for you and you did all for me. Accept this as a slight offering of what I would have done.

Your devoted son
G S Patton Jr
July 9 1927

Letter, Pershing to GSP, Jr., July 12, 1927
No one could meet your father without feeling his personality, and no one could know him, even casually, without recognizing his high character and great ability. I know the high esteem in which you yourself held him and knew him well enough to understand fully the reasons for your great admiration and affection. Please accept for yourself and extend to your mother and sister my deepest and sincerest condolences in the great loss that has come to you, to his friends, to the State of California, and to the nation in his passing.

Letter, GSP, Jr., to Pershing, July 25, 1927
While all sympathy is most grateful when it comes from the first soldier of the age it is truly delightful . . .
I can imagine no more pleasant and instructive place [than Hawaii] to serve. While I am on the Staff—a place for which God never intended me—I can with the Hawaiian Division still see quite a lot of the troops.

CHAPTER 40

Hawaii to Washington

"In war death is incidental: loss of time is criminal."

Letter, GSP, Jr., to Beatrice, November 1, 1926
The order is out to day making me G–3—at last.

He was excited by his assignment to the G–3 post, which he had long hankered after. That staff section was concerned with operations, plans, and training. Although staff work frustrated Patton, the functions of the G–3 were closest to his peacetime interests —preparing troops for combat in a future war. Although he would suffer from the lack of direct contact with units and soldiers enjoyed by commanders, he would at least be directly involved in what he considered to be the most important activity—training. As G–3, he was the division commander's adviser on tactical matters—a subject which encompassed a great many affairs—and as such he could speak in the name of the commander to all subordinate formations and commanders in the division. Relishing his new status, Patton immediately made his presence remarked.

The 22d Brigade of the Hawaiian Division held an exercise in mid-November on how to conduct the advance guard. The demonstration displeased him immensely. As the staff representative of the division commander, he was free to make comments, and according to his observations, certain obvious deficiencies required correction. He minced no words in his written remarks to the brigade commander, who was a brigadier general, and this was a procedural error on Patton's part. He should have had the division commander sign the paper. For a major to "correct" a brigadier general was inadmissible. His action was tactless and created much ill-will toward him.

What he wrote was this:

The normal purpose of an attack is the infliction of death wounds and destruction on the enemy troops with a view to establish both physical and moral ascendency over them. The gaining of ground in such a combat is simply an incident; not an object.

The following remarks are not confined to advance guards nor are they wholly orthodox. They are submitted for what they may be worth . . .

[The attempt by soldiers to use cover was not warranted in most cases, for the] primary efforts are directed to fancied self preservation rather than towards killing his enemy . . . In battle a man going forward enters a lottery, with death the stake, and the odds the laws of probability. The only saving clause in his venture are the time and the effect on the enemy's nerves of his rapid approach; why waste these benefits in futile sacrifices to lost Gods of Indian wars . . .

In battle the dead do not run but the living do and for them to so perform it is necessary that they be scared. These considerations seem to indicate that the present method of using machine guns is not the last word, the best arrangement. Serious thought should be given to supplying each platoon with self contained man transported machine guns . . .

[Howitzer platoons] seem to absorb more men from our depleted regiments than their killing value justifies. . . .

There is much talk to the effect that the fire of guns, machine guns, stokes mortars, etc make certain places impassable. History proves that fighting men can go anywhere. The technique of deploying, fire, cover, etc [in our training exercises] seems to overshadow the paramount idea of KILLING. Advances are too unenthusiastic. This tendency is enhanced by the fact that most exercises stop at the deployment. Actually it is in stages subsequent to the deployment where the fighting and the trouble starts. It is thought that all exercises should be conducted with this idea in view.

Again in his capacity as G–3, Patton instructed all brigade, regimental, and separate unit commanders to correct certain derelictions in military bearing among officers and men: poor adjustment of Sam Browne belts worn at drill; poor saluting by officers who frequently failed to come to attention during the salute; poor manners on the part of officers who smoked while instructing or while supervising instruction—"They shall only smoke during rest periods where the same privilege is allowed the men."

Lieutenant Colonel S. T. Mackall, the acting chief of staff, rated Patton "above average" as G–1, G–2, and G–3—"an ambitious officer, aggressive disposition, well read, perfectly loyal [to his superiors]."

As G–3, Patton tried to solve a problem that plagued all headquarters—how to deal satisfactorily with the mutually conflicting tasks of housekeeping and training, that is, how to have the minimum number of troops on supply and administrative details required to keep a post operating, while at the same time retaining the maximum number at military instruction. At Schofield Barracks, only about half the men were attending drill and other military exercises at any given time; the rest were on kitchen police and similar duties. Patton suggested two alternatives: set aside certain days when all purely administrative and routine activities would cease, thereby having all the men available for training; or form provisional units to train the relatively few men available from each company for military instruction.

These suggestions were probably too radical to be accepted.

A report issued by a board of officers studying how a division could gain protection against low-flying airplanes impressed him unfavorably. The board, headed by Major Henry H. Arnold, who would command the U. S. Army Air Corps in World War II and be a member of the Joint Chiefs of Staff, recommended that ground troops disperse at once when spotted by planes.

Patton wrote in the margin of the report: "This is a poor paper and views the whole thing in a negative way. 'War means fighting and fighting means killing' GSP." What he was saying was that passive defense—dispersing and taking cover—was no solution.

The board also recommended that two .50-caliber machine guns be mounted on light motor vehicles, that these accompany troop units, and that the gunners be ready at all times to engage low-flying planes. Patton's comment on the margin: "only good idea so far."

In May 1927, Patton devoted thought to the problem. In a long memo to the chief of staff, he said that the history of war was replete with lags, that is, periods when a new means of attack or defense gained a temporary ascendancy simply because it was novel rather than irresistible. The latest instance was air attack of ground troops, effective because the sudden appearance of planes gave them the advantage of surprise and because the ground troops offered no opposition. Air attacks were not terribly impressive in lethality; they were more expensive and less productive than ground attacks. Therefore, there was no need to be alarmed that airplanes might replace ground troops. Nevertheless, the vulnerability of ground units to aircraft made it desirable to see what might be done to counter the air weapons.

Most of the important troop movements in the World War, Patton continued, were made at night. This gave soldiers immunity from air observation and attack. But perhaps aircraft had since improved and were now capable of night operations against moving columns, the most lucrative target for planes.

What could be done? It was impossible to think of concealment, for that played into the enemy's hands. Nor was it feasible simply to disregard air attacks, for no discipline was sufficiently strong to keep men from scattering under strafing. The only solution that made sense was to devise some method of attacking the planes from the ground. How?

The speed of planes, which were capable of flying at 200 miles per hour, required ground soldiers to have instant warning of their approach. This meant that at least some troops had to be trained to identify enemy planes and to be on constant lookout for them. Once they gave the alarm, troops had to deploy from their march formation to a fighting formation; they had to do so in less than half a minute. Thus, the transition from march to combat formation had to be a simple procedure that could, with practice, be executed automatically. Whatever combat formation was selected, it had to enable all the men—not just part of them—to participate in the attack against the aircraft. What seemed instantly apparent to Patton was that almost everyone had to turn his weapon against the planes; a few soldiers would have to blindfold the horses and mules to keep them from panicking.

To this end, Patton composed a set of simple principles to regulate the switch from marching to fighting.

He warned, "The purpose of this memorandum is to stimulate thought; not to stifle it with dogma so that the sketchy regulations set out below are to be considered as provocatory rather than manditory in nature."

He added a note:

In writing this a studious attempt has been made to avoid the use of defensive expressions . . . [which] should never be used as they ingender a defensive frame of mind. The same is true of talk of concealment or the avoidance of splinters from bombs. Under normal shell or machine gun fire men do not or should not hide. The same is true in the case of air attacks. It is not recommended that practice against baloons or towed target be indulged in. In peace the hits will be so low asto reduce confidence. In war the volume of wild fire and the less adroitness of war time aviators [likely to be reservists] will secure us more hits. Care should be exercised that enemy aviators shot down should not be taken alive.

Patton proposed an exercise to determine whether his idea was practical, and the Hawaiian Division commander, Major General William R. Smith, after issuing a letter prepared by Patton on the "Ground Attack of Airplanes," ordered a demonstration.

On May 26, as the 3d Battalion, 35th Infantry, and several planes of the 18th Pursuit Group tested the effectiveness of Patton's notion, he observed the maneuver. On the following morning, he wrote a scathing criticism of the results obtained. Having learned his lesson, Patton submitted his comments to General Smith, who had his adjutant general sign the paper and send it to the proper brigade commander.

According to this letter, the officers in the battalion that had taken part in the exercise had failed on a number of points. They had failed to use every available weapon—only one machine gun of the machine gun company had been mounted for firing against air targets; they had failed to arrange to place all the machine guns instantly into action on a stable platform, from which they could fire more effectively against planes; they had failed to guard against a stampede on the part of the animals—the mules had not been blindfolded; they had failed to insure maximum speed and order in assuming the combat formation; they had failed to give fire commands and halts in an authoritative manner.

As a result of these defects, the impression was inescapable that the officers and men had not grasped the spirit of the proposed regulations.

. . . order, volume of fire, and rapidity of transition from march to combat and back to march conditions are the essential elements in the successful combat with air planes. Order depends on instant exact and subconscious obedience to specific commands. Volume of fire depends on the utilization of all available means. Rapidity depends on automatic obedience. Conversation with the officers and men forces the opinion that the men of this battalion were not trained or prepared to combat airplanes and did not visualize the situation. Further that what notions they did have were negative and showed too much thought of danger. The reason stated for the column leaving the road was that in this way they would avoid ricochets. More complete immunity could be secured by not having enlisted. In war death is incidental: loss of time is criminal.

This was strong language, particularly from a relatively young staff officer. It was common knowledge that the exercise was the G–3's baby rather than the division commander's; and so were the comments.

As muttering among some senior officers against Patton grew, General Smith removed Patton from the G–3 position and appointed him G–2, giving as his reason that Patton was too positive in his thinking and too outspoken in his remarks.

The chief of staff, Colonel Francis W. Cooke, rated Patton "average" in all categories as a G–3 and added, "He has had unusual opportunities to acquire both a theoretical and practical knowledge of General Staff work. He is affable and makes friends readily."

But Patton was badly hurt by his removal from the G–3 post. He showed his resentment in a letter to Beatrice: "Gen S. [Smith] must think he was wrong as he had had both Floyd [Parks?] and Capt Coffey tell me that it was only dire necessity which made him relieve me as G–3. Of course he is either a fool or a liar probably both."

Friends of Patton, far more sympathetic to his personality and professional outlook, would soon take control of the Hawaiian Division. Major General Fox Conner would become the commander and Brigadier General George Van Horn Moseley would be chief of staff.

Letter, GSP, Jr., to Brigadier General Harold B. Fiske, September 30, 1927

My dear general Fiske: While I fully realise that generals do not require the approval of majors I am presuming on the fact of my acquaintance with you in France to tell you how very timely your article in the last issue of the Infantry Journal appears. Both my experience in the World War as a training officer and my present occupation as a General Staff Officer . . . have forcibly impressed me with the slowing and emasculating effect on operations and personal leadership inherent in large staffs. As you point out, one of the chief defects in staff work arises from the fact most recent graduates from the different schools seem over impressed with formularism. Their chief concern is to write an order in the nature of an approved solution without regard to the men who must execute it and without considering that successful combat depends on energetic and timely execution rather than on wordy paragraphs. My observation of the schools since the war impresses me with the opinion that this is due, in the vast majority of cases, to the fact that the students have no

background of military knowledge as obtained by reading
. . . instead of applying teachings to pictured situations and
pondering their application they simply memorise the methods . . . better results might accrue were student officers required to read more either at the schools or else before going
to them. Also while at the schools that they were impressed
with the idea that over half of a staff officers responsibility
consists in inspections with a view to assuring his chief that
the orders issued are understood and promptly executed . . .
I hope you will forgive my temerity in inflicting this long
letter on you and attribute it simply to professional interest.
Very respectfully.

GSP, Jr. Lecture, "Why Men Fight," October 27, 1927
With the causes and effects of war we are not concerned.
Its continued existence is inevitable and its results for good
or evil are beyond all human power to avert or change . . .
Help for the helpless springs from love of ourselves . . .
Battle is an orgy of disorder. No level lawns or marker flags
exist to aid us strut ourselves in vain display, but rather
groups of weary wandering men seek gropingly for means to
kill their foe. The sudden change from accustomed order to
utter disorder—to chaos, but emphasize the folly of schooling
to precision and obedience where only fierceness and habituated disorder are useful.

Superiority in all endeavors, particularly in war, was hereditary.
A man's class would show in gentlemanly behavior and sacrifice
and leadership. The lower classes had to be schooled to instant
and unquestioning obedience to authority. Men fought for food
and sex, out of patriotism, habit, or simply obedience, and decorations for valor were important.

. . . a coward dressed as a brave man will change from his
cowardice and, in nine cases out of ten, will on the next occasion demonstrate the qualities fortuitously emblazoned on
his chest . . .
We must have more decorations and we must give them
with no niggard hand . . .
War may be hell; but for John Doughboy there is a heaven

of suggestion in anticipating what Annie Rooney will say when she sees him in his pink feather and his new medal.

The truly great military men were

biological incidents whose existence is due to the fortuitous blending of complementary blood lines at epochs where chance or destiny intervenes to give scope to their peculiar abilities.

Americans were handicapped in their search for leaders because of the absence of class distinctions in American society. Increasing the number of graduates from the Military Academy and from ROTC training at colleges and granting more noncommissioned officers Reserve commissions were methods of conferring class distinctions, and leaders so designated acted in consonance with the highest ideals of gentlemen.

It may well be that the greatest soldiers have possessed superior intellects, may have been thinkers; but this was not their dominant characteristic . . . [they] owed their success to indomitable wills and tremendous energy in execution and achieved their initial hold upon the hearts of their troops by acts of demonstrated valor . . . the great leaders are not our responsibility, but God's . . .
. . . the soul of man is changeless. Our difficulties differ in manifestation but not in nature from those Alexander experienced and Caesar knew. Our success or failure in the next war will depend on our ability to face the naked facts as they exist, and to utilize our means not as we would, but as we may.

This lecture appeared in print, and Patton's friend Sasse commented on the article, saying that men fought because they saw their buddies wounded or killed and they wanted to destroy those who had been responsible. A far less romantic view of men's motivations in combat than Patton's, Sasse's explanation would correspond to the findings of sociologists a generation or so later.

Patton requested a year's extension of his assignment in Hawaii, hoping thus to stay for four years. Was he motivated simply by the extremely pleasant life? Did he cherish the opportunities to observe and participate in relatively large-scale training exercises, which enabled him to have some contact with troops and troop formations? Or did he believe that his staff duties were good discipline, steadying him and restraining his impulses?

Whatever his motives, the War Department turned him down and notified him that he would be transferred to the Office of the Chief of Cavalry in Washington, D.C. at the completion of his Hawaiian tour of duty.

His final few months in Hawaii were notable for his work in amphibious operations, his studies on supporting weapons for assault troops, his thoughts on a reorganization of the division, and a renewed interest in tanks—all of which anticipated developments in World War II.

A series of training exercises on landing an invading force on Hawaii had Patton on the side of the invaders. He issued a series of field orders, signing them "Major General." The situation, sham, of course, resembled in remarkable fashion Patton's invasion of French Northwest Africa on November 8, 1942.

In the same maneuvers, he signed subsequent field orders "Viscount and Lieutenant General" and admonished his subordinate commanders to remember that "violent offensive and rapid movement spell victory."

One set of plans in the war games gave the objective as Pearl Harbor and concluded, in Patton's words: "The Emperor expects the most dauntless courage and vigorous leadership from all his officers. We shall not disappoint him. G. S. Patton, Jr., Viscount and Lieut. General, Commanding [the] Corps." It was a strange intimation of the reality at Pearl Harbor fourteen years in the future.

This was the beginning of Patton's study of amphibious assault techniques, and it would culminate in an expertise that would enable him to plan and lead invasions of North Africa and Sicily in World War II with such conspicuous success.

Devoting thought to the support of infantry assault units in the attack, Patton saw the tank as a vital instrument of firepower support, but was impressed too with its deficiencies.

> Any one who fires tank machine guns in war at 500 yards should be tried [by court-martial]. The best range is from 25 yds down . . .
>
> The idea of two shots is based on the assumption that accuracy is desirable, IT IS NOT. Therefore bursts of five shots are better because they tend to be inaccurate. I cannot refrain from adding the following remarks though I feel that since they are based on war experience they are not apt to be well received by the shooting specialists. The tank is primarily and only a shock weapon. Its efficiency resting on its ability to produce mental shock by the never realised threat of physical shock. For this reason all firing should be from a moving tank at ranges from 150 yards down. A tank which stops to fire gets hit.

This led him to experiment with a device he called a Sled Machine Gun Mount, designed to give the infantry assault echelons adequate self-contained firepower. Infantrymen provided with mobile machine guns capable of accompanying them in the attack and furnishing close and direct fire support—as distinguished from indirect machine gun fire from a distance—would have better fire control, more volume of fire, and, consequently, improved morale. In order to avoid fabricating an entirely new weapon for use up forward where the combat action was—a new weapon would consume time and money—Patton invented his sled mount for the existing machine gun. He had an enlisted blacksmith construct one from scrap material, and it worked quite well. Light, simple, and cheap, it could be pushed along the ground by a single man, packed on a horse, and carried by two men. It was also suitable for antiaircraft fire.

Fox Conner witnessed the sled mount used in a practice maneuver, and recommended to the War Department that it be given a trial and accepted or rejected as it was.

> Attempts to improve it by the addition of various alleged improvements are foredoomed to failure. Major Patton is now under orders to take station in Washington. He will take

this mount with him. It is recommended that extensive tests with the mount be held at some suitable place in the vicinity of Washington.

Letter, GSP, Jr., to Major General Robert H. Allen, Chief of Infantry, January 30, 1928

My dear General Allen: The night after the standings of my class at Leavenworth were published in June 1924 I was talking to you at the dance and you congratulated me in the following words: "Patton, it is a real pleasure to me to see a 'He' soldier graduate in the honors." I have always treasured this remark and have tried to live up to the standard you allotted me. I trust that in sending you direct the enclosed account [description] of a Sled Machine Gun Mount which I have devised I shall not forfeit your esteem. As I see it, the mount is adapted to the use of "He Soldiers" and will, I hope, help them to additional successes in the next war. The original letter was sent to the War Department through channels, but as I felt that you and the Chief of Cavalry would perhaps be interested, I secured permission from Gen Fox Conner to send you and General Crosby a copy direct. Asking pardon for my temerity, I am Very respectfully,

Allen cordially replied and said he was having the Infantry Board look at the sled mount. "I congratulate you on this additional demonstration of your practical ability as a 'He soldier' and wish you continued success along that line."

Letter, GSP, Jr., to Major General Herbert B. Crosby, Chief of Cavalry, January 30, 1928

My dear General Crosby: I have been experimenting on the construction of a machine gun mount sufficiently mobile to accompany the firing line. General Fox Conner was quite pleased with it and I obtained from him permission to send you the enclosed copy of the letter I wrote forwarding it to the Adjutant General. I also sent a copy to General Allen. Due to the lack of pack saddles here I have not been able to experiment with packing this mount on a horse, but I think that it can be readily placed astride the top of a pack. To do this it may be necessary to spread the runners a little. If it proves to be easily packed I suggest that it may prove a much better weapon for the Machine Rifle platoons than the arm they now carry. Its quick adaptability to antiaircraft fire certainly makes it very useful to cavalry. I trust that you will pardon me for bothering you personally with this subject. I was emboldened to do so by the fact that you would perhaps be interested. I am looking forward with great enthusiasm to serving in your office. My tour here ends April 1st and I should be in Washington around the end of the month, depending on the boats. Very respectfully.

Crosby wrote Patton that the sled mount appeared interesting. But far more important to Crosby was his implication of why Patton had been selected to serve in his office—"Mechanization looms very large in the War Department today, and your past experiences will serve you in this." And Crosby, although he left this unsaid, was happy to have Patton because no one could better refute the apostles of mechanization—who were claiming that the horse had become obsolete in modern warfare—than the premier American tank expert in the World War, Patton, widely known to be a proponent not only of the tank but also of the horse.

Probably asked why machine guns on the front line were necessary, why sled mounts were needed, Patton broadened his thinking and considered the larger problem of how best to wage warfare, which to him meant executing the attack. A long paper, entitled somewhat inaccurately "Drills for Fighting," presented the outlook of a mature and thoughtful professional officer. Starting with how to revise training to gain greater realism, that is, how to make exercises approximate actual conditions in combat, he proceeded to look at warfare in the large, what it was and how wars were best fought. This in turn took him into matters of organization, the ideal numbers of men for units, the functions of units, and the nature of leadership.

The study was divided into seven sections and had five tables appended. It was written humorously, sometimes with savage sarcasm, and it represented Patton's distilled thoughts at age forty-two, his prime. Virtually all of the ideas had been expressed previously in piecemeal fashion, but he now brought them together in a unified view of combat that stressed the contrast between the ordered uniformity of the drill field and the chaotic reality of the battlefield.

1. *Battle as per Training Regulations:*

The scouts appear advancing with unerring intelligence despite their unfamiliarity with the terrain, and employing . . . methods of progression often depicted on the burlesque stage as those employed by burglars.

Eventually, this line of tiptoe dancers exasperates the enemy to the point of firing . . .

Crawling and wiggling, on the [scouts] press, the superlative excellence of three months training manifesting itself in the precision with which they invariably avail themselves of the redundant protection of sundry blades of grass and dandelion stems.

Eventually they reach a well sighted [sited] line from which with marvellous accuracy they bring a devastating fire . . . upon the enemy, whose exact location and range they have determined by sundry occult methods well known to map problems.

. . . the leaders in rear . . . assemble their several staffs and, heedless of whispering bullets and bursting shells, engage in erudite cogitation, whose result is . . . academic orders chiefly remarkable for the surprising information they contain relative to the position and intentions of the yet unlocated enemy.

These orders, transmited by all possible means from pantomine to radio, are clearly received and promptly comprehended; with the result that the leading sections of the assault echelon dribble accurately to a line on or near that established by the scouts, and having ascertained the range and targets from these prescient individuals, coolly set their sights and bring to bear on their doomed opponents an accurate and well distributed fire of awe-inspiring intensity.

After . . . this meticulous killing, sundry infallible signs of enemy weakening in the form of diminishing and less accurate fire and movements to the rear become manifest to the Napoleonic corporals and lieutenants. Immediately they engage anew in pantomine while their dauntless soldiers, apprehending the wishes of their leaders by their third eye conveniently placed in the back of their heads, either advance anew or else redistribute their fire to cover those so doing.

. . . A support element materialises itself and, maneuvering with utter disregard to hostile fire, assaults that Achilles Heel, the flank, with a hurricaine of bullets and grenades until the recalcitrant foe becomes quiescent and the line moves on.

. . . that modern Ariadne, the Artillery Observation Officer, moving ever forward at the end of his strand of copper and in collusion with the infantry commander, keeping his guns informed of the changing requirements of the fight. At times the wire is inadequate to voice his emotions and he has recourse to a varied assortment of fireworks which he and his satellites carry with them for such emergencies.

. . . . machine guns which, advancing by bounds on mules bred from salamanders, if one judges from their immunity to fire, support the attack with staccato deluges of distant animosity; while from time to time their cackling is punctuated with the crack of a one pounder or the cough of a stokes [mortar].

2. Obviously in the foregoing we have been guilty of a degree of exaggeration, but our offense was premeditated, for by this means we hope to throw in to sharper relief some features of our present regulations which appear inapplicable to the strident realism of war.

. . . . the manifest inadequacy of the self-contained means at the disposal of the assault echelons for the carrying out of their stupendous task.

. . . while for the purposes of dissection and examination the several acts are treated separately, it is important to remember that they are all mutually interwoven and interdependent.

a. Dispersion:

The deployment into a [firing] line . . . places the large majority of the men . . . beyond the direct physical and moral in-

fluence of the platoon commander. The subsequent operations
. . . must therefore depend on his delegated influence as
diluted and transmitted through section and squad leaders. In
theory . . . [they] are capable . . . In practice . . . this will
hardly ever be the case . . . the sergeants and corporals will
. . . be largely chosen from men of superior educational rather
than moral qualifications; because in the brief time available
for training, mental quickness is more readily discerned than
moral hardihood . . .

In actuality, the principal influences [on a firing line] . . .
will depend on instinct and a sense of duty.

Without in any way disparaging the valor of our soldiers we
affirm that the inexorable record of war proves that neither instinct nor a sense of duty flourish[es] very luxuriantly under
the chilling influence of a corpernical blizzard.

Perhaps the lieutenant and 20% of the men will be sufficiently immune to this numbing influence to advance. In addition a certain proportion of the others . . . will follow the
example of the natural fighters. The rest will stay put or else advance later when the action of their more dauntless comrades
has lessened the danger. With each successive advance a number of the leading spirits become casualties, so the influence of
their example steadily diminishes . . .

b. Cover:
. . . Due to subconscious memories of his prehistoric arboreal
existence, man possesses an inherent instinct for secretive movements. Owing to this fact instructors are prone to display exaggerated interest and ingenuity in hide-and-seek tactics. Who
has not seen a scout or a patrol spend hours in stealthy and
circumlocutory meanderings at places where hostile observation
was highly improbable and completely unimportant; forgetting
while so engaged that time and energy the inexorable functions
of military operations were being ruthlessly squandered.

Over-stressing the value of concealment . . . has a further disadvantage due to the psychological effect produced. Just as
children often evolve terrors from the fertility of their own

imaginings . . . so do soldiers produce in themselves visions of an omnipresent and deadly foe . . . The desire for self-preservation is a fundamental instinct which the first whistle of a bullet impels men to exercise. If, to this natural reaction is added a long course in the avoidance of danger by concealment . . . we shall possibly produce complete invisibility at the cost of absolute cessation of movement . . .

The utilization of cover from fire when that cover is bullet proof is commendable and necessary so long as undue hankering for it does not produce inaction . . .

In battle the soldier enters a lottery, with death the stake . . . the only saving clauses in this gamble lie in time, and the demoralizing effect produced on the shooting and staying qualities of the enemy by the rapid and uninterrupted advance of the attacker.

c. Fire Power:

So far as we are aware, no research of any American attack in the world war substantiates the vaunted assertions as to the death dealing efficacy of small arms fire on the part of the assailent . . . [because] there was nothing much at the actual front with which to fire.

. . . the conditions under which he [the defender] delivers his fire are superior to those of the attacker . . . his firing line is so sighted that all its occupants can fire all the time. . . . his men are not breathless with exertion, he knows the exact range and his machine guns are close enough so that both he and the attacker are audibly and visibly aware of their presence. Under such circumstances . . . the attacker can only advance according to one of the following assumptions.

First, in the case where the defender is morally weak and an outrageously bad shot.

Second, by the result of attrition secured by a constant feeding of the [attacker's] firing line. . . . [this] is bound to be unduly expensive . . .

Third, by the aid of maneuver . . .

Fourth, by means of supporting weapons, mainly artillery . . .

. . . our present firing line does not contain in itself sufficient lethal energy to produce an advance with a normal expectancy of success, due to the fact that it does not contain the killing facilities in adequate density . . .

d. Machine Guns:

The ensanguined ingenuity of our ordnance experts and the fulminations of the pacifists to the contrary notwithstanding, the anomalous fact remains that corpses do not produce panic save in a very indirect manner. It is the fear of becoming corpses that turns men's hearts to water.

. . . this condition is rather generally appreciated [but], we still seem to find our machine guns employed on a generally contrary hypothesis. Furthermore their employment for the ends they seek largely defeats its own purpose . . . as a result of the combined heritage of 1870 when the French used the Mitrailleuse as a cannon because it looked like one, and of the largely defensive traditions of machine guns in the World War our machine guns in the offensive are in but not of the Infantry. This rearward emplacement of our most powerful offensive small arm is further accentuated by . . . the bias of a mechanical age [which] makes men cling with great tenacity to such gadgets as aiming circles, range finders etc. and in the use of these devices to find valid reasons for not exposing his person to the deadly blast of short range hostile retaliation.

The result . . . is that in the inception of an assault, the attacking machine guns are brought well up and the rifleman steps off . . . but from this stage onward they become less and less an integral part of the infantry . . . due to the real and fancied difficulties attached to its [the machine gun's] progression, it usually follows [the riflemen] at too respectful a distance.

. . . As the chorus of his own machine guns dies away the refrain is taken up by those of the enemy, rising ever in volume as he advances . . .

To send men with hand weapons whose accuracy is adversely affected by each throb of physical or mental excitement up against impersonal mechanical means of destruction, while at the same time depriving them of much of the real and all the moral support and threat of their own machine guns, is to ask too much. If, finally, the line does charge home the impetus impelling it is more apt to arise from what Du Picq calls "a retreat forward" than from the creation of fire supremacy.

e. Maneuver . . .

In the many books devoted to the larger military operations . . . what the older writers called "Grand Tactics" we find much reference to maneuver, particularly . . . envelopments and flank attacks.

Unquestionably, much of success in war is due to a just use of such movements, or rather to the fact that, due to these movements, the elan and fighting power of the troops was most happily exploited. But just as the grandeur of a natural landscape becomes tawdry and uninspiring when depicted through the medium of a small water color, so does the maneuver of an army fail to inspire when scaled down to that of a squad.

If, for example . . . the 1st Blue division . . . destroy the first Red brigade by an enveloping attack, we shall always find that, in addition to the invariable stupidity of the Reds certain other conditions were requisite for the success of the masterful maneuver . . . [as] listed by Maurice about 600 A.D. . . .

[These are] . . . the enveloping element . . . moved to its assault position . . . under the cover of darkness, superior artillery fire, or terrain features. . . . [or] the outer flank of the enveloping force was not menaced; or else was covered by a superior force of cavalry. . . . [or] the moral stimulus of a superiority of two to one, measured in regiments, existed. So much for the landscape, now let us consider the water color . . .

It is therefore well worthy of considering whether the losses sustained by the leading element while awaiting the questionable relief due to a menuver [that is, an envelopment], will not exceed those which would have resulted from an immediate [frontal] assault . . . If the firing line is to advance as a result of its own efforts, it must do so by maintaining superior means of killing in its own hands . . . The chief deterrent to the advance is in automatic fire of machine guns. This must be countered by machine guns in the firing line.

f. Supporting Arms:

The firing line in its present may still attain success if its self-contained lack of fire power is made good by that of supporting arms, particularly by artillery.

However . . . it takes from the infantry both prestige and initiative. . . . terrain conditions may well arise which will prevent the massing of sufficient artillery to insure the requisite support.

In the World War the adequate system of metaled roads failed to emphasize different conditions, highly probable of existence in theaters of war where no such roads prevail. Again, in France operations were in general so methodical that ample time could be found for the collection of large stores of ammunition. In a theater where lack of roads prevents the maintenance of continuous fronts, the time element will be much more vital; while the same lack of roads will necessitate much greater periods for the collection of munitions and the movement of guns. In this sort of war, units will frequently engage with only their organic artillery and that limited in ammunition to the amounts present with the artillery batteries . . .

The same considerations which have induced the infantry to hinge their tactics on a practically unlimited artillery support have also predisposed the artillery to utilize methods that will be of doubtful practicability under many conditions of war. What we refer to is the apparent tendency towards the utilization of excessive ranges where the efficacy of fire is contingent on lengthy and unsimple methods of communication . . .

The tendencies towards distant positions received further stimulus from the "gadget" complex . . .

. . . both in consideration of the time lost and of the small

effect secured, better results would accrue were the infantry so
armed and instructed that, once the artillery has made its lift
[lifted its preparatory barrage], they were able and accustomed
to go on without second thoughts as to the possibility of a renewed bombardment.

g. Leadership:

At first blush one would scarcely expect to find in the behavior of a piece of cooked spaghetti an illustration of successful leadership in combat . . . it scarcely takes demonstration to
prove how vastly more easy it is to PULL a piece of cooked
spaghetti in a given direction along its major axis than it is to
PUSH it in the same direction. Further, the difficulty increases
with the size of either the spaghetti or the command . . .

The splendid motto of the Infantry School: "Follow Me"
certainly refutes . . . training and maneuvers . . . [where]
there are a good many backward glances for inspiration.

To us it seems that a fungoid over-growth of that devilish
device the command post is largely responsible for this condition.

. . . when we find commanders as low as company and battalion more interested in securing command post accommoda-
tions than in injuring the enemy, something is wrong . . .

. . . Officers were and are taught that thinking is superior to
doing; that brains outrank guts. The natural corollary to these
notions is that constant reports must flow from front to rear
. . . the message center has replaced the leader . . .

The birthright of leadership is sold for the pottage of formal-
ism.

While to-day battle fields are vast and more or less vacant, a
great deal can be seen by earnest lookers. But . . . All of us are
accustomed to acquire knowledge by reading and listening, not
by seeing; and to impart this knowledge by writing, not by
acting.

. . . [Instead of] "By their deeds ye shall know them" . . .
"By their reports shall they be selected." We are apt to reach a

state of mind in which we will prefer a mimeograph [machine] to a [Stonewall] Jackson.

3. Possible basis of Present System:

. . . our thesis in making the above criticism of present regulation[s] is the belief that the firing line as now armed and used is inadequately equipped for its functions under conditions where artillery support is lacking or insufficient . . .

Prior to the world war, our combat methods were the outgrowth of the legendary ability of all Americans to hit a squirrel in the eye at 100 yards. . . . [Thus we adopted] a doctrine predicated on the belief that the aimed fire of infantry rifles supported in a desultory manner by the fire of a negligible number of cannon and machine guns would be able to secure and retain sufficient fire superiority to permit the advance of the firing line.

On entering the world war, we found these views modified by several circumstances . . .

First; time, facilities, and instructors were lacking with which to train efficient shots.

Second; the foreign instructors who infested our camps had neither experience of, nor confidence in, the efficacy of aimed rifle fire.

Third; the special circumstances existing in France in the way of numerous railroads and metaled highways, permitted the attacker to collect at the desired place such a numerous artillery that its preparatory and supporting fire was sufficient to derange the defense to an extent permitting the advance of the infantry with little actual assistance from the killing weapons in the hands of the foot soldiers.

Since the infantry, following in the wake of the shells, suffered its chief losses from artillery and automatic weapon fires; neither of which it was their primary function to subdue, it became expedient to so spread them over the landscape, that their losses from these agencies would be reduced to a minimum; regardless of the fact that such formations were inimical to the effective use of their own hand firearms.

At the present time, the minds of all military thinkers are still strongly imbued with both our pre-war theories and our war practice; so it seems reasonable to believe that our present attack formations are the fruit of an unholy union between a firing fighting line and a shell-proof formation.

4. Fundamental principles of fighting:

Due to the facility with which men, material, and even situations may be created on paper, many writers produce these on war as admirable as they are impractical. Due also to our school experiences where such intangible factors as morale, training, discipline, fatigue, equipment, and supply cannot be considered, we adopt the simple course of first omitting reference to these factors, and later of assuming them all satisfactory . . .

Duped by the historians who explain defeat and enhance victory by assuring us that both result from the use of PERFECT armies, the fruit of super-thinking, we never stop to consider the inaptness of the word perfect as a definition for armies.

So far as we can recall, only Alexander, Frederick and Napoleon inherited complete armies. Of these the ever victorious Macedonians came nearest laying claim to contemporary perfection.

While the Prussians, though they performed well, were far from being universally successful, and the final outcome of the Seven Years' War was more the result of Allied bickerings than of German superiority.

Napoleon's army was an unwashed mob, whose superiority lay in their elan born of revolutionary exhilaration, which found in the histrionic Corsican a peg on which to drape itself. In each of these armies there was an example of perfection, but it was that of an individual, not of a system. Also, the opponents of each were below the average of their respective epochs . . .

All through history there have been recurring cycles of two schools of war; the one tending towards the adoption of small professional forces relatively well trained. The other toward the utilization of masses and mob psychology. Both schools have usually foundered on the rock of compromise, when the first sought to increase its numbers and the second its discipline . . .

. . . we are personally disposed to favor the use of small trained . . . armies. Certainly, wars conducted with such forces would be more mentally stimulating, much cheaper, and vastly less bloody . . .

Another solution . . . consists in the use of a highly tempered spearhead of long service troops, backed by a horde of amateurs to do the holding and the drudgery . . .

The illusory security of our isolation and the short term of office of our law-makers make them unwilling to burden their constituents and prejudice their own chances of re-election by imposing present financial burdens to fend off future national catastrophies. Under their benevolent despotism our voteless army is bound to pine in a coma of incipient dissolution.

Since, then, our next war will be fought on the quantity rather than the quality basis, it behooves us to determine the best methods of warring with the amateur masses our destiny has foredoomed us to control . . .

. . . victory results from the infliction of a series of moral shocks to which the infliction of death wounds and destruction are but contributory influences . . . we must therefore first demonstrate our ability to kill, and then threaten its inevitable accomplishment.

. . . If the theory of evolution is correct, it is highly probable that our arboreal progenitors did grapple in a mele[e]; but since the dropping of tails, man has always earnestly striven to do his killing at a distance and has devoted incessant ingenuity to the devising of means which will permit [him] to accomplish this desire. None the less, the theory of the necessity of hand to hand fighting is so completely accepted, that resistance can only be overcome by the threat of its imminent accomplishment.

To take a position, we must convince its defenders with our ability to effect an apparently inexorable progression towards physical shock . . . to date the fact remains that victory without movement is as impossible as movement without fire.

In utilizing our horde, then, we must seek SIMPLE means to produce the will to move, and the fire to make it possible.

5. A *solution:*

Our present mobilization plans contemplate the enrollment of masses so vast that the feeding, to say nothing of the maneuvering, of the host envisioned will be impossible save in the most highly civilized locations. Further, while awaiting the advent of our embattled farmers over a period ranging from seven to twelve months, we contemplate holding the foe at bay with our attenuated regulars and ill-trained national guardsmen. . . .

However pacific a citizen may be, he usually becomes quite belicose when first donning a uniform. In order to capitalise on this fleeting emotion we should start warlike training on the first day. That is, instead of saying: "This is a rifle, its nomenclature is thus and so; it takes three counts to put it on your shoulder and four to take it off" and so on, we will have to talk in this wise: "Take this rifle and get into a line even with Corporal Jones. He is your boss. That bush is an enemy machine gun. It is up to you to kill its crew." At this point Private 1/c Brown (regular) will inform his neighbors as follows: "Hey you bozos! Put that wooden part agin' your shoulder. . . ."

To paraphrase the famous remark at Balaclava: "It is horrible but it is war." At first the bush will be fairly safe, but by night the ex-civilians will have an idea of what they are trying to do and till Taps and later they will be arguing, asking questions and, best of all, making fun of each other. Day by day, in every way, they will be better and better. And the men who train them and learn to know them will be the men, who, in the near day of battle, will lead them . . .

Irrespective of plans and organization, all battles quickly resolve themselves into a series of more or less isolated head-on conflicts between small groups of combatants . . .

6. *Proposed training and organization:*

Without in any way aspiring to enter those pellucid regions inhabited by Genius . . . we strive to devise a scheme of: "Utiliz-

ing the means at hand for the accomplishment of the ends
sought."

. . . in our previous paper on "Why Men Fight," we have
striven to divest war of its non-essentials and to strip it to a
tangible, if uninspiring contest between artificially enraged
males . . .

The necessity for this course is particularly important to us as
a nation, since we are congenitally opposed to any form of useful
preparation . . .

[Then followed a detailed discussion of the elements composing a division, with certain recommended changes, including the
elimination of the regiment.]

So far we have assigned to the division three infantry brigades
[each consisting of three infantry battalions] and occasionally perhaps some units of medium artillery. [Actually, the reorganization of the infantry division in the early 1940s, when the so-called
triangular or McNair division replaced the square division of
World War I, eliminated the brigade and retained the regiment
(which, unlike the brigade headquarters that was capable only of
tactical functions, was able to handle tactical, administrative, and
supply duties), each regiment consisting of three battalions of
infantry, plus a cannon company—much as Patton was here suggesting.]

Considering the reduced personnel, considerable curtailments
in the medical regiment will be possible . . .

. . . we propose replacing the engineer regiment with an engineer company plus a detachment of engineer officers to act as
advisers on simple engineering projects, for which the line troops
will furnish the labor . . .

The tank company should be eliminated because, as now armed,
it is inadequate in strength to the tasks proposed and of either
march or combat mobility it is wholly innocent. Moreover, en-
cumbering of a division with the permanent tanks, irrespective of
the intrinsic worth of the type imagined, is as irrational as would
be the permanent issue to all soldiers of arctic overcoats. The
tanks and the overcoats are only an occasional necessity. Tanks

are in reality a modern version of heavy cavalry, as that arm was understood by the first Napoleon. When satisfactory machines are available, they should be formed into a separate corps and used, when terrain permits, for the delivery of the final shock in some great battle; when so used they must be employed ruthlessly and in masses. [This was in striking similarity to Patton's initial conception of how to use tanks in World War II.]

The retention of an air corps unit with the division is vital. We believe that, in addition to the observation squadron which is also capable of a limited amount of attack and light bombing, a pursuit unit should be added as the surest means of safeguarding our marching columns from the growing menace of enemy air attack. [This too foreshadowed Patton's use of supporting air forces in World War II.]

The functions proposed for the augmented air unit are exactly analogous to that of a cavalry unit so frequently required by a division, in that they both furnish reconnaissance and protection in their separate spheres of action, and that by making them integral with the division, the integrity of the main striking force of the arm is left intact, since it will not be constantly depleted by demands for local protection . . .

7. Battle as per proposed regulations:
. . . After a moment's pause to permit this orchestra of death to reach its crescendo the line of bayonets rises and led by the major [in command of the battalion] rushes to its final task gruesome only in anticipation [for the enemy will have fled].

With the semi-stillness of the charge our ear suddenly perceives the insinuating whine made over head by . . . fifty calibre bullets from the brigade machine guns whose devilish whispering is punctured now and again by the hoarser murmur of a lobbing shell from the accompanying howitzers.

Appended to this study were proposed tables of organization and equipment for the infantry rifle company, the infantry battalion, the infantry brigade, and the infantry division. Then followed a comparison of the current and his proposed divisions, showing that the latter, that is, Patton's recommended division, would have a total strength of 9715 men as contrasted with 19,417 in the current organization; at the same time, the firepower of the recommended organization would be far stronger.

This was precisely what the triangular division of World War II sought to attain—more bang with fewer men.

. . .

Several weeks before his departure from Hawaii, Patton delivered a lecture at Schofield Barracks on "Tanks Past and Future." It foreshadowed his forthcoming involvement in Washington with mechanization and motorization, with tanks and armored cars.

Forerunners of the modern tank, he said, were the Trojan horse conceived by "Liarte's" (Laertes') godlike son Ulysses, which was itself the forerunner of the movable towers used by Alexander against Tyre, and certain engines called the Sow, the "Bore" [Boar?], and the Cat, which were intended for siege warfare in antiquity and medieval times.

The British Museum had a picture dated 1456 of a "Cart of War," a vehicle propelled by horses with a platform above their heads to support a weapon and a crew, the platform being protected by sideboards. "So far as I know this machine is the earliest form in which the light or open warfare tank appears. I have been unable to find any evidence that it was ever used in battle."

A similar engine driven by windmills operating wooden gears was described in Italy in 1492. One hundred years later, Simon Stevens depicted a land ship with masts, sails, and guns mounted on wheels. Unfinished notes of Leonardo da Vinci spoke of a land ship or battle car propelled by an engine of some unspecified sort.

As an aside, Patton mentioned that in France in 1918, he had been directed to report on the military value of a machine called the Moving Fort and Trench Destroyer. He examined an elaborate set of blueprints showing a caterpillar-propelled box covered with two-inch armor, bearing six 75-mm. howitzers, twenty machine guns, and a flamethrower. In the midst of the drawing of this contraption was a rectangular box labeled, "Engine not yet devised."

After the laughter of his audience subsided, Patton said,

> I do not know whether atom bursting was known at that date. If it was I feel sure that an engine actuated by that sort of energy must have been intended as no other form of power occupying so small a space could have propelled the 200 ton estimated weight of the fort. In my indorsement I stated that the lack of an engine was considered a defect and further pointed out that while it would unquestionably crush trenches it would just as surely squash a considerable part of France in its journey to the front.

The drill, he continued, for tanks in the British Army—"Colonel J. F. C. Fuller, Chief of Staff of the Tank Corps, is my authority for the following description"—resembled training described by Zenophon and attributed by him to King Cyrus in 500 B.C. But the British tactics at Cambrai were not applicable to American doctrine. The British had the infantry formations conform to the tank capabilities, whereas Patton in France had reversed the conception, primarily because the American tanks were small and unlike the heavier British tanks. He had also rejected the French method of moving tanks behind the infantry until they were needed forward, because this meant that one or two hours elapsed between the need for them and their time of arrival.

Patton had therefore devised an American system of tank employment, which, though far from perfect, had worked satisfactorily. Certain mistakes were nevertheless committed. It was an error to have tanks precede the infantry against weak trenches, for the infantrymen could cross them after an artillery barrage. Tanks were needed primarily for the enemy machine guns sited behind the front.

"In future," he interjected, "it will be better to have the tanks follow the infantry over the front . . . and then deploy ahead for the passage through the delaying area."

This would be the normal procedure in World War II, notably in the COBRA attack, launched on July 25, 1944, in Normandy.

"It is the unconquerable soul of man and not the nature of the machine he uses which insures victory," Patton said. Yet tanks were useful in combat, and he hoped that tanks in the future would be mechanically rugged, have great cruising radius, be light in weight and mobile for roads and cross-country operations, have speed, armor, and gun power.

Finally, ending on a pessimistic note, he was dubious whether the United States would ever have first-rate tanks in sufficient numbers. "The chief drawback under which the whole military profession is now laboring arises from a too unimaginative conception of the probable nature of the next war." The next war was likely to be "trench warfare, which God forbid."

Grading Patton as G–2, Colonel Cooke had thought him "above average." Perhaps because Patton was held in such high esteem by Fox Conner, or perhaps because Cooke now knew Patton better, he marked him "superior" in most categories and "very active both mentally and physically; widely read in military history; an expert horseman. His outstanding qualities are those of a commander."

The endorsement read: "I concur in the above report. I have known him [Patton] for fifteen years, in both peace and war. I know of no one whom I would prefer to have as a subordinate commander. Fox Conner, Major General commanding."

These words from Conner, naming Patton as the subordinate commander he judged best of all the officers he knew in the Army, were exceedingly important for Patton's career. A gray eminence in the Army, whose power was indirect and often concealed, Conner wielded immense authority during the years between the World Wars.

The last efficiency report rendered on Patton for his Hawaiian tour of duty rated him "above average" and "superior." According to Lieutenant Colonel S. T. Mackall, the acting chief of staff, Patton was "an outstanding officer; a student of military affairs, well above the average; intensely interested in his profession; he has taken full advantage of serving in Hawaii to become familiar with the military problem in the Islands."

Letter, GSP, Jr., to Aunt Nannie, March 5, 1928

So far we have not secured a house [in Washington] but hope to do so on the Virginia side [of the Potomac] as it is cooler there and there will be less calling.

Beatrice is still very busy writing her Hawaiian ledgends in french. I hope she succeeds in getting them published. It will be a great dissappointment to her if she does not.

With no horses to ride [apparently the horses were already en route from Hawaii to Washington] I find more time than I have been accustomed to here but as soon we will have to start packing it will be an advantage.

While he was packing the family's possessions, he listed the military, horse, and boat books he owned. There were 321, and from the marginal notations, most of them had been carefully read.

Patton's three years in Hawaii were a pleasant social interlude and a sobering professional experience. The ferocity of his play on the polo field, which became legendary, was in large part the sublimation of his frustrations as a staff and desk-bound—chairborne, the Army calls it—officer, denied the joys of commanding troops. Everyone who mattered in the Army recognized his natural qualities as an active and forceful leader of troops. Everyone also realized that his professional attainments, his loyalty to his superiors, his zeal toward his duty, whatever that happened to be, were outstanding—Patton always gave his best. He had matured but without losing his essential dash.

CHAPTER 41

Washington: The Lure of the Machine

"Oil and Iron do not win battles—Victory is to men not machines."

IN WASHINGTON, after moving into a house at 3117 Woodland Drive Northwest, Patton reported for duty to the Chief of Cavalry and was assigned head of the Plans and Training Division of that office. He left almost immediately for Mitchell Field, Long Island, where he played on the Army polo team all summer.

Lieutenant Colonel H. C. Pratt, probably the nonplaying manager, rated Patton "satisfactory," judged him capable of being a colonel in peacetime and a brigadier general in war—but no higher, and thought him "an unusually energetic and active officer; well-versed in his profession, and always endeavoring to improve himself."

Patton returned to Washington in September and became acquainted with the details and routine of his job.

Letter, GSP, Jr., to Beatrice (in Massachusetts), September 3, 1928
I am delighted that you will not hunt. I realy hate to have you hurt more than to be hurt myself. As a matter of fact it does not hurt me to be hurt . . .

Ike Eisenhower and I are going down the river [sailing] on Sunday.

A month later, on October 6, Mrs. Ruth Wilson Patton died. Patton left no record at that time of his sorrow at the loss of his mother. He would do so three years later.

Sometime during the autumn of 1928 or the following spring, George and Beatrice Patton purchased in South Hamilton, Massachusetts, a house and sufficient acreage for riding and hunting. They named their place Green Meadows, and it became their home, their permanent residence.

By virtue of Patton's assignment to the Office of the Chief of Cavalry, he became intimately involved in probably the most significant controversy that occupied the Army until the eve of World War II. The question constantly debated was the importance of mechanization in future warfare. Should machines replace horses, and if so, to what extent?

The discussions took place in the Army, in the congressional committees concerned with military expenditures, and in the press. On one side were ranged the automobile manufacturers and their lobbyists, the advocates of the car, the truck, the tank, and the airplane, who insisted that machines made horses obsolete. On the other were the polo players, hunters, riders, breeders, farmers, and their associations that publicized the virtues of horseflesh, argued that horses were more reliable and cheaper than machines, and supported congressional parsimony with respect to research and development.

In the center of the debate, Patton would be emotionally torn for more than three years by the conflicting attractions of the intriguing yet contrasting notions over the place of machines and horses in the Army. His superior was the Chief of Cavalry, his own branch was cavalry, he loved horses passionately; he relished the slash of the saber and the reckless abandon of the mounted charge. But he was beguiled by the engines of war too. How could he deny or renounce the achievements of the tanks in France?

As he wrestled with the currents of change, he sought to fulfill his sense of loyalty to the cavalry without betraying his obligation to the Army and its capacity to wage war. On occasion, he mirrored excruciating pain. He preferred not to choose. Throughout his tour of duty, he would seek the path of compromise, trying to offend neither the conservative horsemen nor the radical mechanists.

It was a tricky business, and Patton's gifts were hardly suitable for so devious a course. He was neither subtle nor discreet enough to avoid a wavering commitment, first to one, then to the other.

If a single beacon guided him, it was his loyalty to his boss, the Chief of Cavalry. And in the end, despite himself, he became identified with the horse. This bond to the horse cavalry almost cost him his chance for fame in World War II.

For Patton, the whole disagreeable yet fascinating activity started in November 1928. He worked on the War Department Mobilization Plan and suggested that the cavalry secure young and vigorous accomplished horsemen to form "an aristocracy of valor, vital to the success of Cavalry." He was also appointed to a board of officers—with Lieutenant Colonel James J. O'Hara, Majors C. C. Benson and Harry A. Flint—to inspect the Christie caterpillar mount for its suitability as a heavy armored car; as before, he found Christie's machine a promising development.

There was little difference between the Christie tank and the Christie car except semantics. The proponents of change in the cavalry were restricted to armored cars because the tanks had been transferred to the infantry. Forbidden to have tanks, the cavalrymen simply called them armored cars. Yet they were smaller and lighter than tanks, consequently more mobile and more appropriate for a branch of service that prided itself on its ability to move and maneuver.

Thus began a persistent fiction, also a continuing struggle between the infantry and cavalry for control of the means of armored warfare, no matter how the vehicles were designated. The contest would eventually be decided by the branch of the officers who would be selected for and assigned to the armored forces. That fight would take place largely within the Office of the G–3, the War Department Plans, Training, and Operations Section. There, Major Adna R. Chaffee, son of a former Army Chief of Staff, old friend of Patton, and well-known cavalryman, horseman, and polo player, would play a principal role in the activity.

The question of mechanization had become important because the Secretary of War, Dwight F. Davis, had observed during the summer of 1927 the maneuvers in England of the British Experimental Armored Force, a rudimentary organization of mechanized units. Davis was impressed by what he saw. Influenced also by the advances in the motor vehicle industry, the advent of better roads in the United States, the abundant American oil resources, and the increasing displacement of horses and mules by farm machinery, Davis directed the Army to create an armored force in 1928.

The Army assembled at Camp Meade a composite force made up of small units—tanks, cavalry, field artillery, air corps, engineers, ordnance, chemical warfare, and medical corps. Because of insufficient funds and obsolete equipment, little was done in the way of welding these elements into a single unit of combined arms. Yet merely gathering the force together was a symbolic act that would prove beneficial to the Army.

Absorbed by both horses and machines, Patton was sufficiently enthusiastic over the horse cavalry to propose:

> The use of Army Cavalry in driblets or for indefinite missions is to be deprecated. When opportunity for decisive results offers, or occasion demands, cavalry must be ruthlessly expended.

At the same time, he cherished and saved the paper that announced the Secretary's approval of a plan—after tests at Fort Leonard Wood, Missouri, and Fort Myer—for the Chief of Cavalry and the Chief of Ordnance, in cooperation, to procure the Christie chassis and equip it as an armored car.

Patton copied this letter and kept it in his personal papers. He wrote on it: "Probably a very momentous paper. GSP Jr. Feb 21 1929."

He was destined to be disappointed, for the Army would fail to buy the chassis in sufficient numbers to keep Christie solvent, and he would eventually be forced to sell his invention elsewhere, to the Russians, English, and Japanese.

Armored cars seemed an obvious solution to the major problem of funds; cheaper to build than tanks, they offered mobility and firepower, plus a degree of protection to their crews. Stimulated by the Secretary's decision, Patton listed their advantages and disadvantages, probably to clear the air of misconceptions.

A normal armored car rolling on wheels was an effective offensive weapon capable of rapid movement on roads; gave partial protection to its machine gun or small cannon; had a relatively long cruising range; provided secure and rapid messenger service; could delay enemy units operating without tanks, penetrate enemy rear-guard forces, ambush enemy troops and transport, and make distant raids; was an excellent rear-guard weapon; added firepower to mounted units; and was cheap to manufacture, thereby easy to build in large numbers.

The special tracked and wheeled vehicle, Christie type, was expensive to manufacture, therefore wasteful to employ for messenger service. Its ability to move off the roads improved its capacity for reconnaissance, helped it to avoid ambush and gain surprise. It could menace deployed lines of troops, launch independent raids, accompany cavalry, thereby adding fire and shock, cover a withdrawal, and act as a powerful mobile reserve.

A normal or wheeled armored car was liable to stall on unimproved, frozen, or wet roads; could be stopped by simple obstructions; had limited mobility at night; was susceptible to ambush, useless in swampy, rocky, or forested country, and certain to provoke enemy attack. Its killing power was limited.

Having set forth the characteristics of armored cars, Patton pushed forward in a paper entitled "Tactical Employment of Armored Cars, Experimental." He prefaced his remarks with a typical opening:

> Oil and Iron do not win battles—Victory is to men not machines. No perfection of mechanism nor metriculosity of training can replace courage. The heart which animates a chauffe[u]r is only a bilge pump. If the A.C. [armored car] degenerates into a perambulating source of fire power it has belied its cavalry birthright. Movement, not fire, is its primary weapon.

The armored cars had to have complete liberty of action and "act with the uttermost boldness." They moved by bounds, by accordion or by inchworm methods. The armored car commander had to consider his machine and its weapons as a trooper regarded his horse and arms. "The analogy is complete: grooming, cleaning, feeding, oiling and fueling; training; adjustment."

Armored cars personified "the age old dread of monsters." They should follow the precept "Audacity and the threat of contact are far more potent means of combat than are fire or armour." Fire fights should take place only at close range.

After accompanying several armored cars making an experimental march from Washington, D.C. to Camp Meade, Maryland, Patton set down additional remarks. He warned against making the vehicle too heavy—"any military machine has a tendency to overload itself with spare parts, whether they are men or material." He recommended against having crew members equipped with the Thompson submachine gun, for that would encourage them to fight as infantrymen rather than as armored car operators. Fuel was as important as ammunition, if not more so, because "an armored car which stops to fight is lost."

He was caught up rather short in his enthusiastic promotion of the armored car by a question asked by General Crosby, the Chief of Cavalry. Would Patton consider the "Limitations of Mechanization"?

Responding, Patton offered a key thought:

Without in any way detracting from the capabilities of mechanical and mechanized units when employed under conditions of terrain and weather which render their use possible, it is none the less pertinent to point out certain characteristics of the machines which detract from their universality and limit their spheres of action.

He said what he had said often before. Machines could not operate in certain kinds of weather and terrain, and thus horses were still necessary for military forces that wished to preserve their capacity to fight anywhere and any time.

This became the standard cavalry formula—no objection to developing gas-engine weapons like tanks and armored cars so long as the proponents of mechanization and motorization recognized the basic contribution of the horse.

This led to the idea of using machines with horses, and in 1929, the cavalry tentatively adopted the Christie car, which could go

40 miles per hour cross country on tracks and 70 miles per hour on highways on wheels.

Asked to write an article on the new vehicle for the Hearst papers, Patton turned out an unpublishable effort. In it he justified the development of war machines by his own peculiar logic:

> . . . it must never be forgotten that all weapons and devices are only of secondary importance. Now as ever the fate of the nation depends on the heroic souls of its sons not on the weapons they wield. None the less in order to justify ourselves in demanding of them the supreme sacrifice we must in honor see to it that we give them every assistance which our wealth and ingenuity can provide.

He meant not only the armored car but all the weapons and equipment that enabled the American fighting man to face with confidence any enemy equipped with first-rate matériel and weapons.

So drawn was Patton to the need for machines in the Army that he worked on a table of organization for a mechanized cavalry regiment designed to operate with horse cavalry units.

Early in 1929, Patton said that Americans in peacetime could afford only the essential parts of the military machine. In wartime, with large funds and great numbers of men available, "we may indulge ourselves in experimental accessories, but, in peace, any part which cannot meet this question of absolute indispensability must be ruthlessly scrapped." If all that was claimed for all sorts of new machines and weapons were true, there would be no reason to retain the horse cavalry. Yet this could hardly be the case.

"It is pretty well agreed that the next war will be a war of movement." Since air forces and mechanized forces were bound to play important roles in the future, it was necessary to understand both the powers and the limitations of those new means of waging war.

> I wish it distinctly understood that nothing I shall say is spoken in disparagement of these branches. We recognize the extreme importance of the air corps and mechanized forces . . . we go further—we are endeavoring with all our

might to include in our [cavalry] scheme of things all air and mechanization developments.

In all wars, no matter what sort and where fought, certain functions had to be performed, and only cavalry was capable of doing them in all kinds of weather and terrain. Therefore, cavalry remained an indispensable part of the military establishment.

Patton developed this theme in a paper he called "Cavalry in the Next War." In his opening he established his belief that

the ROAD in all its forms from marble to chicken-wire has played a predominant role in the bellicose meanderings of mankind. The invention of the motor car and its variants has not only failed to alter this condition but has in fact emphasized it.

Contrasting as he had before the experiences in Mexico, where roads were primitive, and in France, where the roads were so good that they "give us an exaggerated idea" of how easy it was to use trucks, he said that in both areas the roads did not come under attack—"so that in this respect our experience lacks finality." Yet it was certain that the general condition of roads "in any theater save Western Europe" would approximate more nearly those in Mexico. It would, therefore, be foolish to expect mechanized vehicles to move with facility.

It is realized that these statements will be challenged by the vast fraternity of motorists who spend their Sundays in pleasant perambulations along our arterial highways. But let these skeptics try our vastly more numerous byways and the valor of their ignorance will be abated. Moreover, let them remember that the difficulties they encounter are as nothing to the conditions that would confront the hundredth truck of convoy [that has churned up and destroyed a road].

Roads were the alpha and omega of military operations,

and their number and condition will absolutely determine the character of the next war . . .

Vast concentrations [of men], such as we saw in Europe cannot exist if they cannot be fed. Hence in most parts of the

earth contending forces will be smaller or else tied like unborn babes to the placenta of a railway or river line. This
reduction of forces will result in making . . . flankless lines
[as on the Western Front] impossible.

As a consequence, maneuver will reappear. Time will again
become the vital factor [in war].

Emphasizing that he had no intention of belittling the importance of motor transport in war, recognizing the need for "the
employment of the utmost usable number of motor vehicles,"
Patton foresaw difficulties "undreamed of on a holiday tour."

. . . it seems relevant to advert on[c]e more to history in
order to definitely confound lithesome theories of the self-
styled mechanists or academic warriors who are so exhilarated
by the gaseous exhalations of their pet machines as to be
oblivious to the necessity for more prosaic arms.

It is confidently asserted that if any one of these gentlemen
will take the trouble to personally examine the districts
made famous by the Peninsular and Bull Run campaigns . . .
of the Wilderness campaign . . . he will have to admit that no
machine yet made or dreamed of could have replaced to any
appreciable degree the man on foot or the man on horseback. . . .

Having had the honor of commanding tanks in action we
are the last to belittle their importance, but knowing their
limitations as we do we are unalterably opposed to the assigning to them of powers which they do not possess. Such
action not only foredooms them to failure but also condemns
the army which relies solely on them to disaster and defeat . . .

Of yore the chariot, the elephant and, later, gunpowder
were severally acclaimed as the mistress of the battlefield.
Within our memory the dynamite gun and the submarine
were similarly lauded. Now gas, the tank and the airplane
share . . . this dubious honor. The glory of the skyrocket
elicits our applause; the splash of its charred stick is un-
noticed . . .

The wrestling adage that: "There is a block for every hold"
is equally applicable to war. Each new weapon demands a

new block and is mighty potent until that block is devised. The development these new weapons and their counters . . . are desirable in that they add to the repertoire of our attack and defense. They are dangerous when they cause us to pin our whole faith on their efficacy . . .

The proportion of automatic weapons in our cavalry is now much larger than in any other cavalry of the world. This will have most striking results. Formerly we were weak in fire power and that which we attained was paid for at the price of immobilizing a large number of our men. Now the use of automatic weapons permits us to develop a formidable fire effect while at the same time leaving the great majority of our men mobile, thus giving us a double threat in the offensive and making us more tenacious on the defense.

We have already incorporated the wheel-type armored car into our cavalry divisions and at this writing are carrying the process one step further by adopting a combined wheel and track machine for use with cavalry corps and, perhaps, divisions. This latter weapon is ideally suited to play the part of an offensive reserve and may on occasion be used for reconnaissance.

Finally, the partial motorization of cavalry supply trains will have a far reaching beneficial effect on our mobility.

From here, Patton went into a consideration of "the several functions of cavalry in the sequence in which they will occur during our next attempt to insure the peace of the world by combat."

Cavalry, he wrote, was useful for distant reconnaissance despite the airplane, which was useless in storms, fogs, darkness, and forests. Planes were properly regarded as the ally of cavalry for strategic reconnaissance, and they would help cavalry troops to gain and maintain contact with the enemy, to locate and report the enemy's movements and condition. When the road network permitted their use, wheeled-type armored cars would "add strategic feelers to the cavalry." They enjoyed an intermediate place between the plane and the horse, but they were unable to live off the country and a mechanical breakdown was likely to be disastrous. In contrast, "A lame horse loses one trooper." Still, they were excellent for supply and messenger services, and they could fight "as naval cruisers, possibly in pairs," fighting enemy cars by "Nelsonian tactics and close shooting rapidly."

The essential idea governing the use of these reconnoitering detachments is to furnish a control force and mobile base for patrols. Perhaps if we picture an ambulatory beehive moving down the road with small groups of bees going in and out searching for the honey of information, we will form an accurate notion of such a detachment. Like the hive, too, it can be stirred into vindictive activity against any interference with the endeavors of its members . . .

. . . in story books, map problems, and other works of fiction, patrols are supposed to move over hill and dale like a skiming swallow or agile fox examining . . . every hedge, barn and manure pile, and maintaining at the same time the fabled rate of five or six miles an hour.

In practice this is impossible because horses lack spare parts. Roads are where the enemy will be; why seek him in bogs?

As for the masked batteries and lurking machine guns which are popularly supposed to make movement by roads impossible, they do not exist. No enemy, however malign, has enough of such trinks [tricks or trinkets?] as to be able to secrete them about the countryside in the fond hope of bagging poor Corporal Smith and his trusty squad.

Patton then described the correct method of patrolling. "Notice," he said,

that there is no Boy Scouting, no crawling or entwining the hat with a wreath of poison ivy in a futile endeavor to impersonate some Pan or Satyr. In war men will have neither the training nor the time for such frivolities.

If the patrol met a small enemy force or an enemy patrol of like size, he continued,

Instantly the corporal should gallop at this with all his men, emitting while so doing ferocious noises . . .
If our corporal gallops the enemy and does it first, and hell for leather, the chances are 99 to 1 that the foe will run and

later justify his tumultuous departure by reporting to those who sent him that he was attacked by a platoon or possibly a troop—such is the nature of man.

If the patrol encountered a machine gun in position, "it must take its losses, which will be surprisingly small, and beat it out of range." But then the patrol must discover the size and nature of the force grouped around the gun.

In an aside, Patton gave his opinion that "Night patroling should be more emphasized in peace training." Then he made a statement, later to be quoted widely and frequently misunderstood because of being taken out of context. "Our personal feeling," he said, "is that even if the enemy were not trying to stop us, we would attack him. War is a question of killing, and the sooner it starts the better." What he meant was that victory usually belonged to the side on the offensive, and the side that got the jump on the enemy in launching an offensive was more likely to win.

He also summarized his tactical thinking in a single aphorism, and it too would be quoted later in World War II—usually in vulgar form—as personifying Patton's unorthodox and fiercely aggressive views:

> In reading of the tactics appropriate to . . . a fight we are apt to find ourselves enmeshed in a mob of strange words, such as the "Pivot of Maneuver," "The Mass of Maneuver," etc. If instead of this we describe the tactics appropriate by saying: "Grab the enemy by the nose and kick him in the pants," we sacrifice purity to precision but we express the idea.

Once a position had been gained in the enemy's rear, "there is but one solution: the mounted charge."

For this attack the saber is more appropriate than the pistol because the psychology of the bayonet and saber are identical— you have to get close to use them. The actual killing potentiality (not effect) of a line of infantry firing from the hip while charging is far greater than a similar line trusting to the bayonet, but human nature being what it is a charge so conducted would never get home. For when the bolt refuses to close, signaling an empty magazine, the hero will stop to reload and in nine cases out of ten he will never restart . . .

. . . [the charge] should be executed at the utmost speed of every horse. To follow the theory that the pace should be that of the slowest horse in order to attain so-called cohesion, is foolish. By such methods all the fierce elemental emotions of the stampede are lost. To charge effectively a man must be in a frenzy; you cannot have controlled frenzy . . .

In our opinion the headlong charge applies also to operations against mounted opponents. The efficacy of the charge rests in very great measure on the psychological effect produced. There is an exhilaration in speed and it utilizes the enthusiasm of the natural fighters both to afright the enemy and to hearten their more cautious comrades . . .

If the unlikely happens and a melee follows the charge, it is individual killing ability and savagery—not formations which will determine the issue.

Patton noted that "the increased use of machines [in future wars] will put a high premium on gasoline. Its destruction will be worth a great effort."

The German Ardennes counteroffensive in December 1944 would threaten important stocks of Allied gasoline.

Mechanized forces, Patton predicted, would have difficulty forcing the passage of obstacles, for example, creeks and gulches, and would have to do so by establishing bridgeheads. These would require the presence of "portee infantry" or "Tank Marines" or, more simply, motorized infantrymen. These in turn would demand "numerous non-fighting vehicles, with a corresponding elongation of the [marching] column." And this would seriously delay the speed of march and the rate of deployment.

Furthermore, "Without gasoline machines are junk." They could not fight at night. And "the battle command of Mechanized Forces offers tremendous and as yet unsolved difficulties."

Cavalry, Patton indicated, could fight mechanized forces if the cavalrymen followed certain principles—attacking only at night, harassing tankers, giving them no rest, destroying bridges behind them, intercepting their supply columns, and the like.

Of course the cavalry will not get off scatheless. Sad to say no effective means of fighting without killing and getting killed has yet been invented.

. . . it is our firm belief that the independent employment of Mechanized Forces is so largely illusory that it will never be seriously employed. Certainly not after a few trials.

The true metier of these forces is in the form of effective reserves to be used in the final stages of a general battle to strike the decisive blow.

The effect of airplanes on cavalry, Patton prophesied, would be to force cavalry units to move while dispersed into small march units and concentrate at a desired point, no great difficulty. Bivouacs would have to be spread to offer poor air targets. "The days of nicely ordered cavalry camps on the open sunny slopes of a hill are as defunct as the buffalo among whom they used to flourish."

The best method of countering enemy aviation was to have "our own" aviation—but whether he meant planes controlled by cavalry or simply Army air forces, he did not specify.

As for command, communication, and supply, he stressed that objectives "must be few and simple; the means of attaining them must be vigorous and direct." Simple orders and personal example were the keys to success.

We can give men ideas if not brains. In this case we must imbue our officers with restless energy. An old football coach once said to a lineman: "If you don't know what else to do, throw a fit—do something."

Approvingly, he cited Marshal Foch as having said that most military information was received from historians—after the war. But "Lack of orders is no excuse for inaction. Anything done vigorously is better than nothing done tardily."

Thus, more than a decade before World War II, Patton's thought and expression had attained mature originality. In the "next war" he so confidently expected, he would apply with conspicuous success these beliefs he phrased as aphorisms.

Replying to a published article advocating mechanization, Patton wrote:

> It would be foolish for us to be uncompromising toward mechanization with non-existant vehicles when we can still utilize existant horses. There is a probably psychologic influence at work in favor of mechanical war which takes its sources in the natural reluctance of mankind to be killed. Consequently man attributes great efficiency to machines which he thinks will reduce the number of combatants and, therefore, materially lessen his chances of being called to fight. Also there is no question but that all of us today feel the lure of the machine.

Chairing a conference in the Chief of Cavalry's Office on the impact of mechanization on cavalry, Patton repeated most of what he had already said in writing. He had some additional materials.

> The statement that most regular officers know everything about the last war and nothing about the next was never truer than to-day. The sooner we disabuse our minds of trenches and barrages; of endless lines of boundless supplies; of cigarettes and chocolates—and get back to mud, marches and bacon—the better are we apt to be off the next time Mars sounds revellie on a disillusioned world.

He gave special attention to the armored-car squadron. "Much of the experimental work on its component parts," he said, "was done right here," and the squadron was now an integral part of every cavalry division. There were 36 fighting cars in each armored-car squadron, divided into three 12-car troops (or companies). There were two types of cars, light and medium.

After discussing the various functions carried out by units, Patton closed "with a brief excursion into the unexplored realms of tomorrow." He touched upon the effect of airplanes on marching columns, admitting that his ideas were "largely conjectural." Any theorist would be biased, depending on whether he was a pilot or a horseback rider, but since Patton was both an amateur pilot and a rider, he was likely to be less biased. Thus, he believed that planes would force the cavalry to march in shorter columns, to make more marches at night, and to disperse its units. Yet

the multiplicity of missions which fall to the air corps in war will not leave it with unlimited time or planes in which to chase columns. Furthermore, if all columns fight back instead of running, the joy of column strafing will diminish—there is no pursuit so keen as that of the unresisting. Finally, our own air forces will certainly afford the best and surest protection against their kindred of the clouds.

He believed "beyond the shadow of a doubt" that mechanized forces would be used in the next war, but how they would affect cavalry or how cavalry would influence mechanized forces was

problematical. Having both the cavalry and the tank viewpoint I shall not try to argue either way but shall simply point out certain phases of the question which appear to warrant more notice than our army has so far given them.

He remarked the congestion of mechanized forces on roads, the difficulties of supply and command, and the virtual impossibility of fast cross-country movement. But, he warned, if "a mechanized force gets deployed in fair country, cavalry will have to clear out." The armored cars, light and medium, Patton concluded, were weapons of the future, and he looked for

a combined wheel and track vehicle capable of real work across country as well as high speed on the road, where it will normally be used. Obviously such a vehicle is in no sense a tank, since the mobility we demand of it will inhibit the use of really bullet-proof armor. We also realize that since such a type will be a non-commercial product we shall never have very many of them, certainly not at the beginning of a war.

Such a weapon will restore the cuirassiers to the cavalry and I confidently believe that at no distant day we shall see troops or squadrons of them charging in line as of old and bursting a hole through which our equine squadrons will thunder to victory.

It was a thrilling vision; part of it would come true.

Undoubtedly he managed to establish an equilibrium within himself on the conflict between horses and machines. It permitted him to ride horses and be their advocate while at the same time it enabled him to keep a notebook filled with materials on the Christie tank and the tactical employment of mechanized forces.

The armored car was imperfect, but "Mechanical progress can only result from physical experiment." During the spring of 1929, the 1st Armored Car Troop of the 1st Cavalry Division—the only armored car unit in the Army—was patrolling the border between El Paso, Texas, and Hachita, New Mexico, with five small, open cars, five small pickup trucks, and one larger truck, all quite innocuous.

The Christie car was better, even though some highly theoretical factors still remained to be solved.

> The reason for this state of uncertainty is due to the fact that in the Christie car we are buying a principle not a vehicle. The vital thing is the track and wheel suspension. This we have secured and will build around it an appropriate body with armament, armor, crew, engine, gasoline supply, etc. in proper proportion.

"The use of armored forces," he wrote, "is likely to restore mobility to its preeminent place in warfare." The greatest chance for victory would lie with the side that had developed mobility to the maximum extent. For mobility enhanced surprise. Sweat saved blood, and so would gasoline.

He disagreed with his old friend Brett, who wrote on "Anti Tank Defense" and suggested using tanks to counter enemy tanks. To Patton, tanks were not defensive weapons, they were offensive tools. Bodies of water, marshes, forests, and mountains would serve as strategic tank defenses, and in actual tank combat, delayed fuze shells and white phosphorous rounds (which burned at extremely high temperatures) would be the best defenses, especially if command tanks were singled out and knocked out and if tank assembly points were bombed by planes.

Reacting to an article by Colonel C. M. Bundel on strategy, Patton found himself in disagreement on four points. Bundel said that surprise was unnecessary if a military force had sufficient superiority; beside that statement, Patton wrote: "But it adds to superiority." Bundel said that every commander in contact with the enemy had to hold forces in reserve to counter unexpected developments; Patton wrote: "I do not at all agree with this." Bundel said that it was essential for a soldier in a republic to keep the head of government accurately informed on all military matters; Patton added: "Or to depose him." Bundel said it was necessary to use every man in combat; Patton wrote: "Twice."

An article by Marshal Foch on the conduct of war prompted Patton to observe that the fundamental truths underlying the art of war remained unchanged, that victory came from the ability to prepare for offensive battle, then to launch the decisive attack during that battle, and that generals who fought willingly were not easy to find.

Material describing the British experimental Mechanized Force led him to postulate that the human factor in war could not be disregarded, that long-service professional soldiers were necessary for mechanized units, that mechanized forces were sensitive to ground conditions, that all the functions of the horse were still unable to be borne by machines, that a stationary gun always had the advantage over a moving gun, and that tanks had to become cheaper to manufacture and less cumbersome to operate if they were to become the decisive factor in combat.

Another treatise caused him to agree that war games were valuable for training, that it was difficult to design problems for practicing command in a war game, and that commanders were likely to control ground troops from the air in the future. But he was unimpressed by the tendency "to use the word 'VAST' in speaking of the numbers of tanks. (One could win a war with a 'VAST' number of trained worms.)"

Patton acquiesced warmly with a statement that a mechanized force was useful only in the attack and that cavalry units bolstered by mechanized elements were doubled in value. He noted that during the siege of Rhodes in 304 B.C., Demetrius had constructed an enormous rock-throwing machine moved by 3400 men; the enemy destroyed the engine by making it fall into a hole.

He cited Seeckt, father of the postwar German Army, as authority for the statement that mechanization was a catchword against which thinking soldiers had to fight. The Army of the future was sure to be small, professional, well trained, and highly mobile, with cavalry a vital element.

After looking at the courses offered by the Air Corps Tactical School, Patton commented on the need for armor-piercing ammunition for all antiaircraft guns. He noted that radios and planes still failed to work well together. He felt that an observer in an aircraft being used for reconnaissance had to be an expert in radio, photography, flying, the tactics of all the other arms, and a good machine gunner—"for which profundity of knowledge he only gets 50% increase in pay and that only for a little while." Observation missions in the air would, he thought, be hampered by fear of interference from hostile pursuit planes.

Patton believed that an effective military leader was an artist rather than a scientist. Unfortunately, the intricacies of mechanization were apt to involve soldiers in techniques that were more scientific than artistic. While the fighting value of units depended on many elements, the prime determinant was the sort of leadership they had.

It is very easy for ignorant people to think that success in war may be gained by the use of some wonderful invention rather than by hard fighting and superior leadership.

Fifteen years later, when signs multiplied that Germany was losing World War II, Hitler would constantly promise and the German people would believe that new miracle weapons were about to appear and change the course of the war.

Emphasizing leadership, Patton wrote:

. . . the attempt to make mahoginy boxes out of pine is analogus to the attempt to make leaders out of a large percentage of students [in the military schools] . . . Leadership demands a balanced consideration of all means—a

complete mastery of technique. The military specialist who is
blind to the defects or virtues of all arms but his own is a
menace, a dangerous menace . . . Wars are not won by
maneuvers but by fighting. Education cannot make though it
can help a genius . . . It is cheaper to beat an enemy by war
of maneuver than by trench warfare but in our enthusiasm
for maneuver we must not forget that trenches will be used to
defend vital localities and most of all as points around which
to maneuver.

The papers, articles, and reports he studied reinforced his long-
held beliefs in the importance of mobility, speed, and surprise,
the importance of the soldier rather than the machine, the importance of command, communications, and supply, the importance of air warfare and ground mechanization, and the
continuing importance of the offensive, the attack.

Had the environment—the United States, the Army, the cavalry, his own friends and associates—been more stimulating, less
negative, more open, less constricting, more alive, less bound
by tradition and inertia, more encouraging in funds and in spirit,
what contributions might Patton have made to the military
thought and the art of war of his times?

CHAPTER 42

Washington: Cavalry and Tanks

"It is just Tank propaganda and was hard to write as I did not want to do any thing that could be used against the horse."

Letter, GSP, Jr., to Henry L. Stimson, Secretary of State, March 29, 1929

My dear Mr. Secretary: Knowing, by previous experience, your fondness for exercise and riding, I am taking the liberty of offering you the use of my horses and squash court, at any time and as often as you may find convenient. The court and horses are situated at 3000 Cathedral Avenue (the old New-lands Place), not far from the War[d]man Park Hotel. Of course the court cannot move but the horses can meet you either at my house or at any other place you may elect . . . Please believe me when I say that in accepting either of these invitations you will be conferring a favor upon me. Both the court and the horses need exercise. Mrs. Patton joins me in sincere regards to Mrs. Stimson and yourself. Very respect-fully,

Letter, Stimson to GSP, Jr., April 6, 1929

My dear Major Patton: Many thanks for the kind offer of horses and squash court. Some time in the near future I hope to be able to avail myself of the use of the horses . . .

It has been a pleasure to get back to Washington and to have the privilege of enjoying the hospitality of my old Army friends . . .

[Handwritten] P.S. Apr 8. I had a delightful ride on Gay-lord yesterday.

Patton attended the twentieth reunion of his class at West Point, then traveled to Fort Riley to inspect training activities for the Chief of Cavalry. He talked with many officers, "all old friends," on how well the Cavalry School was fulfilling its missions, and he observed the classroom and outdoor activities.

When he returned to Washington, he recommended certain changes. Assigning students to the Advanced Equitation Class, he thought, should be deferred until later in the school year because some students developed slowly. Horses should not be classified as jump or school horses but be used for whatever purpose was required. More time ought to be set aside for riding during the year-long course—"After all, the chief characteristic of the cavalry-man is his horse-induced mobility."

> Due to the constant change in station, to the small pay and the great amount of duty at stations where horses may not be maintained, the present cavalry officer gets far less riding and knowledge of the horse than did his predecessor of ten or twenty years ago.

More riding halls, whether temporary or permanent in construction would help. Polo received insufficient official encouragement; the Cavalry School should have the best polo team in the Army.

> I realize that in making this statement I can be accused of bias. However, I honestly believe that my opinion in this particular case is impartial. Polo is . . . the great equestrian game, and it seems therefore very appropriate . . . at our great equestrian school.

Better quarters on post were required for the noncommissioned officers.

> Even the very senior non-commissioned officers are forced to inhabit buildings of a very temporary and dilapidated nature. The class of non-commissioned officers at the Cavalry School and with the school detachment is particularly high and every effort should be made to facilitate their comfort and self-respect.

More cavalry maneuvers were needed. The students who came from the 1st Cavalry Division were better prepared for their studies because of the frequent exercises along the border.

Discussing the school programs for the coming academic year, Patton said that "long and intimate association with scholastic subjects leads to an obliteration of perspective. The purpose of instruction (killing) becomes lost in the means of imparting it (talking)." Therefore, he recommended that the courses be reduced from 180 to 140 hours in length, with the exception of military history, which should be increased "as a means of inculcating esprit de corps and of developing a resourceful mind." He thought it made sense to increase the hours devoted to mounted and combined arms warfare, to decrease the hours concerned with staff and logistics. As for fortifications, "The less cavalry knows about digging the better." Cavalrymen had no need of technical knowledge of machines, but they needed to know how to employ armored cars tactically. He recommended that riding and scouting classes be held at night and in bad weather at least ten times during the school year.

Crosby rated Patton a "superior" officer who was competent to hold the rank of major general in the cavalry and brigadier general in any other arm and who was capable of holding any General Staff position. He was:

> A most energetic and forceful officer with a thorough knowledge of his profession. He possesses a combination of physique, determination and daring, coupled with a knowledge of his own and other arms that make him one of the few officers I know who would make an ideal commander of a Cavalry Division in war.

The campaign in the Army, the Congress, and the press to modernize the military establishment by machines seemed to pick up in intensity, and a rebuttal appeared in the Washington *Post* of Sunday, July 7, 1929. A story called "The Juggernaut of No-Man's-Land" purported to show what had been learned about tanks since the World War, what the latest developments were, and how they would be used in the "Next Great World Conflagration." There was a large photograph of Patton standing in front of a tank in France. The reporter had obviously talked with Patton, and certainly it was from Patton that the following sentence came: "In a country like the United States, which owns 21,000,000 horses and 4,000,000 mules, the tank and the motor vehicle will not soon supplant all animals for military purposes."

In a formal rebuttal of the case for mechanization in August, Patton referred at length to the inability of machines to traverse all kinds of terrain in all conditions of weather. He offered the observation that horses required no experimental or developmental costs. The horses necessary for a patrol of four men cost $600; an armored car capable of carrying four men cost at least $1500; a tank cost anywhere from $12,000 to $15,000. Furthermore, "It would be folly and a great hardship to the farmers if we fail to utilize the natural and existing productions in the shape of horseflesh." He concluded with words that had become second nature to him:

> . . . each new invention from the chariot to the airplane—from gunpowder to the gas engine—has been heralded as the final solution, and yet in no instance has the adoption of a new weapon materially affected war. The wrestling maxim that "there is a block for every hold" still holds true. We may say without exaggeration that the first appearance of any new weapon in combat marked the zenith of its effect, though usually the nadir of its efficiency. This is due to the fact that now, as always, surprise is the primary means of attaining military success.

He worked much the same thought into a somewhat different format in a paper entitled "The Value of Cavalry." He started by quoting "expert opinion"—statements by high-ranking officers who testified to the continuing importance of cavalry. The list of cavalry supporters was impressive—Pershing, Harbord, Summerall, Liggett, Parker, Haig, Allenby, French, Foch, Pétain, Hindenburg, Weygand, Ludendorff, Kluck, Seeckt, and others. For example, Summerall had said, either in a letter to Patton or in an address: "There has been a great deal of misinformation broadcasted relative to the cavalry. It is a fact that cavalry is of far more importance than it has ever been."

Continuing, Patton must have been hurt by his need to turn so savagely on Fuller and Liddell Hart who were espousing theories of tank warfare in England.

> There is not a single known statement of any soldier of combat reputation which is derogatory to Cavalry. Surely the remarks of Colonel J. F. C. Fuller (British Army) who during the course of four years' war replete with opportunities attained only the rank of Lieutenant-Colonel, or the opinions of such a hack-writer as Captain Lyle Hart seem puerile when compared with the forceful statements of the elite of the military world. Despite this fact the effects of often repeated misstatements and halftruths are so far reaching and so readily swallowed by a gullible and motor minded public that a critical examination of the value of cavalry as compared with or modified by the so-called scientific arms is necessary in order to reach a definite conclusion.

He then went into his song and dance. Cavalry could operate anywhere whereas "Mechanical forces do not possess this universal availability." Unimproved roads were hard on motor transport, for they reduced the rate of speed, deteriorated rapidly under military wear, destroyed vehicles "through unwonted stresses," and exhausted drivers. Bridges were rarely strong enough to sustain the weight of motor vehicles. Vehicles could neither ford nor swim streams. "In the next war the destruction of roads and road bridges will be as common as was the destruction of railways and railway bridges in the last."

The last statement was an accurate prediction.

Cavalry, Patton went on, had augmented its firepower by increasing the number of automatic weapons it handled, now used armored cars, and was hoping to obtain tracked armored cars to form strong mobile points of maneuver.

> The limitation inherent in . . . vehicles, such as their inability to operate at night, to live off the country, or to penetrate wood and mountains indubitably stamp them as auxiliaries and not as supplanters of Cavalry.

The individual mobility of cavalry and its universal adaptability are unaltered . . .*

Patton's paper was vehement because the cavalry was fighting for its existence. Lack of funds since the National Defense Act of 1920, and reductions in authorized personnel had cut the mounted arm back, and the advocates of mechanization, particularly the airmen, were clamoring to decrease the horse cavalry even more. As authorized numbers of wagons and pack animals were severely limited by public and congressional pressures, the cavalry compensated for its losses by adding small trucks and automobiles.

Coming events cast long shadows. Even though the combined arms assembled at Camp Meade to test concepts of mechanization were unable to accomplish much, a War Department Mechanization Board, appointed to study the results of the experiment, recommended that a permanent mechanized force be established despite the general lack of funds.

It was even impossible to keep the tanks (infantry) as a large and concentrated striking force. When the War Department decided to send eleven tank companies to various posts in order to facilitate training with infantry divisions, there were insufficient machines and men to carry out the plan. Tank companies were dispatched from Camp Meade to four Army installations. But the tank "companies" transferred to five others, as well as that left at Camp Meade, consisted only of tank platoons—five tanks instead of twenty.

For a few weeks during the summer of 1929, Patton was in charge of the Army polo team at Mitchell Field. Putting aside his visions of tanks and armored cars, forgetting for a short time the

* Appended to this paper was an Addendum in Patton's handwriting: "Note: a great friend of mine was in G–3 when this paper came in. He simply had it coppied and submitted it as the belief of his section. Gen. Edward King then G–3 took the paper to Gen. Crosby Chief of Cav and showing it to him said this is a great paper why can't one of your office write it. Gen. Crosby showed Gen. King the original with my name to it. Neither King nor my friend A.R.C. [Adna R. Chaffee] ever apologized to me. GSP Jr."

collection of photographs, drawings, and blueprints of experimental machines in his files in Washington, he concentrated on horses, the joy of riding, the thrill of competition. He played hard.

At the end of the polo season, he went to Green Meadows for a month of leave. While there, he answered a letter from the Chief of Cavalry.

My dear General Crosby: Pardon my delay in sending you the following answers to the questions . . . It is only too true that when one has lots of time one has no time.

He sent Crosby a ten-page staff paper on organization, division trains, motor equipment, vehicles, roads, marksmanship, gunnery, courses of instruction, motorized infantry, and national defense. "Aviation cannot take prisoners or hold ground," he wrote. "Again therefore it can aid but not replace cavalry." He was perfectly frank when he could not answer a question—"I have no data here on which to base recommendations for motorizing Cavalry Division trains." He admitted that "the consolidation of the Field and Coast artilleries is not susceptible of discussion by me." He thought that certain economies could be gained by reducing unit movements and personnel transfers, by cutting the number of officers attending service schools, and by abolishing military bands.

Early in October 1929, he traveled to Fort Bliss, where he attended meetings of the Polo-Horse Show Association and observed maneuvers held by the 1st Cavalry Division.

Letter, GSP, Jr., to Beatrice, October 9, 1929
Darling Beatrice: We had a very interesting manuver yesterday. The 8th Cav in trucks went up to Finlay to stop the 1st Cav mounted. There were 4 armored cars with the eighth [Cav]. Due to the utter lack of imagination of the Colonel of the 1st . . . the cars so delayed them that there was no battle. However it proved that my ideas both asto fighting with and against armored cars was correct . . .

Our old house at Sierra Blanca is still standing but you would hardly know the town. It has grown to be quite a place

and has a golf club. Dick Love now lives in Mexico and Dave
Allison has at last been killed.

I am getting on fine. I love you   George.

Letter, GSP, Jr., to Beatrice, October 12, 1929

The value of the commander is most evident. When he is
active the manuvers are fine. When he is slow . . . they are a
wash out.

Letter, GSP, Jr., to Crosby, October 18, 1929

My dear General: Feeling that you will not now be able to
attend the maneuvers and knowing your great interest in
them I am sending you this [which] is a brief and probably
ill-digested account of the features which have attracted my
notice thus far.

Armored Cars: These vehicles have an almost unprecedented capacity in this terrain. They function not only as cars
but are also capable of assuming frequently the role of
tanks. They are much more effective on the defense than in
the attack. In combating them it is axiomatic that troops
(Cavalry) must refrain from playing their game. That is the
cavalry must keep off the roads—well off. Captain Holt has
established excellent relations with the Ordnance. If he can
secure two hundred dollars from the Ord. he can make some
most desirable changes in the cars here. I believe Gen. Williams [Chief of Ordnance] will let you have this money . . .

Pursuant to your ideas I persuaded Col. Brown . . . to put
his saddle packs in the train in one maneuver. The effect was
marked in the excellent condition of the horses . . .

Envelopment: It is my opinion that in some cases cavalry
is too timid about extended deployments. Too much memory
of distances used in the schools . . . A notable exception was
an attack made by the 10th Cav. under Lt. Col. L. Brown.
In that case he got completely behind the enemy before he
was ever seen . . .

So far as I can see control and mobility are inimical. We
should admit this and . . . let the two principal elements
work independently . . .

Comments from some of the Corps and War Department
heads harped on the subject of more caution. This is an error.
All men are cowards; the first whisper of a bullet will awaken

all the caution we need, probably much more than we want. At maneuvers we should be over bold so that in war the tendency to over caution may to a measure be counteracted . . .

If a division can't operate 18 miles from a good road it is in a hell of a fix . . .

The training of the [cavalry] division is excellent, the discipline fine, the conditions of the mounts exceptional . . . The arrangements were worked out in the most minute details and worked without a hitch. The umpires and observers were cared for to a superlative degree. If we had had this division in Mexico in 1916 there would be no border question to-day. All officers were most regretful that you could not be present. In closing I repeat that this is a very hasty summary liable to error. The general impression [I have of the Cavalry Division] is of an efficient contented and powerful machine. Very respectfully,

After refereeing a polo game, then giving a dinner party for eighteen people to pay off social debts—it was expensive, cost $83, "but they all had a good time," Patton departed by air for Los Angeles and a brief visit with his sister and aunt. While flying over Arizona, he wrote Beatrice: "You can see the tops of all the hills we have so often wished to climb and look into the secrets of all the little can[y]ons. One gets so much better an idea of the lay of the land."

Letter, GSP, Jr. (Woodley, Washington), to Beatrice (Green Meadows), no date.

Enclosed is a copy of an article I wrote for the Hearst papers by request. It is just Tank propaganda and was hard to write as I did not want to do any thing that could be used against the horse.

As I wrote it in two sittings and failed to have your help either in criticism or punctuation it is not much good but if it is accepted I get $250.00.

The untitled article started with a sketch of tanks moving to position for jump-off in battle:

. . . a machine gurgles and dies while its frantic crew, sobbing curses like apoplectic mule skinners, wiggle and sweat to replace some refractory magneto or erring fanbelt. Presently an officer arrives to lend his muffled profanity to the task of rekindling the defunct spirit of the motor . . .

She tops the parapet and exposing six feet of slimy belly teters for a moment until with the grace of a baby hippo she plunges forward and courtesying clangorously to the void wabbles on again for all the world like some huge Galapagos turtle, swaying the gun proboscis of its turret head from side to side in search of prey . . .

The "Baby Tank" as the French affectionately called the little Renault [during the war] was an infant in more respects than size . . . all the faults of adolescence; feeble clumsy and near sighted, it only survived due to the indomitable will of the men who fought and tended it . . .

[Those at Camp Meade recently saw the latest example of] the metal saurian make its debut . . .

Long, low, its eight wheels articulating with the rhythmic abandon of the legs of a water beetle it flew past us not at four, but forty miles an hour.

Report, GSP, Jr., to Crosby, Tactical lessons derived from the Cavalry Division maneuvers, October 1929, November 27, 1929

Armored Cars. In dry weather the country along the western section of the Mexican border—that is from Marfa to the Pacific Ocean—is particularly well adapted to the employment of armored cars. Their ability to move over this region is extraordinary and permits them to partake of the nature of fast, light tanks. The operations are further facilitated by the fact that few of the roads are ditched so that they may be entered and left at will . . .

The best place to locate barricades for the purpose either of checking or upsetting armored cars is on the far side of blind curves, or just beyond the brow of a steep rise . . . A tree or telegraph pole felled across the road will serve as a basis for such a barricade.

In engaging armored cars by fire the targets should be the tires, wheel-hubs, eye slits, and differential or radiator, even when protected . . .

Envelopments. Excessive pursuit of "A's" [good grades] at sundry schools have had the pernicious effect of making our officers timid . . . The function of cavalry is to get behind the enemy . . . wide and risky movements are necessary . . .

Advances by bounds. This method of progression exists only on paper . . .

Control. There was much comment by all the observers upon the lack of control in action . . . we have for so long been accustomed to . . . the dream soldiers of map problems that we forget the many defects in poor human flesh. As a matter of fact, in war we shall have much less control than at the maneuvers. The sooner we accommodate ourselves to this fact and arrange our methods of war so that they will function despite lack of information, the better we'll be off.

Camps. No effort was made to cover or protect camps from air attacks . . .

Supply . . . Unfortunately, when rain occurred, making the roads difficult, the maneuvers were called off; so no test of supply during inclement weather was obtained . . . some engineering trucks . . . were stuck for some two days not over seven miles from a hard road.

Due to the ill-advised attempt to make World War conditions of static combat applicable to cavalry, staff command was overstressed . . . Much time was wasted. The essence of cavalry combat as has been demonstrated by all successful cavalrymen, of whom there are a very limited number, depends upon spontaneous cavalry leadership. Attempts to smother and delegate authority and staff command is fatal.

GSP, Jr., Lecture to the Pennsylvania National Guard Convention at Reading, December 6, 1929, "Cavalry in the Next War"

. . . should any of you chance to believe one-tenth of the current bunk about cavalry and war, you might well paraphrase the title of my remarks into: "The Extinct in the Impossible." . . . piffle to the contrary notwithstanding, cavalry will bear its part in that war as it has done in all that have preceded it. For, as Field Marshal Earl Haig once said to me: "My boy (I was one twelve years ago) Infantry and Artillery can win battles, but only cavalry can make them worth winning." Less cryptically he meant that the man who runs in fear of death can always outstrip the man who pursues, unless the pursuer can provide more rapid means of locomotion . . .

Battles without successful pursuit are futile . . .

I have had as much experience with mechanized forces, both in war and peace, as has any man in our army; therefore when I tell you that machines have defects as great as their advantages, I deserve your attention . . .

An unfed motor stops; a starved horse takes days to die.

Remount magazine carried a piece by Patton on hunting, "The Sport of Kings." It was marked by humor—"the first horse a man owns is apt to share the fate of the first child and be killed by misplaced attentions and undigested education"; by common sense— his fears over his adequacy to complete a course of schooling were countered by the remark "Just look at the dumb-bells who have graduated"; by exaggeration—a small error leads to "folly"; by individual turn of phrase—timidity was "intuitive reluctance to adventure in the unknown"; and by the need to be perfect in every action undertaken—one became perfect by constant study and practice.

By the end of the war, Patton had completed what he called the "First Phase of Study" of a long treatise entitled "A Study of the Combat of Cavalry up to and Including the World War." An ambitious project, the initial part alone consisted of 249 typed pages, single space. It was typically Patton in phraseology and content. For example: The mission of armies was to win battles, for all military operations culminated in battle. Cannae was won "by a supreme confidence [of the soldiers] in their leader, Hannibal." At Pharsala, Pompey and Caesar exemplified that "Strategy merely leads up to battle. The end of all effort and maneuver in war is successful combat or to cause the enemy to give up because of his fear of that combat."

A lecture he wrote early in 1930 re-used parts of earlier papers. There was nothing new except his form of expression. For example, novelty was a form of surprise, "and it is surprise, not power which appalls us." Airplane observers saw a great deal but very badly. Armored cars went fast and far but only if and when the roads permitted. Seeing a charging line, troops would usually act like Macbeth's dinner party and depart without waiting on the order of their going . . . Think . . . of how few places there are in the world, except target ranges, where one can see every foot of ground from zero to a thousand yards . . . Extensive obstacles such as creeks, gullies, and wooded draws should be held in force. At such places mechanized forces can be stopped. If they know their business, however, they will not attack but go around . . . [Command] must be extremely personal and extremely decentralized . . . Anything done vigorously is better than nothing done tardily.

These statements had become his clichés, and he reiterated them constantly. Whether he actually believed that the horse had a place in modern warfare, or, as everyone was saying, in the next war, or whether he was forced into defending the horse against his convictions with respect to tanks and armored cars was probably something he himself could not have said with assurance.

There is no doubt that he believed in mechanization to some extent, perhaps to a large extent, and to this end he worked actively with Christie, perhaps even to the degree of partially subsidizing his work.

So he straddled the issues. And was apparently comfortable enough in his dual role as traditionalist and innovator to handle both sides with ease. In February, while he was working on the proper sequence of training regulations for mounted troops, he marked one of six glossy prints of Christie tank bodies in his handwriting as "My model of Christy Type for Cavalry." Whether he was expressing a preference or whether he had actually contributed to the Christie design by advice or funds remains a matter of conjecture.

In March, Patton was appointed a member of a board to review and revise the development, organization, and equipment of the permanent mechanized force that the War Department had approved. Perhaps it was this that led him to come close to conceding defeat for the horse cavalry. In a memo on antitank and anti-armored car operations, he wrote: "Mechanization is now so universally adopted that we will probably encounter a certain number of fighting vehicles in the ranks of any possible enemy."

How successfully he had managed to defend the horse and to advocate the machine was obvious in Crosby's rating of his performance. Crosby repeated what he had earlier written—that Patton would make "an ideal commander of a Cavalry Division in war." This time Crosby added: "While he is an outstanding horseman he is also outstanding as an authority in mechanization due to his varied experience in France with the Tank Corps and to his continued interest in and study of the subject of mechanization."

CHAPTER 43

Washington: Horses and Machines

*"It would be cheaper to dress our men in overalls,
but it would be a saving too truely bought, for without pride soldiers are useless."*

WHATEVER PATTON'S DIFFICULTIES may have been with respect to
machines and horses, a way out suddenly appeared in a letter from
an old friend.

*Letter, Ralph I. Sasse (West Point) to GSP, Jr., March 18,
1930*

Dear Patton: For the last two months my tongue has been
tied on a definite promise to one of rank here at West Point
—yesterday I heard additional news which may be stale to
you, however here goes. Richardson is due to leave here as
Commandant of Cadets. The following have been mentioned
to replace him—Charlie Thompson—Tom Catron—Jake Devers, Buckner and yourself. General Rivers [Patton's former
commanding officer] has probably gotten wind of what is taking place, as he told me last Saturday evening that he had recommended you to the Superintendent, though no reaction
was obtained. Col Whipple, The Adjutant here is one of my
best friends and the Supt. acts upon his advice in many matters. Accordingly I have swung Whipple in line for you. I
would like to see you come here. The place needs some red
blood and hard common sense. With you as Commandant I
believe we could produce a few soldiers. Besides I need a
squash partner. Best to Beatrice and the gang. Cordially,

Patton tucked away Sasse's phrase "red blood and hard common sense" in his mind, then went to see General Crosby. He
asked Crosby to recommend him for the job.

It was not a moment too soon. Crosby was retiring from the Army in two days. He wrote immediately to the Superintendent, Major General William R. Smith, who had commanded the Hawaiian Division and who had removed Patton from the post of G–3. Being Commandant of Cadets, Crosby wrote, was the most sought after assignment among young field officers, and many had asked him to recommend them for the position. He felt he could at last recommend two officers,

> either Chaffee or Patton—two of our outstanding cavalrymen—for the place. Both of them, as you know, had brilliant records in France and Patton especially, one that should make him a hero to the Cadet. As a result of his service under you in Honolulu his friends tell me he is less positive in his ideas and in his expression of them. He is certainly loyal to you and has been most loyal to me during his two years in my office. With apologies for butting in to what I know you will decide and decide properly for yourself, I am, Cordially,

For the second time, Patton would fail to get the assignment. Major General Guy V. Henry, an old friend of Patton's became Chief of Cavalry, and the pleasant relations Patton had enjoyed with Crosby would continue.

Patton's professional study during his years in the Office of the Chief of Cavalry was enormous. He now wore glasses when reading. In the spring of 1930 when he suffered from a slight conjunctivitis, an inflammation of the eyes, the doctor recorded that the probable cause was Patton's staying up with his books until one o'clock every morning.

He avidly went through G–2 reports compiled from military attachés in England, France, Germany, and Japan, and appended to many of these papers, which Patton kept in his personal files, were his own typed notes, usually a page or half-page, sometimes more, generally a digest of the substance. For example, one sheet was headed "Thoughts aroused by the foregoing" and contained the statement that advocates of mechanization believed they would have a monopoly on heroes in the future. "Mobile A.A. [antiaircraft] units are excellent Anti Tank Units," which was a concept for a dual-purpose gun able to engage both air and ground targets.

With cavalry under heavy attack and Patton busy fending off efforts to declare the cavalry obsolete, he wrote draft lectures for Henry to deliver. He had Henry saying that machines, guns, tanks, armored cars, and planes only made cavalry stronger.

We are now the most powerful cavalry and, in my opinion, the most powerful arm in the world. The path to fame and glory lies before us, if we have but the intelligence to follow it.

As a committee member studying the development both of weapons and of communications and their influence on strategy and tactics, Patton stated:

A Study of the evolution of tactics . . . naturally [but it would be natural only to someone like Patton who was steeped in military history] leads me to use the Seven Years War as a mile stone since at this point we just find the powder propelled missile assuming a predominant place in warfare.

A summary of conclusions appended to a report on firepower read:

In art it often happens that a sketch by the very baldness of its portrayal gives a better likeness than does a finished painting. Just so when we view war objectively . . . we denude it of its non essentials and bring into vivid relief the thoughts of Frederick and Napoleon which we still paraphrase to read: "Fire is every thing as a means to securing victory through movement."

He thought it a mistake to expose immobile masses of humanity to machines and believed that as science placed additional inventions at the disposal of the Army, greater demands would be made on the soldiers who used them.

His miscellaneous notes written on various occasions, most of them undated, contained aphorisms, including:

. . . articles and pictures . . . far out horror the reality of war.

. . . rifle fire in war . . . is not to be taken too seriously, because in addition to the almost complete absence of targets all the participants have their nerves and muscles strained to the breaking point by fatigue, sleeplessness and lack of food to say nothing of the insinuatingly suggestive hissing and screeching of shell fragments and bullets.

. . . in a war of position cavalry is about as useful as railway artillery would be in a war of movement.

Battles are won by fear.

[Victory in the Boer War was actually a] triumph of discipline cohesion and the offensive spirit.

In April 1930, he delivered a speech to the American Remount Association, and it was music to the ears of his listeners. He cited progress in breeding, the numerous horse shows, the flourishing state of polo competition, the popularity of horse racing, the appeal of hunting, the growth in bridle paths in cities, and called this equine revival pleasing to horsemen everywhere because it benefited the population in health and pleasure, brought wealth to breeders and to the farmers who grew the forage, and helped train young men for the next war.

He then swung into his sermon, a hard-hitting talk consisting of arguments "to refute the blithe assertions of the motor enthusiast that the horse has no place in war and hence is not a necessity," to rebut the "unlimited belief in and enthusiasm for machines as a cure-all for future unpleasantness."

The World War was not the first conflict that prompted the inventive genius of mankind, and he recalled the chariot, longbow, ballista, armor of various sorts, Greek fire, and gunpowder—all of which in their day had much the same impact on warfare as gasoline motors, tanks, gas warfare, airplanes, and machine guns.

To me it seems that a person who says that since machines are faster than horses, horses should be scrapped and machines only secured is on a mental parity with the poor man who on seeing an overcoat of undoubted warmth in a second hand store sells his pants to purchase the coat only to find that in summer it is burdensome and not wholly satisfying even in December . . .

The horse is not useless neither is the machine. What is wanted is better types of both run by men who know their powers and limitations and who instead of decrying each others capacities aid one another.

In May, Patton wrote a lengthy rebuttal to a study submitted by Colonel James Kelly Parsons, who proposed the creation of six tank divisions, one for each of the six field armies envisaged in the General Mobilization Plan. Patton's major objection was that there were "only three [possible] theaters of war in which we could utilize such a mass of men"—Western Europe, Asia, and the United States, and he showed in great detail why he thought six tank divisions would be "redundant." Furthermore, tanks like battleships became obsolete. At the close of the World War, the Army had had 900 Renaults and 100 Mark VIII tanks; their current value was "zero." The tank, he said, was a better machine in 1930 than in 1918, but it was less effective, because there would be many heavy machine guns in the next war—they were "cheaper and quicker to make than tanks," and they could knock out tanks.

The expenditure of twenty seven million [dollars] on lightweight .50 caliber machine-guns would probably do much more toward the winning of the next war than will the expenditure of two hundred and seventy million on tanks.

Soldiers were trained in the Great War to fire at the hulls and eye-slits of tanks. "This was playing the tank-man's game." In the next war, soldiers would aim at "the running gear and will secure results for less ammunition. A stalled tank is junk!"

Exactly how conservative Patton was—whether by necessity or by inclination—became apparent when he rejected the idea of having "infantry integral with the tank division." Unlike the Germans who were organizing units of closely coordinated tanks and infantry, Patton felt this was "a grave mistake." He would change his mind in World War II.

Attached without comment to a letter from Patton to Beatrice in June was a newspaper article. The clipping was headed "Joe Angelo Pleads for Veterans."

Angelo appeared before a congressional committee investigating unemployment and the bonus claims of veterans. According to the reporter, "The veteran [Angelo], who weighs 107 pounds, said he had walked 180 miles to Washington to state that the ex-soldiers 'do not want to rob the treasury. We just want to work.'"

He had been out of work for a year and a half. He was married and had a child. He had built a home when he returned from France, but he was likely to lose it because he was unable to pay the taxes he owed on the property.

Medals covered Angelo's breast. When asked how he had won the Distinguished Service Cross, he replied that he had saved the life of Colonel Patton, who was now stationed at Fort Myer. Angelo showed a watch he had received from the colonel's wife and a stickpin with a bullet mounted in gold from the colonel's mother.

Angelo said he could make money bootlegging. Or he could go to Fort Myer and get all the money he wanted or needed from Patton. But that wasn't right. He wanted to work. Or if work was unavailable, he wanted the money due him according to his service certificate. He wished to have at least part of the $1424 coming to him for his war service.

Congress refused to authorize an immediate cash bonus for veterans. For the moment there was little more than vague unrest about the hard times in the country. But demands for the federal government to ameliorate the economic conditions would soon reach a strident insistence, and Joe Angelo would figure in it. He would have a symbolic confrontation with his old Tank Corps colonel.

In the War Department, Patton was considering "the tactical role of armored cars and the characteristics deducible therefrom."

It is patent that any assumptions made must be tentative, until the test of battle shall have given its verdict. None the less it is believed that we now have enough information to justify us in certain assumptions. Such a course will at least service the purpose of giving us a datum plane from which to measure progress . . .

The history of war is a history of an age-old duel between

defensive and offensive devices. Each new arm traces its birth to the necessity of countering some temporarily decisive invention. The tank was conceived and born to counter the .30 caliber machine-gun. Conversely, the .50 caliber machine-gun was devised to counter the tank. To continue the construction of vehicles only capable of resisting .30 caliber fire is absurd. On the other hand, an attempt to wholly protect them against short range .50 caliber projectiles is impossible. A compromise must be effected on grounds analogous to those used in the Navy. That is, we must make an harmonical arrangement of our four defensive means: armor, speed, gun fire, and low silhouette.

. . . The nose of our machine must then be heavily armored. To do likewise to the tail would not only overload our machine, but also would have a bad moral influence. Remember Cortez and his burned ships [which forced his men to advance into the interior of Mexico].

Together with C. C. Benson, Patton wrote a paper entitled "Mechanization and Cavalry." It was published in the *Infantry Journal* in June 1930. The final paragraph read:

The fighting machine is here to stay, and if our cavalry has not lost its traditional alertness and adaptability, we will frankly accept it at its true worth. If the 14th Century Knight could adapt himself to gunpowder, we should have no fear of oil, grease, and motors. Confident of our own power, we should give the fighting machine the serious thought that it deserves.

Letter, GSP, Jr., to Beatrice, June 30, 1930
Darling Beat: Our [boat] trip was most successful We left . . . at ten minutes to 5 Sunday morning and got to our destination Smith's Creek, beyond St. Mary's at 10:30. We looked over Col Latrobes prospective place for a couple of hours got gas and returned . . . at 7:15 having gone 160 miles in 10½ hours. The moku [boat] went fine.

The place on Smiths creek is very beautiful though terribly run down and owned by the largest man I ever saw. Remind me to tell you about him. The house is on a peninsula with a private bay nine feet deep right at the house.

There are private oysters in the bay.

Col Latrobe and Palmer Swift make a fine crew. Palmer loves to steer and Col Latrobe to cook so I had nothing to do. This did not keep me from missing you and thinking how much nicer a trip it would have been had you been there . . .

It is realy very hot here but not too much so.

I love you   George.

Henry rated Patton a "superior" officer—"outstandingly energetic and forceful. A thorough student of his profession—dependable and loyal. Suitable for most any duty."

Over the long Fourth of July weekend, Patton met and talked with John Pell, associate editor of the *North American Review*. Pell was impressed by the thesis that Patton articulated—that every weapon was most useful though least effective when it was introduced into combat. Would Patton write an article for the journal emphasizing the application of that theory to the airplane? Patton agreed.

He sent the article, saying:

In accord with your suggestion . . . I have attempted to express my views . . . I fear without too happy results. My chief critic and leading punctuator, Mrs. Patton, is away so that probably much is left to be desired in this connection.

Entitled "The Effect of Weapons on War," the article opened beautifully:

When Sampson took the fresh jawbone of an ass and slew a thousand men therewith he probably started such a vogue for the weapon, particularly among the Philistines, that for years no prudent donkey dared to bray.

Although the rest of the piece was vigorous in language, it was so obviously addressed to military men that the *Review* could not publish it.

Letter, GSP, Jr. (Washington), to Beatrice (Massachusetts), July 21, 1930

Darling Beat: It is 108 in this office so they have closed the offices and I am only waiting to write you before I take to the cellar at home. The heat is something fierce . . .

I hope I did not leave you with the impression that I thought you were either a poor sailor or mother. I think you are perfect in these rolls as in all others. I will even "bend" so much as to sail with you in the Dont Esk if you want me.

I love you. George.

Letter, GSP, Jr., to Beatrice, August 5, 1930

Gen Douglas MacArthur is announced as the next Chief of Staff. I don't know just what effect that will have on the cavalry. He is not favorable to polo but I heard that he said that if he became chief of staff he would try and convince the army that the war was over. Meaning that now too much work is required.

In a memo to Henry he argued that automatic weapons, contrary to general belief, enhanced rather than reduced the need for and value of cavalry. Speaking of economy, he said: "Unquestionably it would be cheaper to dress our men in overalls, but it would be a saving too truely bought, for without pride soldiers are useless."

Patton could well have said he had gained an international reputation as a military expert, for the British *Cavalry Journal* in its October issue gave a précis of an article of his in the American journal and called it a well-reasoned paper with a sane outlook.

When Captain B. H. Liddell Hart stated that cavalry had become too susceptible to air attack for continued usefulness in war, Patton took issue.

In my opinion Captain Lydell Hart assumes his conclusions and then writes articles to prove them. This is a very common practice among all writers. I think that he probably overstates his ideas with a view of creating argument.

Asked to comment on a new experimental cavalry saber, he said it seemed superior because it was lighter and stiffer, but actually it was inferior because the hilt was attached to the sword by an outmoded method instead of by the kitchen-knife method used in the 1913—his—model.

I am very much opposed to the fancy grip suggested. For several thousand years men have been killing each other with out finding thumb grooves or finger bumpers necessary. A simple hard rubber grip is cheaper better and lighter . . .

Note: In 1912 when I was working on the saber I designed one almost identical with the Experimental model. I also had a metal scabbard. Gen. H. T. Allen and E. St. J. Greble were on the G.S. [General Staff] and insisted that I make a double edged sword so it would pull out easier (This was theory as they had never tried in bodies of pigs as I had—the single edge pulls out equally well). These same two also forced the wooden scabbard. The temper refered to by the board is not very essential. Softness is better than brittleness. It is a simple matter to straighten a saber blade with a foot. We also do it with dueling swords.

He wrote, probably on instruction from Henry, to several influential commanders asking them to exert pressure on the War Department to help keep the cavalry branch from losing men to the air corps. To Fox Conner, commander of the First Corps Area, he added:

You told me years ago that the next war would be fought with smaller armies of professionals. Now is a chance to save a few of the "Brutal and licentious soldiery" for that happy occasion.

Under his signature, he wrote, jokingly of course, "Maj[or] of Pac[i]fists."

GSP, Jr., Lecture, "New Developments in Cavalry," delivered at the Quartermaster School, Philadelphia, December 17, 1930

Were I to begin by saying that there are no new developments I should probably both surprise and please you, while at the same time I would be telling the truth—but not the whole truth . . .

Our so-called new developments . . . are not new, only recurrent . . .

The trench is but a rampart upside down while belts of wire are moats . . .

. . . the railway train is the epitome of reliable speed. Yet if the coal fails, the tracks are pulled up, or the engine injured, our mighty contrivance becomes junk. Moreover, it has no liberty of direction: it follows a predestined course.

The same thing applies in varying degrees to all machines. Further, being devoid of intelligence and sensory nerves machines can not move freely at night without lights—what lovely targets headlights make! Finally, they have no ears and their own noise deadens those of their operatives.

. . . A Swallow can out-maneuver an eagle but he is not feared. Speed and mobility not linked with fighting capacity are valueless. Wars are won by killing. . . .

Some bewail the advent of machines while others proclaim them as the final solution to the age-old problem for safe success. As usual both are wrong. The new abets but does not supplant the old.

. . . In the cavalry we are doing everything financial restrictions will permit to develop to the full our part of mechanization . . .

. . . success depends very little on complicated tricks of procedure and very much on stark fighting ability. Victory comes to rough and simple methods executed by disciplined and heroic soldiers. The Bosch call it: "The will to victory." The vulgar call it "guts."

. . . many writers on mechanization picture the enemy as static and unarmed, while gasoline grows on trees and bridges are constructed by a wave of the hand.

A battle in which the enemy is not destroyed is a more or less futile affair . . .

I invariably find myself feeling sorry for the enemy: he seems in such an awful fix. But really my tears are wasted. His cavalry with its cars is on hand to oppose ours, so it is a fight once more and the best man wins . . .

In closing I can but repeat that the ends we seek and the methods we employ are as old as winter and as young as spring. Only the technique and the weapons change a little, but neither are vital. Battles are won now as always by the indomitable heart of man, the oldest weapon.

Memo, GSP, Jr., to Chief of Cavalry, December 31, 1930

The other day while hunting in the snow I saw some people putting cup grease in the bottom of their horses feet. On asking the reason I was told that it prevented the snow from "Balling." I tried it and found that it worked. [It cut down slipping. Some winter campaign in the future might depend on some such expedient for success. Recommends test at Cavalry School.] No expense is involved as grease is expendable or at the worst waste cylinder oil can be used.

GSP, Jr., Lecture, "Modern Cavalry," delivered at the Marine Corps School, Quantico, Va., January 9, 1931

. . . the saber and the bayonet are . . . the symbols of implacable determination . . . but it is more the fear of their questing points than the wounds they produce which induces the enemy to leave . . .

The mobilization, feeding, and movement of [huge armies] . . . is a stupendous task, while the cost and delays entailed are out of all proportion to the results attained.

For example, the ratio of men behind to men in front increases out of all reason. At time[s] during the war it reached the ridiculous figure of five behind the three fighting. [In World War II, the proportion required would be, roughly, ten to one.]

The inertia inherent in such armies leads inevitably to stabilization with its attendant high costs and lack of conclusiveness.

The inert human masses become fodder for their equally inert masses of machines. The only road to victory lies in attrition—the sausage machine method.

Again, while the development in weapons is continuous, the cost of perpetually rearming hoards [hordes] with new arms is beyond the powers of the richest; so mass armies must, perforce, fight with obsolescent tools.

Finally, the complexity of the new weapons and of the methods best adapted for their employment is beyond the capabilities of short term troops.

The outstanding lesson of the World War was its indecisiveness and, since this is largely traceable to the use of "Nations in Arms," soldiers seeking a solution tend more and more towards a return to smaller mobile armies capable of maneuver . . .

In closing let me say that the greatest ill-luck I can wish those who think cavalry is dead, is to be against us in the next war. They will be the corpses, not we.

Letter, Fox Conner to GSP, Jr., January 1931
I hope that the powers that be will never lose sight of the fact that we need, above all, things that will work under all conditions.

This was exactly what Patton had been preaching.

In mid-January, Patton almost had the dubious distinction of being challenged to a duel. A member of the Spanish embassy, Ramon Padillo, had unexpectedly stopped at a jump during a hunt and had almost caused Ruth Ellen Patton to collide with him. She barely avoided the possibility of serious injury. Her father who was nearby rode up and gave Padillo a severe and profane tongue-lashing.

Apprised immediately afterward that the Spaniard would be quick to take umbrage, Patton wrote him a note, asking him please to accept his apologies for any remarks he may have made. In sport in America, Patton explained, it was the custom to speak out and those who did so were not considered impolite. Had he known that Padillo was a foreigner, he would not have so spoken. He gave renewed expressions of his regret.

He was, more than likely, himself disturbed by the savagery of his outburst.

Padillo answered on the same day, addressing his note to "Major G. S. Patterson, Jr." He thanked Patton for his letter. "I did not consider myself the least offended by your remark at the hunt." He explained his own behavior by saying that he had not known whether it was the custom in Washington to halt at each jump.

A potentially nasty situation was avoided.

Commenting on March 4 on a draft manual, Patton wrote, with some unnecessarily harsh words:

A manual should state WHAT to do and HOW to do it. It should not state WHY nor should it give alternative methods. Men who will use this manual in war will belong to the honest 80%. The smart 10% need no manual; the stupid 10% cannot use one.

Letter, Vice President Charles G. Dawes to GSP, Jr., March 22, 1931

My dear Patton: I hope you will excuse my delay in answering your letter but my sister, Mrs. Gann, informed me she had accepted your invitation for dinner and told you we would attend the Polo Ball. She looks after all my social engagements. It will be a pleasure to attend the Ball and indeed a great pleasure to have dinner with you and Mrs. Patton. With kindest regards, I am Very truly yours,

In April 1931, the argument over machines and horses seemed to come to some kind of tentative resolution. Following the recommendation of the War Department Mechanization Board and shortly before his retirement, General Summerall, who was then Chief of Staff, directed in October 1930, that a mechanized force be stationed permanently at Fort Eustis, Virginia. A strong proponent of the infantry-artillery-machine gun team, which had been effective in the World War, Summerall was convinced that tanks must be included in that team of combined arms. Since the infantry presumably was less interested in mobility than the cavalry and since mobility was the rage in conversation about how to avoid in the next war the static conditions of the last, a cavalry officer, Colonel Daniel Van Voorhis, was appointed the first commander of the mechanized force. Yet to insure infantry participation in the venture, the executive officer or second in command was Patton's old friend Sereno E. Brett, an infantryman who had taken command of the tank brigade in France after Patton was wounded.

Perhaps to press the issue of mobility, to confirm the control of cavalry over mobile mechanized forces, and to guarantee the notion that horses and machines would work together, Patton composed a memo entitled "Notes Regarding Cavalry." It was for Henry, the Chief of Cavalry, to submit to the Chief of Staff, now General MacArthur. In great detail, Patton analyzed the occasions when machines were superior to horses and when the reverse was true. He concluded:

> As a result of derogatory articles, preposterous claims by inventors and loose talk by officers, many junior cavalrymen are greatly exercised over the future of their arm. My purpose in submitting these notes to the Chief of Staff is the hope that he will either approve my ideas or else give me definite instructions as to those changes he may elect. Armed with such a statement I can calm my juniors and shape my course to conform to the wishes of the Chief of Staff.

Henry was apparently dissatisfied with this paper and asked Patton to turn out another. Patton wrote a memo called "Information on Mechanized Forces," which in slightly altered form took a somewhat different approach.

These two papers were put together and revised, then sent to MacArthur. The Chief of Staff returned it at once. What he wanted to know was how much progress had been made on re-armament and re-equipment in the cavalry. He meant mechanization and motorization.

Henry, probably with Patton's help, complied.

By then, the future of cavalry seemed altogether precarious. The War Department proposed to consolidate the cavalry, field artillery, and coast artillery branches. In a staff paper, Patton argued heatedly against the idea. His reasons were less than cogent and somewhat superficial, but actually amalgamation made very little sense and had been prompted by a desperate search for economy.

With the swing accelerating toward mechanization, and perhaps because his tour of duty in the Office of the Chief of Cavalry was coming to an end, Patton decided that machines could no longer be wished away, that the cavalry had best make peace with that fact, and that more armored cars had to become part of the old horse cavalry. Categorically, he wrote: "At the beginning of a war with any first-class power armored fighting vehicles will be met."

For Henry's information, Patton noted the composition of Van Voorhis' Mechanized Force at Fort Eustis. There were a headquarters company, a troop of cavalry armored cars, a company of tanks (infantry), an infantry machine gun company, a self-propelled artillery battery, an engineer company, an ordnance company, and signal, chemical warfare, and quartermaster detachments.

The whole contained 36 officers, 648 men, and 167 vehicles—20 passenger cars, 11 armored cars, 15 motorcycles, 23 tanks, 7 caterpillar tractors, 33 carrier cart trucks, 2 generator trucks, 4 kitchen trucks, 4 radio trucks, 5 trailers, 3 antiaircraft machine gun trucks, 15 tank carriers, 1 machine shop truck, 1 wrecking truck, 1 caterpillar wire-layer, 11 six-wheel machine gun trucks, 11 Class B trucks, and 31 additional vehicles due to arrive, mostly light quartermaster trucks with four-wheel drive.

It was by any standard a pitifully small force.

Writing to the captain who commanded the armored car troop, Patton wanted to know whether a car could cross a river even if the exhaust was six inches below the water's surface. Could a hose be attached to the exhaust and raised above the water level? If the batteries, generator, and self-starter were first removed, was it possible to tow an armored car—by man, horse, or motor power—across a river when the water covered the engine?

No doubt the captain experimented.

Patton closely followed the activities of the Mechanized Force. He kept a file of newspaper clippings on its work and the comments it prompted. He exchanged notes with others interested in the experimental composite Force. He was quite well aware of the politicking that surrounded its efforts.

Despite the appointment of Van Voorhis as commander, which made the cavalry the dominant arm, the infantry was still trying to gain control of the Force. Despite the dubious effectiveness of the Force, which had yet to be proved, congressmen were increasingly talking about abolishing the cavalry horse regiments.

These were perhaps peripheral matters to the real work required, but Van Voorhis had to deal with them in order to carry out his experiments. Furthermore, he had to be careful not to destroy the horse in the process.

Beyond that, Van Voorhis had to grapple with the problem of developing a doctrine, a methodology of how to plan, as Patton phrased it, "the use of machines for which there is no historical precedent." Doctrine could emerge only after units of precise size and composition were firmly established.

What hampered Van Voorhis, Patton believed, was that his tactical "ideas are extremely nebulous." Van Voorhis, for example, thought of mobility as meaning speed, whereas the correct definition, according to Patton, was fluidity, a more inclusive term derived from the French language.

> Finally I believe that Colonel Van Voorhis attaches too much importance to the technical skill of officers and men serving in mechanized regiments. If war were as difficult as specialists seem to think we would need no League of Nations to prevent fighting.

Patton cautiously conceded in May:

> the advent of the airplane and radio have so facilitated the transmission of information that raids other than local night affairs cannot in the future be effectively executed by horse elements of cavalry.

In the same month, Chaffee, Patton's old friend, left Washington for Fort Eustis to replace Brett and help Van Voorhis cope with the problems of the Mechanized Force. For Chaffee it would be the beginning of a new career. During the next ten years, he would work extremely hard to develop and promote concepts of mechanized warfare. He would sponsor and champion mechanization, motorization, armor, and the use of the combined arms in a hard-hitting striking force. In the process he would become known as the Army's foremost tank expert. He would thus hold the position at the beginning of World War II that was comparable to Patton's place in World War I.

Late in 1931, General MacArthur dissolved the Mechanized Force because of a lack of funds. Harking back, probably unknowingly, perhaps not, to a suggestion made in passing by Patton, MacArthur directed all the arms and services—that is, all the branches within the Army, whether combatant or noncombatant—to adopt mechanization and motorization as far as they could with the limited appropriations, men, and equipment at their disposal.

In compliance, the cavalry in 1932 would adopt the mechanized regiment as its basic experimental unit. Similar in organization to the horse regiment, the new unit would have 35 combat or armored cars. Later, an armored car troop would be added to the cavalry division, along with a tank company, and still later an air observation squadron would be programmed. Retained with these mechanized forces were two horse brigades.

Thus, the idea of using horses and machines together, a cherished notion of Patton's, came into being.

In 1933, the cavalry would develop and test combat vehicles at Fort Knox, Kentucky, and early that year, the 1st Cavalry Regiment would arrive from Texas and begin to replace its horses with machines. The movement toward the Armored Force had begun. In the course of that development, Chaffee, as the cavalry's expert in mechanization, would figure prominently, Patton would arrive late.

Letter, GSP, Jr., to Colonel Pierre Lorillard, Jr. (Tuxedo Park, New York), May 14, 1931

Dear Pete: All this stuff [in the press] against the horse hurts the General [Guy Henry] beyond words, both because of the discouraging effect it has on his officers and also because, while many of the quotations used in the papers are authentic, they are frequently removed from their proper contexts with a deceiving effect. As you know, the General has more physical and moral courage than any Chief we ever had. Also, he is the preeminent horse-soldier of the Army. On the other hand, he is intensely loyal and, since the statements quoted, however perverted, are alledgedly those of his military superiors, his hands are absolutely tied insofar as making rebuttal statements in the press. The same things apply to any of us here in the office. Anything we write or say is of necessity attributed to him. Personally, I think that we will have to grin and bear it until the accumulated effect causes horsemen outside of the Regular Army to write the "powers that be"—namely, the Secretary of War, the Chief of

Staff, and General Moseley—explaining to them the vital need for further explanatory statements to the press by way of correcting the idea that the horse is to be immediately supplanted. The inclosed copy of a radiogram sent to all cavalry regiments is clear and self-explanatory. Since it is confidential it should not be quoted but it can guide you in forming any letters you may write or cause to have written. You probably feel that I am passing the buck. Honestly, Pete, I am not; and, most emphatically, General Henry is not. We are "muzzled." The only comfort we can get is our belief that you and your friends will again come to the front and help us with the same enthusiasm which you have always shown. This is not "Bull."

Throughout the spring of 1931, Patton enjoyed considerable success and publicity as a horseman. He won first prize in a show in nearby Virginia. Near Baltimore, he scored what the New York *Times* called "a notable triumph" in hunter trials.

That summer, his tour at the Office of the Chief of Cavalry came to an end. Henry judged him "superior"—"A man of outstanding energy. A hard-worker and a great reader of military literature. Very progressive and has an extensive knowledge of various subjects. He will accomplish what he sets out to do."

After a month of vacation in Massachusetts, he would enter the Army War College as a student in the 1931–32 academic course. This was the top Army school. Attendance would terminate his formal military education. Selection to attend the school meant that he was deemed suitable and completion of the course would make him eligible for command at the highest levels.

CHAPTER 44

Army War College and
the Bonus March

*"If you must fire do a good job—a few casualties be-
come martyrs, a large number an object lesson."*

Letter, GSP, Jr. (Washington) to Beatrice, August 31, 1931

Darling Beat: I got here last night at 9:30. I had to leave
the boat at Cape May the entrance to the Delaware.

The winds were light and heading all the way so we had to
use the motor all the time except one day.

I had a devil of a time persuading Capt S. [Stimpson, paid
skipper] to leave N.Y. [to sail] down the Jersey coast. We
waited 24 hours while he tried to hire an extra man. At last
I said I was going alone if necessary so we started going down
the bay. He swore the compas was 20° out and wanted to
turn around but I said we would allow for that and we kept
on.

I think that he is a fair weather sailor who hates to loose
sight of land. When we got to Deleware and he heard it was
all in side he was full of fire again.

At Gravesend Bay I met a Bolshiviki sailor working on a
fishing scooner. My costume led him to believe I was a sailor
too so he told me how wicked it was to own a yacht and be a
capatalist when he was only getting seven dollars a day rig-
ging a boat. I told him it was wrong all right but that the
wrong part lay in his getting 7.50 for a job worth 1.50 and
that I was a capatalist and that if his theory was correct we
ought to fight it [out] at once and see who was best and that
I was redy to start. He then got very friendly and offered to
work for me at 8.00 dollars a day.

I liked the boat very much. She keeps you busy and is very

good in a sea and a blow. Though we had only moderate ones. Capt S. with a toothless wonder I hired to help him up the [Potomac] river will arrive on Wednesday.

I have hay fever.

I love you. George.

Soon after Patton entered the Army War College, he began to maneuver to get the post of Commandant of Cadets at West Point upon the completion of his course of study. General Harbord wrote to Major General William D. Connor, Army War College commandant, who was rumored to be the next Superintendent of the Military Academy:

> I consider him [Patton] the outstanding man among his contemporaries that I include in my acquaintance. He has always been an outstanding soldier and has had such a broad experience for a man of his age that I am sure his fitness for the duty has probably already occurred to you. He has a very charming wife, and it is no drawback to the family that they have means enough to keep up their end, as the saying goes.

General Drum, who now commanded the Fifth Corps Area, spoke with Connor about Patton's desire and extracted the promise that if Connor could make the selection, he would put Patton's name second on his list. If Connor's first choice was unable to accept, Patton would have the appointment. "Will you please keep this confidential?" Drum asked Patton.

This effort too was in vain. Patton would fail to get the assignment.

General Henry confided to Patton that he feared he had reached the end of the line as Chief of Cavalry and would receive no further promotion. Patton sent a confidential letter in behalf of Henry to Malin Craig, who had been Chief of Cavalry and who now commanded the Ninth Corps Area. Could Craig, Patton asked, offer any advice that Patton could pass on to Henry?

Craig acknowledged "your very thoughtful, generous note concerning General Henry." He understood Henry's concern, and he suggested that Henry go directly to MacArthur and tell him frankly that he hoped his current tour would not interfere with his selection for promotion, which had always been his ambition.

I did the same thing with the Chief of Staff the very day I reported in Washington to take over the duties of Chief of Cavalry, and while the Chief of Staff seemed a bit startled he, nevertheless, recommended my promotion at the time he thought I was entitled to it . . .

I wish to repeat that MacArthur is absolutely straight-forward and fair and, to the best of my knowledge, he will never play a favorite at the expense of his fairness while he is Chief of Staff.

Henry, it turned out, would receive no further promotion.

Aunt Nannie Wilson, who was a dear old lady and rather pathetic in her later years, addicted somewhat to sherry, died on November 26, 1931. Patton traveled to California for the funeral, staying while he was there with his sister Nita.

When he telephoned his daughter Ruth Ellen to inform her of Aunt Nannie's death, he said, "I never knew, until I saw her in the majesty of death, what a noble face she had."

During his visit to the family home, Lake Vineyard in San Marino, Patton wrote a letter to his mother, deceased for three years, and put it in her trinket box.

Letter, GSP, Jr., to his mother, November 30, 1931
Darling Mama. Here with your things before me you are very near. I never showed you in life the love I really felt nor my admiration for your courage and sporting acceptance of illness and losses. Children are cruel things. Forgive me. I had always prayed to show my love by doing something famous for you, to justify what you called me when I got back from France, "My hero son." Perhaps I still may, but time grows short. I am 46. In a few moments we will bury the ashes of Aunt Nannie. All the three who I loved and who loved me so much are now gone.

But you know that I still love you and in the presence of your soul I feel very new and very young and helpless even as I must have been 46 years ago.

Nothing you ever did to me was anything but loving. I

have no other memories of you but love and devotion. It is so sad that we must grow old and seperate.

When we meet again I hope you will be lenient for my frailties. In most things I have been worthy.

Perhaps this is foolish but I think you understand.

I loved and love you very much.

Your devoted son G. S. Patton Jr.

Patton worked hard at the Army War College. At the end of February 1932, he passed in a 56-page study entitled "The Probable Characteristics of the Next War and the Organization, Tactics, and Equipment Necessary to Meet Them." It was an ambitious work that drew together his cherished beliefs.

As was his practice, Patton started by drawing on history. Armies, he said, had oscillated between those based on quantity and those based on quality. Mass armies were composed of hastily raised and incompletely trained individuals who looked upon war as a secondary occupation. Since the World War, it appeared that smaller, more mobile, better trained armies would fight short, decisive wars. The current interest in mechanization reflected this feeling.

Size and strength, he said, were not synonymous. Small professional armies were thoroughly trained, gave their members long association together that enhanced solidarity and mutual confidence in the ranks, were suited for mobility and maneuver, were ready immediately in time of emergency, and had a better chance of achieving quick and decisive victory. They would be used in the next war, he predicted, because equipment was becoming more complex and costly. Equipping masses of men with the latest weapons was financially impossible, but smaller armies could be kept up to date.

According to some military thinkers, it was useless to study warfare before 1870, for the lessons before that date were no longer relevant and practical. To Patton, history moved in cycles; therefore, styles in warfare recurred. Without perspective a painting was valueless; and so it was with things military. Ancient tactics were hardly to be copied, but professionals had to be familiar with them and with the reasons for their adoption. For the basic nature of man had changed but little during the course of recorded history.

Starting with 2500 B.C., Patton classified wars after the types of armies involved, that is, mass or professional. He ran through the Egyptians, Syrians, Greeks, Macedonians, Romans, Africans, Goths, Byzantines, Franks, Vikings, Mongols, Swiss, Turks, British, French, Spanish, Dutch, Germans, and Americans—ending with the Boer War. From these historical examples, he extracted certain lessons. For example, professionals fought better in protracted operations, in campaigns where supply was difficult, and in wars where discipline was more important than emotional inspiration.

He had asked many officers, including students and instructors at the War College, why mass armies were desirable. No one could say.

So far as he could tell, the advantages of large conscript armies were: 1) the sense of power and security raised in the popular mind by an armed force numbering in the millions; 2) the opportunity to arouse popular enthusiasm and support by placing the burden of war on all alike; 3) the benefit of producing a homogeneity of national character among recruits; 4) the safeguard afforded political leaders, who could say, if things went wrong, that everything possible had been done to insure success; 5) the widespread conviction that a national army was the cheapest form of national security; 6) the fact that a large army could fight on several fronts simultaneously; and 7) the belief that big battalions were the same as strong battalions.

On the other hand, small, highly trained, lightly equipped, professional armies were more easily supplied, less tied to the roadnet, and better disciplined. They had the ability to disperse on the battlefield, a requirement now forced on ground troops by the airplane; the capacity to maneuver in order to gain surprise and, as a consequence, decisive victory; the capability to function in dire cases of stress, when habitual or automatic responses to emergencies were necessary. They could, in short, better cope with all the conditions of war, for "Battle is an orgy of organized disorder."

Small, mobile, largely self-contained units were therefore indicated for the next war. They were better too because they offered military leaders the opportunity to exercise great initiative. Commanders could operate on the assumption that "a simple mediocre solution instantly applied is better than a perfect one which is late or complicated."

Frequent conferences between an overall commander and his subordinate commanders were necessary in order to indoctrinate all concerned in the methods selected to meet a few general situations. Battles were fought mainly by junior officers who carried on without specific orders. The overall leader, Patton believed, could personally influence only one or two units. He therefore had to depend on subordinates who exercised command by their personal efforts—through the influence of example. Inspiration for them and for the troops came not from coded messages but from the visible personality of the overall commander.

For the history of war was a history of warriors, few in number, mighty in personality. In small professional armies, leaders would often be killed, but the death of high-ranking officers whose primary aim was to win, not simply to survive, had great inspirational effect on men.

In sum, small professional armies would restore mobility to the battlefield in the next war, which, as a consequence, would be shorter and more decisive than the World War.

The sincerity of purpose and the hard work that went into this paper were obvious, and in April the commandant of the War College informed Patton:

> An examination of your individual staff memo recently submitted indicates that it is of sufficient merit to warrant consideration by the War Department. Accordingly the memo, by direction of the Chief of Staff, has been forwarded to the War Department for such use as the Department may see fit to make of it. You are hereby commended for work of exceptional merit.

This was high honor indeed.

Patton was also chairman of a student committee, which, as part of the regular course work, presented a report on mechanized units. The Patton touch was everywhere in evidence. For example: "The Austro-Prussia War of 1866 furnishes the only instance, in wars between two civilized opponents where weapons played the decisive role."

The task of the committee was to study and assess the current interest in mechanization and to make several direct and practical recommendations to the General Staff on the subject.

Since "mechanical warfare," "mechanization," and "motorization" were terms often used interchangeably, the committee first defined them. A mechanized force "not only . . . [is] transported in motor vehicles, but also fights from some or all of its vehicles . . . having armament [weapons] and protective armor." A motorized force, in contrast, was transported, in whole or in part, in vehicles to the scene of action; the troops dismounted from their vehicles to fight.

In the following year, the War Department would accept these definitions and make them official.

The tank in the World War and mechanized forces in the postwar period, the committee said, were attempts to restore maneuver to combat in order to shorten wars and lessen attrition.

Armored fighting vehicles were special, costly machines with no commercial use. Of them, the tank was "peerless" for shock action. In order to stimulate as much experimentation as possible, the committee believed that each arm should develop its own mechanized units according to its own missions and expected capabilities.

This was what Patton had earlier recommended and what MacArthur had directed the Army to do.

The committee's conclusions, which were very much like Patton's convictions, were: a large and independent mechanized force had no role in current warfare; mechanized units assisting infantry and cavalry had vital roles; mechanized units could not replace existing arms; mechanized units should be developed by the existing arms.

The committee's single recommendation was that the mechanized units developed by each arm should be used in combined maneuvers to determine their tactical and strategic capabilities and characteristics.

Rating Patton's performance as a student, the War College commandant judged him "superior." He was, Connor wrote,

> An aggressive and capable officer of strong convictions. An untiring student. Proficiency in theoretical training for High Command: Superior, for War Department General Staff: Superior. Special aptitude for any particular class of duty: Command. Qualified for duty with any civilian component. Academic rating: Superior.

He was, in short, a first-rate, all-around officer capable of exercising high command and competent to discharge the responsibilities of an important staff position.

In his official personal file was noted "Work of Exceptional Merit."

Now Patton had completed his formal military education. If there was to be a next war, he would be assured of a high and important place in it. Unless, of course, he failed somehow to measure up to the high standards he had set for himself or failed somehow to meet the high expectations of his superiors.

On July 8, 1932, Patton reported for duty to Fort Myer, Virginia, as executive officer, second in command, of the 3d Cavalry Regiment. Less than three weeks later, he was a central figure in the Bonus March incident.

With the country in the depths of the Great Depression and economic distress rampant, several thousand members—somewhere around 20,000—of the Bonus Expeditionary Force, an informal organization, arrived in Washington. Unemployed and poverty-stricken veterans, they came to the capital to influence Congress into voting each former serviceman a cash payment, a bonus, computed according to length of war service. The money had been voted, but only for disbursement in 1945. The Bonus Marchers wanted it at once.

The influx of veterans, who camped in a "Hooverville" of shacks and tents on the Anacostia Flats, who occupied abandoned and partially dismantled buildings in the heart of downtown Washington, and who lived in other parts of the town and on the outskirts, seemed to threaten the peace. It was not so much that they were disorderly or unruly; it was rather that they were present, a large and restless group of surly men who might turn into rioting mobs. President Hoover, Secretary of War Patrick J. Hurley, and Chief of Staff Douglas MacArthur regarded them as subversives and potential revolutionaries.

When Congress adjourned without voting the bonus, many marchers departed Washington, probably more than half, and the attitude of the government, War Department, and city officials hardened toward the veterans who remained. On July 28, there was a scuffle between police and some marchers who were camping in and refused to leave government buildings being demolished for a park downtown. A panicky policemen fired his revolver and killed a man. This triggered a call for troops to help the police restore order.

According to an account written by Patton, he said, to "commemorate" the successful "quelling of the domestic disturbance," the operation, from a military point of view, was a complete victory.

> Owing to a total misconception of mob psychology General Glassford, then Chief of the Metropolitan Police Department, temporized with the Marchers. As time went on they violated more and more laws and regulations, and finally marched on the Capitol and the White House . . . In my opinion, the majority were poor, ignorant men, without hope and without really evil intent, but there were several thousand bad men among them and many weak sisters joined them.

Like Hoover, Hurley, and MacArthur, Patton believed that Communist agents had infiltrated the ranks of the Bonus Marchers and were inciting them to revolution.

> For some weeks . . . the troops here [at Fort Myer] were held in the Post in readiness to move. The horses had

been practised in moving against mobs, and the men were equipped with gas masks and a few gas grenades.

Therefore, the men were ready for action on July 28 when the 3d Cavalry commanding officer, Colonel Cootes, received a telephone call at 1:45 P.M. from the 16th Infantry Brigade commander, General Perry L. Miles. Miles asked that all available cavalry troops on the post be sent to the Ellipse, just west of the White House. Accompanied by Patton, the troops crossed the Memorial Bridge into Washington and reached the Ellipse 55 minutes later.

. . . we moved in column of fours without security detachments; the tanks in trucks followed by themselves at [a distance of] about one mile. No outpost was established. We dismounted at the Ellipse.

While the cavalry—a total of 14 officers, 217 enlisted men, and 213 horses—waited for infantrymen to arrive from Fort Washington, about twelve miles below the city on the Maryland side of the Potomac, Patton rode off alone. Stiffly and unsmiling, he trotted down Pennsylvania Avenue to 3rd Street, where several thousand veterans were congregated. They greeted him with mixed cheers and jeers.

Having made a reconnaissance of the terrain and an estimate of the situation, Patton returned to the Ellipse.

. . . the battalion of 12th Infantry from Fort Washington arrived in trucks, having passed right through the Bonus Camps. After a pause of another hour the troops were ordered to march up Pennsylvania Avenue and clear it as far as 3d Street. So far as I know this was the only order issued for the first operation.

The clearing action started at 4:05 P.M. Cavalrymen wore steel helmets, carried gas masks and carbines at the sling, and held drawn sabers. Infantrymen wore gas masks and carried rifles with bayonets.

The cavalry moved first in column of troops with the tanks in trucks between the last two troops [companies]. The in-

fantry followed in colum of fours. The avenue was a sea of
people. It took us half an hour to clear them out, and we . . .
had to use force. As we passed the occupied buildings [where
the scuffle had taken place] the Marchers cheered us and
called, "Here come our buddies." The civilians in the crowd
hissed us in a mild way.

After a halt of half an hour at 3d Street the infantry put
on their gas masks and, advancing in assault formation in two
waves, using gas grenades, began clearing the buildings . . .
Soon the gas got to work, and they all ran and formed along
the second street south of the Avenue. Major Surles [who
commanded the 2d Squadron] then moved his cavalry to
push them on. We were doing very well when the infantry
halted to reform, and the mob, angry by now . . . were very
nasty and brandished clubs, iron bars and bricks, and cursed
us in a most wholehearted manner. The soldiers were magnificent. They set grimly on their horses and made no reply
except to poke an occasional Marcher who tried to grab a
horse by the head. Things kept looking worse as the infantry
was still not up and our flank was turned. Suddenly, without
a word of command, the whole line surged forward. Bricks
flew, sabers rose and fell with a comforting smack, and the
mob ran. We moved on after them, occasionally meeting serious resistance. Once six men in a truck threw a regular barrage of bricks, and several men and horses were hit. Two of
us charged at a gallop, and had some nice work at close range
with the occupants of the truck, most of whom could not sit
down for some days [afterwards].

The cavalry, moving via the streets, and the infantry,
through the shacks, pushed the crowd to the railroad where
all resistance ended.

It was then decided to capture the camp [across the Anacostia River] at night. The men were fed, and General Mac-
Arthur came up and gave explicit orders for the operation.

When we crossed the bridge at the Navy Yard the infantry
was in front and had to use grenades to force the spectator
crowd out of the way.

The cavalry formed at the north end of the [Bonus Marchers'] camp with its right flank on the river, while the infantry
moving south along the edge of the water turned by the left

flank and started to clear the camp. At this moment we were ordered to halt as the Marchers said that if they were given an hour they would withdraw. During this hour many left but some set fire to their tents.

When the time was up the infantry moved forward in a long line of skirmishers, using grenades from time to time. If, during this operation, a single shot had been fired many would have died, for in the dark on a flat plane [plain] fire discipline could not have been maintained, and there was no cover.

It speaks volumes for the high character of the men that not a shot was fired. In justice to the Marchers it should be pointed out that had they really wanted to start something they had a great chance here but refrained.

On the following morning, groups of veterans began to leave the city. Troopers from Fort Myer routed out a large encampment at Oakcrest, Virginia, and these Bonus Marchers crossed Key Bridge into the city and walked up Wisconsin Avenue and out of Washington.

It so happened that Joe Angelo was in Washington, and the newspapers played up the Angelo-Patton relationship. One headline read: "Major Ousts Vet Who Saved Life; Bonus Seeker Flees before Officer He Rescued on Battlefield."

From this moment on—if not already as early as the occasion when Angelo had appeared before a congressional committee two years before—Patton became hostile to his wartime orderly.

If any letters came to Patton expressing objection to his role in the action against the Bonus Marchers, he saved none. But he kept a letter from Al C. Stiller.

Writing on stationery headed Stiller & Strickland Tire Company, El Paso, Texas, Stiller said that he had been the initial First Sergeant in charge of the Casual Company (soldiers awaiting assignment) at the tank center in France and later First Sergeant of two other companies. He had been wounded at Varennes, where his tank was destroyed. He had thought often of Patton since the war, would be mighty glad to see him again, and hoped that Patton had fully recovered from his wounds. He added that he would have liked to have been with Patton to throw the veterans out of Washington because they were "rif raf" and not the kind of men who had done the job over there in France.

Ten years later, Al Stiller would be Patton's aide-de-camp. He would serve with Patton throughout World War II.

Sometime after the election of November 1932, probably immediately thereafter, Patton wrote a paper on "Federal Troops in Domestic Disturbances." It was designed as two lectures to officers, one on the history and training of this type of duty, the other on the tactical aspects of operations of this sort. It was, in many respects, a savage document.

From the Whisky Rebellion, he wrote, until the Bonus March, federal troops had been called out more than one hundred times

> to participate in that most distasteful form of service . . .
> We of the Army should take pride in the fact that not once
> in all these cases have our predecessors either failed or been
> guilty of unnecessary violence. It must be our aim to main-
> tain this proud tradition whenever it shall be our unfortunate
> duty to be called on for such onerous service.

When the Army was effective, Patton continued, liberty flourished. When soldiers failed in their duty, insurrection and national chaos ensued.

> When, under Marius, Rome's first Regulars blotted out in
> blood the mobs roused by those generous and misguided
> brothers, the Gracchae, she prospered, and, from a debating
> society, became the mistress of the world, and so remained
> until at last the venal and disloyal Praetorian Guard sold the
> purple to the highest bidder and thereby destroyed the power
> no foe could conquer. When the foolish and genial Louis
> XVI lost his head and the Seine ran crimson to the sea, the
> fault lay not with the people but with the soldiers . . . the
> success of the Bolsheviki in 1917 was due wholly to the hesi-
> tating and weak character of the Russian officers. While in
> Germany, on the other hand, a loyal and well led Army de-
> stroyed the course of Communism ere it could raise its ugly
> head above the ruins of a war weary nation . . . [Soldiers]

have never yet bitten the hand which starved them, or failed in any way to support constituted authority. Even in the Civil War when more than twenty percent of the officers went south not a single enlisted man deserted the flag . . .

The military is used [in domestic disturbances], not to *displace* existing laws, but to *sustain* them when by reason of obstructions their effectual administration by normal legal methods becomes impossible . . .

TRAINING REGULATIONS: Strange as it seems this loquacious document is very reticent on Domestic Disturbances. All it has to say is found in TR 10–5, paragraph 9— "Troops of the combat branches, in addition to their training for war, will be trained in the tactics for the suppression of domestic disturbances, the guiding method to be employed being a demonstration of force, followed, if necessary, by its application in a speedy and decisive manner."

HABEAS CORPUS: This is the next item that arises to plague us . . . If you have captured a dangerous agitator and some misguided judge issues a write of Habeas Corpus for him . . . there is always danger that the man might attempt to escape. If he does see that he at least falls out of ranks before you shoot [him]. To be soft hearted might mean death to your men. War is war after all . . .

Throughout history, good soldiers have quelled riots and often, as a result, have achieved promotion and fame. Bad soldiers have failed, and as a result their countries have perished . . . As juniors we simply obey the orders of our superiors. As independent commanders, there is a very remote possibility that we may have to back our judgement with our commissions. Officers in command of troops on riot duty should remember the following points:

Civil officials and National Guard and Reserve officers could give Regular troops proper and legitimate orders only if they had been mustered into the federal service. Regular officers were to cooperate with police and state troops, but the Regulars, not the police or state troops, were to judge the amount and character of the cooperation to be rendered. They were to insist on having all orders in writing.

Before firing at a mob warn them of your intention, and tell innocent people to "beat it" . . . Designate in advance certain sharpshooters to kill individual rioters who fire on or throw missiles at your men. Have even this firing done only on your order, or that of a commissioned officer . . . Should some orator start haranguing the crowd and inciting them to violence grab him even if it brings on a local fight. Small fights are better than big ones. Words cunningly chosen change crowds into mobs . . .

Do not enrage reporters . . . They dislike tear gas and are not provided with masks. Finally, do your full duty as you see it, and damn the consequences.

Crowds could usually be dispersed by strong patrols and kept from reforming. But if a crowd suddenly became violent and destroyed a patrol, it had to be punished instantly. Otherwise, it would develop a false sense of power and become dangerous.

. . . try to arrange your axis of approach so as to drive the mob into the poor quarter [of the city] and away from vital areas . . . Gas is paramount . . . While tear gas is effective, it should be backed up with vomiting gas.

If gas failed to move a mob,

open fire with one man per squad from a frontal attack while, at the same time, have men previously stationed in nearby buildings shoot into the rear ranks selecting apparent leaders. Always fire for effect [that is, to kill] . . . If you must fire do a good job—a few casualties become martyrs, a large number an object lesson . . .

When a mob starts to move keep it on the run, but always leave it a line of retreat—a cornered rat will fight desperately, while on the other hand movement to the rear engenders panic . . . use the bayonet to encourage its retreat. If they are running a few good wounds in the buttocks will encourage them. If they resist they must be killed.

When guarding buildings, troops should mark a line and announce clearly that those who crossed would be killed. "Be sure to kill the first one who tries, and leave him there to discourage the others."

If intelligence indicated that mob leaders were gathering for a meeting, "A night raid . . . will be most useful—no prisoners should be taken."

FINALLY: Never take a drink at any time, or allow your men to do so. Close all drinking establishments. This is illegal but necessary . . . An armed mob resisting federal troops is an armed enemy. To aid it is treason. This may not be law, but it is fact. When blood starts running law stops, because, by the fact of bloodshed, it has demonstrated its futility.

His ultimate judgment on the action against the Bonus Marchers:

In spite of faulty methods the high training and discipline of the soldiers and officers secured a complete and bloodless (mostly) triumph, which, by its success, prevented a war and insured the election of a Democrat [Franklin D. Roosevelt].

CHAPTER 45

Fort Myer, Hawaii, Massachusetts

"I think that a little blood and gutts would be good for cadets."

PATTON spent nearly three years at Fort Myer, and they were filled with social and sporting events and activities. He played polo, sailed in the Chesapeake Bay, participated in horse shows in Washington, West Point, Tuxedo Park, and elsewhere, hunted in the lovely countryside of nearby Maryland and Virginia—Mrs. Curtis Dall, President Roosevelt's daughter, presenting him on one occasion with the first place ribbon for winning the Hunter Trials at Bradley Farms, Maryland. Beatrice was prominent as a sailor, and, with her daughters acting as crew, raced in the Women's National Sailing Championship competition at Cohasset, Massachusetts.

For the Pattons, the highlight of those years was the Cobbler Hunt, an organization he and Beatrice formed of civilians and military people who rode to the hounds, usually twice a week. The course was on the adjoining estates of friends who lived near Delaplane, Virginia.

Patton kept a diary for the 1932–33 season and recorded the first hunt, taking place on September 26, when the Pattons and two others gathered at 7 A.M. "This was the first time I acted as M.F.H. since 1912 at Fort Riley."

October 1: "The jumps were very hairy and pace fast."

October 19: "The best run so far and one of the best I have ever had."

The cub hunting having ended, the regular season opened with 41 riders present, and many more spectators in motor cars, coming for breakfast. According to a newspaper account, the Pattons were "clad in scarlet coats and derbys"; a photograph in the New York *Times* showed them dressed alike in formal hunting attire.

Patton attended a dinner in New York for Masters of the Fox Hunt. At the end of March, the season closed with the Cobbler Hunter Trials, various races and competitions arranged and directed by Patton.

The Cobbler Hunt had another successful season in 1933–34. A message posted at Fort Myer by Patton invited all officers and their ladies to hunt with the Pattons. "Any horse able to jump three and one-half feet is capable of hunting in Virginia."

Letter, Colonel C. L. Scott to GSP, Jr., no date ("after Cherry Blossom Festival Show, 1934")

Dear Georgie. Want to thank you and your whole family for your entries and support in the Hunter Trials last Saturday . . . the winning of the class or the loosing of the class was a small matter compared to the sportsmanlike way in which the Patton family accepted the judges decision—after all the kicking and crabbing one generally sees and hears in events of this nature it is a pleasure and an encouragement to occasionally see some real sportsmanship show up.

Young Beatrice was married to Lieutenant John Knight Waters on June 27, 1934, at St. John's Church in Beverly Farms, Massachusetts, and a reception took place immediately afterward at Green Meadows, South Hamilton.

Letter, GSP, Jr., to Beatrice, July 7, 1934

From my view point as "wedding guest" I want to say again what a realy great organizer I think you are. No show could have gone better and it was a very large show too. Also no mother of a bride ever looked better or cried less.

The Cobbler Hunt had a third season. According to Patton's diary, there were seven runs during the cubbing and 39 during the regular season, ranging in duration from 15 minutes to an hour and a half. The twelve horses belonging to the Pattons were all scrupulously noted on a work sheet so that each was exercised regularly.

The opening of the season had 50 guests gathered on a spacious lawn against a background of the Cobbler Mountains. After the hunt, about 2500 persons assembled for a giant barbecue. Later, a tournament featured charging knights, about 30 horsemen driving forward to place a lance through a ring. Among those present were General Leon B. Kromer, the Chief of Cavalry, Colonel Kenyon Joyce, commanding Fort Myer, General Hugh Drum, Deputy Chief of Staff, and General Billy Mitchell.

On November 27, Patton recorded that the weather was rainy with a heavy fog on that scheduled hunt day. He waited until 10 A.M. for the field to show, but no one came, so he went out with two attendants. "Coming back I tried to shut a gate on Hukupu [his horse] and he got mad and rearing fell on a woven wire fence with me under him. He got all four feet caught but kicked himself clear and ran away till he hit a second fence when I caught him. Neither of us was hurt."

The Pattons resigned as masters at the end of the season. "Beatrice and I both feel that the cost of hunting for the last three years as Masters has been more than offset by the pleasure abtained which no inflation or confiscation can ever take away from us."

Letter, Walter Huston (a leading actor on Broadway, writing from the Waldorf-Astoria Hotel, New York) to Beatrice, February 1, 1935

Dear Mrs Patton. We will be very happy to join you after the show Thursday Feb. 7th. We Both send our Regards to you and your family and will be glad to see you again. Sincerely,

. . .

GSP, Jr., Speech to the American Legion, Alexandria, Virginia, November 11, 1932

To most of us November 11 is a day full of mixed emotions.

Joy when we think of it as commemorating the victorious termination of the World War.

Sorry when we remember all the young lives extinguished to achieve the victory . . .

Certainly no one who was privileged to see, as I did, the solumn grandure of todays ceremonies at Arlington could help being deeply moved. Though possibly in my case the remembrance of the fact that I very nearly caused my dear mother to wear a gold star may have enhanced my appreciation . . .

Until we have more, much more tangible proof of a change of mental attitude disarmament is folly. Perpetual peace a futile dream.

Yet . . . groups of internationally minded pacifists are constantly working to change Armistice day into Disarmament day.

A limited number of these deluded [persons] . . . unsatisfied with making us physically helpless . . . are seeking to render us morally unworthy . . . They hold to scorn the deeds of our fighting ancestors, of our dead comrades. They make a mock of courage, a joke of patriotism. This too we must combat or else contend with China for the prize as leading jellyfish of the world.

Do not misunderstand me for in spite of the fact that I am what is sometimes referred to as a brutal and licentious mercinary I am not hunting trouble or advising others to do so. I do however regard with horror a state of affairs which would make our country both unready and unwilling to defend its honor . . .

Most of us think of [the next war] in terms of France, of conflicts between huge immobile masses of men engaged in a butting match and abundantly supplied with every sort of contrivance from Gas, Tanks and Airplanes to cigarettes, chocolates and Red Cross girls . . .

There will be much more walking than fighting [in the next war] and armies will be numbered by thousands rather than by millions. Similarly . . . we will have less shells, less gas, less chocolates and less Girls. It will be a most unpleasant war. An investigation of the Bolsheviki-Polish war of 1920 or of the operations in China last year proves this contention. Man as an individual not munitions decided those conflicts.

Also it is well to disabuse our minds of the fanciful picture of wholesale destruction conjured up by certain writers and

attributed to such inventions as Gas, Tanks, and Airplanes
. . . It is man not his machines that conquers.

Most men and all armies are goosey, they fear an attack
from the rear. Since the continuous fronts in France prevented rear attacks stalemate resulted.

Many eminent soldiers realizing this fact are now seeking
not bigger but more mobile armies. The very evident dread
with which France with her large conscript army views Germany with her small professional one is cumulative evidence
on this point.

Hence since we are not particularly likely to again fight in
Europe and since if we do we are apt to meet small highly
trained forces it seems reasonable to turn our minds to the
need of such a force ourselves . . .

Personally I believe that our form of preparation lags in
the maintenance of the adequate and immediately available
regular army and navy with which to get to the fire [war]
quickly and hold it in check until our national man power in
smaller numbers and with better training becomes available.

. . . there are countless other solutions equally good. The
point is to adopt one of them and then see that it is carried
out . . .

When our time comes to sleep in Arlington we can lie
down with quiet minds content in the knowledge that as soldiers and citizens we have done our full duty.

A long letter, with illegible signature, reached Patton in January 1933, and bemoaned current military trends, asking how in
the world the dedicated horsemen in the Army could stop mechanization. The field artillery was ready to become motorized. The
National Guard was motorizing its field artillery units. "We [in
the cavalry] may soon be the only mounted arm." Congressmen
were talking of having lots of machines—planes, tanks, armored
cars—in storage and a small army of highly trained, technical personnel ready to wheel them out when needed. What they failed
to realize, these advocates of mechanization, was that machines,
not horses, became obsolete. But the lobbyists, especially General
Motors, were exerting pressures, and "these are critical hours for
our cavalry."

GSP, Jr., Lecture, "Mechanized Forces," delivered at Fort Myer, Fort Humphreys, and Washington, D.C., January, March, and August 1933

Many soldiers are led to faulty ideas of war by knowing too much about too little.

A picture without a background is both uninteresting and misleading. Hence in order to paint for you an intelligent picture of Mechanization as it exists today we must provide an historical background . . .

. . . the want of perspective . . . still induces most of us to visualize future battles as simple repi[ti]tions of the butting matches of the World War while soldiers who talk of forces smaller than groups of armies are considered pikers . . .

New weapons are useful in that they add to the repertoir of killing but be that tank or tomahawk weapons are only weapons after all. Wars may be fought with weapons but they are won by men. It is the spirit of the men who follow and of the man who leads that gains the victory.

Cootes rated Patton "excellent" and capable of being a colonel in peacetime and a brigadier general in war. "Possesses force, fine military bearing, excellent horseman, superior as instructor in tactical work. Fine leadership. Excellent in every way, very loyal and outstanding officer."

Letter, William Floyd, Arlington, Virginia, to GSP, Jr., December 13, 1933

[Sincere thanks] for every consideration shown my son in his severe moment of distress. When you came into the room where Captain Hickey, myself, and the boy were the night of the tragedy I thought you might be a stern, severe officer extending little sympathy, but when you called me out and had a little talk with me I appreciated what a real flow of sympathy there was in your heart and, Major, you will possibly never know what your words meant to me at that time.

On March 1, 1934, having been a major almost fourteen years, Patton was promoted to lieutenant colonel.

GSP, Jr., Lecture, "Mechanization," April 11, 1934

Let us not become so bemused with technical and administrative details that we forget this fact. In the last analysis the successful soldier is the courageous fighting man—the killer.

GSP, Jr., Lecture, "The Probable Characteristics of the Next War," 1934

The object of maneuver is to get . . . behind [the enemy] . . .

Men not machines win battles. Let us strive to be men and worthy leaders of the other men who follow us.

Patton spent almost the entire month of May 1934 at the Cavalry School, Fort Riley, Kansas, observing a series of maneuvers by mechanized cavalry units belonging to the 1st Cavalry Regiment (Mechanized). "Just to be around with a bunch or rather selected lot of officers who talk and think nothing but of war," he wrote to Beatrice, was exciting. He was going out on the first exercise that evening, an all-night affair, "and [it] promises to be very wet as it is raining hard now and is quite cold."

He spent a weekend at Fort Leavenworth, where he visited a horse show, watched a horse race, and saw a lot of old friends. He learned that he might be sent there the following year

as a chief of section. Gen [Guy] Henry thinks I should go if asked for. I hate the idea but it might be worse I suppose . . . Most every one on the post was "oiled." I was not. We leave at 8:00 o'clock A.M. for a three days manuver. As it is raining hard I think we will have quite a time . . . I smashed my little finger in the lock of the car but it is not serious.

Colonel Kenyon A. Joyce, who had replaced Cootes as commander of the 3d Cavalry and of Fort Myer, rated Patton "superior." Patton was "an officer of outstanding physical and mental energy who is intensely interested in his profession. I believe this officer should be counted upon for great feats of leadership in war."

As Patton's tour of duty drew to a close, Joyce rated him once more. Again he scored Patton "superior." He changed his description but slightly, saying, "an officer of broad attainments who has extraordinary mental and physical energy. In my opinion he is absolutely fearless and could be counted upon for great feats of leadership in war."

Patton was then fifty years old. His weight varied between 170 and 180 pounds. He wore a partial denture. His hairline was receding. His vision was myopic.

When Patton learned he was to be assigned to Hawaii again, he purchased a 52-foot schooner, the *Arcturus,* and had it moved from New England to the west coast by steamer. With Beatrice, Mr. and Mrs. Gordon Prince of Boston, and Joe Ekeland as crew members and himself as navigator, he sailed from California in May 1935 and reached Honolulu a month later.

The Pattons discovered that Hawaii was as pleasant as they remembered it. They found many old civilian and military friends. It did not take them long to settle down.

Patton was detailed to the General Staff Corps and assigned G–2 or intelligence officer of the Hawaiian Department at Fort Shafter.

He arrived in Hawaii in time to observe the June maneuvers. Since the commanding general asked all staff officers to report their personal reactions, Patton was quick to oblige. His observations, all critical, ran to five single-spaced typed pages.

He criticized the lack of mental flexibility among commanders. They showed "rigid adherence to methods of procedure current in the World War and applicable, if at all, only to situations involving very large bodies of troops in semi-stabilized operations." For example, while the division was launching a counterattack of five battalions of infantry, the staff remained in the headquarters 4½ miles from the scene of the combat, made no effort to conduct ground reconnaissance, and established no forward command post.

He pointed out the absence of imagination in the exercise. The troops demonstrated "utter disregard for the probable effect of enemy fire." For example, "From 4:00 P.M. on, Kolekole pass and the road leading to it was jammed with transportation. It is certain that any enemy capable of forcing a landing would have the means and intelligence to interdict the pass . . . artillery units adjacent to the road were making meticulous efforts to camouflage their battery positions, which . . . they had moved into in broad daylight with columns well closed up." Infantry and artillery counterattacking forces camped in close formation and made no attempt to conceal their bivouacs. "Camps were brightly illuminated and their fires unscreened." The units posted no gas sentries and employed no security detachments.

He cited the misuse of motor transportation. All units used vehicles greatly in excess of the number required, and many carried equipment inappropriate to war, for example, iceboxes, field safes, and the like.

He deplored the pervading philosophy of "comfort first." "Sumptuous eating, sleeping and clerical conveniences everywhere" included folding cots, bedding rolls "of monumental proportions," blackboards, mess tables, chairs, and typewriters, all of which "took transportation—needless transportation."

He was pained by the appearance of "Undigested Education." "Many officers have acquired information that they are either unwilling or mentally incapable of using. The result is that they try to remember rather than to think." The brigade field order was far too long, drawn without the benefit of reconnaissance, and issued too late. "The operation was conducted as a map problem because our officers are familiar with them, not as a war problem because our officers are not familiar with maneuvers."

He remarked the excessive use of signal wire. "The craze for wire is largely due to the inordinate demands made by higher units for reports from the front . . . If higher commanders would go up and look they would do some good, at least they would inspire the men . . . the place of the brigade commander is with his men, not with his telephones."

He made some pungent comments on the effect of motorization on war. "To utilize the full power of strategic mobility inherent in trucks, columns must move under fire or else we must readjust our estimates as to their speed of employment." As for tactical mobility, "the normal human tendency to avoid perspiration is very apt to induce the utilization of machines in tactical situations where their use would be suicidal."

He concluded: "The army exists to kill men—not to groom vehicles."

GSP, Jr., Speech to the American Legion Convention, August 7, 1935

The chief trouble with the thousands of honest peace advocates is that, due to lamentable ignorance of history, they confuse the apparent with the actual causes of wars . . . the causes leading to wars are as obscure and far more malign than are the germs which result in cancer or tuberculosis. The pimple or the cough to which the uniformed attribute their ailment is but the last and superficial evidence of the long continued presence of the disease within their system . . . [War is] the culmination of convergent commercial and political interests. Wars are fought by soldiers but they are produced by business men and politicians.

GSP, Jr., Paper, "The Causes of War," November 27, 1935

. . . it seems hardly fair to assume that through all those bloody years thousands of Trojans should have laid down their lives in order that a somewhat discredited prince might enjoy the bedfellowship of a lady; or that countless Greeks were equally willing to die in order that Menelaus might regain his lost, aging and besmirched light o' love. In actuality the causes which produced the war may be ascribed to the fact that the Trojans were becoming too successful in competing with the Greeks for the carrying trade of the Aegean Sea.

Patton went on and talked of the destruction of Carthage, the First Crusade, the long years of undeclared war between Spain and England, the rivalry between English and Dutch fleets, the American Revolution, the Napoleonic conflicts, the war with Mexico (due chiefly to land hunger, he said), the Civil War (King Cotton not Uncle Tom), and the Franco-Prussian War.

[It is impossible to predict] just where or when on sea or land some trivial incident will once more induce Mars to sound his tuneless horn . . . Our lack of prescience is immaterial and we can but regret and, if we are wise, zealously prepare for the cataclism which will inevitably occur when any pair of the several nations now moving on lines of convergent political and commercial interests collide.

A classmate of Patton, Lieutenant Colonel Robert L. Eichelberger, who was serving as Secretary of the War Department General Staff and who would command the Eighth Army in the Pacific during World War II, sent Patton a radiogram in February 1936 to tell him that the post of Commandant of Cadets at West Point would soon become vacant.

Without waiting to hear further details, Patton dispatched an immediate telegram to the War Department:

> Just learned that I am on list for Commandant. If I am otherwise acceptable hope you can prevent the use of any Adjutant General policy from preventing my detail on the ground that I am on foreign service or the General Staff. I have had more foreign service than most officers of my grade and this is my second tour on the General Staff. Am willing to return [to the United States] at own expense. Please do what you can.

Eichelberger had already mailed a letter explaining the situation more fully to Patton. It was that Simon Bolivar Buckner—who would command the Tenth Army in the Pacific during World War II and be killed on Okinawa—was the current Commandant of Cadets and would soon leave West Point. The job had been offered to Eichelberger, who found it tempting but was unable to accept. Patton was being considered but, unfortunately, he was out of the country on what was considered a foreign assignment. Someone had been chosen to succeed Buckner for only a year. Eichelberger would be going to West Point for a visit in the spring, and he would let Patton know what he could find out about the next appointment. "I feel that you would grace the job with your usual 'becoming dignity and efficiency.'"

Upon receipt of Patton's telegram, Eichelberger cabled him:

> Prior to receipt of your radiogram General Connor [West Point Superintendent] had asked for detail of Colonel Mc-

Cunniff as Commandant of Cadets and his detail has been approved for one year.

There was nothing to do but wait. By November, feeling that McCunniff's tour of duty was drawing sufficiently toward its close, Patton solicited Pershing for help in obtaining the appointment.

Letter, GSP, Jr., to Pershing, November 2, 1936
    I hate to be always asking favors but as I still am anxious to amount to something before I retire I am going to do it . . .
    You were good enough to write Gen. Conner in my behalf last year so I hope you will feel able to do it again this year and if you will, also write to Gen. Craig. The best argument I have for my selection is based on the fact that I think the fact of having had close in battle service under you in both Mexico and France would be a drawing card with the cadets. Since the World War none of the officers detailed as commandant have had such service. True it was not their fault but their misfortune but none the less I think that a little blood and gutts would be good for cadets.
    Trusting that you will forgive my bothering you and with all good wishes, I am, Very respectfully,

Five days later, Patton wrote Pershing again. He had heard that General Connor had recommended Captain Butler of the engineers to be Commandant of Cadets. Butler was "a very nice man," but his service had consisted for the most part as aide to Connor, and this, to Patton, appeared inadequate preparation for the position. Butler was a member of the class of 1920, which had graduated in November 1918, after two years at the Military Academy, and this was hardly enough time, in Patton's opinion, to absorb the West Point tradition and outlook. Butler had not graduated from the Command and General Staff College and therefore probably lacked maturity. Butler had no war experience comparable to Patton's, and officers with active combat such as Patton were much more looked up to by the cadets.

If Pershing wrote to Connor in Patton's behalf, would he please refrain from mentioning Butler's name because that would implicate Patton's friend at West Point who had tipped him off.

Meanwhile, Patton had written to Craig telling him the whole story. If Pershing could talk to Craig, it would certainly help Patton's case.

"I have only wanted three things in my life very much," Patton concluded. "The first was to go to Mexico with you, the second was to accompany you to France."

Pershing's aide answered Patton on December 1, saying that Pershing had left Washington for Lincoln, Nebraska, and from there was going to Arizona to spend the winter. The aide in Washington had forwarded Patton's letter to Arizona.

The letter reached Pershing, and he answered. A handwritten note on Patton's letter contained these words of Pershing: "Wrote him [Patton] in general terms nothing definite as there is nothing definite I could write. J.J.P."

On February 25, 1937, Patton acknowledged with thanks—he could not thank Pershing enough—Pershing's letter, which the general had written in his own handwriting. Patton was having it mounted between two pieces of glass, not to exhibit it but "to pass on to my descendants as a priceless souvenir of our greatest soldier."

He was pleased to learn that Pershing and Harbord had both recommended him to be Commandant of Cadets. But he was pessimistic over his chances.

> I have gained the impression that possibly the fact that I am very outspoken is held against me in some quarters, but as I never noticed you doing very much pussyfooting, I do not take this criticism to heart as much as I should. Possibly the candor of a fighting soldier is not too well received in peace.

At the end of March, he wrote Pershing to tell him he had just learned that Charles W. Ryder—who would command the 34th Division in World War II—was to be Commandant of Cadets. When some people failed to get something they wanted, Patton continued, they lost interest in those who had tried to help. "I want to assure you that I appreciate your efforts very much and only regret that I put you to unnecessary trouble." He hoped to be in Washington soon and "shall give myself the pleasure of calling on you to thank you personally."

A job he wanted with all his might, it escaped him for the fourth and final time simply because of chance. What was important about this last effort on his part to obtain the post was the emergence of the term he coined—"blood and gutts."

Although Patton wrote several papers on mechanization—in one he predicted accurately the development of self-propelled howitzers—his notable professional preoccupation at Hawaii was his study of amphibious operations, a subject into which he had delved during his earlier tour of duty in the Islands. It was a natural interest, for the defense of Hawaii was very much on the minds of those responsible for this American outpost. Yet, characteristically, Patton was concerned less with how to repel an invasion than with how to get ashore.

His first step in 1935 was to look into history. He selected several landing operations, summarized the salient facts, and extracted, then evaluated the lessons. Sir Francis Drake, he found, succeeded at Cartagena, Colombia, in 1588, because he utilized surprise, command of the sea, and ferocious attack. The French took Cartagena in 1697 even though they failed to gain surprise —because they had command of the sea and met no resistance on the beaches. The British admiral Vernon was defeated at Cartagena in 1741 for a variety of reasons. The British attack at Antwerp in 1809 was significant for command of the sea and beach resistance. Winfield Scott's invasion of Vera Cruz in 1847 showed careful planning and cooperation between Army and Navy, was mounted on a broad front, and profited from command of the sea.

Patton considered the French and British operations 40 miles south of Sebastopol in 1854, during the Crimean War; the Japanese landings in 1904, against Russia, and particularly the Japanese capture of Tsingtao; the British crossing of the Tigris River in February 1917; the German operations in the Baltic in September and October, 1917; and the Japanese amphibious behavior in the Shanghai incident of 1932.

What interested him most of all was the Dardanelles operation, usually called the Gallipoli campaign:

> Foisted on a reluctant government by an enthusiastic but visionary politician [Winston Churchill] who did not scruple to use disingenuous methods to attain his desires. Conducted by a gallant but incapable general [Ian Hamilton] initiated without plan or adequate means. The operation was still born and preordained to failure . . . more repleted with a strange mixture of valor and stupidity, of sacrifice and unselfishness, than any other campaign of which history has a record.

Patton then summarized the lessons he had derived. Command of the sea, surprise, night landings, energetic leadership, Army-Navy cooperation, naval fire support, broad front landings, artillery and machines with the leading waves, special boats and other equipment, and transports close to the landing beaches were all necessary for successful invasion. In the future, the side that had command of the air would have an overwhelming advantage.

Daylight landings, an absence of surprise, landing on a narrow front, the failure of naval fire support, inflexible plans, inept leadership, and poor Army-Navy cooperation led to defeat.

Applying his observations to Hawaii, he concluded that if the Japanese attacked the Islands, they would utilize air attack and try to block the sea channels in the Pearl and Honolulu harbors.

Actually, his forecast of amphibious doctrine in World War II was accurate. Allied operations, uniformly successful during that war, capitalized on all the factors he listed—command of the sea and of the air, surprise (gained by elaborate deception plans), close inter-service cooperation (gained by the principle of single or unified command), heavy naval fire support of ground forces, broad front landings, a large proportion of artillery and tanks and other heavy weapons going ashore with the leading elements, a variety of special equipment, and the anchorage of ship transports relatively close to shore. Night landings were at first deemed essential, but as the Allied domination of the sea and air became overwhelming, later amphibious operations were conducted during daylight.

To what extent Patton's study influenced the amphibious doctrine during World War II, or whether it had any impact whatsoever, is impossible to say. At the very least, his informal discussions and conversations with his fellow officers stimulated thought of a technique that was to have an important bearing on the outcome of World War II. Certainly his knowledge of amphibious operations was a factor that led to his selection as commander of the Western Task Force, which invaded the coast of North Africa near Casablanca in November 1942. By 1943, after the invasion of Sicily, where he led the American troops ashore, Patton was regarded as one of the leading amphibious experts on the Allied side.

Fascinated by the Gallipoli operation, Patton studied it more deeply. In August 1936, he completed a paper of narrative and analysis that ran 128 pages. So thorough and thought-provoking was this work that it was mimeographed, bound into a booklet, and disseminated to officers in Hawaii for their instruction.

Patton's conclusion on Gallipoli:

> At Suvla Bay it was not the Turkish army which defeated the British, but it was Von Sanders, Kemal Pasha and Major Willmer who defeated Hamilton, Stopford, Hammersley and Sitwell. Had the two sets of commanders changed sides it is believed that the landing would have been as great a success as it was a dismal failure.

Leadership, above all, he was saying, was the decisive factor in warfare.

After the annual major exercise in April 1937, Patton specifically investigated Hawaii's vulnerability to attack. Crediting Drum, who was the Hawaiian Department commander, with the vision to draw attention to the strategic importance of the Islands, with the knowledge of amphibious operations to understand Hawaii's danger, and with the foresight to warn of Hawaii's value as a hostile advance base, first for enemy aviation, later for

amphibious forces attacking the United States mainland, Patton
wrote of

> the inescapable assumption that complete surprise offers the
> greatest opportunity for the successful capture of these is-
> lands. It is reliably reported that during the last four years
> three or more Japanese divisions were embarked, moved to
> the coast of Asia and disembarked without any military
> attache, consular agent, foreign press correspondent or any
> other foreigner living in Japan being aware of the fact until
> the troops were in action in Asia. Some of the Mandated
> Islands, about which absolutely nothing is known, are only
> 2500 miles distant, seven days' streaming over the loneliest
> sea lanes in the world. Who can say that an expeditionary
> force is not in these islands now?

He invited attention to "the necessity of establishing certain
precautionary measures against surprise attack," including provid-
ing infantry, artillery, and air troops with at least half a day's fire
in ammunition—actually in the hands of the troop units; storing
lamps and candles in barracks and supply rooms, flares or flood-
lights for depots and hangars; and creating an alarm system designed to get troops to their wartime posts in a hurry.

For the Japanese, he demonstrated in some detail, could invade
and occupy Hawaii.

> It is realized that the events above enumerated [how the
> Japanese could take Hawaii] are not likely of occurrence. On
> the other hand the vital necessity to Japan of a short war and
> of the possession at its termination of land areas for bar-
> gaining purposes may impel her to take drastic measures. It is
> the duty of the military to foresee and prepare against the
> worst possible eventuality.

The attack on Pearl Harbor was four and a half years in the future, and Patton's estimate was a shrewd and thoughtful perception.

The world seemed to be marching toward war. Japan had conquered Manchuria and invaded China. Italy took Ethiopia by

force. Civil war had broken out in Spain. And Hitler in Germany was preparing for violent expansion.

The U. S. Army, long dormant, was beginning, but slowly, hardly visibly, to reawaken and rearm.

Patton's ratings at Hawaii were uniformly high. Brigadier General Daniel Van Voorhis, chief of staff of the Hawaiian Department judged him an "excellent" G–2—"ambitious, progressive, original, professionally studious; conscientious in the performance of his duties—fine appearing—the most physically active officer I have ever known . . . An officer of very high general value to the service."

Colonel James A. Ulio, who succeeded Van Voorhis as chief of staff, graded Patton twice "superior" and called him "an outstanding officer of high professional attainments. An indefatigable worker and reader as to his profession. A most active officer physically. Loyal, zealous and efficient."

Drum wrote: "Heretofore I have noted on this officer's Efficiency Reports a weakness in 'Tact.' In the last year he has overcome this weakness in a satisfactory manner. Colonel Patton has those qualities so essential to a superior combat leader."

Patton was reassigned to the Cavalry Board at Fort Riley, and in June 1937, he, Beatrice, young George, Francis "Doc" Graves, cook Suzuki, and deckhand Joe Ekeland sailed from Hawaii in the Patton *Arcturus* and headed for the mainland.

Beatrice Patton, Voyage of Arcturus, *Honolulu to San Pedro (California), 1937 (in the form of a letter to the children)*
June 13: We left on the dot yesterday at nine A.M. . . . over two hundred people on the dock to wave us goodbye. We had 180 leis and presents galore, books, soap, (salt and fresh water), iced cakes, candy, liquor, lifesavers, grapefruit peel, cap nets, jam, macademia nuts and everything you ever dreamed of. Joe said we had more flowers than a gangster's funeral! We were making one giant lei of all the little ones to throw overboard off Diamond Head, when all of a sudden . . . seven airplanes swooped out of nowhere and sailed right

over us, all changing their positions directly overhead—an Aloha!

[Escorted now by porpoises and birds. Ran engine 10 hours to get clear of land. Have to go north 600 miles before turning east with the westerly winds.]

June 15: so far this cruise is just the way I have pictured a cruise ought to be—lovely weather—everyone happy and comfortably sunburned—and the whole situation most pleasant and congenial.

June 22: Doc is a great joker, he swore he could see Latitude 34 when he looked over the side . . . (Back in 1898 on the River Nile, Uncle Freddie and I took turns all one day hanging over the rail of the Dahrobiyeh, watching in the muddy water for the Tropic of Cancer. Our tutor, Mr. Bentinck Smith told us to look for a dotted line.)

June 27: [third wedding anniversary of B and Johnnie Waters, who were at West Point.] we shall probably have to drink to your health in lavender water, as the regular stuff is running low.

July 9: [getting radio stations; learned that aviatrix Amelia Earhart had crashed.]

July 12: [arrived Los Angeles and were met by Ruth Ellen and Nita and others.]

Patton had arranged in Honolulu to sell the *Arcturus* on the mainland, and this was done. After a brief stay at San Gabriel, the family traveled to Massachusetts. Patton had a leave of absence for one month and fifteen days, to end early in August.

On July 26, he telephoned the headquarters of the First Corps Area in Boston to report that he was in the hospital at Beverly with a broken leg.

His stay in hospital, he said, would be without expense to the government, he wished his status changed as of July 25, the date of his accident, from leave to sick in hospital, and since he was under orders to proceed to Fort Riley for duty, would the War Department notify the commanding general of his injury.

The corps area commander assumed that Patton had broken his leg playing polo, and he so advised the War Department. About a month later, on August 19, he instructed the commanding officer of the Harbor Defenses of Boston at Fort Banks to appoint a board of officers to determine whether Patton's injury was in line of duty. A normal procedure, the investigation would establish whether there was a good reason and just cause for the accident or whether Patton was hurt as the result of some foolishness.

Two coast artillery officers and a Medical Corps officer, comprising the board, proceeded to the Beverly Hospital. Patton appeared before them and was sworn to testify.

On Sunday, he said, July 25, he, Mrs. Patton, and Lieutenant John K. Waters were riding on his estate near South Hamilton when Mrs. Patton's horse, which was just ahead of him, bolted suddenly, kicked, struck Patton's right leg, and inflicted a compound fracture of front and back bones. An ambulance was summoned, and it carried him to the hospital.

The doctor who had been on duty when Patton was admitted to the hospital was then called and sworn in. He said that Patton was absolutely sober and not under the influence of narcotics when he arrived. The doctor had administered anesthesia for an operation to reduce the fracture of the right tibia and fibula before applying a plaster cast. He believed there might be some permanent partial disability as the result either of the fractures or of a subsequent swelling in the pelvic veins.

The medical diagnosis was fracture, compound, right tibia, middle third; fracture simple, multiple of right fibula, upper and lower thirds; thrombo phlebitis, acute, of the pelvic veins, with resultant edematous swelling of the right leg.

The board of officers returned to Boston, met again, and reported their findings. Their unanimous verdict was that the injury had been incurred in line of duty. There was no misconduct on Patton's part. He had not been under the influence of drugs, narcotics, or alcohol at the time of the accident.

Letter, Lieutenant Colonel W. J. Froitzheim, commanding General Dispensary, U.S. Army, Boston, Mass., to Commanding General, Fort Riley, Kansas, November 15, 1937, subject: Sick Report

Report that Lieutenant Colonel George S. Patton, Cav . . . was admitted to the Beverly Hospital, Beverly, Mass., from July 25th to November 4th, 1937, inclusive. Upon his discharge from this particular hospital he was marked "sick in quarters" and at the present time is remaining in quarters . . . LD [Line of Duty]—yes.

Date of final disposition will be furnished by this office at the proper time.

Pershing wrote to Patton in December, saying he had just heard of Patton's accident and hoped he was on the road to recovery. General Kromer, the Chief of Cavalry, had given a small dinner at the Army and Navy Club the night before to which were invited several men "with whom I have been rather intimately associated . . . You would, of course, have been one of the party if you had been available."

Letter, GSP, Jr., to Pershing, December 30, 1937

My leg is realy much better and though I still have to wear an iron brace I can put a little weight on it and expect to go to Riley on dismounted duty about the tenth or fifteenth of January.

Now I have to bother you with a personal problem. Gen. Drum has always been more than kind to me and took me to Hawaii on his staff. As you know he is most anxious to follow Gen. Craig as Chief of Staff. So far as I can see the choice lays between him and Gen. De Witt. Yesterday Gen. Drum wrote me and asked if I could find out from you how you felt toward him in respect to his ambition. My loyalty to Gen. Drum makes it incumbent on me to ask you this question but since you are the center of all my loyalty I do not wish to place you in a position which might prove inconvenient to you. If you care to write me some statement which I could quote to Gen. Drum it would be helpful to me in my relations with him. If however you do not feel disposed to say any thing I shall understand your position and will simply have to say to Gen. Drum that I did not feel able to ask you such a question. I trust that you will forgive me being thus frank and assure you that what ever action you will take will be perfectly satisfactory to me.

Pershing chose to make no response. Eventually, in 1939, George C. Marshall would succeed Malin Craig as Army Chief of Staff.

On January 31, 1938, having been ordered to report to the Fort Banks Hospital for a medical survey to determine his fitness for active duty, Patton entered the hospital. He walked with a decided limp, although his general condition appeared good. He complained of a slight weakness in his right leg while walking and of a slight pain and swelling after walking.

According to the notes of his medical history, he had been under treatment in the Beverly Hospital for 103 days, and after discharge had been at home, walking on a caliper splint and cane. During his hospitalization, he had had a severe phlebitis due to an embolus in his right leg and a pulmonary embolus had lodged in his left lower lung. Recovery from both was complete. He appeared capable of limited duty, that is, of work requiring neither constant standing nor riding.

His eyesight was 20/30, uncorrected for distant vision, but corrected by glasses for near vision. His figure was medium, his frame heavy. He was 73 inches tall, weighed 196 pounds, and his normal chest measurement was 40 inches, 42½ inches when expanded, 38 at exhalation.

As for his recent injury, his recovery was very satisfactory. The function in his right leg was good. There was a limitation of motion in the right ankle because of the prolonged fixation of the leg. At the moment he was not qualified for duty. He was to have moderate exercise and refrain from riding. He was to elevate his foot and leg when his edema (swelling) was troublesome. He should be under medical supervision until he recovered completely.

On February 2, the War Department relieved Patton from assignment to the Cavalry Board and detailed him to the staff and faculty of the Cavalry School and to additional duty with the 9th Cavalry, which was stationed at Fort Riley as school troops.

There is no personal record of this six months of enforced inactivity resulting from Patton's broken leg and, what was frightening, his embolism. He must have read a good deal. He must also have pondered his future with a depression close to despair. He must certainly have wondered whether he would recover sufficiently to exercise his profession, to sustain the active pursuits that were the heart of his active duty. He must have painfully relived all his disappointments, his failures, his errors, and the occasions where he had displayed a lack of tact.

The world seemed to be drifting toward "the next war" he had anticipated with relish. And there he was, isolated and incapacitated, fifty-three years old, and perhaps over the hill. Could he recover his élan, his spirit, his robust health, his stamina, his zest for physical exertion? And could he do so in time to answer with confidence and vigor the peal of opportunity, the call of his destiny, his fate?

XI

The Approach
of War

"The thing we want is to retain our mobility."

CHAPTER 46

Fort Riley, Fort Clark, Fort Myer

*"He certainly seems to have taken a shine to me
and I have developed into the greatest YES MAN."*

PATTON'S RECOVERY was quicker than might have been expected. He arrived at Fort Riley on February 8, 1938, and became executive officer of the Academic Division and of the 9th Cavalry, and a member of the faculty and staff of the Cavalry School. Although he remained at his desk much of the time, he soon took brief rides, which he lengthened progressively. By March he had regained much of his old form and was displaying his customary energy and enthusiasm. After being examined by a board of officers, he was certified qualified for promotion.

In July, Colonel Clarence Lininger, assistant commandant of the Cavalry School, rated Patton "superior" in all categories except physical endurance. "Broken leg last summer from kick of horse," Lininger explained. "Rapidly approaching recovery. He rides hard now and it interferes little or not at all."

Letter, GSP, Jr., to Major General John A. Herr, Chief of Cavalry, spring 1938
My dear General: The three swords of which I wrote you are forwarded today under separate package for your inspection. They are not made of sword steel but are simply mild steel which I procured from the Union Pacific shops, roughed out with a cutter and then ground to shape. At first I made wooden models but decided that I could not judge the balance so had to revert to the steel . . .
. . . There are several advantages to this bayonet idea. In the first place it might be easier to issue a bayonet to the cavalry than it would be to restore a saber. In the second place

it would give the cavalry a very nasty arm for close combat dismounted should they become involved in such an operation, which heaven forbid. Third, it has the greatest chopping leverage of any blade I have ever seen . . .

Trusting that the models may be of some satisfaction to you, and assuring you that it was a great pleasure for me to make them, I am Very respectfully,

That spring, for his own edification or for the consideration of the staff, he set down his thoughts on what was wrong with the methods of instruction at the Cavalry School. The teaching was generally colorless, without emphasis on leadership and individuality. Not enough time was devoted to the personality of leaders. The problems to be solved by the students were too long and far from clear cut; too much information was given—"It is not necessary to have a history of the war to fight it." He had the impression that staff officers were becoming operators and were tending to usurp the functions of commanders. "Only God can make generals," he wrote, reversing his thought of two decades earlier, "the duty of this school is to make captains and majors."

Letter, GSP, Jr., to Beatrice (with her daughter Beatrice at the birth of the second Waters child), April 27, 1938

Here is George's report card which as he feared is not too good but on the other hand it might have been worse . . .

I had all the Heads of departments, the Gen., Col Rodney, Col. Holderness and Col Stayer and their copious wives in yesterday afternoon to drink the health of the offspring . . . Honeycutt and Nelly Richardson got promoted. So did Gens Van Voorhis, Ben Lear and Walter Grant all Cavalrymen. Col. Lininger was pretty well cut up as the selection of Richardson definately passes him up as it does Col Rodney too. Someday I may be in their shoes so feel sorry for them.

Significant changes were occurring throughout the military establishment as Japanese and German aggression pushed the world toward war, and the promotion of Van Voorhis to major general —he would receive his second star in July—was linked to a decision respecting mechanization. Early in 1938, the War Department directed the cavalry and infantry—no other branches—to develop mechanized forces. In compliance, the cavalry formed two mechanized regiments at Fort Knox and organized the 7th Cavalry Mechanized Brigade. Because of Van Voorhis' earlier experience with the Mechanized Force at Camp Meade and Fort Eustis, he was given the command of the unit.

Van Voorhis would remain a short time. In September, he would move on to Columbus, Ohio, to command the Fifth Corps Area.

Chaffee would take his place. Chaffee had served at Forts Eustis and Knox for three years, then on the War Department General Staff for four. When he replaced Van Voorhis, he would be promoted to brigadier general. Soon Chaffee would be put in charge of mechanized units of both the cavalry and infantry, and he would, in effect, recreate a new Tank Corps augmented by motorized infantry.

Despite Patton's interest in mechanization, he appeared to remain wholly a cavalry man. This too had its rewards. On May 12, in a memo addressed to the Adjutant General, subject: George Patton, General John K. Herr, the Chief of Cavalry, wrote that he wanted Patton promoted so that he could command the 5th Cavalry. He considered Patton "the only suitable officer for this assignment." Since no one in the military was supposed to be indispensable, Herr crossed out the "only" and substituted "most available." Therefore, Herr was recommending that the restriction currently in force against giving an officer a permanent change of station until he had served at least two years at his current duty post be waived in Patton's case.

On July 1, 1938, Patton was promoted to colonel. Ten days later he was assigned to the 1st Cavalry Division. He arrived at Fort Clark, Texas, on July 24, and assumed command of the 5th Cavalry.

Letter, GSP, Jr., to Beatrice, July 24, 1938
San Antonio is very quaint and I think you will like it . . . [Fort] Clark is 138 miles due west . . . I think we will like it. Gen J. [Joyce] runs the post and I run the regiment which

makes it very nice. The Joyces were delighted to see me and are more human than [they were] at [Fort] Myer . . . All one can do here is to Ride-Read Write & Swim.

Letter, GSP, Jr., to Beatrice, August 4, 1938

One of us [Joyce or Patton] has to be here as . . . the next ranking officer is not considered suitable to command the post. However he is doing all right for me . . .

[The house is beginning to look] swell. I had a new room built for a butler's pantry and bought a sink for it. I also am having the garden fenced with a 6 foot latice fence which should be finished by the end of September. All work here has to be done by soldiers. So as not to make them hate me I have them do the work on their own time and pay them for it. I got an extra month's furlough for George Meeks [his orderly] so he will be here until I return. Last night the Joyce's and I went to Eagle Pass and had dinner at El Moderno with Gen. Canones the Mexican commander. You will like him and his wife and also the town. It is just as foreign as Saumur or more so. I am striking up numerous friendships with the ranchers who while crude are real people and have plenty of shooting and fishing to trade for a little politeness. The Joyce's cant see this which is their misfortune. The sherrif and the County judge and the policeman are already my friends.

Letter, GSP, Jr., to Beatrice, August 8, 1938

[Brigadier General Kenyon A. Joyce] certainly seems to have taken a shine to me and I have developed into the greatest YES MAN unhung but it is the best way to get along with him and as a matter of fact he is very nice but I am makeing mental notes what I will do to two members of his staff if he ever leaves them in my clutches. He seems to think he will get Gen Lears job commanding the Division in November or december and if he does I may be in command here for a long time alone which will be somewhat less complicated than at present.

Patton had been sent to Fort Clark in order to take part in a series of maneuvers staged by the Third Army in Texas. The overall aim of the sham battles was to test concepts of troop mobility, concentration, and deployment under conditions of simulated warfare.

Letter, GSP, Jr., to Beatrice, August 15, 1938

This is the second day of the [mock] war. Yesterday we marched 35 miles in the worst heat I have ever seen and secured our objective with out a fight. Said objective is a stunted oak forest on a ridge but owing to ground rules we have to sit in a windless vally. I have been here ever since 5 A.M. I think that the infantry wont get up for another 18 hours and as the enemy who is 4 miles north of us wont fight I guess we will just sit. Tomorrow night we may march around his flank but it will be a very long trip over slippery roads. Still at night it is cool.

Letter, GSP, Jr., to Beatrice, August 23, 1938

We are now at Savenal which is sixty two or three miles from [Fort] Clark. So as I am making two thirty mile marches we will be in on the 25th. Actually I am at Clark now having driven in the regimental Car to get a bath which God knows I needed . . .

The last day of the Maneuvers I had a swell time. The 12th was in front on a flank march which I had advised the first day and was only put over on the fourth. It got held up for three hours and then they put B [Troop] and the Machine Gun troops of the fifth [cavalry] in the advance guard. I went along as sort of huntsman. We moved about ten miles mostly at a gallop and one horse died but we got right into the enemy rear areas and captured two battery kitchens one battery one battalion all of National Guard artillery and then scooped up the colonel and the command post of the 69 Regular artillery AA [antiaircraft]. In galloping over a wire fence the man next me got a bad fall but I was having such a swell time I never saw the fence which was low and my horse jumped it all right. The colonel of the 69th was very mad and refused to surrender to Capt Doyle till I came up and stuck my white pistol in his face then he was very quiet especially as I paroled him as I had no men to guard prisoners.

Gen Joyce expects to get back the 13th [of September] and I can start [on leave] immediately . . . Let me know what

riding and evening clothes I have at G.M. [Green Meadows]
as I expect to fly and want as little baggage as possible.

At the close of the maneuver, Major General George Van Horn
Moseley, the Third Army commander, conducted the critique and
concluded that the horse cavalry had demonstrated its continued
usefulness for close-in reconnaissance. Patton's strenuous endeavors had, no doubt, contributed to that judgment.

Letter, GSP, Jr., to Beatrice, August 27, 1938
Last night I had my first experience in twenty years of being the old man [senior officer] at a party. I drank beer till
my teeth floated but nothing else and along about midnight
I found it expedient to go home . . .
The awnings have made the house cooler but still you sit
and drop from two to four daily which is the hottest part of
the day.

*Letter, GSP, Jr., to Major General Daniel Van Voorhis, Fort
Knox, Kentucky, August 29, 1938*
We had a great war in the Third Army Maneuvers and on
the last day got right back of the enemy and into his gun positions. It was great sport and the funny thing was to see the
utter surprise of the enemy. They had so absorbed the bull
butting tactics of the World War that they forgot they had
to keep their pants buttoned or else get buggared. The more
people decry Cavalry, horse or mechanized, the more we will
bust them up next time. The thing we want is to retain our
mobility for the last ten miles.
You can count on me to keep the torch burning [for mechanization?] . . .
The only out about Fort Clark is the heat but I suppose it
is no worse than Brownsville and you survived that. Anyhow,
it is swell for the figure; mine has dwindled perceptiably . . .
Some times I almost think that there will be something
doing here [along the border] in a little while. Of course I
have hoped so more or less ever since 1911 and it has only
happened once, but now again I think there may be a flare
up. If you command the army of occupation don't forget to
take the Fifth Horse and loan us a few combat cars; anything
you can spare.

With sincere regards to yourself and love to the family, I am Very respectfully,

Letter, Major General Ben Lear, commanding 1st Cavalry Division, to GSP, Jr., October 30, 1938

My dear Patton: Before leaving the Cavalry Division I desire to personally express to you my appreciation for the most generous loyalty, the many kindnesses, and the real assistance which you have given to me and to the Cavalry Division throughout the period we have served together . . .

I have the warmest feeling of friendship towards you and your personnel, and wish for you and the members of your command much real happiness and success in the days to come.

Please permit me the privilege of sharing with you an admiration of your splendid command, and a gratification over it's many outstanding accomplishments.

Sincerely yours,

Patton enjoyed Fort Clark and its outdoor life, which restored him to health. He thrived in a position of command, and commanding the 5th Cavalry Regiment gave him great satisfaction, particularly because it was a combat organization, a tactical unit that was expected to be ready at all times for operations. Although Patton experimented with new organizational and operational concepts, he had plenty of time to hunt and fish and ride. He enjoyed his associates and friends.

His hopes for remaining in Texas, close to Mexico, where he continued to expect hostilities to break out, came to an abrupt close. On November 1, the War Department suddenly relieved him from assignment with the 5th Cavalry. He was instructed to report to Fort Myer, Virginia, in December, and take command of the post and of the 3d Cavalry stationed there.

Shortly before he left Texas, a board of officers examined him and found him qualified and eligible for promotion to brigadier general.

Letter, GSP, Jr., to General of Brigade Jesus Jaime Quinones, Piedras Negras, Coahuila, Mexico, December 2, 1938

I regret from the bottom of my heart that circumstances

are such that I cannot call on you in person but can only express my gratitude by the written word. I must also take this occasion to bid you farewell. It is a source of profound sorrow to me to leave here and so deprive myself of seeing more of you. With renewed expressions of thanks and esteem, I am, my dear general, your devoted admirer.

Joyce, who succeeded Lear in command of the 1st Cavalry Division, hated to see Patton leave. "Professionally it was grand to have you with me and personally it was a real joy."

He rated Patton "superior" and "an outstanding leader who has great mental and physical energy. Because of his innate dash and great physical courage and endurance he is a cavalry officer from whom extraordinary feats might be expected in war. A deep military student who is intensely interested in his profession. He is thoroughly qualified for the grade of brigadier general. Of outstanding value to the service in every way."

Patton reached Fort Myer on December 10, just as General Jonathan Wainwright, the previous commander, was leaving. The 3d Cavalry was drawn up in trim lines from Wainwright's house to the post gate, and his automobile was preceded and escorted by four scout cars.

The formation, while indicating the respect his officers and men had for Wainwright, reflected in large part the ceremonial nature of the duties performed at Fort Myer. During Patton's tour, he and his men would serve as escorts to the President of Nicaragua and to the King and Queen of England during their visits to Washington in 1939, they would provide the solemn trappings for military funerals, and they would lend military glamour and security to official receptions at the highest levels of the government.

While absorbed with these details and with the normal preoccupations of a post and unit commander, Patton was able to meet with important persons in the capital. The Army Chief of Staff had his quarters at Fort Myer. The War Department was nearby. And the city and its dignitaries were close at hand.

Drum, who was at Governors Island in New York and who was hoping to succeed Craig as Army Chief of Staff, wrote Patton and expressed pleasure that he was back in Washington, where he knew many influential people in high social and government circles.

He was glad, Patton said in reply, that Drum thought his stay at Fort Myer would work out well. He added that he would

> do my best to make your wish come true. Also, I am most hopeful that the opportunities to see one another, of which you speak, will not be those resulting from my occasional visits to New York, but rather will be the consequences of having you living at Fort Myer [as Army Chief of Staff].

To Chaffee, who commanded the 7th Cavalry Mechanized Brigade at Fort Knox, Patton wrote: "My dear General Adna," he was grateful to have Chaffee's letter welcoming him back to the Washington area. He would have preferred to serve under Chaffee, for together they could have made the brigade "a very warlike rather than a show-off outfit. However, don't tell General Van Voorhis what I have said." As for his assignment to Fort Myer, "I was as much surprised as anyone when I was ordered from Clark here, and have yet to find out why it happened."

It was all too obvious why Patton had been brought back to Fort Myer. The post was a show place. It featured a ten-week season of drill rides, mounted spectacles featuring impeccable troopers and spirited horses, that attracted congressmen and other governmental officials. The social obligations of commanding the installation were such that no colonel living solely on his Army pay could handle the position. Patton had an outside income. Wainwright, it was rumored, had departed from Fort Myer in debt.

The exhibition drill season opened in January, and Patton invited Major General James Kelly Parsons, the area corps commander, to come down from Baltimore as the guest of honor. He and Mrs. Patton, he wrote, would be happy to have Parsons and his wife, his chief of staff, and anyone else Parsons wished to bring, to lunch at their home.

Early in February, Patton informed General Malin Craig that the members of the Senate Military Affairs Committee and their wives were to attend the drill after lunching with the Pattons at their quarters.

Since I thought it might prove a good chance for favorable propaganda, I have asked the Deputy Chief of Staff, the Assistant Chief of Staff G–3, the Chief of Cavalry, the Chief of Field Artillery (who cannot accept), and Gen Murray [who commanded the troops stationed in the Washington area] to have luncheon with us at one o'clock and attend the Drill afterwards. Mrs. Patton also asked Mrs. Craig who is coming. I wonder if it would be too much of a favor to request that you, too, come. I would have asked you sooner but I hated to keep bothering you.

General Orders 5, Fort Myer, Virginia, March 18, 1939
The Commanding Officer congratulates all the members of the command on the superlative quality of the individual and combined efforts demonstrated by them during the exhibition drill season just concluded. The outstanding success of these drills was wholly due to the fine spirit of discipline, initiative and cooperation for which this garrison is famous. Troops animated by such spirit are invariably successful in peace or war.
Signed: G. S. Patton, Jr., Colonel, 3d Cavalry, Commanding

[Handwritten on one copy sent to Joyce] Dear Gen Joyce: How is that for a little back slapping that I learned from a former Colonel of the Third [Cavalry—meaning Joyce] . . . GSP Jr.

[Handwritten from Joyce] Dear Georgie: Done like the master that you are! . . . KAJ

Whatever Patton's efforts in behalf of Drum, Brigadier General George C. Marshall, the Deputy Chief of Staff, was selected to succeed Malin Craig as Chief of Staff on September 1. Early in May, Patton wrote to Marshall. Extra funds, Patton said, had been allocated for the Chief of Staff's house at Fort Myer, and

Patton suggested that the money be used to replace the coal furnace by an oil furnace, to repair two bathrooms, and to paint the rooms. He thought this could be done without disturbing General Craig. He also told Marshall who the servants were—the drivers, the cook, the butler, and so on. "I trust you will forgive me for bothering you with these details, but I believe that your knowing of it now will permit you to make more intelligent plans."

The announcement of Marshall as the new Chief of Staff led to some inevitable jockeying among Army officers. Patton, who was on the scene, who was in contact with Marshall, not on policy matters but rather on housekeeping affairs, and who was, by virtue of his position, rank, experience, and standing very much in the social swim, thus became important to his friends. A chance remark or a private conversation might provide that slight push that could bring about a choice assignment or an advancement in rank.

Joyce, for example, wondered in a letter to Patton where he would be transferred if he were promoted to major general. He preferred, he said, the Ninth Corps Area. "How is Marshall in the matter of the horse and horse cavalry? While I know him very pleasantly I know him but slightly in an official way."

"It would certainly be splendid if you could get the Ninth Corps Area," Patton replied. "What I say will possibly carry little weight but I shall find occasion to bring the subject up in conversation with General Marshall, whom I know very well."

Joyce, it turned out, would be transferred to that post the following year.

There was more involved than a gesture for a friend. International tensions provoked by the aggressions of Germany and Japan were having their effects on the U. S. Army. During his tenure as Chief of Staff, Malin Craig had succeeded in securing increasing budgets for military expenditures. Although the Army was still small and ill-equipped, it was growing.

The National Defense Act of 1920 had authorized 280,000 enlisted men on active duty, but the actual strength of the Army

had remained far below that figure. General MacArthur had recommended in 1933 that the Army be built up to at least 165,000
men, and that level was finally attained five years later. Not until
June 1939 would the Regular Army total 200,000 officers and
men.

Even though the troops were scattered in relatively small par-
cels among 130 camps, posts, and stations, the Army was stirring
after years of doldrums. There was serious talk of preparedness
for the next war. New units were being formed, large-scale maneuvers—such as the ones in Mississippi and Texas in 1938—were
being planned, and for the Regular officers, an invisible excitement that contrasted with the sober demeanor of the newly selected Chief of Staff ran like a tremor through the military
establishment.

Happy to be near the center of power although constrained to
operate on its fringes, Patton looked longingly toward the horses
—the 1st Cavalry Division, which Joyce commanded; and toward
the machines—the 7th Mechanized Brigade, which Chaffee commanded. Both were operational units devoted to training, and it
probably would have made no difference to Patton if he could
have worked with either—or, for that matter, with any of the units
that were scheduled to participate in a variety of exercises to test
combat doctrine, weapons, and equipment. He waited impa-
tiently, hoping desperately to be chosen for a field command,
where he could dispense with the glitter and pomp of a show place
like Fort Myer and get into the excitement and reality of combat
preparation.

While waiting, while performing diligently and loyally the functions of his assignment, he wrote numerous letters of congratulatory flattery to old friends and new, trying somehow to attract
notice so that he too could be part of the almost imperceptible
expansion of the Army that was starting.

He wrote to Van Voorhis to express regret that he had been
away when the general had visited the post. Patton hoped that
what the general had seen of Fort Myer "accorded with your own
standards insofar as copying perfection is possible."

He wrote to Brigadier General Robert C. Richardson, Jr., to say that he had heard that Richardson was doing "wonderful things for the [Cavalry] School as we all knew you would."

He congratulated Frank Andrews on his promotion to brigadier general. He congratulated John Millikin, who was elevated to colonel and who would command a corps in World War II. He congratulated General George Grunert, Fourth Army commander, who wrote back, "we oftimes wish you were here to pep up action and add color to the otherwise drab exercises." He congratulated Thomas M. Robins, George R. Allin, and others. His good wishes were genuine, yet there was an unmistakable undertone of query: when would he have something important to do? When would he enter into the ranks of the general officers?

His most faithful correspondent, and probably his best friend at this time, was Joyce. Soon after leaving Fort Clark, Patton had conveyed his thanks:

> I always find myself quite incoherent in expressing my appreciation and gratitude, and when I say that never have I had more delightful and instructive service than during my two tours under you I am understating it. I sincerely hope that I may again have the honor and pleasure of serving under you and in a war.

Joyce cautioned him about his health. "Don't be a nitwit and play any hard polo with that leg! In other words, be sane and don't jeopardize your chances for the sake of a little fun. My advice would be to do some equitation and jumping but otherwise confine yourself to indoor sports."

"I intend following your advice about polo," Patton replied, "and shall only play enough to keep my stomach under control."

When Patton learned, unofficially, of course, that Joyce's chances for promotion were good, he wrote, "I am saving up for your extra stars."

In the midst of his correspondence, Patton found time to look after his subordinate officers. For example, he wrote to Richardson about a captain who was a member of Patton's command

and who had recently been detailed to Fort Riley. The captain, Patton said, was

> an outstanding competition rider. He has the rare ability of doing better under pressure, and I believe that the Cavalry School is fortunate in getting his services. As a Troop Commander I rated him very satisfactory [not a high rating] due to the fact that his interest in individual horsemanship somewhat clouded his attention to troop duties. I am writing this letter because I feel that should you see his efficiency report without having the information contained in this letter you might possibly get an adverse reaction to him. I think this would be a mistake for on the job on which [he is] detailed I consider him very superior. Trusting that you will pardon my writing to you, I am, Very respectfully,

He wrote to one of his lieutenants who was temporarily at Fort Riley, telling him not to worry for even a moment about asking for an extension of leave because of his wife's condition; he was not to hesitate to ask for another extension if necessary.

He wrote to Colonel W. C. Crane, who was vacationing at Woods Hole, Massachusetts. The recent movement of Crane's battalion from Fort Belvoir to Fort Myer had resulted in the loss of fourteen horses in one battery because of heat exhaustion. A board had been convened to determine the responsibility for this excessive loss. What were the exact orders, Patton asked, that Crane had issued for the march? Was the entire battalion to move as a unit? Or were the batteries to proceed separately? "I do not believe the situation demands your return [from vacation], but write me all the information that occurs to you."

Patton managed to give some attention to professional matters outside the scope of Fort Myer. He sent the Chief of Cavalry a copy of the new "Infantry Drill Regulations" and suggested that the cavalry ought to have a similar book "instead of having to look through a public library to find out how things should be done." Seen handling the new cavalry saber-bayonet in the Office of the Chief of Cavalry, he was asked to submit a short article for the *Cavalry Journal*.

He found time to look into the case of three soldiers who annoyed two visitors to Washington. "I personally feel," Congressman Anton J. Johnson of Illinois wrote Patton, "that it was through your untiring efforts that these soldiers were apprehended and punished, and the way the whole thing was expedited speaks again of the high efficiency of the United States Army."

"Probably no one," Patton replied, "regrets the incident more than I do. I am proud of being a soldier and therefore I particularly dislike incidents tending to bring disgrace on that splendid profession."

Letter, GSP, Jr., to his son (at the Hill School, Pottstown, Pennsylvania), May 19, 1939

Your frank and manly letter was very pleasing to me, and I was glad to get it. If you can't like the Smith boy, leave him alone, because no matter how good a fighter he is, the people at the school consider him an under dog. It never pays to fight an under dog. You can fight for them, but never against them. It is very foolish, but quite understandable that one should run around raising h——l, but it gets one nowhere and betrays a lack of self-confidence. A man who is self-confident does not run around with a gang. It is much better to be a lone wolf than a coyote. Thanks for the money you sent me. I have already spent it. Hoping that you will not get into any more trouble, I am, Very affectionately,

He and his daughter Ruth Ellen rode at horse shows, and during a single week, between them, collected fourteen ribbons and a reserve championship, plus what he called several pieces of tin.

He rejoined the Capital Yacht Club. After spending a month of leave in Massachusetts, he and Beatrice sailed their boat, a two-masted schooner named *When and If*, from Cape Ann above Boston through the Cape Cod Canal, past Cape Charles, into the Chesapeake Bay, and up the Potomac to Washington.

Brigadier General Maxwell Murray, who commanded the Washington Provisional Brigade, judged Patton "superior" in all categories and qualities. Patton was "a vigorous, forceful and conscientious officer, whom I consider an outstanding leader. He is loyal, courageous, and gives his best effort to his profession."

General Parsons endorsed Murray's rating.

In the midst of Patton's activities came a poignant reminder of the past.

A former captain living in Merchantville, New Jersey, wrote Patton that he had met Joseph T. Angelo, who had a job with the Works Progress Administration "pushing mud on the riverbank." He had tried to help Angelo because of Angelo's war record and sunny disposition, which the captain found attractive despite the man's lack of education. Angelo had asked nothing, "as he seems to still have some pride." But any financial help that Patton could send would be a good deed. Angelo lived at 834 Homan Avenue, Camden.

Instead of writing directly to Angelo, Patton wrote to the former captain. He referred in some disdain to Angelo

who I believe saved or materially aided in saving my life there [in France]. I am sorry to hear that he is on relief. As he told you, my mother and I helped him considerably, but due to changed conditions I am not able to do as much for him now as then. I am enclosing a check to his order for $25.00 which I should appreciate your handing to him.

Angelo was capable of the grand gesture too. He spent more than he should have to send Patton a telegram: "Thanks for money much needed now hope you are well. Joe Angelo."

Letter, GSP, Jr., to General G. C. Marshall (Acting Chief of Staff, U.S. Army), July 20, 1939

Major Gay, the Quartermaster here [at Fort Myer], informs me that your property will be moved to the house from town on the 28th. That being the case, it occurs to me that you will have no place to stay. All my family are away, but my house is open and running, and I am there. I can give you a room and bath and meals, and should be truly delighted to do so. I shall not treat you as a guest and shall not cramp your style in any way. Hoping that you will give me the pleasure of your company, I am Very sincerely yours,

Letter, Marshall to Patton, July 24, 1939

I have just found your letter of July 20th, with its hospitable invitation for me to "batch" with you while I am getting my house established at Myer. I will be glad to accept and will talk to you later over the 'phone. You are very kind to invite me. Faithfully yours,

Letter, GSP, Jr., to Beatrice, July 27, 1939

I have just consumated a pretty snappy move. Gen George C Marshall is going to live at our house!!! He and I are batching it. I think that once I can get my natural charm working I wont need any letters from John J. P. [Pershing] or any one else.

Of course it may cramp my style a little about going out but there are compensations . . .

You had better send me a check for $5000.00 as I am getting pretty low.

Letter, GSP, Jr., to Beatrice, July 29, 1939

Gen M.[arshall] is just like an old shoe last night he was dining out and instead of having a chauffeur he drove him self

He is going out in the boat with me to day [Saturday]. He does not seem to have many friends.

CHAPTER 47

Fort Myer to Fort Benning

*"If we can get the platoons so they can fight anywhere
and the men convinced that they are the best on
earth and are willing to get killed to accomplish their
missions, we will be a great success."*

As PEOPLE EVERYWHERE during the summer of 1939 watched with
growing indignation and anguish the threatening posture of
Adolf Hitler, Patton pursued his normal occupations, waiting all
the while for some mark of attention, some sign of notice, some
gesture of assurance that he was deemed worthy of something
more than the direction of ceremonial duties at Fort Myer. He
seemed to have reached a dead end in his career. Out of the main-
stream of military developments, he performed his official functions, mingled with the upper elements of society, and pined for
excitement.

His most interesting activity that summer took place near Fort
Belvoir and Manassas, Virginia, where he participated in maneuvers conducted by the III Corps. These games were a smaller off-
shoot of a major exercise engaging the First and Second Corps
near Plattsburg, New York. The entire training program was under the direction of the First Army, commanded by Drum, and
its chief aim was to give the staffs of higher headquarters—divisions, corps, and field armies—practice in moving and deploying
units in simulated combat.

As early as May, when Drum was planning the exercises, Patton wrote him to make a suggestion. He had been studying maps
of the probable areas of the summer maneuvers, and he thought
that if Drum imposed imaginary boundaries on the flanks of the

troops involved, he would be committing a mistake. Arbitrary lines confining the maneuver area would inhibit and limit the possibility of flanking marches, and thereby seriously handicap the cavalry units, whether horse or mechanized. Similar restrictions placed on the maneuver forces the previous year in Texas, he said, had prevented the proper use of mobile troops.

Knowing your interest in realism [in training] I am taking the liberty of making the above suggestion so that we can attack from the rear, which, in my opinion, is the proper direction of attack for horse and mechanized Cavalry. Trusting that you will forgive my temerity in writing you direct, I am, as ever, Devotedly and very respectfully yours,

Drum replied that he was glad to have Patton's remarks, which, he said, he would bear in mind.

But Drum was less interested in mobility than Patton was. At the conclusion of the maneuvers, Drum would report to the War Department that it would be desirable to develop the highly mobile, hard-hitting striking forces that intrigued Patton. But Drum's overall conclusion was that the bulk of the Army ought to be organized for sustained and prolonged combat much in the manner of World War I.

During the exercises in Virginia, called the First Army Maneuvers, Third Corps Phase, Patton commanded a mobile unit— probably at least part of his 3d Cavalry—supported by attached artillery. He carried out his assignments with vigor and verve, playing hard, conducting in his aggressive way wide, sweeping movements designed to outflank his opponents.

In the course of the war games, he was unintentionally brusque, perhaps even rude, to Albert H. Stackpole, a well-known National Guard officer and military writer. Concerned over the possible damage to his public image, for he was highly conscious of Stackpole's power with the pen, Patton later apologized. Stackpole gracefully acknowledged Patton's note, saying, "Apologies are not at all necessary. I fully appreciate that while a war is being fought the commanding officer can't be bothered with casual observers."

At the conclusion of the maneuvers, Patton wrote to Major

General Edward Martin, who commanded the 28th Division, Pennsylvania National Guard, which had been on the opposite side of the sham battles. Patton congratulated Martin on the spirit and efficiency of his men. Martin replied, "I can reciprocate the remark relative to the enthusiasm, energy, and sportsmanship shown by our command. The same applies to your officers and men."

Brigadier General Maxwell Murray sent a "Commendation" to the War Department to cite the "superior" performance of Patton during the exercises. "His tireless energy, prompt decision, and clear grasp of the situations presented were noteworthy," Murray wrote, "and I consider that his work as commander . . . in most difficult terrain, was outstanding. I recommend this officer for early consideration for appointment to the grade of brigadier general."

Letter, J. W. Stilwell (Carmel, California) to GSP, Jr., August 23, 1939

My dear Patton, That was really an unfair advantage I took of you and Carberry [when they were cadets at West Point and returning at night from an unauthorized expedition]; I was running on a nice smooth path, and you were leaping over rocks all the way. And how you two did put out! My belated thanks for an exceptional feat of agility and an interesting recollection. [Stilwell had then been an instructor and was nice enough to have pretended he could neither recognize nor catch Patton and Carberry; otherwise, he would have had to report them for punishment.] Many thanks for your kind words about my promotion, which is of far less importance to me than the approval of old friends. I appreciate your having taken the trouble to write. Best wishes, and hoping to see you again some where soon.

Joyce wrote on August 25 to thank Patton for the delightful party he had given for him several weeks earlier when Joyce had been in Washington. "Our mutual friend is most interesting, and I am sure will make a great Chief of Staff . . . Do not fail to get Pa Watson [Brigadier General Edward Watson, soon to be promoted. He had graduated in Patton's original class of 1908, had been Roosevelt's military aide and was now his Secretary] on your side. This is confidential, but most important. As things are now you are nicely fixed [with influential friends] I know."

Letter, GSP, Jr., to Colonel James A. Ulio, Office of the Adjutant General, Washington, D.C., August 31, 1939
My dear Jimmy: Paragraph 4 of the enclosed letter of commendation is, I believe, of vital importance to me, because, while General Murr[a]y gave me a wonderful efficiency report on June 30th, he failed to mention the general officer part. Since it is highly probable that I shall be up for consideration [for promotion to brigadier general] prior to next June 30th I wish you would discover some way of getting a copy of this letter before the Chief of Staff, or at least have it recorded with my current efficiency report. This letter is certainly doing me no good sitting in Baltimore [at Headquarters, Third Corps Area]. On the other hand, I cannot ask the new Chief of Staff, Col Allin, to do anything as he might consider that I am stealing his thunder [affecting Allin's eligibility for promotion]. Since you are sure of being made [a general officer], I believe that I can call on you without misgiving. Do your damnedest. Most sincerely,

The German invasion of Poland on September 1 opened the hostilities of World War II. And still Patton remained unaffected by the hectic changes occurring everywhere.

Early in September, as German mobile mechanized forces were overrunning Poland, President Roosevelt raised the U. S. Army's authorized strength to 227,000 men. At the same time, General Lesley McNair started planning a program to reorganize the combat divisions from square to triangular type. Instead of four regiments, a division would now have three, and each regiment would have three battalions instead of four. The result was a saving in manpower and a gain in flexibility. Improved weapons would increase the division's firepower, and more vehicles would give it greater mobility.

McNair's program would be carried out late that year, and the new look would make possible genuine corps and army maneuvers in 1940, something more than the earlier extemporized exercises.

Meanwhile, Patton was writing to the Chief of Cavalry to suggest that four officers at Fort Myer ought to attend the Army War College. However, one of the four, he said,

will probably be taken care of by the President, or could be if you had no hole [space] for him. In any case he is of more value to the Cavalry in his present position as a riding companion for Mrs. Roosevelt than he would be at the War College, at least for the next few years.

Patton wrote to Chaffee on a flimsy excuse. Chaffee was coming to Washington to give a talk at the War College, and the Pattons hoped he would stay with them.

Chaffee was unable to avail himself of Patton's hospitality. "I am counting on seeing you, though," Chaffee wrote, "and talking over a lot of things with you." He was, no doubt, referring to armored things, for Chaffee was working hard on mechanization at Fort Knox.

When Marshall officially assumed his post as Chief of Staff and became a four-star general, Patton had a set of sterling silver stars —eight in all—sent to him from New York. Patton also presented a set of stars to Joyce upon his promotion to Major General.

Letter, General G. C. Marshall to GSP, Jr., September 23, 1939

Dear Patton: As I told you yesterday, I tried to get you over the 'phone to thank you for that whole firmament of stars you presented to me. I appreciate very much your thoughtfulness and generous gesture, and I trust that I will wear these stars with satisfaction and honor to the Army.

Letter, Joyce to GSP, Jr., September 27, 1939

[Thanks a thousand times for the stars.] I trust I shall be able to return the compliment with a pair for your own wear in the very near future. I have just returned from [Fort] Clark where I had two glorious dove shoots on Otto Postell's ranch. They tell the story at Clark that when Mrs. Postell recently used some strong language she promptly explained that she had learned the words from you.

Letter, GSP, Jr., to Marshall, October 12, 1939

My dear General Marshall: With the rapid approach of the social season in Washington it occurs to me that you might require the temporary service of an aide to attend to your engagements and to keep the appointment book for both yourself and Mrs. Marshall.

First Lieutenant Loren F. Cole has had considerable experience, knows everyone in Washington, and is a very charming gentleman. Should you see fit I would be very glad to detail Lieutenant Cole as an acting aide until such time as your permanent aide reports for duty.

Trusting that you will not consider me too intrusive, I am Very respectfully,

Letter, Marshall to GSP, Jr., October 16, 1939

My dear Patton: I received your note of the 12th regarding Cole. I appreciate your thoughtfulness and I will talk to you about it at some later time. Faithfully yours,

Letter, Sterling Larrabee, Master of the Fox Hounds, The Old Dominion Hounds, Crest Hill, Virginia, to GSP, Jr., October 15, 1939

Dear George: Your question as to the best ration for foxhounds is indeed a nice one, and probably has as many answers as there are Masters of Hounds. After experimenting with various rations during the past fifteen years, I have arrived at the ration as shown below, which has proven satisfactory in this particular country and this climate—I fancy the climate and other conditions at Fort Knox are somewhat similar . . .

[Then followed a detailed, three-page, single-spaced, typed letter on the feeding of hounds.]

I sincerely trust that you may get some dope out of the above which you can cull over and pass on to Adna Chaffee, who (Hitler permitting) may get some good sport out of organizing a pack at Fort Knox. Those mechanized gents ought to get some real exercise, anyway.

Life went on as usual for Patton. In November, he went to New York and attended the National Horse Show in Madison

Square Garden, participating in several events and judging the Open Jumpers Classes.

In December, a board of officers certified that Patton was eligible and qualified for promotion to brigadier general. This was the second year he had been so designated. What he needed was a job, an assignment, that called for that rank.

He was well regarded. His official file was full of "superior" ratings and comments. "Everywhere I hear mention of the fine record you have built up and are continuing to maintain," Colonel J. A. Green, editor of the *Infantry Journal*, wrote him.

Yet nothing happened. His status remained unchanged. Marshall seemed to ignore him even though he searched for young and vigorous officers to fill vacancies in an expanding Army. Perhaps it was because he thought Patton too old, or too wedded to the horse cavalry; perhaps because he was aware of Patton's efforts to impress him; it may have been that Marshall was testing Patton's patience, or, indeed, that nothing suitable for him was open. Then too there was vague talk—from Pa Watson?—that the White House considered Patton too outspoken, too flamboyant, possibly even erratic; and his social and political connections through his wife to prominent Republicans in Massachusetts would hardly have worked in his favor. Whatever the reason, Patton stayed at Fort Myer.

The new year arrived, and he conducted the drill exhibitions. In his spare time, for his own amusement, he drew up his "idea of what the proper course of instruction" in the pistol should be.

Letter, Lieut. Col. John J. Bohn, Cavalry School, to GSP, Jr., March 22, 1940
Dear George: Your recent study on instruction of the pistol has just passed over my desk en route to the Cavalry Board. I cannot refrain from expressing to you in a personal note my appreciation of your succinct murder of the present valueless course in cavalry pistol instruction. In addition, I strongly feel that the simple, sensible and practical course of instruction proposed by you for cavalry pistol instruction should be adopted at once. The plan needs no selling. The

improvement is apparent to anyone who has ever fired a pistol, and I look forward to its speedy adoption.

Several events in the spring of 1940 would finally change the direction of Patton's career. First, the Third Army Maneuvers in Georgia and Louisiana in April and May precipitated a break in the close relationship between Patton and Joyce.

The split had become visible, although it was far from a rupture, as early as the previous autumn, when the tactical thinking of Joyce and Patton began to diverge. Joyce's 1st Cavalry Division had engaged in war exercises in Texas, and shortly thereafter, Joyce summarized for Patton's information some of the relevant experience.

He himself had commanded the cavalry division, which had opposed a force of motorized and mechanized infantry and artillery. In the course of a "battle," a relatively small task force of "enemy" infantry and artillery had made a wide turning movement of 100 miles to get on the flank of Joyce's horse cavalry. If successfully prosecuted, the sweeping advance would have struck the cavalry flank and thereby have, theoretically, destroyed Joyce's unit. Yet when the "hostile" task force arrived in position to menace Joyce, his troops stopped the flanking movement cold and separated the enemy task force from the main enemy body, thereby, again theoretically, making the small outflanking force vulnerable to destruction. In short, the mobile unit had failed to carry out its aim, and Joyce's cavalry had "won" the battle.

Knowing Patton's penchant for wide envelopments or turning movements, Joyce admitted in his letter that there were, of course, many good arguments in favor of this sort of venture. But personally he believed that it was too risky.

Joyce then tried to smooth over the difference. Both sides, he wrote, had made mistakes, "as there always will be in maneuvers or in wars, and all learned by the experience. The good soldier does not make the same mistake the second time."

If Patton felt offended by Joyce's having questioned one of his deepest convictions—the value of mobility to permit hard-hitting forces to strike at the enemy's flank and rear—he made no immediate retort.

In February 1940, as evidence of his friendly feeling toward Joyce, Patton passed along some news, some inside information that, strictly speaking, it was not altogether fair to disclose. John S. Wood, chief of staff of the Third Army and a friend of Patton, had been in Washington and had talked about the maneuvers to be held that spring. According to Wood, Joyce's 1st Cavalry Division would participate and have the assignment of covering or protecting the assembly and concentration of an infantry corps. Joyce's division of horse cavalry would oppose Chaffee's mechanized brigade. Wood has said that the initial concentration points of the opposing forces were 100 miles apart. But he had hinted that the covering action by Joyce would start before the main troops on both sides reached those positions.

This was valuable advance knowledge that Joyce was not supposed to have, for it gave his forces an unfair advantage over Chaffee's. Patton promised to let Joyce know anything further that he might learn.

Patton continued:

It occurs to me that, since mechanized cavalry depends for its success on a very large use of radio, much advantage could be obtained over them should you be able to set up radio interference. I am informed that the sets in the scout cars are strong enough to be used for this purpose if they are tuned in on the same bands. I think it would be a great joke if our friendly enemy on wheels and tracks could be totally deafened [by radio jamming]. Colonel Wood also informs me that there is a river running through a considerable portion of the maneuver area, and that this river will probably be unfordable except by swimming. Perhaps you could find some place near [Fort] Bliss where you could practice this and so steal another march on Chaffee, Millikin and Company . . .

Trusting that you will not consider me presumptuous for the foregoing and with all good wishes for the success of the horse cavalry, I am, as ever, Very respectfully yours,

Thus, Patton was motivated in his desire to have Joyce win both by his friendship for Joyce and by his attachment to the horse cavalry.

Letter, GSP, Jr., to Lieutenant Colonel John S. Wood, Third Army, Atlanta, Georgia, March 19, 1940
Dear P: While I have not received my order I definitely know that I shall be an Umpire [in the forthcoming maneuvers], so don't forget to give me a good job.

Write me prior to March 25th as to what uniforms I should take, do I need woolen o.d. blouses as well as breeches, do I need a cap as well as campaign hat; do I need a bedding roll, and any other pertinent information that you may think will be of value to me. Please answer at once.

As ever, in a hurry, yours,

On the following day, he received the order detailing him to the Third Army on temporary duty as a control officer or umpire.

Upon receipt of Patton's letter, Wood wrote that mimeographed instructions had probably reached Patton. There was little he could add, except that it was chilly in Georgia in April and hot in Louisiana in May. "Please give my love to Bea. I hope that you are both well. It was a great pleasure to see you two again and to have had such a delightful evening with you."

The Third Army Maneuvers were staged in two phases, the first near Fort Benning, Georgia, between April 12 and 25, the second near Camp Beauregard, Louisiana, between May 5 and 25. These games had as their prime purposes the testing of organization, doctrine, equipment, and the performance of units, commanders, and staffs. They were designed to train the new type of corps, composed of triangular divisions, to deploy large bodies of troops over long distances against a mobile enemy, and were particularly oriented on the operations of the few mechanized units in existence. The maneuvers would help in determining how mechanized forces and combat aviation could best work together. They would also evaluate the usefulness of horse cavalry against motorized and mechanized troops.

These aims stemmed from the shocking success of the German

blitzkrieg in Poland the previous year, which was a sobering sight
for the U. S. Army. An isolationist Congress, niggardly with
funds, had deprived the Army of the means with which to develop and produce in large numbers tanks, self-propelled artillery,
trucks, close-support planes, and other new weapons and pieces
of equipment, together with the units to use them. There were
but few mechanized forces with rudimentary equipment, and they
had had little experience working with close-support airplanes.

Chaffee's 7th Mechanized Cavalry Brigade from Fort Knox
and a Provisional Motorized Tank Brigade created by the infantry at Fort Benning dominated the Third Army maneuvers. These
two units were formed into an improvised armored division, and
the success of this force coincided with the crashing explosion
that marked the end of the Phony War in Europe. In May, as
Chaffee's machines were defeating Joyce's horses, the German
forces attacked France. In six weeks, with an astonishing rapidity,
the Germans defeated the British, Belgian, and French armies
and forced the evacuation from Dunkerque. Professional soldiers
in general and tank enthusiasts in particular advocated with increasing clamor the need to form true armored divisions.

This was what the Third Army commander, Lieutenant General Stanley D. Embick, recommended—that the mechanized brigades, one cavalry-sponsored, the other infantry-sponsored, be
expanded into armored divisions. Embick also suggested that the
horse cavalry be retained to perform the subordinate and limited
function of reconnaissance, and that the horse units be further
motorized and mechanized.

Patton's presence as an umpire in the maneuvers was extremely
beneficial to him. He saw precisely how the new mechanized units
were organized, how they operated, and what could be expected
from them. Joyce's horse cavalry had been unable to stand up
against them, in part because Joyce lacked the punch and the
slashing, driving aggressiveness that characterized Patton's
thought and behavior. Yet, no matter what the deficiencies of
Joyce as a commander, no matter whether Patton might have
done better if he had been in command, it was obvious to every-

one, and to Patton as well, that the machine had replaced the horse in warfare.

Disenchanted with Joyce's leadership and with the horse cavalry operations during the maneuvers—the two were tied together— Patton nevertheless made an effort to keep his friendship with Joyce intact and close. In the following month, Patton sent Joyce a training memo he had drawn up for his own regiment of horse, the 3d Cavalry at Fort Myer.

Joyce's reaction to Patton's training program was negative. The memo, Joyce wrote, contained much advice for the young, but some statements were so general as to be misleading.

> What you say in paragraph "M" relative to saddle bags and cantle rolls is just 100% wrong. The individual mounted soldier should not be dependent on a truck in any way for periods up to 48 hours . . . This belief that the cavalry soldier must have a truck with him all the time is as bad as the infantry soldier having to ride up to the firing line in a truck. We must get away from such stuff. Save the horse—YES, but in any active service have the individual fighting man self-supporting in every way and ready to go.

A decided gap had opened between the doctrinal thinking of the two men. Joyce remained conservative in his views. Patton modified his traditional outlook by broadening his focus and by adjusting to the reality that Chaffee's machines had made Joyce's horses look bad.

This perception prompted Patton to switch his allegiance. He began to look with increasing longing toward Chaffee's tanks. This was the second event that affected Patton's career.

Meanwhile, Patton was collecting "superior" efficiency ratings and commendations for his manner of performing his duties. As an umpire in the maneuvers, he was graded "superior" for his contributions to the successful exercises. Shortly thereafter he received an official compliment on the appearance of his troops during a parade.

Letter, Brigadier General Maxwell Murray, Washington Provisional Brigade, to GSP, Jr., June 5, 1940, subject: Commendation

The review held at your station [Fort Myer] on the morning of June 4, 1940, in which the 3d Cavalry . . . 1st Battalion, 16th Field Artillery, 3d Battalion, 12th Infantry, and Troop F, 10th Cavalry participated, was a superior demonstration of precision and nicety of detail, always desired in Army ceremonies, yet too seldom achieved. The appearance of the troops, their precision of march and exactness of formations were so exemplary in every detail as to unequivocally establish claim to a high state of training, morale and discipline. Mindful that such standards of proficiency are only attained through long and tedious hours of instruction and training, with a high spirit of cooperation throughout, I wish to commend you and through you the commanding officers and enlisted men of the units concerned.

Two weeks later, Murray composed for Patton's official file another "Commendation" in appreciation of Patton's faithful discharge of duty. Patton, Murray wrote,

has filled this difficult assignment [at Fort Myer] in a manner which reflects great credit upon himself and the military service . . . I feel that I have been very fortunate in having had Colonel Patton serve under me in the important post he has occupied.

Still later that month, Murray formally rated Patton "superior" in all categories, and called him

a most enthusiastic, energetic and able officer. He has decided opinions, and expresses them frankly but carries out loyally any decision of his superiors. He maintains himself in remarkable physical condition, and through personal leadership builds a high esprit in his command. He is well fitted for higher command in peace or war.

But a "higher command," for the moment at least, eluded him.

The training memo he had sent to Joyce appeared in the *Cavalry Journal* under the title "Training Memoranda to His

Regiment." It was an attempt—his last—to restore the faltering prestige of the horse cavalry. "My observations at the Maneuvers in Georgia and Louisiana," Patton wrote, "induce me to re-stress the following points which are so obvious they are never remembered."

Scout cars, he said, were not combat cars. They were supposed to find and report information about the enemy. They were to fight the enemy only when combat was unavoidable. "It is not necessary," he said in illustration, "to push your nose against the glass to see through a window. Observation from a distance is just as efficient and much safer."

Reconnoitering elements, he counseled, should stop on the friendly side of a crossroads so that the enemy could not use the lateral road to cut them off. Units had to guard their security by putting out flankers during a halt. "If attacked by enemy planes, fire at them with everything you have. If you are under cover [and undetected] keep quiet." Crew members of scout cars ought to fill their gasoline tanks at every opportunity. If withdrawing, they should destroy all the gasoline they could not use.

"The secret of success in mounted operations," he reiterated, having made the same statement several years earlier, "is to GRAB THE ENEMY BY THE NOSE AND KICK HIM IN THE PANTS." As soon as horse cavalry struck opposition, it had to pin down the enemy in the front with a minimum of force and get around the enemy flanks. Against motorized columns, the objective was always the trucks, which were usually just around the first bend or just behind the first hill. If the wind was favorable, troopers could set fire to anything that would burn toward the enemy.

Imbedded in his text were aphorisms:

Always fell trees and burn bridges on roads leading to your position or bivouac . . .

Anti-tank guns are deadly at 1000 yards. The guns in tanks are not . . .

Next to a windshield a khaki tent is the most visible object from the air . . .

It is not soldierly to send a two-ton truck for a can of beer, but it is done all the time. This must stop . . .

It must be borne in mind that the surest way to avoid losses is to inflict losses on the enemy by your own fire.

These were hardly profound observations. They were practical, down-to-earth statements that were immensely applicable to field soldiering. They repeated his continuing belief in the efficacy of mobility, the value of wide sweeping maneuvers, and the benefit of overwhelming firepower to defeat the enemy.

Despite his continuing interest in horses, his responsibilities as post commander, his satisfying contacts with prominent people in Washington, Patton was restless. He had been at Fort Myer a year and a half. He had everything under control. His life was pleasant enough, but offered little challenge. His duties were routine. Furthermore, the dedicated horsemen with whom he had been closely associated throughout his career seemed to have lost touch with and to be out of step with the times.

Motivated by his boredom and by his newly awakened appreciation of the capabilities of mechanized forces, Patton wrote on June 26 to his friend Chaffee. Perhaps Patton had learned informally that Chaffee would on July 10 become Chief of a newly organized Armored Force, which was built around the 7th Mechanized Cavalry Brigade and the 6th Armored Infantry Regiment at Fort Knox, a force that would be authorized 530 officers and 9329 men. Perhaps Patton had heard unofficially that Chaffee was to take command on July 15 of a newly formed I Armored Corps, which would control the 1st Armored Division (successor to the Mechanized Brigade) at Fort Knox and the 2d Armored Division (successor to the Provisional Tank Brigade) at Fort Benning.

Precisely what Patton said in his letter to Chaffee toward the end of June has been lost. No doubt, he sent his congratulations. He probably added that people were saying good things about Chaffee's work. He may have mentioned an observation or two from the Georgia and Louisiana maneuvers. And he invited Chaffee to stay with the Pattons whenever he was in Washington.

Although he may have included a jocular remark to the effect that he wished he were helping Chaffee, Patton would not have asked for anything specific. The entire tradition and custom of the service argued against direct pressure or subservient pleading of this sort for a favor. The purpose of Patton's letter was to remind Chaffee, in an indirect fashion, of Patton's interest in Chaffee's endeavors and of his availability for a new and exciting challenge.

Chaffee replied two days later. He talked about his frequent visits to Washington and elsewhere—"I have been so busy with two trips to Washington in the last three weeks that my head is going around. I work all week and travel on Sunday." He thanked Patton for the invitation—but "I usually go to the Club or to a hotel, in order to be footloose, because my time is never my own."

Finally, he came to the heart of the matter, and what he said was probably more than Patton could have expected.

> I put you on my preffered list as a brigade commander for an armored brigade. I think it is a job which you could do to the queen's taste, and I need just such a man of your experience in command of an armored brigade. With two light armored regiments and a regiment of tanks employed in a mobile way, I think you could go to town. We have an enormous job in front of us to get this thing organized, trained, and going in a minimum of time. I hope things will work out favorably for you. I shall always be happy to know that you are around close in any capacity when there is fighting to be done. Good luck to you always and I will be seeing you soon, I hope.

This was the third event that would change Patton's career.

The fourth occurrence was the appointment early in July by President Roosevelt of Henry L. Stimson as Secretary of War. Patton immediately sent Stimson, an old friend, a congratulatory letter. Stimson acknowledged with thanks Patton's "very encouraging message which you sent me concerning my appointment." He sent affectionate good wishes to Patton and to Beatrice.

It is highly probable that Patton's note led Stimson to wonder why a proved fire-eater like George Patton was being kept at Fort Myer. And no doubt he mentioned this thought to Marshall.

Certainly there was increasing need for an officer of Patton's ability and experience. And certainly there were increasing opportunities for men of his caliber. In July 1940, the War Department activated General Headquarters, U. S. Army, under the command of General McNair to supervise the training of tactical units. In the following month, Congress would authorize the President to call National Guard units to active federal service. And in September, the President would sign the Selective Service Act permitting the induction of 630,000 draftees, would muster 270,000 National Guardsmen to the national colors, and would enlarge the Regular Army to 500,000 men. A total of 1,400,000 troops would soon be on active duty and preparing for war.

France had surrendered, and the battle of Britain had begun. The United States was finally awakening to the danger of Axis aggression.

Meanwhile, Patton left Washington on July 2 for fifteen days of leave in Massachusetts. Four days later his daughter Ruth Ellen married Lieutenant James W. Totten. The wedding was held at St. John's Church in Beverly Farms, and it was followed by a reception at Green Meadows.

As was his practice, Patton requested that his leave be extended for ten days. Permission was granted.

On July 15, while he was reading the morning newspaper at Green Meadows, he saw an item about himself. With mounting excitement, he learned that he had been assigned to the 2d Armored Division at Fort Benning, Georgia. He was going back to the tanks.

It took him several hours to restrain his joy, to compose himself, to consider the sudden turn in his career. Perhaps he made several telephone calls to Washington to confirm the information.

Letter, GSP, Jr., to Brigadier General C. L. Scott, commander 2d Armored Division, Fort Benning, Georgia, July 15, 1940

My dear Scotty: You can imagine my great delight at reading in the paper this morning that I had been assigned to your outfit. I am sure that I owe the detail to you. It is probably needless for me to say that I will do my uttermost to give satisfaction.

His leave expired on July 27, he informed Scott; he would like to stay in Massachusetts at least until the 22d, but he could be at Fort Benning within 36 hours if Scott wanted him at once. He concluded: "With best regards and looking forward to a short and bloody war, I am Very sincerely."

Letter, GSP, Jr., to Brigadier General Adna R. Chaffee, Fort Knox, Kentucky, July 15, 1940
Dear General Adna: I deeply appreciate your nice letter of the 28th [of June]. In this morning's papers I note that I am to go to Benning to take one of the armored brigades. I am sure that this most happy detail was due to your efforts and I appreciate it very much indeed. You may be sure that I shall do my damndest to justify your expectations of me.

Chaffee had put Patton's name on his preferred list, but it was Scott who had the vacancy in the 2d Armored Division. Scott had selected Patton from among those whom Chaffee considered qualified and eligible for the job.

It was quickly obvious to Patton that his assignment to the 2d Armored Division would have been impossible unless Marshall approved. He therefore wrote a letter of thanks to the Chief of Staff.

Letter, Marshall to GSP, Jr., July 19, 1940
Dear Patton: I have just received your note of July 16th, thanking me for your assignment to the brigade of an armored division. I am glad this arrangement is pleasing to you, for I thought it would be just the sort of thing you would like most to do at the moment. Also, I felt that no one could do that particular job better.

I am looking forward to seeing you and having a talk with you before you leave for the South.
Hastily,

Patton arrived at Fort Benning on July 27. He moved into quarters at 601 Baltzell Avenue, and assumed command of the 2d Armored Brigade.

Two days later, the War Department revoked Patton's Mobilization Assignment—that is, the position Patton would take if the country went to war—as commanding officer of the 3d Cavalry, thereby cutting the cord that had tied him to the horse cavalry.

It must have occurred to Patton soon after his arrival at Fort Benning, if not earlier, that Pershing had probably had a hand in his transfer. It was Marshall's practice periodically to visit Pershing, who was then living permanently at the Walter Reed Hospital in Washington. With Pershing, Marshall discussed the qualities, qualifications, and capabilities of officers who could be brought along rapidly to assume positions of high command and responsibility. Certainly Pershing must have talked of Patton's success in training and leading the tankers in France.

Patton wrote to Pershing early in August. "This command," he said, "is a very fine one and I am most fortunate to have landed it." His brigade had two light tank regiments, one medium tank regiment, a field artillery regiment, and a battalion of engineers— 350 officers, 5500 men, 383 tanks, 202 armored cars, and 24 105-mm. howitzers. Some equipment was lacking, but more tanks were promised soon, and men were coming in at the rate of about 100 each day. General Scott, the division commander, was full of energy and wonderful to work for. All the officers were a carefully selected lot.

> The whole thing is most interesting as most of the tactics have yet to be worked out and there is a great chance for ingenuity and leadership. As I see it we must be able to fight any place and in any manner either alone or in close association with infantry or cavalry. I think if we can get the platoons so they can fight anywhere and the men convinced that they are the best on earth and are willing to get killed to accomplish their missions, we will be a great success . . .
>
> Just at the moment the military appearance of the men and to a degree of the officers leaves something to be desired.

I am trying to set an example of being smart and soldierly and hope the rest will copy me—if they dont I will have to use stronger methods.

I seem to have inflicted a rather long letter on you but my excuse is that I am so interested in the job that I love to tell you about it.

I am quite sure that you had a lot to do with my getting this wonderful detail. Truly I appreciate it a lot and will try to be worthy of having served under you.

He added a postscript, his usual self-depreciating remark: "As my office is not yet running I had to type this my self—please excuse the mistakes."

Letter, GSP, Jr., to Pershing, August 7, 1940
Last Sunday I had a sudden impulse to turn on my radio and the very first thing I heard was some one introducing you. I heard all of your address and it was the finest and most manly statement I have ever listened to. The country is to be congratulated that it has a man like you to tell the truth and to tell it so forcefully.

Letter, Pershing to GSP, Jr., August 12, 1940
My dear Patton: Thank you very much for your kind note, which I have read with a great deal of interest. I can understand your enthusiasm for this new job, and am sure that you are going to thoroughly enjoy the experience.

Patton was on his way to fame, although probably no one, except surely himself, was aware of it. How could anyone but he know, how could anyone guess?

Hardly anyone, even in the Army, remembered that Patton had once been with tanks, that he had personified the tanks in World War I. Seemingly more important and more than apparent were his prowess as a horseman, hunter, and polo player; his attachment, his strong loyalty, to the horse cavalry; his high jinks, exuberance, and grandstanding on the polo field; his personal wealth that enabled him to keep a string of ponies and to own a yacht. He appeared to be a playboy, a socialite. His intemperate remarks outraged many persons. Some believed that he flaunted his money. Impulsive, outspoken, and aggressive, he had the facility to provoke distaste for his behavior and mode of life.

Largely forgotten were his dedication to his profession; the depth of his military knowledge and the variety of his experience; the ability he had to inspire, especially among those who worked closely with him, admiration, respect, and warm liking. Even the increasing frequency of his almost uncontrollable rages, his outbursts of temper, his periods of depression and moodiness, his extreme swings from overriding anger to abject contrition affected but slightly his friendships, never his performance of duty or his efficiency as a soldier. Georgie, his friends said, had always been eccentric.

He drove himself still, as he always had, and he realized, no doubt better than anyone else—with the single exception perhaps of Beatrice—the challenges he would face in the coming months: the challenges of his work, of the war itself, and of his personal destiny, which was coming within his reach. He would have to grasp it now, for this would be the last time he could hope to attain the glory that, in the measure he aspired to, had so far escaped him.

He was fifty-five years old, the same age that Pershing had been in 1916, the time of the Punitive Expedition into Mexico, the eve of the American entrance into the Great War. It was, then, not too late for Patton to gain achievement.

He had completed the necessary formal military education by attending the institutions of higher Army learning and succeeding in his courses with high distinction. He had served on every organizational level, from platoon to corps, both as a commander and as a staff officer. He had read far more than the average officer, had thought more deeply than most.

Yet he seemed to have moved not at all since he had left the tanks in 1920. Twenty years later, he was again with tanks, once more in command of a brigade, and still a colonel.

His classmate Devers was a brigadier general and in command of the Provisional Brigade of Washington, D.C. His classmate Eichelberger was a colonel in command of the 30th Infantry Regiment and would soon become Superintendent of the Military Academy. His friend Eisenhower, much younger than Patton, was an obscure lieutenant colonel with the 15th Infantry at Fort Lewis, Washington, and about to start his meteoric rise in rank. Mark Clark, also young, was a lieutenant colonel, an instructor at the War College, but he would soon join McNair and become his right-hand man. Omar N. Bradley was a diffident lieutenant colonel who was the Assistant Secretary of the War Department General Staff.

Fame would beckon to all of these and to others. Yet in mid-1940 it appeared to Patton that he had moved scarcely at all during the past twenty years. The two decades had been full of professional disappointment and frustration. It had taken him fourteen years to advance from major to lieutenant colonel. He had become identified with the wrong branch and the wrong bunch—the horse-cavalry men. He had backed the wrong people—Crosby and Henry, then Drum. Yet he had had the great luck to be close to Pershing, to Hines and Summerall and Craig. And finally, Stimson, Marshall, and Chaffee had smiled at him.

He had wasted time, it must have seemed to Patton, as a General Staff officer. His self-advertising at polo, sailing, hunting, and riding appeared to have backfired. The last few years of his career had been aimless, without direction.

Even the mere passage of time had changed him considerably for the worse. The two decades since the Great War had coarsened his figure—he had put on 20 pounds and weighed nearly 200. He had lost his youthful good looks.

Yet he was vigorous, energetic, and enthusiastic, even boyish. He was also somewhat chastened, less outspoken, more diplomatic, less spontaneous, more calculating. If he had had to serve the interests of the horse soldiers rather than those of the mechanized troops, to his own disadvantage, he had known how to keep rein on his impatience, to serve with loyalty, to satisfy the desires of his superiors, to practice—to an enormous extent—self-abnegation.

Patton had suffered the bitterness of the postwar years, and they had scarred and tempered him.

It was, rather, the U. S. Army that had failed to advance between the wars. The main function of tanks, as Patton had so clearly enunciated it in France, as he himself had been so largely instrumental in formulating it, was to assist the infantry. After 1918, the chiefs of the Tank Corps, of the infantry, and of the Ordnance Corps tried repeatedly to have the War Department take and support an official position on what tanks were supposed to be and what they were supposed to do. Finally, in 1922, the War Department fell back on the established rule and stated that the primary mission of tanks was "to facilitate the uninterrupted advance of the riflemen in the attack." Official doctrine in 1939 was quite the same: "As a rule, tanks are employed to assist the advance of infantry foot troops, either preceding or accompanying the infantry assault echelon."

This could not stand in 1940, not after the swift successes of the German blitzkrieg. Catching up to, overtaking, and ultimately surpassing the Germans would in large part be the work of Patton. How he would do so was quite unclear to him at the beginning of his World War II adventure at Fort Benning.

American tank production between the wars had also been gripped by inertia. Christie's tank, operating on removable tracks and also on large removable solid-rubber bogie wheels, and built on a system of independently sprung wheels, was never accepted in the United States. The infantry and the cavalry both adored the Christie tank, but the ordnance believed that it was mechanically unreliable and that its dual-purpose equipment violated good engineering practice. Controversy raged until 1938, when the convertible Christie principle was abandoned.

The Mark VIII heavy and American Renault light tanks of World War I were standard until the 1930s. From 1920 to 1935, only thirty-five tanks were built in the United States. Most were hand-tooled test models. Not until 1938 would an American designed tank be accepted and standardized. To meet the armored challenge of the age, the United States would have to design and produce a host of modern and reliable tanks quickly.

This task would belong to others. Patton's function would be to use them—to employ tanks, armored and mechanized troops, motorized infantry, self-propelled artillery, close-support aircraft, and the other elements of the combined arms team in order to out-blitzkrieg the Germans.

He would have to prove himself capable. But he had always had to do that. He had forever had to drive himself, to show himself that he was able, competent, and knowledgeable.

And now that the "next war" had come to Asia and to Europe and threatened—or, from Patton's point of view, promised—to draw in the United States, he faced the unknown with a confidence that was more apparent than real. He would reinforce his strong and vital sense of duty and devotion by his close identification with his personal destiny or fate.

It was, he was certain, his destiny or his fate to become a great captain, and he would do his uttermost, as he would have said, to make that destiny, that fate, that dream come true.

A Brief Note
on Military Terms

George S. Patton, Jr.,
His Military Chronology

A Brief Note on Military Terms

A PLATOON is a unit of about 40 soldiers and is commanded by a lieu-tenant, either a second lieutenant (who wears a gold bar) or a first lieutenant (silver bar).

A company—called a troop in the cavalry—consists of four platoons and is usually commanded by a captain (two silver bars).

A battalion—called a squadron in the cavalry—consists of four com-panies (or troops), and is under the command of a major (who wears a gold leaf) or lieutenant colonel (silver leaf).

A regiment consists of two battalions (or squadrons) and is com-manded by a lieutenant colonel or a colonel (silver eagle).

A brigade is composed of two regiments and is commanded by a colonel or a brigadier general (whose insignia of rank is one star).

A division is an organization of two brigades; the commander is usually a major general (two stars).

A corps consists of two or more divisions and is commanded by a major general or a lieutenant general (three stars).

An army, sometimes called a field army, contains two or more corps and is under a lieutenant general or a general (four stars).

In the early part of the twentieth century, the U. S. Army was headed by the Secretary of War who was a member of the President's cabinet and who advised the President on military matters. The War Department, located in Washington, D.C., consisted of civilians and military men who assisted the Secretary. The top man in uniform was the Army Chief of Staff, who was the principal military adviser of the Secretary of War.

The Chief of Staff presided over the General and Special Staff Sections, each of which was headed by an officer who was responsible for a specific function, for example, Personnel, Intelligence, Plans and Operations, Supplies, Ordnance, and the like.

Staff officers were also assigned to field armies, corps, divisions, brigades, regiments, and battalions (squadrons) to help the commanders of these organizations.

There was, and is, a distinct difference between commanders and staff officers. Only commanders have the authority to direct units; only commanders bear the responsibility for unit performance. It is the commander who makes decisions and who is held responsible for success or failure. Staff officers are the commander's advisers. They help him reach his decisions, and they take action only in the name of their commander.

George S. Patton, Jr.,
His Military Chronology

1885 November 11	Born, San Gabriel, Los Angeles County, California
1897–1903 September–June	Student, Stephen Cutter Clark's Classical School for Boys, Pasadena, California
1903–1904 September–June	Cadet, Virginia Military Institute, Lexington, Virginia
1904 June 16	Entered U. S. Military Academy, West Point, New York
1905 June	Turned back to repeat initial year
September	Re-entered as Cadet, U. S. Military Academy
1906 June 13	Appointed Second Corporal, Cadet Corps
August 27	Appointed Sixth Corporal, Cadet Corps
1907 March 14	Appointed Second Corporal, Cadet Corps
June 14	Appointed Sergeant Major, Cadet Corps
1908 February 14	Appointed Battalion Adjutant, Cadet Corps
1909 June 11	Graduated U. S. Military Academy; commissioned Second Lieutenant, 15th Cavalry

September 12	Joined 15th Cavalry, Fort Sheridan, Illinois, and assigned to Troop K
September	Qualified as Expert Rifleman
December	Qualified as Expert Revolver Shot
1910 November 2–December 23	Commanding Officer, Machine Gun Platoon, 3d Squadron, 15th Cavalry
1911 May–November	Acting Commanding Officer, Troop K, 15th Cavalry
December 3	Joined Troop A, 15th Cavalry, Fort Myer, Virginia
1912 March 12	Appointed Quartermaster, 1st Squadron, 15th Cavalry, Fort Myer
June 14	Sailed for Europe to participate in Olympic Games, Stockholm, Sweden
July 7–July 17	Participated in Modern Pentathlon, Olympic Games
July–August	Received individual instruction in fencing at Saumur, France
August 22	Returned to United States
December 14–1913 March 22	Temporary Duty, Office of the Chief of Staff, U. S. Army
July 9–Sept 17	Study of Swordsmanship at Saumur, France
September 23	Reported to Mounted Service School, Fort Riley, Kansas, as Master of the Sword and as Student, First Year Course
1914 May 8	Graduated First Year Course
September	Master of the Sword and Student, Second Year Course
1915 June 17	Graduated Second Year Course
September 15	Joined 8th Cavalry, Fort Bliss, Texas
September 25	Assigned Troop D, 8th Cavalry

October	Appointed Squadron Adjutant and Quartermaster as additional duties
October 19– 1916 January 22	Stationed at Sierra Blanca, Texas
March 13	Detached from 8th Cavalry and attached to Headquarters, Punitive Expedition, Mexico
May 14	The Rubio Ranch Affair
May 23	Promoted to First Lieutenant
June 8	Transferred to 10th Cavalry, continuing duty with Headquarters, Punitive Expedition
1917 February 1	Transferred formally to 7th Cavalry, Fort Bliss, Texas
February	Returned with Punitive Expedition from Mexico
February 27– April 14	Commanding Officer, Troop A, 7th Cavalry
May 15	Promoted to Captain
May 18	Ordered to report to Pershing in Washington, D.C.; appointed Commanding Officer, Headquarters Troop, AEF
May 28	Sailed for Europe on *Baltic* with Pershing's headquarters
June 8	Reached Liverpool; departed for London
June 13	Departed London; arrived Paris
September 1	Moved with Headquarters to Chaumont
September 13	Additional duty as Post Adjutant, Chaumont
October 3	Requested assignment to Tank Service
November 10	Detailed to the Tank Service

November 18	Relinquished command of Headquarters Troop, AEF
November 19–December 1	Observer, French Tank Center, Chamlieu
December 16	Moved to Langres to open Light Tank Center and School

1918 January 1–

January 7	Visited French and British Tank Centers
January 23	Promoted to Major
February 14	Formally assigned to command the Light Tanks, AEF (302d Light Tank Center)
February 22	Moved Tank Center and School from Langres to Bourg
March 4–March 10	Visited British Tank Center in England
April 3	Promoted to Lieutenant Colonel
April 28	Organized 1st Light Tank Battalion with himself in command
June 6	Organized 2d Light Tank Battalion, with himself in command of the regiment
June 17–August 20	Student, General Staff College, Langres (completed course)
August 24	Organized and commanded 304th Tank Brigade (1st Tank Brigade)
September 12–September 15	St. Mihiel Offensive
September 26	Wounded near Cheppy, Meuse-Argonne Offensive
September 26–September 30	Evacuation Hospital #11
October 1–October 17	Base Hospital #49
October 17	Promoted to Colonel

October 17–	
October 28	Base Hospital #24
December 16	Awarded Distinguished Service Cross
1919 January 17–	
February 7	Detached Service, Second Army
February 26–	
February 28	En route to Marseille
March 2	Sailed for United States
March 17	Arrived Brooklyn, New York; to Camp Mills, Long Island, New York
March 25	To Camp Meade, Maryland
April 22	Temporary duty, Washington, D.C.
June 16	Awarded Distinguished Service Medal
September 4	Relieved from temporary duty; returned to Camp Meade
1920 June 30	Reverted to Regular grade of Captain
July 1	Promoted to Major
September 30	Relinquished command of 304th Tank Brigade
October 3	Joined 3d Cavalry at Fort Myer, Virginia, as Commanding Officer, 3d Squadron
1922 December 18	Departed Fort Myer
1923 January 10	Student, Field Officers' Course, Fort Riley, Kansas
June 3	Completed Field Officers' Course
September	Student, Command and General Staff College, Fort Leavenworth, Kansas
1924 June 30	Honor Graduate, Command and General Staff College
July 5	Joined First Corps Area Headquarters and assigned as Assistant Chief of Staff G–1 (Personnel)

1925	March 4	Sailed from New York for Hawaii
	March 31	Reached Hawaii; assigned G–1 and G–2, Hawaiian Division
	October 30	Detached Service, Acting G–1, Hawaiian Department
1926	September 30	G–1, G–2, and G–3, Hawaiian Division
1928	April 7	Departed Hawaii
	May 7	Joined Office of the Chief of Cavalry, Washington, D.C.
1931	September	Student, Army War College, Washington, D.C.
1932	June 2	Awarded Purple Heart for wound in 1918
	June	Distinguished Graduate, Army War College
	July 8	Executive Officer, 3d Cavalry, Fort Myer, Virginia
1934	March 1	Promoted to Lieutenant Colonel
1935	May 7	Departed Los Angeles in yacht for Hawaii
	June 8	Arrived Honolulu; assigned G–2, Hawaiian Department
1937	June 12	Departed Honolulu in yacht
	July 12	Arrived Los Angeles
	July 25	In hospital, Beverly, Massachusetts, with broken leg
	November 4	Discharged hospital; sick in quarters
1938	February 2	Returned to duty status
	February 8	Executive Officer, Academic Division of the Cavalry School and 9th Cavalry, Fort Riley, Kansas
	July 1	Promoted to Colonel
	July 24	Commanding Officer, 5th Cavalry, Fort Clark, Texas

December 10	Commanding Officer, 3d Cavalry, Fort Myer, Virginia
1940 April	Umpire, Spring Maneuvers, Fort Benning, Georgia
May	Control Officer, Maneuvers, Fort Beauregard, Louisiana
July 26	Commanding Officer, 2d Armored Brigade of 2d Armored Division, Fort Benning

Index

Index